THE
CHRISTIAN
SPEAKER'S
TREASURY

THE CHRISTIAN SPEAKER'S TREASURY

A Sourcebook
of Anecdotes
and Quotes

RUTH A. TUCKER

1817

HARPER & ROW, PUBLISHERS, SAN FRANCISCO

New York, Grand Rapids, Philadelphia, St. Louis,
London, Singapore, Sydney, Tokyo

FIRST EDITION

Library of Congress Cataloging-in-Publication Data

Tucker, Ruth, 1945–
    The Christian speaker's treasury.

    1. Homiletical illustrations. I. Title.
BV4225.2.T83   1989   251'.08   88-43273
ISBN 0-06-250862-8

89   90   91   92   93   RRD   10   9   8   7   6   5   4   3   2   1

To
My Sisters
By Birth and By Marriage
Jeannine
Kathy
Sharon
Sooky

ABORTION

Biblical References to the Unborn

The question of when life begins is debated among philosophers, medical specialists, and authorities in other fields, but the Bible seems to be very clear that God recognizes the unborn child's full personhood. Martha Zimmerman documents this perspective in her book *Should I Keep My Baby?*

"The Bible often mentions children, both unborn and born, and it never refers to them in any way other than as full-fledged people. Psalm 139:13–16 describes God's personal involvement in David's *unborn* life: 'For Thou didst form my inward parts; Thou didst weave me in my mother's womb. . . . My frame was not hidden from Thee, when I was made in secret. . . .' If David had been the only person to write this thought, we might say he was just being poetic. But other Bible writers said the same thing. The prophet Isaiah wrote, 'The Lord called me from the womb' (49:1); God said to Jeremiah, 'Before I formed you in the womb I knew you, and before you were born I consecrated you' (1:5); and the Apostle Paul, hundreds of years later, wrote, 'He who had set me apart, even from my mother's womb . . .' (Gal. 1:15). The beginning or meaning of 'personhood' did not seem complicated to these men."

[Martha Zimmerman, Should I Keep My Baby? *(Minneapolis: Bethany House, 1983), pp. 21–22.]*

Changed Views on Abortion

Dr. Jean Garton, who at one time advocated a pro-choice position on abortion, became a pro-life activist after studying the evidence and after being challenged by her preschool son on the issue. It was a challenge that made an indelible impression on her and changed the course of her career. She tells the story in her book *Who Broke the Baby?*

"All our children were in bed; the late television news was over, and I was putting the finishing touches to a presentation for medical students scheduled to be given the next day. As I reviewed some slides which might be used, there appeared on the screen a picture of an abortion victim, aged two and one-half months' gestation; her body had been dismembered by a curette, the long handled knife used in a D&C abortion procedure.

"Suddenly I heard, rather than saw, another person near me. At the sound of a sharp intake of breath, I turned to find that my youngest son, then a sleepy, rumpled three-year-old, had unexpectedly and silently entered the room. His small voice was filled with great sadness as he asked, 'Who broke the baby?'

"How could this small, innocent child see what so many adults cannot see? How could he know instinctively that this which many people carelessly dismiss as tissue or a blob was one in being with him, was like him? In the words of his question he gave humanity to what adults call 'fetal matter'; in the tone of his question he mourned what we exalt as a sign of liberation and freedom. With wisdom which often escapes the learned, he asked in the presence of the evidence before his eyes, 'Who broke the baby?' "

[Jean Staker Garton, Who Broke the Baby? (Minneapolis: Bethany Fellowship, 1979), p. 7.]

Early Penalties for Abortion

Historically, there is mixed evidence regarding society's concern for the welfare of the unborn child. If the child was accidentally killed by someone who was doing bodily harm to the mother, the penalty was sometimes merely a fine, but if the mother purposely terminated the life of her unborn child, the penalty was high. Indeed, in many pagan societies abortion was viewed as a heinous crime.

" 'When men strive together,' said the book of Exodus, 'and hurt a woman with child, so that there is a miscarriage, and yet no harm follows, the one who hurt her shall be fined. . . . If any harm follows, then you shall give life for life, eye for eye, tooth for tooth. . . .' " (21:22–24). In Assyria, any man who struck a wellborn lady and 'caused her to cast the fruit of her womb' was liable to a heavy fine, a beating, and a month's forced labor; if the lady was not wellborn, the only penalty was a fine. The Hittites were coolly businesslike. Ten shekels of silver if she were near full term, only five if she had not yet passed sixth moon month.

"Abortion was a criminal offense. For an Assyrian woman, the penalty was 'to be impaled and not to be given burial.' If she died of the abortion, the same punishment was meted out to her corpse. But no one was much interested in infanticide, presumably because it was a fate usually reserved for girl children, while miscarriage or abortion might prevent a boy from being brought into the world. Only the Hebrews ruled against it by forbidding children to be given to Molech—not a demon, as was once thought, but a technical term for child sacrifice—which amounted to much the same thing."

[Reay Tannahil, Sex in History *(New York: Stein & Day, 1980), pp. 69–70.]*

Guilt Associated with Abortion

Dr. Susan Stanford, a practicing psychologist who works extensively with women who have had abortions, has found that the emotional trauma in the aftermath of an abortion is much greater than most pro-choice advocates would ever acknowledge. "Depending on the situation the research shows that most women suffer one of several of the following symptoms after an abortion: unresolved grief, chronic guilt, anniversary depression, psychosomatic illness, drug and alcohol abuse, suicide attempts, psychotic breakdowns, or other lesser resultant effects.

"One of the most universal aftereffects of abortion is the feeling of guilt and loss. In my own practice some post-abortion women may initially deny feeling guilty and consequently avoid the topic of their abortions early on in the counseling relationship. However, invariably the topic comes up, perhaps around the anniversary due date or death date. When I've asked my clients how they feel about it in retrospect more than 90 percent share they feel some level of guilty feelings."

[Susan M. Stanford, with David Hazard, Will I Cry Tomorrow? Healing Post-Abortion Trauma (Old Tappan, N.J.: Revell, 1986), p. 135.]

Historical Acceptance of Abortion

Abortion in the early weeks of pregnancy has not always been viewed as a crime by religious leaders, as illustrated by the trial of Bathsheba Spooner in Massachusetts, in 1778, who was convicted of murdering her husband. She sought to postpone her execution, claiming to be pregnant. She was examined by two men and twelve "discreet matrons," who were directed to determine not only if she was pregnant but also if she was "quick" with child. "It was a fine distinction but an important one. Quickening was the coming to life of the fetus, the point at which church authorities recognized it as a living being which it would be sinful to destroy. That crucial moment was thought to occur at about thirty to forty days for female fetuses, eighty to ninety days for males. Before quickening, the fetus was only a lump of protoplasm. Consequently, no church (not even the Catholic Church) objected to aborting the fetus before it quickened or to hanging a women in the early weeks of pregnancy."

[Ann Jones, Women Who Kill (New York: Holt, Rinehart & Winston, 1980), p. 61.]

Limited Justification of Abortion

While the Roman Catholic church and a vast number of evangelical Protestants take a strong stand today against abortion in any circumstances, some in both camps would argue that there is limited justification for abortion. While they would strongly condemn abortion as a means of birth control as it is widely practiced, they would maintain that the issue cannot be determined with absolutes that permit no exceptions. The well-known theologian Carl Henry is an example of those who hold this position.

"When childbirth would endanger the mother's life abortion can be morally justified. The fetus seems less than human, moreover, in cases of extreme deformity in which rational and moral capacities integral to the *imago Dei* are clearly lacking. The scriptural correlation of sexual intercourse with marriage and the family, furthermore, implies an ethical basis for voluntary abortion in cases of incest and rape. But the ready sacrifice of fetal life as a means of sexual gratification and of birth control is monstrous.

"Abortion on demand has become an earthshock to the structures of marriage and the family. It restructures the role and duty of parents, it undermines the virtues of motherhood, and it accommodates a breakdown of conscience that can readily dispense also with the elderly once they become senile and, like fetuses in their weak and helpless condition, cannot protect and maintain themselves."

[Carl F. H. Henry, The Christian Mindset in a Secular Society *(Portland: Multnomah, 1984), p. 103.]*

Opposition to Abortion

We cannot diminish the value of one category of human life—the unborn—without diminishing the value of all human life. . . . There is no cause more important.

—PRES. RONALD REAGAN

[Quoted in Nancy Leigh DeMoss, ed., The Rebirth of America *(Philadelphia: Arthur DeMoss Foundation, 1986), p. 114.]*

Sorrow and Trauma for the Mother

In her book *Will I Cry Tomorrow?* Susan Stanford shares her own personal trauma of having an abortion. She had just received her Ph.D.

in counseling and psychology from Northwestern University and was embarking on a career as an assistant professor at that same institution when she realized she was pregnant. She was separated from her husband, and the pregnancy had resulted from an affair with a fellow doctoral student. To many young women in that situation, an abortion might seem like a simple and uncomplicated solution to a potentially explosive problem. It was not. The trauma of the abortion itself and the aftermath were the most devastating ordeal she had ever endured, and her experience was not unique.

"I slipped into the gown, sat down, and stared at the wall. The nurse had said 'in a few moments.' Why had her tone sounded so cool, so businesslike? In a few moments it would be all over. I could forget this day. I could get on with my life, with efforts to reconcile with Frank. Things would be normal again.

"But things would not be normal for a long, long time. More than my baby would die in that room. And my own mental strength would not be able to give life where death had come.

"It would take a power far greater than I had ever known.

"I waited in silence, trying to think of nothing. It was futile. . . .

"In the next hour-and-a-half my body slowly recovered from the pain and shock of the suction machine. Not so my psyche. The counselor, Julie, had warned me that I might experience a sense of loss. But this was emptiness. Desolation. Or something worse that can never be named. Once I had had a personality, a life, a soul. Now I was a body with broken pieces inside. It was that sense of shattering that I could not get a grip on."

[Susan M. Stanford, with David Hazard, Will I Cry Tomorrow? Healing Post-Abortion Trauma (Old Tappan, N.J.: Revell, 1986), pp. 17–18, 72.]

ABUSE

In Marriage

Abuse in marriage is not confined simply to physical abuse. While that is a serious problem in marriages, perpetrated usually by the husband, who is generally physically stronger than the wife, the problem of psychological abuse can often be even more devastating. Dr. Susan Forward, a well-known therapist, has given a definition of abuse and told of its effects on women. "The current definition of *abuse* in the mental-health profession covers both psychological and physical violence. *Abuse is defined as any behavior that is designed to control and subjugate another human being through the use of fear, humiliation, and verbal or physical assaults.* In other words, you don't have to be hit to be abused. . . .

"I do not use the term *abuse* loosely. I am not using it to describe an occasional bad mood or the expression of angry feelings that exist in any relationship. I am using it to describe *the systematic persecution of one partner by another.* Verbal abuse has not received the attention that it warrants, given how devastating it can be to a person's mental health over a period of time."

[*Susan Forward and Joan Torres,* Men Who Hate Women and the Women Who Love Them *(New York: Bantam Books, 1986), p. 43.]*

ADOLESCENCE
Difficulty of Becoming a Woman

Frances Willard, the great temperance leader of the nineteenth century, wrote in her autobiography of the difficult struggles she endured as she entered her teen years. She was now a lady, and that meant a completely different way of behavior. "No girl went through a harder experience than I, when my free, out-of-door life had to cease, and the long skirts and clubbed-up hair spiked with hair-pins had to be endured. The half of that down-heartedness has never been told and never can be. I always believed that if I had been let alone and allowed as a woman, what I had had as a girl, a free life in the country, where a human being might grow, body and soul, as a tree grows, I would have been 'ten times more of a person' every way. Mine was a nature hard to tame, and I cried long and loud when I found I could never again race and range about with freedom. I had delighted in my short hair and nice round hat, or comfortable 'Shaker bonnet,' but now I was to be 'choked with ribbons' when I went into the open air the rest of my days."

She recorded her despair in her journal. "This is my birthday and the date of my martyrdom. Mother insists that at last I *must* have my hair 'done up woman-fashion.' She says she can hardly forgive herself for letting me 'run wild' so long. We've had a great time over it all, and here I sit like another Samson 'shorn of my strength.' That figure won't do, though, for the greatest trouble with me is that I never shall be shorn again. My 'back' hair is twisted up like a corkscrew; I carry eighteen hair-pins; my head aches miserably; my feet are entangled in the skirt of my hateful new gown. I can never jump over a fence again, so long as I live. As for chasing the sheep, down in the shady pasture, it's out of the question, and to climb to my 'Eagle's-nest' seat in the big burr-oak would ruin this new frock beyond repair. Altogether, I recognize the fact that my 'occupation is gone.' "

[*Frances E. Willard*, Glimpses of Fifty Years: The Autobiography of an American Woman *(Chicago: Smith, 1889; reprint, New York: Source Book Press, 1970), pp. 69–70.]*

Need for Reassurance

The know-it-all attitude that teenagers commonly display can disguise their insecurity and the need they have to be reassured that they are special and praiseworthy young adults. In *Traits of a Healthy Family,* Dolores Curran speaks to this issue. "Many adolescents feel ugly and unlovable most of the time. They need constant reassurance that they are attractive and loved. I remember particularly the great number of teenage girls I taught in high school who were never made aware of their unique and appealing traits, such as an engaging smile, a special zest, or a keen wit. But they knew about their acne or their extra five pounds, and that was all that counted."

[*Dolores Curran,* Traits of a Healthy Family *(Minneapolis: Winston Press, 1983), p. 45.]*

Self-Centeredness

As youngsters enter their teenage years, many parents and teachers despair over their behavior. They fail to understand the peculiar circumstances and problems that children in this age group confront, and they do not understand that some of the most disagreeable character traits that suddenly appear are common to adolescence and generally pass as the child matures.

"Egocentrism reaches its peak during early adolescence. The more egocentric a teenager is, the less objective he can be. The junior high school student often is not yet able to generalize, to use symbols, or to process information with objectivity. Most have not yet matured enough to go beyond concrete approaches to learning. Because of this, they are often 'typed' as being difficult to teach. Their lack of objectivity and their excessive involvement with themselves makes them inconsiderate of others and difficult to engage in an extensive conversation. Parents and teachers who don't take the level of maturity into consideration may hold out unrealistic expectations that the teenager is not capable of meeting. Then, when the teenager can't meet the expectations, she feels inadequate, which fuels her already-heightened sense of self-criticism.

"Contrast these conditions with the circumstances of the high school–age adolescent. Older adolescents have no distinctive new adjustments or changes in status to endure. Most have completed their physical growth and development. Their interpersonal relationships are more mature and constructive, and they are more highly critical in their evaluation of their peers. They are experimenting and learning new roles, but they plan and choose more thoughtfully."

[Brent Q. Hafen and Kathryn J. Frandsen, Youth Suicide: Depression and Loneliness *(Evergreen, Colo.: Cordillera Press, 1986), pp. 55–56.]*

ADOPTION

By Single Women

The recent stories about single women adopting children are viewed with skepticism by some who believe that a proper upbringing must include both a father and mother. The practice, however, is not new. It was not uncommon for single missionaries of the nineteenth century to adopt native children. Mary Slessor, who served for many years in West Africa, is an example. She had several "adopted" children, whom she reared from their infancy. But single women in the United States also adopted children, with Elizabeth Blackwell being a case in point. As the nation's first female medical doctor, she had many obstacles to overcome, and she was convinced that she could not succeed as a married woman, whose chief occupation would have been domestic concerns. Yet, she was unwilling to deny herself all the joys of womanhood. Indeed, her nurturing instincts were strong, and she believed that a child would give her fulfillment while she carried on her medical career.

Elizabeth's decision to adopt was not without controversy; even some among her own family were very critical. "Women were meant to be mothers," they argued; "it was a perversion of nature to deny it, and this craving for a child proved it." Elizabeth viewed the situation from a different perspective. She "dared to suggest it proved something quite different—that society was wrong to expect self-realization in one sphere to go automatically with self-denial in another.... She was saying that although self-sacrifice was necessary if a woman wished to have a career there was no need for it to be total. . . .

"The adoption [in 1856] of Kitty, aged seven, was Elizabeth Blackwell's indulgence to herself. She was thirty-five years old and had long ago renounced all thoughts of marriage. To this she was quite reconciled. But what she found hard to reconcile was being childless as well as husbandless. Her carnal desires, while acknowledging their existence, she could control and sublimate but her maternal ones were not so readily dealt with. She felt she must have somebody who was hers to love and be loved by. Her family was not enough. And so she began going down to Randall's Island, where four hundred orphans were housed, and looking for a child to be hers. She finally settled on Kitty Barry, who everyone thought plain and stupid. Kitty described years later how a 'very pleasant voiced lady' with gentle hands came up to her and asked her if she would like to be her little girl and come home with her. Kitty said yes but would the lady please wait until she had finished watching the sunset."

From that beginning the relationship developed into a deep and caring bond of affinity. They played and worked and traveled together, and in 1910, when Elizabeth was dying, Kitty, who was then in her sixties, was at her bedside seeking to make her final moments more comfortable.

[*Margaret Forster,* Significant Sisters: The Grassroots of Active Feminism, 1839–1939 *(New York: Knopf, 1985), pp. 77–78, 85.*]

AGING

Physical Activity

Dr. Ida Scudder, the famous Reformed church missionary who founded the Vellore medical complex in India, kept physically fit well on into her eighties. Yet, she knew all too well the indignity bestowed on elderly people. When she was sixty-five, she was involved in a tennis tournament. Before the match began, she overheard her teenage opponent complaining to the officials for putting her opposite a "grannie." So incensed was Ida that she played her hardest and unmercifully trounced the young woman, winning every game in two sets.

[*Dorothy Clarke Wilson,* Dr. Ida: The Story of Dr. Ida Scudder of Vellore *(New York: McGraw-Hill, 1959), p. 243.*]

AIDS

Sympathetic Response to AIDS

It is sometimes tempting to think that we are the first generation to deal with a massive problem of a contagious life-threatening disease such as AIDS. In the time of Jesus, however, lepers were the disease-ridden outcasts of society who were kept away from public exposure, an exclusion that continued through the centuries. There was little sympathy expressed for these unfortunate people. One who stands out for her caring concern is Katherine Zell, an outspoken pastor's wife and reformer in her own right in Reformation Germany. She wrote tracts and edited a hymnbook, but she also used her gift of writing in more personal ministries. When a city official who was a longtime acquaintance of hers was quarantined from Strasbourg because he had contracted leprosy, she visited him and spoke to local magistrates about improving his situation. She also wrote to him, and one of these writings later appeared in tract form. It was a letter of reassurance and consolation that could be applied to many situations, including that relating to AIDS today.

"My dear Lord Felix, since we have known each other for a full 30 years I am moved to visit you in your long and frightful illness. I have not been able to come as often as I would like, because of the load here for the poor and the sick, but you have been ever in my thoughts. We have often talked of how you have been stricken, cut off from rank, office, from your wife and friends, from all dealings with the world which recoils from your loathsome disease and leaves you in utter loneliness. At first you were bitter and utterly cast down till God gave you strength and patience, and now you are able to thank him that out of love he has taught you to bear the cross. Because I know that your illness weighs upon you daily and may easily cause you again to fall into despair and rebelliousness, I have gathered some passages which may make your yoke light in the spirit, though not in the flesh. I have written meditations on the 51st Psalm: 'Have mercy upon me, O God, according to thy loving-kindness,' and the 130th 'Out of the depths have I cried unto thee, O Lord,' and then on the Lord's Prayer and the Creed."

Katherine's meditations on Scripture were brief and to the point. They were designed not to be scholarly commentary but to be a practical source of encouragement to a downcast soul.

[Roland H. Bainton, Women of the Reformation in Germany and Italy *(Minneapolis: Augsburg, 1971), p. 69.]*

Turning the Pain into Productive Efforts

In her book *The Screaming Room,* Barbara Peabody tells of the months of agony that she endured during her son's painful struggle with AIDS. Peter was twenty-eight, and he had his whole life ahead of him. She first heard the news through an early Sunday morning phone call from her former husband. " 'Oh, my God, no-o-o!' My cry pierces the quiet, San Diego morning. I am cold, shaking uncontrollably. I clutch the blankets around me."

Eleven months later, she relates how the awful nightmare is coming to an end. "Peter will die today. I know.

"I look at the lavender-gray hollows in his temples, his cheeks, his eyes, the skin stretched taut over the contours of his bones, and I know. My only remaining hope now is for a beautiful day, a brilliant sunset, and a soft, dark night. He deserves that."

The knowledge of his impending death does not ease the pain of losing him. " 'Oh, Peter . . . ' I finally wail, and the tears come, falling on his hair, his tortured face, dripping on the pillow, his chest, his arms, as my whole body wilts, crumbles, caves in. I don't have to be strong anymore, the strengths built up during months and months of tension, of angry energy, dissolve, and I am just another mother who has lost her child, who holds his empty, wasted body in her arms and mourns, grieves, cries for loss of part of her own body and soul."

For Barbara and her family, however, Peter's death was not the end of their struggle with AIDS. They determined that they would not allow his memory to be swallowed up in their grief. Each one found a way to move ahead with life while giving something back to him in the form of service to others, as Barbara explains.

"My mother, 82, helped establish an AIDS support organization in Portland, Maine, when the first patient was diagnosed there in the winter of 1984. The hospital calls her in to talk with patients' parents, to console and advise.

"All my children, though busy with work and school, have found time to work with AIDS organizations where they live. It's not easy. They see their brother in the eyes of other patients.

"Walter [Peter's father] has lectured on AIDS to students at Virginia Polytechnical Institute, where he works in student health, and is helping establish an AIDS Task Force there.

"I gradually found my way out of my screaming room by sorting out and writing down all that happened to us. I have closed the door, but scars and bruises will always remain inside. Tears still come when least expected."

[Barbara Peabody, The Screaming Room: A Mother's Journal of Her Son's Struggle with AIDS: A True Story of Love, Dedication, and Courage *(New York: Avon Books, 1986), pp. 1, 269, 273, 278–79.]*

ALCOHOLISM
Effect on Women

Recent clinical studies and medical research have revealed that the effect of alcoholism on women is quite different from its effect on men. In some cases the differences are culturally determined; in others there appears to be an inherent difference in the ways women and men relate to the disease. Rachel V. reaches this conclusion in her book *A Woman Like You: Life Stories of Women Recovering from Alcoholism and Addiction.*

"A woman's experience of the disease is markedly different from a man's, and the response of the world around her is very different as well. It is still much more unacceptable for a woman to be an alcoholic than a man. The stigma further delays recognition and treatment of the disease, meaning that often women have deteriorated much more than if the disease was recognized and treated early on. A woman who falls prey to the disease may seem to have forsaken her expected societal role of virtuous wife and mother. There is almost universal assumption that the woman who drinks heavily must be promiscuous as well. That is one of the reasons why in certain Moslem countries a woman discovered to have been drinking could be killed on the spot by her male relatives. In ancient Rome, she could be starved or stoned to death."

There are physiological reasons why women are affected differently by alcohol as well. "Men and women also have a different distribution of fat and water in their bodies, so that women are indeed more affected by drinking than men. Women seem to be more vulnerable to the toxic effects of alcohol on the body, because the liver is more sensitive to alcohol in the presence of estrogen and thus more likely to be damaged than a man's. There's a 'telescoping' effect of alcohol that has been noted in women. The disease tends to run its course more rapidly in women, so that the time from the onset of regular drinking until the development of serious problems with drinking occurs in a shorter or 'telescoped' time span. . . .

"Another difference in the experience of alcoholism in women is the phenomenon of 'cross-addiction.' Men can be and are cross-addicted as well, but it seems that there are more reports of this among women than men. Since most of the tranquilizers in this country are prescribed for women, it would not be surprising to have this problem. The terms *cross addiction, dual addiction,* and *polyaddiction* refer to multiple dependencies such as on alcohol and drugs whether prescribed by a doctor or procured on the streets. Cross addiction is a growing problem, particularly with young people."

[*Rachel V.*, A Woman Like You: Life Stories of Women Recovering from Alcoholism and Addiction *(San Francisco: Harper & Row, 1985), pp. xviii, xx.]*

Historical Roots of Alcoholism

We sometimes think of drinking as a problem of the modern age, when people often seek to drown their depression and overcome their stress through alcohol. But drinking has been a far greater problem for our ancestors than it is for the modern generation. Indeed the Founding

Fathers of our country—often spoken of as having strong Christian values—were heavy drinkers.

"John Adams was the most abstemious of the Founding Fathers, but even he regularly drank a tankard of hard cider with breakfast every morning. Hard cider has about twice the alcoholic content of beer. George Washington was, among other things, a whiskey distiller; Thomas Jefferson had one of the first vineyards in America, and he customarily drank three glasses of wine a day.

"The British claimed, with considerable justification, that the American Revolution was hatched in taverns. The common men met in taverns to toast freedom, organize a militia, and plot their revolution."

Even before this time, the Puritans of the Colonial era were known for their love of liquor. "Drunkenness was quite common among God's Saints, and while public drunkenness might be condemned and punished, drinking itself was not."

The argument can be made that the heavy consumption of alcohol was natural, since good drinking water was in such short supply. Indeed, "the image of a pre-industrial America of clear streams and unpolluted wells is a false one. In St. Louis the drinking water came from the Mississippi, but before people could drink it, they had to allow it to 'settle,' and the sediment often filled a quarter of the container." Nevertheless, there is no justification for the excessive drinking of our forebears.

"There was no such thing as an eighteen- or twenty-one-year-old drinking age. Indeed such an idea would have seemed absurd to nineteenth-century Americans. 'I have frequently seen Fathers,' wrote one traveler, 'wake their Child of a year old from a sound sleep to make it drink Rum or Brandy.' American parents began trying to accustom their children to drinking practically from infancy, at least partly in the hope that this would protect them from becoming drunkards later on."

As the nineteenth century progressed, the drinking patterns in America slowly began to change, and moderation became more acceptable. This change was due in large part to the temperance movement, which was conducted largely by women.

[Susan Cohen and Daniel Cohen, A Six-Pack and a Fake I.D.: Teens Look at the Drinking Question *(New York: Evans, 1986), pp. 80–84.]*

Mother's Problem with Alcoholism

Statistics show that alcoholics are often the children of alcoholics. Parents who set a bad example in the home often discover that their children develop the same type of behavior as they mature. If parents could look into the future and see how their drinking would affect future generations and society at large, they might be more motivated to change their habits. Indeed, the mother of President Franklin Pierce should have taken such a view. "In one respect, Anna Kendrick Pierce differs from every other Presidential mother. She drank. Nor is this a matter of only limited pertinence, because her son Franklin had the same failing—and he attributed it to maternal example. Since there was nothing else that particularly distinguished New Hampshire's sole occupant of the White House, the weakness he shared with his female parent can hardly be overlooked."

Some would argue that Franklin Pierce should at least be credited for making it as far as the White House, but the promises he made on the campaign trail and the charm he exuded in public were not translated into the kind of leadership the country needed. "In the White House the little that Pierce had to offer was not enough, and his own party would not even pay him the ritual compliment of nominating him for a second term; he died in obscurity twelve years after leaving office. Much before then, but many months after descending into what was charitably called senility, his mother had preceded him."

[Doris Faber, The Mothers of American Presidents (New York: New American Library, 1968), pp. 210–12.]

Outdated View of Alcoholism

In his book *Heavy Drinking: The Myth of Alcoholism As a Disease,* Herbert Fingarette, a professor at the University of California who is recognized internationally for his research on addictions, maintains that "*no* leading research authorities accept the classic disease concept" of alcoholism. According to one researcher he quotes, "There is no adequate empirical substantiation for the basic tenets of the classic disease concept of alcoholism." Another expert insists that the concept of alcoholism as a disease is "old and biased."

Fingarette compares alcohol abuse with such compulsions as excessive eating, spending, gambling, drug use, and caffeine intake. "The pattern of chronic heavy drinking seems at least somewhat analogous to these other patters of behavior, all of which we tend to refer to as addictions, compulsions, or dependence. And some researchers are starting to conceive of all these forms of 'excessive appetite' as variants on one theme, to be incorporated in a 'unitary theory.' "

But if alcoholism is not a disease, why is it so often identified as one? One of the most important reasons for this, according to Fingarette, "is the concern that revealing the bankruptcy of the classic disease concept might discourage heavy drinkers from seeking help. The essence of this rationale is that if chronic drinkers are told that there is no disease of alcoholism, they will see their drinking as a personal failing; out of guilt and shame, they will tend to hide or deny their problems." In actuality, he points out that the opposite may be true. Thinking their problem is a disease may cause heavy drinkers to blame their problem on their genetic makeup.

Do alcohol abusers have control of their drinking? "The public has been so indoctrinated by the idea of loss of control that few dare to seem naive by carefully observing alcoholic conduct and acknowledging that heavy drinkers often do moderate and limit their drinking. We may be close to people who have been labeled alcoholics, but we discount our observations of the times they show self-control because we have been told that alcoholics have no control. Or if we do recognize evidence of control, we decide the drinker in question cannot really be a 'true' alcoholic."

What is the value of recognizing that alcoholism may not be a disease as has been assumed for so long? "Once we leave behind the disease concept, which emphasizes medicine and individual treatment for a supposedly involuntary symptom, we can adopt a broader view: that what takes place in the drinker's environment may be more important than what takes place in the drinker's body."

[Herbert Fingarette, Heavy Drinking: The Myth of Alcoholism As a Disease *(Berkeley: University of California Press, 1988), pp. 3, 4, 7, 24, 45, 142.]*

ANGER

Comes from Within

It is natural for people to blame others for their anger and to avoid taking responsibility for it themselves, but it is important to realize that anger is a conscious or conditioned response to circumstances or other individuals, and we do ourselves a disservice if we fail to realize that fact. Anger, as Marie Chapian and Neva Coyle point out in their book *Free to Be Thin,* comes from within and must be dealt with as such.

"Has anyone or anything made you angry lately? Anyone or anything made you upset, worried, furious, miserable, frustrated, depressed or anxious? . . .

"It's the mature person who can stop blaming people and situations for his/her own sins. The responsibility for our happiness is on our own shoulders. Nobody else holds it for us. We do.

"People don't actually *make* you angry. You make yourself angry. Imagine driving in your car with a friend. This friend is telling you every turn and stop to make, as if you had never been behind a wheel before. He is being a backseat driver *par excellence.*

"You think to yourself, 'This guy is really making me angry. In a minute I'll explode.'

"Explode you may, but not because he makes you angry. You may want to throw your Indie 500 trophy at him, as well as your international chauffeur's license, but please, as you do, say the truth and tell him, 'I *make myself* angry when you tell me how to drive.'

"Nobody else *makes* you anything. You make *yourself* feel, think, say, act and do what you do."

[Marie Chapian and Neva Coyle, Free to Be Thin *(Minneapolis: Bethany House, 1979), pp. 137–38.]*

Many Faces of Anger

The injustice that women face in everyday life produces anger, and this anger is often so submerged that women are not even aware of it.

Anne Wilson Schaef gives examples of the different faces of anger in women in her book *Women's Reality*. Among them is the chemically dependent or overweight woman, who "vents her anger by abusing herself and her body. She also punishes those around her with her erratic and self-destructive behavior. Her anger seems passive, but she uses it effectively to control her world.

"There is also the depressed woman. Depression in women almost always goes hand in hand with rage turned against the self. The depressed woman suffers and she has learned to use her depression as a weapon, making sure those around her suffer as well.

"The neighborhood gossip expresses her rage by talking maliciously about other women—but rarely about men. By attacking almost everyone else around her, she believes that she can win male approval.

"Finally, there is the 'Good Christian Martyr.' This embodiment of anger is generally supported by our culture—especially by the church. The Good Christian Martyr releases her rage through sacrifice and suffering. She always takes the smallest piece of meat at mealtime. If there is not enough dessert to go around, she does without. She never buys any clothes for herself because she is not important, but she always makes sure that her children and her husband have new clothes. She gains control over others by inducing guilt. She is perhaps the most manipulative and powerful of all angry women. Some of the most damaged women I have worked with in therapy are those who have had Good Christian Martyr mothers. They try but they can never live up to the image of their perfect mothers who sacrificed so much."

[*Anne Wilson Schaef,* Women's Reality: An Emerging Female System in a White Male Society *(San Francisco: Harper & Row, 1985), p. 45.*]

Myth of Letting It All Out

It has been common among some counselors and therapists in recent years to encourage people to let their anger come out through emotional explosions. The reasoning has been that bottled-up hostility causes physical and psychological stress that is far more detrimental than the explosions themselves. This view, according to Carol Tavris, is a myth. She argues that suppressed anger is no more harmful than that which is not suppressed.

"The popular belief that suppressed anger can wreak havoc on the body and bloodstream has been inflated out of realistic proportions. It does not, in any predictable or consistent way, make us depressed, produce ulcers or hypertension, set us off on food binges, or give us heart attacks. I am not saying that constant, excessive feelings of rage are good for you; constant anxiety or depression aren't good for you, either. But that is different from maintaining that *suppressed* anger is responsible for our ills."

Tavris argues that anger that is not suppressed has dangerous social consequences and therefore can be much more detrimental to a person's well-being. "In the pop-psych discussions of the danger of suppressed anger, the content of the anger is regarded as less important than what we do with it. This mistaken emphasis ignores the lessons of history, anthropology, and Freud, all of which show that sometimes suppressed anger makes social life possible. The idea that it is always medically bad for you has, unfortunately, led to some odd conclusions that are less likely to produce emotional health than emotional tyranny. One man, for example, rationalized his twelve-year-old son's tantrums to me by saying that they would stave off ulcers and heart attacks later."

[Carol Tavris, Anger: The Misunderstood Emotion *(New York: Simon & Schuster, 1982), pp. 118–19.]*

ANIMAL CRUELTY
Associated with Criminal Behavior

Researchers have found that there is a correlation between a child's abuse of animals and later criminal behavior. It is frequently discovered that prison inmates have had a history of cruelty to their own pets and animals in the neighborhood. This was true of Clyde Barrow, of the infamous Bonnie and Clyde outlaw team, who left a dozen people dead in his violent and bloody rampage through the back roads of the South.

According to his biographer, he revealed "an innate cruelty when as a child he was seen by some neighbors 'torturing pet animals.' " He tortured the calves on the farm where he lived, and witnesses claimed that "one of his pastimes was to break a captured bird's wing and watch the wounded creature attempt to fly. Another was to half wring the necks of chickens and enjoy their prolonged agony."

[John Treherne, The Strange History of Bonnie and Clyde *(New York: Stein & Day, 1984), p. 36.]*

Cruelty to Animals Accepted in Past Centuries

Cruel treatment of animals, which is viewed today as deviant behavior, was widely practiced historically. Indeed, cruelty in general was often regarded as an amusement, and people and animals were the objects of torture in public arenas, where multitudes of people watched with apparent delight. This same perverse enjoyment was practiced throughout history on a much smaller scale and was accepted as a legitimate form of entertainment—with no apparent remorse for the pain inflicted on the hapless victim.

"The torture of animals, especially cats, was a popular amusement throughout early modern Europe. You have only to look at Hogarth's *Stages of Cruelty* to see its importance, and once you start looking you see people torturing animals everywhere. Cat killings provided a common theme in literature, from *Don Quixote* in early seventeenth-century Spain to *Germinal* in late nineteenth-century France. Far from being a sadistic fantasy on the part of a few half-crazed authors, the literary versions of cruelty to animals expressed a deep current of popular culture.... All sorts of ethnographic reports confirm that view. On the *dimanche des brandons* in Semur, for example, children used to attach cats to poles and roast them over bonfires. In the *jeu du chat* at the Fete-Dieu in Aix-en-Provence, they threw cats high in the air and smashed them on the ground. They used expressions like 'patient as a cat whose claws are being pulled out' or 'patient as a cat whose paws are being grilled.' The English were just as cruel. During the Reformation in London, a Protestant crowd shaved a cat to look like a priest, dressed it in mock vestments, and hanged it on the gallows at Cheapside."

[*Robert Darnton,* The Great Cat Massacre and Other Episodes in French Cultural History *(New York: Basic Books, 1984), pp. 90–91.]*

ANIMAL WELFARE

Exaggerated Concern

Winston Churchill, one of the greatest statesmen of all times, who fearlessly led his country through the devastation and horrors of World War II, became almost calloused to the pain, suffering, and death of his soldiers in the field. Amid all his other concerns, however, he could not bear the thought of children or animals suffering. "The Churchill children were never spanked. The worst that could happen to them, according to Sarah [his daughter], was banishment from his presence. Like many another great captain who has sent thousands of men to their deaths, he shrank from personal violence."

This concern almost reached the point of fanaticism when it came to insects. "Once during a division in the House, Anthony Head, the first man out of the chamber, spied a ladybug on the carpet. Realizing that a thunder of MP feet would soon pass this way, he bent down to rescue it. At that moment the prime minister arrived and instantly grasped the situation. Taking charge, he said, 'Put her out the window.' But since the introduction of air conditioning the windows had been permanently locked. 'Use the Chancellor's office,' he said, 'and report back to me.' Head did, but when he returned Churchill was in conference with the French foreign minister. The secretary told him he could look in for a moment. Head did and told Churchill: 'She escaped. I let her out through Macmillan's window. Nobody touched her.' 'Good, good!' the prime minister boomed. To this day Head wonders what must have passed through the foreign minister's mind."

[*William Manchester,* The Last Lion: Winston Spencer Churchill, Visions of Glory, 1874–1932 *(Boston: Little, Brown, 1983), p. 37.]*

Role of Animal Welfare in Mission Outreach

In some cultures animals are regarded highly—sometimes more highly than other people. This is what Ann Croft discovered when she sought to reach out with the Christian gospel to people in the Fulani tribe in Nigeria. Other missionaries had established human health services, but she quickly realized that the health of their cattle meant more to the people than their own health. She devoted her time to upgrading veterinary services and taught the people how to care better for their animals. As she shared her religious faith with them, she emphasized Old Testament passages that referred to nomadic cattle-herding peoples. Her ministry was very effective, and many in this Muslim tribe converted to Christianity.

[Ruth Tucker, "Female Mission Strategists: A Historical and Contemporary Perspective," Missiology: An International Review 15, no. 1 (January 1987): 85.]

ATTITUDE

Key to Success

Recent studies have shown that the key to success is not so much talent or natural gifts but rather one's drive and enthusiasm. A researcher studied the top performers among tennis players, neurosurgeons, pianists, and other fields of endeavor and found that "these superstars, who were rarely the best in their school classes and often appeared not to be physically or mentally qualified, succeeded because they cultivated proficiency. Practice and motivation determined their success. . . . There are three key factors that help us cultivate proficiency: enthusiasm, optimism, and creativity."

[Jo Berry, Becoming God's Special Woman (Old Tappan, N.J.: Revell, 1986), pp. 128–29.]

AUTHORITARIANISM
Associated with Certain Personality Types

Most people who are authoritarian by nature justify their actions through an ideological rationale. It may be a biblical argument, or it may be some other philosophical line of reasoning, but rarely would they admit that their style of behavior is based largely on their personalities or backgrounds. Patricia Gundry speaks to this issue in relation to women in ministry in her book *Neither Slave nor Free.* "You will find, if your experience matches mine, that most of the opposition to your efforts to open doors for women in the Church comes from people who have an authoritarian mind set. I find authoritarianism an interesting subject for study. Much can be learned about how to deal with authoritarians by examining their mind set.

"They tend to come from rigid parental backgrounds. Early on, they were required to obey strict parents. They always had to determine between two choices: the right way and the wrong way. Since much of the time that is almost impossible for children to do, they were frequently punished. And they were made to feel guilty about doing wrong, failing to do right, and failing to *know* how to make the right choice and do them. They thus feel insecure without rigid structures to tell them where boundaries for behavior are. They will look to an authority figure to tell them 'the truth' rather than find it for themselves. They tend to believe there is always a higher authority from which they must extract direction.

"But most of all, authoritarians think in black and white. . . . For example, they give themselves only two choices whenever possible. They will notice one and then determine its opposite. They then decide between the two."

Their virtual inability to compromise makes authoritarians very difficult to deal with when seeking to effect change in an organization or policy.

[Patricia Gundry, Neither Slave nor Free: Helping Women Answer the Call to Church Leadership *(San Francisco: Harper & Row, 1987), p. 103.]*

AUTHORITY

Matriarchal

The authority a mother wields over her children sometimes has little bearing on their age, their independence in activities not scrutinized by her watchful eye, or their status in society. This was true of Rose Kennedy and her children. "To my surprise," wrote her personal secretary, "Mrs. Kennedy's children seemed to be almost as much in awe of her as I was." Long after they had children of their own to discipline, they were careful how they spoke and behaved in front of their mother. "Sometimes I found it hard to believe that her children were so daunted. After all, although she called them 'the children,' they were in their forties and fifties. Eunice Shriver, Pat Lawford, Jean Smith, and Ted Kennedy were fully mature individuals with significant accomplishments and responsibilities of their own. They themselves had almost grown children; they were independently wealthy; they held important positions in government and administered a major charity.... But back in their mother's house, these world-renowned figures reverted to the status of children, seeking to please the woman who to them symbolized the powerful authority of the adult world. That frail octogenarian, who weighed less than one hundred pounds and stood barely over five feet tall, easily dominated them all."

[Barbara Gibson, with Caroline Latham, Life with Rose Kennedy (New York: Warner Books, 1986), pp. 31–32.]

BEAUTY

Advantages

Making an effort to enhance one's attractiveness pays dividends. It has been well documented that attractive people have many advantages in life over those who are less attractive. Unattractive people are more likely to be viewed by strangers as "unhappy, cold, insensitive, and dull." Unattractive people are less likely to be hired for a job than attractive people; jurors are less likely to accept the testimony of unattractive individuals, and they, on the average, receive longer prison sentences than attractive individuals; and people involved in service professions, including medical and educational, give less attention to patients and students who are unattractive. This data should challenge people to be concerned about their outward appearance, but it should also cause them to be more cautious about judging people too quickly by what they see.

[Norma Kvindlog and Esther Lindgren Anderson, Beyond Me *(Wheaton: Tyndale, 1987), p. 47.]*

Higher Standards of Beauty for Women

Christine Craft, who worked as an anchorwoman for Metromedia, a large broadcasting company in Kansas City, was informed very bluntly that her appearance was not acceptable for television journalism. She was in effect told that she was to have more beauty but fewer brains than her male counterparts. The words were stinging and brutal. "Christine, our viewer research results are in and they are really devastating. The people of Kansas City don't like watching you anchor the news because you are too old, too unattractive, and you are not sufficiently deferential to men. We know it's silly, but you just don't hide your intelligence to make the guys look smarter. Apparently the people of Kansas City are more provincial than even we had thought. They don't like the fact that you know the difference between the American and the National League! We've decided to remove you from your anchor chair effective immediately. You can stay on and continue your reporting and earn the rest of your contracted salary, but just remember that when the people of Kansas City see your face, they turn the dial."

Although she had been interviewed in person and told by the television executives that they liked her "look," almost immediately Christine found herself embroiled in a controversy centering around her facial features and her mental capabilities. "From the very beginning of my tenure at their midwestern television station, my attention began to be drawn repeatedly to the fact that my squarish jaw and somewhat uneven eyes made me a less desirable commodity than they had originally thought." This naturally had a negative effect on her self-confidence, but she realized from the start that the hassle she was facing was nothing short of sex discrimination. "The men could be balding, jowly, bespectacled, even fat and encased in double-knit, yet the women had to be flawless. Moreover, there was the expectation that I should pretend not to know certain facts just because I was female. The unveiled implication was that not to do so would be unfeminine."

[Christine Craft, Christine Craft: An Anchorwoman's Story *(Santa Barbara: Capra Press, 1986), pp. 9–10.]*

Importance of Inner Beauty

How should women react to the emphasis in today's world on outward beauty? This is a difficult aspect of life to deal with because there is so much pressure from society to conform. Yet, most women recognize that the emphasis on physical beauty is superficial and that a proper balance is needed for a healthy, well-rounded attitude. "Women are exploited emotionally about physical beauty. Badgered by Madison Avenue's manipulation of a natural desire to be attractive, women go through painful anxieties over their appearance. . . . And that's not all bad. Every woman ought to look as good as she can. Sloppiness is no virtue; neither is a head of hair that needs a good styling job. Perfume smells better than body odor. Too many rolls of fat are neither healthy nor pretty; and a scrubbed-looking face is pleasanter than an overly-painted one. Looking our best makes us stand taller and gives us more confidence. Our mistake comes when we derive our value from our physical appearance. If we believe that an unattractive nose makes an unattractive person we've lost the battle at the first pass. Don't be found hating thick ankles more than an ugly soul!"

[Gladys Hunt, Ms. Means Myself *(Grand Rapids: Zondervan, 1972), pp. 107–8.]*

Lack of Beauty

As a child, Carol Burnett was ever conscious of her looks. She envied the beauty of her cousin who later became a homecoming finalist at UCLA, and she often wished that her parents' good looks had been passed down to her. She was different, and she was never allowed to forget that fact, even though she had a real beauty of her own. "I was gangly and skinny. All bones and no meat.

"A true 'Burnett,' according to Nanny and Mama.

"I also had the famous 'Burnett lower lip.' It meant I had no chin. Andy Gump. Gopher Girl.

"Ugly.

"It didn't make sense to me. Daddy was good-looking. Grandma Nora didn't have a Burnett lower lip. Daddy's brothers, Uncle John and Uncle Jimmy, had chins. Didn't look like a Burnett trait to me.

"It was a trait that was mine, all mine.

"Mama backed down a little when she said I probably got the buckteeth from sucking my thumb so much. And she thought she made me feel better when she told me, 'It's great that you can draw so well 'cause no matter what you look like, you can always be an artist.' "

[Carol Burnett, One More Time *(New York: Random House, 1986), p. 112.]*

BEHAVIOR

Actions Speak Louder Than Words

Queen Victoria, who reigned in England for sixty-three years during the nineteenth century, proved by her example that women could wield great power and, in doing so, could generate monumental changes in society. Yet, "she was the despair of the women of her century, being one of those strong-minded women who could not let anyone else be strong." She stood in forceful opposition to the woman's rights movement, and in 1870, when the women's suffrage bill was being debated in Parliament, word was sent out that "the Queen is most anxious to enlist everyone who can speak or write to join in checking this mad, wicked folly of 'Woman's Rights' with all its attendant horrors, on which her poor feeble sex is bent, forgetting every sense of womanly feeling and propriety.' " But despite her verbal opposition to woman's rights, women took a very active role in society—"evidence that women learned to model themselves on her deeds rather than on her words."

[Elise Boulding, The Underside of History: A View of Women through Time (Boulder, Colo.: Westview Press, 1976), p. 618.]

BIRTH CONTROL

Early Defense

Because there was so much opposition to birth control in past generations, some extraordinary attempts to justify the practice developed, and some of the most fervent of these came from medical doctors themselves. Writing in 1929, Dr. William J. Robinson warned that failure to prescribe birth control could lead to dire consequences, and he presumed that birth control was the remedy for problems that were far deeper than ones that could be solved by birth control alone. He gave ten case studies to prove his point, most of which were pitiful cases that seemed to have a substantial amount of merit, although some seemed perhaps to be overdrawn. The following is an example:

"Case 3. A young woman was married to a man who besides being a brutal drunkard was subject to periodic fits of insanity. Every year or two he would be taken to the lunatic asylum for a few weeks or months, and then discharged. And every time on his discharge he would celebrate his liberty by impregnating his wife. She hated and loathed him, but could not protect herself against his 'embraces.' And she had to see herself giving birth to one abnormal child after another. She begged her doctor to give her some means of prevention, but that boob claimed ignorance, and the illegality of the thing. The woman finally committed suicide, but not before she had given birth to six abnormal children, who will probably grow up drunkards, criminals or insane.

"And because we object to such kind of breeding, we are accused of being enemies of the human race, of advocating race suicide, of violating the laws of God and man."

[William J. Robinson, Woman: Her Sex and Love Life *(New York: Eugenics Publishing, 1929), p. 254.]*

Early Methods

Birth control has been practiced for thousands of years. An Egyptian papyrus recorded how women used crocodile dung and material dipped in honey to block the sperm from entering the cervix. In China, women used tea leaves and bamboo paper for the same purpose, and Jewish women, getting their instructions from the Talmud, used spongelike materials. Not until the sixteenth century was the first reliable form of birth control developed. It was a male sheath made of fine linen invented by Gabriello Fallopius (who discovered the Fallopian tubes) and was initially intended for protection from venereal disease. Not until a century later was a similar sheath, manufactured from sheep's intestines, developed specifically for a birth-control device. The inventor in this instance was a Dr. Condom, and his clients were nobles in the court of Charles II in England. Like the earlier models, these were used most frequently by men seeking sexual pleasure outside marriage, and thus they were "colored as gaily as possible, with green or scarlet ribbons threaded through the top end."

[Madeline Gray, Margaret Sanger: A Biography of the Champion of Birth Control *(New York: Marek, 1979), pp. 94–95.]*

Need for Birth Control

The campaign for birth control was born out of desperation. Women were dying from childbirth and self-inflicted abortions at an alarming rate. Someone had to rise up against the opposition from moralists and lead the way in offering women a safe method for family planning. Margaret Sanger was that individual. She herself was one of eleven children. Her mother died in her forties, while her father lived on past eighty. This background influenced her to consider family planning, and she chose to have only three children. She had trained to be a nurse, and after twelve years of homemaking and childrearing, she went back to that profession as a public-health nurse in the slums of New York City. She was deeply moved by the plight of poor women, and she later wrote of the many tragic experiences she encountered.

"Pregnancy was a chronic condition among the women of this class. Suggestions as to what to do for a girl who was 'in trouble' or a married woman who was 'caught' passed from mouth to mouth—herb teas, turpentine, steaming, rolling downstairs, inserting slippery elm, knitting needles, shoe-hooks. When they had word of a new remedy they hurried to the drugstore, and if the clerk were inclined to be friendly he might say, 'Oh, that won't help you, but here's something that may.' The younger druggists usually refused to give advice because, if it were to be known, they would come under the law; midwives were even more fearful. The doomed women implored me to reveal the 'secret' rich people had, offering to pay me extra to tell them; many really believed I was holding back information for money. They asked everybody and tried anything, but nothing did them any good. On Saturday nights I have seen groups of from fifty to one hundred with their shawls over their heads waiting outside the office of a five-dollar abortionist.

"Each time I returned to this district, which was becoming a recurrent nightmare, I used to hear that Mrs. Cohen 'had been carried to a hospital, but had never come back,' or that Mrs. Kelly 'had sent the children to a neighbor and had put her head into the gas oven.' Day after day such tales were poured into my ears—a baby born dead, great relief—the death of an older child, sorrow but again relief of a sort—the story told a thousand times of death from abortion and children going into institutions. I shuddered with horror as I listened to the details and studied the reasons back of them—destitution linked with excessive childbearing. The waste of life seemed utterly senseless."

[Margaret Sanger, An Autobiography *(New York: Norton, 1938), pp. 87–88.]*

Objecting to the Use of Condoms

One of the strongest arguments against birth control in the nineteenth century was that it would potentially liberate women. Frequent pregnancies kept women in their place—in the home managing domestic affairs—and anything that prevented pregnancies was viewed as dangerous to family life. One of the strongest proponents of this view was Augustus Kinsley Gardner, who, in his book *Conjugal Sins,* warned married couples against the sexual vice of using condoms. He deplored the "use of intermediate tegumentary coverings [condoms] made of thin rubber, or gold-beater's skin, and so often relied upon as absolute preventives. . . . Their employment certainly must produce a feeling of shame and disgust utterly destructive of the true delight of pure hearts and refined sensibilities. They are suggestive of licentiousness and the brothel, and their employment degrades to bestiality the true feelings of manhood and the holy state of matrimony. . . . Furthermore they produce (as alleged by the best modern French writers, who are more familiar with the effects of their use than we are in the United States) certain physical lesions from their irritating presence as foreign bodies, and also from the chemicals employed in their manufacture."

[Augustus Kinsley Gardner, Conjugal Sins *(New York: Redfield, 1870), p. 109.]*

Opposition to Birth Control

When Margaret Sanger traveled throughout the United States speaking out for birth control during the early decades of the twentieth century, she confronted strong opposition—especially by Roman Catholic clergy. On one occasion when she was on a speaking tour in Massachusetts, a meeting was canceled because of the following declaration that the church had ordered to be read before all masses in the local Catholic congregations: "We have been informed on good authority that a campaign is about to be launched in Western Massachusetts in the interests of the detestable practice of birth control. It is understood that a nationally known defender of this vice, Margaret Sanger by name, is to arouse people to pass a new state law permitting this vice to be practiced. Those who are sponsoring this lecture are engaged in a work that is unpatriotic and a disgrace to the Christian community. Catholics, of course, will be guided by the mind of Christ and His Church, and will *actively oppose* any attempt to label this locality as a center of such immoral doctrine."

[Madeline Gray, Margaret Sanger: A Biography of the Champion of Birth Control *(New York: Marek, 1979), p. 383.]*

BIRTH DEFECTS
Caused by Parental Neglect

It was widely believed during the Victorian era that birth defects, infant death, or even the sex of the child was a result of parental attitude or weak semen. "A Victorian child who showed weakness or defects was seen as suffering not from unknown or God-inflicted causes, but from its parents' neglect of duty before, during, or after pregnancy. Infant or early death was now viewed as the result of inherited deficiencies deriving from weak seminal fluids on the father's part and an unresponsive attitude during impregnation on the mother's part. Some doctors believed that strong semen produced boys and weak semen, girls. Dr. Trall's advice on achieving joyful sex included the warning that indulging on a full stomach could result in the birth of a deformed child."

[Annegret S. Ogden, The Great American Housewife: From Helpmate to Wage Earner, 1776–1986 *(Westport, Conn.: Greenwood Press, 1986), p. 86.]*

BITTERNESS
Resulting in Wasted Life

David and Svea Flood, a young Swedish missionary couple, were "on fire for God" when they arrived in Africa in 1921. They were determined that they would do pioneer evangelistic work with an unreached tribe, but they quickly discovered that the Africans were hostile, and the climate was deadly. Soon after the birth of their second child, Svea died. The emotional stress was too much for David. Doubts consumed him. He could not understand why God had let him down. Had God turned his back on him? Had he and Svea been on a fool's errand? For all their work they had only one convert, and he was a child.

In a spirit of anger and bitterness, David left Africa with his young son, leaving behind Aggie, his baby girl, who was too weak to travel. A missionary couple took her in, and when they subsequently died, she was passed on to another missionary couple, who later raised her in America. In the meantime, David, now back in Sweden, renounced the church and his commitment to God. He lived a life of drinking and debauchery. After his second marriage dissolved, he began living with a mistress, and his children forsook him. He seldom thought about his daughter, whom he had not seen since infancy.

Aggie, however, often thought about her early years and the father who had abandoned her. She loved the family who had cared for her, but something in her life was missing. After high school and further study at North Central Bible College, she married Dewey Hurst, and together they served in various ministries with the Assemblies of God. But she longed to go home and to tell her father a story about Africa that she hoped would change his life.

Finally, she was able to make the trip to Sweden, where she met her older brother and half-brothers and half-sister. In Stockholm she found her 73-year-old bedridden father in a run-down dingy apartment with liquor bottles lining the window sills. It was a pitiful and disgusting sight. But he was her father. She took him in her arms and told him she loved him and explained how God had taken care of her through the years. Indeed, God had done far more than that. There in his grimy bed, with tobacco juice running down his unshaven face, he heard for the first time that the little boy who had been converted through his and Svea's ministry had won his village of 600 people to Christ. This young boy had gone on in the faith and had become a great leader in the church. It was an emotional moment for David, and through his daughter's urging, he recommitted his life to God. There was joy in that tiny apartment that day, but also sadness that a life had been wasted. In the weeks that followed, his health declined, and six months later he was dead.

[Aggie Hurst, One Witness *(Old Tappan, N.J.: Revell, 1986), pp. 106–9.]*

BREAST-FEEDING

Benefits

In her book *Dr. Mom: A Guide to Baby and Child Care,* Marianne Neifert presents many benefits of breast-feeding over artificial infant formulas. She points out that the value of breast-feeding was not questioned until the early decades of the twentieth century, "due to a combination of social and cultural factors." Indeed, "by the 1950s and 1960s, only one in five mothers elected to breast-feed her baby and bottle feeding was the norm." This pattern began to change by the early 1970s "in that back-to-nature and health awareness era. . . . Breast milk was literally rediscovered by the medical profession, and its benefits to the infant were widely publicized to both lay and professional people. With this new knowledge, many mothers chose to breast-feed, so that nursing one's baby has again been established as the norm."

Among the many benefits of breast-feeding are nutritional factors. Even before the milk "comes in," the breasts offer the newborn colostrum, a fluid that "is higher in protein, vitamins, and minerals than breast milk and lower in fat and the milk sugar, lactose." It is "a perfect, easily digestible first food for a new infant. It helps protect her from infections and prepares her intestines for breast-milk feedings."

When the milk does "come in," it contains the necessary ration of protein, fat, and carbohydrates for "optimal infant growth." Likewise, "other elements in breast milk, including vitamins, minerals, enzymes, and water, are present in the exact amounts that a newborn needs and can best utilize." And still another important benefit of breast milk over that of artificial formulas is the immunological effect. Components in the milk protect the baby from various illnesses, infections, and allergies.

There are psychological benefits as well. "Breast feeding won't guarantee bonding. But the early, loving, skin-to-skin contact that breast feeding affords may enhance the process."

Neifert sums up her position on breast-feeding with some obvious advantages. "Breast feeding is the easiest, most convenient way to feed a baby. Breast milk is highly portable; it never needs heating or refrigeration. The container is sterile, self-cleaning, and unbreakable. There's no mixing, no mess, no trips cut short because you didn't bring along enough to feed your baby, no cold kitchen floors to walk at 3:00 A.M. while you prepare a bottle of formula." If that is not enough to convince the prospective mother, she points out that breast-feeding is the cheapest way to feed the baby. "Six months of not buying formula can save enough to buy a major household appliance."

[Marianne E. Neifert, with Anne Price and Nancy Dana, Dr. Mom: A Guide to Baby and Child Care (New York: Putnam's Sons, 1986), pp. 131–35.]

CAPITAL PUNISHMENT

Killing a Rehabilitated Criminal

One of the most powerful arguments against capital punishment is that innocent people may be executed without being given an adequate time to overturn their guilty verdicts. But there is another argument against capital punishment. What about those people who have been rehabilitated and whose lives have been dedicated to making this world a better one? Taking the life of such an individual is destroying one of society's most precious assets. This was true in the case of Velma Barfield. Billy Graham tells her story and how she had an impact on his own family.

"Velma Barfield was a woman from rural North Carolina who was charged with first degree murder; no one could have surmised the effect her life and death would have upon so many people. In 1978 she was arrested for murdering four people, including her mother and fiancé. She never denied her guilt, but told the chilling story of her drug-dazed life, beginning with tranquilizers which were prescribed following a painful injury.

"Velma was a victim of incest as a child and the abuse of prescription drugs as an adult. After she admitted her guilt, she was taken to prison and confined in a cell by herself. One night the guard tuned in to a twenty-four-hour gospel station. Down the gray hall, desperate and alone in her cell, Velma heard the words of an evangelist and allowed Jesus Christ to enter her life. She wrote, 'I had been in and out of churches all my life and I could explain all about God. But I had never understood before that Jesus had died for me.'

"Her conversion was genuine. For six years on death row she ministered to many of her cell-mates. The outside world began to hear about Velma Barfield as the story of her remarkable rehabilitation became known. Velma wrote to Ruth and there developed a real friendship between them. In one letter Ruth wrote to Velma, 'God has turned your cell on Death Row into a most unusual pulpit. There are people who will listen to what you have to say because of where you are. As long as God has a ministry for you here, He will keep you here. When I compare the dreariness, isolation and difficulty of your cell to the glory that lies ahead of you, I could wish for your sake that God would say, 'Come on Home.'

"My daughter, Anne, received special permission to visit Velma Barfield many times and was touched by the sadness of her story and the sincerity of her love for Christ as well as the beauty of her Christian witness in that prison.

"Before her final sentence, Velma wrote to Ruth: 'If I am executed on August 31, I know the Lord will give me dying grace, just as He gave me saving grace, and has given me living grace.' On the night she was executed, Ruth and I knelt and prayed together for her till we knew she was safe in Glory.

"Velma Barfield was the first woman in twenty-two years to be executed in the United States."

[Billy Graham, Facing Death and the Life After *(Waco: Word Books, 1987), 113–14.]*

CAREER
Married and Single Women

In an age when a combination of marriage, career, and family seems to be the norm for vast numbers of women, it is sometimes startling to hear voices of strong opposition that seem almost to come from another era or another planet. Yet, these voices need to be heard and responded to. An example is Elisabeth Elliot, a well-known missionary and author.

"There may be a few exceptional women who successfully combine career and marriage, but to give full attention to both at the same time is an impossibility. If a woman wants her career to have priority she will do better to stay single, for the simple scriptural reason that she was made to adapt to a man (made 'for him') if she has a man."

[Elisabeth Elliot, Let Me Be a Woman *(Wheaton: Tyndale, 1976), p. 113.]*

CELIBACY
For Birth Control

For many centuries celibacy has been the practice of men and women who desired full-time ministry within the Roman Catholic church. The decision was generally made before marriage and before children had been born, but that was not always true. Margery Kempe, a late-medieval mystic, made the decision to live in celibacy and devote the remainder of her life to the pursuit of holiness as a wandering evangelist after she had been married for many years and had given birth to fourteen children. Indeed, her decision to live celibate may have been prompted by her desire to avoid pregnancy, as abstinence was the only viable method of birth control for women at that time. She left her husband and went on a pilgrimage that lasted some twenty years and took her as far north as Norway and as far south as the Holy Land.

One of the reasons she left home was that she feared she would not be able to maintain her vow while living with her husband at home.

[Edith Deen, Great Women of the Christian Faith *(New York: Harper & Row, 1959), pp. 316–17.]*

CHARITY
Greatest of All Virtues

A visionary miracle influenced the conversion of a fourth-century Hungarian cavalry officer who later became the Bishop of Tours. St. Martin, as he is generally remembered, was leading his troops, when he came upon a poorly clad beggar suffering from the frigid temperatures. "Moved by the man's suffering, Martin took off his own elegant cape and put it on the beggar, and he was about to go on his way when he was stopped by an amazing sight: the beggar was Jesus Christ, searching among men for evidence of the charity He had said was the greatest virtue." Soon after that incident Martin resigned his position in the military and became a monk. He founded a monastic community and became known for his healing miracles and good deeds to the poor. So popular was he that he was later chosen to be bishop, an office that he very reluctantly accepted.

[Glenn D. Kittler, The Woman God Loved: The Life of Blessed Anne-Marie Javouhey *(Garden City, N.Y.: Hanover House, 1959), p. 16.]*

CHILD ABUSE
Abuse versus Legitimate Discipline

One of the tragic aspects of child abuse is that some parents seek to justify it by quoting the Bible. Indeed, in some instances children have actually been killed, and the parents insisted that they were following the biblical injunction not to "spare the rod." Kay Marshall Strom speaks to this issue in her book *Helping Women in Crisis.*

"Surprisingly, Christians are some of the most difficult people to convince that child abuse exists to any serious degree. Many feel that anyone who speaks out against child abuse is against spanking and therefore against the Bible. The problem is that some parents are driven by such an out-of-control spare-the-rod-and-spoil-the-child philosophy that they truly believe abusive punishment is the only way to discipline their children properly. Many of these parents argue that as children they were beaten or strapped and that the experience, though painful, was 'good for them.' This idea is reinforced by some Christian leaders, one of whom tells parents, 'Welts and bruises are a sign that you are doing a good job.'

"As counselors, is it possible for us to draw a line between a disciplining smack and an act of abuse? It isn't easy. One expert offers this guideline: 'If an hour after the spanking you can see a red mark, or if a bruise appears, you have crossed the line between discipline and abuse.' The goal of discipline is loving guidance, not injury."

[Kay Marshall Strom, Helping Women in Crisis *(Grand Rapids: Zondervan, 1986), p. 42.]*

Mothers' Abuse of Daughters

Today, parents who physically abuse their children are under penalty of law, but in decades and centuries past, brutal treatment of children was viewed as a proper way to discipline. Sometimes the physical home environment was a factor, as in the sixteenth century, when families lived in very close quarters. Houses were tiny, and families were large, and "in the compressed life spaces available there were high tension levels and frequent expressions of physical violence." Indeed, the literature of the period refers frequently to the brutalizing of children, especially instances of mothers' beating their daughters. "Daughter beating was often in connection with a child's resistance to parental marriage plans. Even the gentle peace queen Marguerite of Navarre beat her daughter daily for weeks on end to make her agree to a politically designed marriage choice. Lady Jane Gray's mother beat her. Agnes Paston . . . beat her daughter so badly that 'her head was broke in 2 or 3 places.' It would seem that women of this period were subject to a lot of emotional pressure which they vented by child beating. Putting daughters out to other families as servants was one of the few available means of relieving the strain, but this required reciprocity, in that such a mother must accept someone else's daughter into her home."

[Elise Boulding, The Underside of History: A View of Women through Time (Boulder, Colo.: Westview Press, 1976), pp. 552–53.]

CHILDBIRTH
Archaic Practices

Many advice books for women were being published in the late nineteenth century, some of which included strict admonitions for pregnant women and women who had already given birth. One such book, written by G. H. Napheys, cautioned new mothers not only to stay in bed but also to remain "rigidly in the recumbent position for the first few days, not raising her shoulders from the pillow for any purpose." Indeed, she was instructed to remain so still that she was not even permitted to change her birthing gown until the fourth day, but even then she was not to lift her head off the pillow. Precautions were also taken to protect her pubic area, which was swabbed with goose grease and wine every few hours and then wrapped in heavy fabric so that it would not be exposed to air. After a week in bed she was encouraged to sit up, and after two weeks to get out of bed for short periods each day. After a month of recuperation she could safely resume household duties, but she was to continue wearing her heavy muslin sanitary napkin for months in order to avoid the affliction of a fallen womb. That such precautions were taken is not surprising in light of the high death toll that women suffered in childbirth, but such precautions were not feasible for vast numbers of women—especially the pioneer women, who had no choice but to return to housework soon after giving birth.

[G. H. Napheys, The Physical Life of Women: Advice to the Maiden, Wife, and Mother (Walthamstrow, Mass.: Mayhew, 1879), pp. 141–93.]

Early Theories and Modern Facts

As with other areas related to science and medicine, much incorrect information about conception and childbirth was disseminated before the true facts were actually known, and in many instances, the early theories reflected a sexual bias that has long since had to be abandoned. In her book *Woman of Tomorrow*, Kathy Keeton discusses this history in scientific terminology.

"It hasn't been that long since we figured out how babies are made. A little over 150 years ago, scholars, all men of course, still believed that men made them. Their theory was that each male sperm was actually a complete little person—a homunculus. Unseen within the glands of each tiny male homunculus were even smaller homunculi, and so on—all future generations of man packaged like Chinese nested boxes within boxes and waiting to be deposited in the womb and grow. Women served only to incubate the little male-begotten creatures to birth. ('Male pregnancy envy' is how researcher John Money characterizes the theory.)

"In the 1820s, scientists using microscopes discovered the female egg and set that theory to rest. So sperm fertilizes egg to create an embryo. But that didn't provide any clues as to why some embryos turn out female and some male. The answer to that came in 1902, with the discovery of the X and Y sex chromosomes. Two X chromosomes cause an embryo to begin developing as a female. An X and Y set in motion the development of a male. The egg always carries an X, so it's the X or Y contributed by the sperm that makes the difference. Notice how tentatively I said 'set in motion the development of a male.' The pairing of the X or Y chromosomes is only the first step in a chain of events that has to go off smoothly in order to produce an individual we'd recognize as male or female.

"*Every embryo starts life prepared to develop into a female.* Within it are two clusters of cells that, left to themselves, will develop into ovaries. The job of the Y chromosome is to interfere with this feminine development plan and cause the embryonic clusters to develop into testicles. (It wasn't until 1976 that researchers discovered how. They found that a gene carried by the Y chromosome sets up production of a substance called H-Y antigen. This antigen coats the clusters, and by the sixth week of fetal life begins to virilize their development.) Once testicles have formed, they take charge of the masculinizing process, blocking development of another embryonic structure that would have become the womb and turning out testosterone, which spurs the development of sperm ducts and male sex organs.

"So it takes a nine-month remodeling effort to make a male. . . . If anything interferes with the work of the H-Y antigen or the testosterone, the fetus reverts to its original female development pattern."

[Kathy Keeton, with Yvonne Baskin, Woman of Tomorrow *(New York: St. Martin's, 1985), pp. 34–36.]*

Effect of Alcohol on Childbirth

Only in recent years have medical specialists discovered the detrimental effects alcohol can have on the unborn infant. This is a very serious problem in the United States today because the highest increase in alcoholism is among young women.

"We are now in a position to understand that drinking is one of the three most common causes of birth defects in this country and the only one that is preventable. This information is tremendously important news that every woman today needs to be aware of. Fetal alcohol damage is so common that it affects one in every two hundred live births in the United States. For American Indian women, the figure is one out of fifty live births. Damage can range from mild mental retardation to severe physical deformation as well. The full effect of fetal alcohol syndrome (FAS) is relatively rare and primarily affects the children of very heavy drinkers. There is increasing evidence that heavy drinking on the part of the male can result in damaged sperm and probably in an abnormal fetus as well, yet women are the ones who must carry the possibly alcohol-damaged fetus to term or make the difficult decision not to do so. A knowledgeable physician can say with certainty that there is no known safe amount of drinking for a woman who is pregnant or who is trying to conceive. This is recent knowledge, and far too many women were and still are uninformed. They will live with the tragic consequences."

[Rachel V., A Woman like You: Life Stories of Women Recovering from Alcoholism and Addiction (San Francisco: Harper & Row, 1985), p. xxi.]

Natural Childbirth (Lamaze)

The so-called natural childbirth, or Lamaze method, is not for everyone. Sylvia Ann Hewlett, who holds a Ph.D. in economics, believes her experience is common among women. "During my first pregnancy Richard and I took Lamaze classes, faithfully immersing ourselves in the techniques and philosophy of the natural childbirth movement. We absorbed the message that modern obstetrical practices were at best unnecessary and at worst a conspiracy on the part of the male medical establishment to deny women the 'great experience' of birth.

"Fired up by such a worthy cause," she anticipated childbirth with great optimism. She was not prepared, however, for the "seven excruciating hours" of labor or for the doctor's conclusion that she was "hysterical" and that her behavior was an attempt to "impress" her husband. Finally, her husband was able to locate an anesthesiologist who agreed to give her a local anesthetic. "Within minutes I was a different person. The incredible, unbearable pain just drained away. I became calm and reasonable, even joyful. The epidural left me completely conscious and with a great deal of control over my body so that when the time came, I was able to help push my baby out. Lisa was born pink, noisy, and beautiful." Sylvia soon discovered that she was not alone in her inability to go through natural childbirth. Out of the thirteen expectant mothers in her Lamaze class, three underwent cesareans, and seven required medication to relieve the agony they were suffering. "Only three of the thirteen had been able to deliver their children according to the Lamaze blueprint, and subsequently many of us had to deal with bouts of depression. At some level we truly believed that we were the weaklings that had failed."

[*Sylvia Ann Hewlett*, A Lesser Life: The Myth of Women's Liberation *(New York: Morrow, 1986), pp. 35–36.]*

Postpartum Depression

After the birth of a long-awaited baby—at a time when women should be on a high emotionally—many mothers experience an unexpected and unexplainable depression. As they are forming the strongest love bond that they are capable of experiencing, they are at the same time feeling unhappy and listless. There is a medical reason for this, and women should prepare themselves for this normal aspect of the childbearing process.

"The emotional fragility that occurs during postpartum is sometimes referred to as 'the baby blues.' The baby blues aren't experienced only by women who already happen to be maladjusted or psychologically unsteady. Research indicates that there's a difference during this time even for ordinarily stable and well-functioning women. Following the birth of the baby, there is an abrupt drop in levels of different endocrine agents that have been circulating in a woman's plasma. This is a biologically induced state similar to what happens to a person coming off drugs. In this case it is a female-hormone withdrawal."

[*Brenda Poinsett*, Understanding a Woman's Depression *(Wheaton: Tyndale, 1984), p. 108.]*

Premodern Techniques of Childbirth

The history of childbirth, especially in Colonial America, is replete with amazing techniques and innovations used by midwives in order to relieve pain and avoid complications that often resulted in the death of the infant or the mother. In some instances these techniques may have done more harm than good, but in many cases there may have been at least a positive psychological effect that aided women during this most difficult time. "Judge Samuel Sewall mentions in his diary that the midwife brought a collapsible 'birth stool,' a chair, in use since medieval times, designed to support the laboring woman's back while encouraging the force of gravity to expedite birth. The device also featured a cut-out seat to provide the midwife with access to the birth canal. She knelt down to receive the baby from below, under the long skirts that kept the mother warm and preserved her modesty. The stool was probably a rather common aid to birth. An adjustable version, called the 'portable ladies' solace,' was used in Philadelphia as late as 1799. In some instances women attendants took its place, supporting the mother's back and legs during labor. There is even one reference to a husband's acting as a substitute for the birth stool by holding his wife in a sitting position on his lap and pressing down on her abdomen, but this occurred in the nineteenth century on the Midwest frontier and may have been uncommon earlier. Colonial women were able to move about and assume a variety of positions to help their labors along.

"The female attendants provided food and drink for the laboring woman to keep up her strength, offering such things as toast, buckwheat gruel, mutton, broth, and eggs. Cordials and red wine produced relaxation and eased pain. Too many cordials could make a woman drunk, and some English midwives were accused of administering an excess. Warm cloths on the stomach or an enema served to dilate the birth passage. The midwife might put a quill full of 'sneezing power' (snuff or white hellebore) up the woman's nose to make her sneeze and so dislodge a difficult birth. A child born as a result of this practice was known as a 'quilled baby.' "

[Richard W. Wertz and Dorothy C. Wertz, Lying-In: A History of Childbirth in America (New York: Schocken Books, 1979), pp. 13–15.]

View of Childbirth as Sinful and Unclean

The joyous occasion of childbirth that, in recent years, husbands often observe in the delivery room or at home was not always thought to be the ultimate in God's creative handiwork. In fact, it was thought to be such an ugly and unclean bodily function that theologians in the Middle Ages argued that the Virgin Mary, to whom they ascribed sinless perfection from the time of her conception, could not have given birth to Jesus in the normal way through the birth canal. The "closed uterus" theory developed, which held that Mary's womb remained closed and that Jesus miraculously emerged without the messy "unclean" aspects of childbirth.

[Ruth A. Tucker and Walter L. Liefeld, Daughters of the Church: Women and Ministry from New Testament Times to the Present *(Grand Rapids: Zondervan, 1987), pp. 168–69.]*

CHILDLESSNESS

Perspective of a Single Woman

The desire to bear children comes naturally to most women whether they are married or single, and in recent decades more and more single women have been choosing to have children and raise them on their own. Yet, there are mixed emotions for most single women on this issue, as is illustrated by the response one such woman gave Jane Howard, a journalist and author. This woman confessed that a child would interfere with her life-style. "Now my whole life is geared to being flexible and free—not just free to travel, though that's part of it, but free to *grow,* whenever and in whatever ways may seem necessary."

Howard identified with those feelings and reflected on her own mixed emotions regarding children. "That's how my life has been, too, and the price I have paid for freedom is childlessness. On bad days I brood over children I might have had. On good days I think about her or him or them whom I might someday still bear. On all days I reflect with gratitude on the existence of a certain few, borne by others, whose company matters as much to me as anything in the world. I need kids in my life as much as I need men. To hold a snuggling, trusting child on one's lap is to feel a deep and peaceful intimacy as necessary, to me at least, as any feeling I know."

[Jane Howard, A Different Woman (New York: Dutton, 1973), p. 124.]

CHILDREARING

Decrease in Importance

Women today with traditional values often seek to argue that their work in childrearing is as important today as it was in generations and centuries past. In many respects this is true, but in terms of a woman's lifetime responsibilities, the function of childrearing has become a less and less significant part of the whole. Kathy Keeton makes this point in her book *Woman of Tomorrow.* "That's not a conspiracy on the feminists' part, and it didn't happen overnight. It's simply a reflection of changing economic times, and ironically, our own longevity. In an agricultural age, when children were valued as economic assets on the farm, infant mortality was high, and women themselves expected to die in their forties, childrearing was truly a vital and lifelong profession. But today we live to be nearly eighty and average one and a half children apiece. That's hardly a lifetime job. I find it tragic that many girls . . . are still being raised to think that childrearing is their major contribution to society."

[Kathy Keeton, with Yvonne Baskin, Woman of Tomorrow (New York: St. Martin's, 1985), p. 113.]

Theories of Childrearing

The frustration of rearing children has changed very little over the centuries, and the realities rarely correspond with the various theories of how best to deal with particular circumstances. John Wilmot, a seventeenth-century Earl of Rochester, wrote of this frustration in his own life. "Before I got married, I had six theories about bringing up children; now I have six children and no theories!"

[Marion Stroud, Please Tell Me How You Feel *(Minneapolis: Bethany House, 1982), p. 137.]*

CHILDREN

Authoritarianism and Dependency

Few would argue with the concept that parents should have authority over their children, but raising them in an authoritarian environment is a different matter. There are some serious pitfalls associated with authoritarianism, one being that "it requires the presence of an authority to keep the child in line. It is well-known but frequently ignored that 'When the cat's away the mice will play.' Some of the most mischievous children are those whose parents try to control them through anger, force, and pressure." Another peril of authoritarianism is that it "prevents the child from developing a set of love-motivated controls." Children "lack the incentive to develop their own inner values. They conform not because it is good for them or for others, but because they are afraid to do otherwise.

"A third problem of authoritarianism is that it stunts psychological growth and fosters immature dependency. If children do not rebel against the rigid control exercised in an authoritarian home, they will succumb to mindless conformity. They will blindly follow the wishes of their parents and others, while at the same time losing touch with their own individuality, spontaneity, and flexibility. Instead of learning to confront difficult decisions with their own resources, they respond mechanically according to an imposed code of conduct. . . . Even as adults, they cling to the standards and teachings of their parents because they have proven neither their own adequacy nor their own ability to make decisions.

"The final difficulty in authoritarian parenting is its negative effect on a child's self-esteem. Parents who dominate and pressure their children and who do not respect their capacities and gifts undermine the child's attempts to gain confidence and to develop self-esteem."

[*Bruce Narramore,* Parenting with Love and Limits *(Grand Rapids: Zondervan, 1979), p. 39.*]

Bonding during Infancy

In recent years there has been much discussion on the importance of bonding between an infant and its parents. Studies have indicated that lack of bonding in the early weeks and months of an infant's life can have serious repercussions later on. "Bonding," writes Marianne Neifert, "is the emergence of profound love between a parent and child, the surge of affection that calls a parent to respond to every infant need despite their own physical sacrifice." Some misconceptions regarding bonding, however, cause some parents undue stress. "Unfortunately, the bonding process, which really begins before birth and can take weeks to complete, has been commonly thought of as taking place in the first few minutes or hours of life. A false concept of 'epoxy bonding,' effected by holding an infant immediately after birth and allowing some magical exchange to occur between parent and child, has been popularized. The large number of parents who are separated from their infants at birth because of medical reasons, who had Caesarean births, or who adopted babies have recently come to doubt whether they 'fully bonded' to their infants. In fact, true bonding is a long-term process. It almost never goes awry among well-intentioned, committed parents, even in the worst of delivery circumstances. Almost all of our mothers gave birth to us under general anesthesia and had very limited contact with us during the first week of life, and still they managed to 'bond.' Bonding can be made more difficult when an infant is sick or premature or has a birth defect, and it can occur more easily when the birthing experience is enjoyable, the infant remains with the parents immediately after birth, and the family has easy access to the infant during the entire hospital stay."

[*Marianne E. Neifert, with Anne Price and Nancy Dana,* Dr. Mom: A Guide to Baby and Child Care *(New York: Putnam's Sons, 1986), p. 78.*]

Death of a Child

Some researchers maintain that the greatest stress or sorrow known to humankind is that involving the death of a child. This is true whether the offspring is an infant, a youth, or an adult, and the sorrow is deeper when there has been a close relationship between the parent and the child. The mother of President James A. Garfield had such an experience. She doted on him when he was small and helped teach him to read the Bible by the time he was four. When he ran away to become a sailor at the age of sixteen, she faithfully prayed for him, and he later credited her prayers for turning him around. She nursed him back to health after a severe illness and helped pay his way through seminary to train for the ministry. But instead of becoming a great preacher, as his mother had dreamed of his doing, he went into politics and was elected president in 1880.

Eliza Garfield was filled with pride "the following March when she sat on the flag-draped platform erected over the Capitol's steps watching her son take the oath of office as President of the United States. Although five women before her had lived till they had a son in the same position, she was the first to see the actual ceremony—and just four months later, she became the first who had to hear that her son had been struck down by an assassin." It was a traumatic ordeal for her. "Just a few months after her son kissed her at his inauguration, he was shot by a disgruntled office seeker." He "was on the brink of death for eighty days, suffering unspeakably, before finally succumbing. He was forty-nine when he died, and she was within two days of her eightieth birthday. How she summoned the strength to bear that long and terrible vigil must be imagined, for she did not write about it; her venture into autobiography had been undertaken to please James, who no longer could read her words."

[*Doris Faber,* The Mothers of American Presidents *(New York: American Library, 1968), pp. 124, 132.*]

Denying Guilt Common to Children

It is a common trait of children (and adults) to deny guilt and place the blame on someone else. Miriam Neff writes of this tendency in her own household.

"There is a fifth child who lives at our house called 'Nobody.' I was cleaning under the basement stairs on my once-every-two-years cleaning plan. On the dark cement in a corner I found moldy apple cores, black, brittle banana peels, and peach seeds. It looked like someone had been operating a fruit stand or collecting compost to fertilize a garden. I called our offspring to give accounts of themselves. By the time the lineup had all had his/her turn to reply, the unanimous decision was that 'Nobody' had done it. 'Great,' I wanted to scream, 'Will Nobody please crawl back there and clean it up?' Within a few days I discovered that 'Nobody' also liked to eat in the attic. I stumbled across assorted containers with remains of spaghettios and chocolate pudding.

" 'Nobody' breaks windows, eats the frosting off cakes before company comes, leaves gallon boxes of ice cream on the kitchen counter before we leave the house for three hours, and delights in parking bicycles behind the car. 'Nobody' puts crayons in the clothes dryer and is not even tax-deductible!"

[Miriam Neff, Women and Their Emotions *(Chicago: Moody, 1983), pp. 193–94.]*

Difference in Treatment of Children

Women sometimes fail to appreciate the liberation they now enjoy in comparison to their forebears, who suffered so many indignities in life. Fashion is just one of the areas of discrimination that women have had to endure down through the ages.

"Before the thirteenth century, all children were enclosed in swaddling clothes. Swaddling clothes bound the baby completely so it could not move its limbs; they offered an early and ineradicable experience in constriction. This lesson never ended for women. Boys went from swaddling clothes to a little dress and long hair until they were shorn and breached at seven—the age of reason—but girls went directly into adult clothes. Their tiny bodies were imprisoned in bodices and corsets reinforced with iron and whalebone that molded them into the prevailing female fashion. They were expected to maintain a dignified posture, a slow and graceful walk, and generally to conform to the standards of adult females. 'The contraptions used to achieve these ends often frustrated them, leading instead to the distortion or displacement of the organs, and sometimes even death.' Boys, however, were left free to play."

[Marilyn French, Beyond Power: On Women, Men, and Morals *(New York: Summit Books, 1985), p. 174.]*

Difficulty in Rearing Children

Bill Cosby, who is known for his kid-oriented television commercials and his top-rated family-oriented television program, writes humorously of the struggles he has faced in raising his own children. He begins a chapter entitled "Sweet Insanity" with the following words: "Yes, having a child is surely the most beautifully irrational act that two people in love can commit. Having had five qualifies me to write this book but not to give you any absolute rules because there *are* none." He goes on to discuss the futility of thinking there actually are hard and fast rules that aid in childrearing. "Raising children is incredibly hard and risky business in which no cumulative wisdom is gained: each generation repeats the mistakes the previous one made. . . . We parents so often blow the business of raising kids, but not because we violate any philosophy of child raising. I doubt there can *be* a philosophy about something so difficult, something so downright mystical, as raising kids. A baseball manager has learned a lot about his job from having played the game, but a parent has not learned a thing from having once been a child. What can you learn about a business in which a child's favorite response is 'I don't know.'

"A father enters his son's room and sees that the boy is missing his hair.

" 'What happened to your head?' the father says, beholding his skin-headed son. 'Did you get a haircut?'

" 'I don't know,' the boy replies.

" 'You don't *know* if you got a haircut? Well, tell me this: Was your head with you all day?'

" 'I don't know,' says the boy."

[Bill Cosby, Fatherhood *(Garden City, N.Y.: Doubleday, 1986), pp. 18–20.]*

Falling Short of Parental Expectations

The Nobel-prize-winning physicist Dr. William Shockley, who is known for his support of genetic breeding in order to produce superior offspring, has himself donated sperm to a sperm bank. Women of high intelligence are permitted to draw on the resources of the bank to increase their chances of having superior children. "Asked whether his own children were superior, he had no compunction in announcing for publication that they constituted 'a very significant regression.' His daughter was graduated from Radcliffe, one son had a Ph.D. in physics from Stanford—but with academic distinction only of the second rank, Shockley said—and another son was a drop-out. The flaw, he said, was in their mother, who 'had not as high an academic-achievement standing' as he."

[Marilyn French, Beyond Power: On Women, Men, and Morals *(New York: Summit Books, 1985), p. 326.]*

Need for Children to Feel Needed in Family

One of the negative influences the modern age has had on family life is that children no longer feel needed. There simply is not enough work in most households for children to develop a sense that their membership in the family is a necessary ingredient. This situation also has a negative impact on the child's preparation for adulthood.

"A very serious problem in today's 'traditional' family is that children do not feel useful or needed (they aren't). They are assigned inane chores like taking out the trash, but otherwise are allowed to 'play.' I can think of numerous young people who have spent their entire adolescent years taking lessons in this and that, playing basketball, football, or any sport they can get into, but always *playing* at something. Their families love them, enjoy them, are proud of their 'achievements.' But their families do not *need* them, except as darling pets. And the kids know it. Being needed is basic to a person's sense of worth but it cannot be faked. Knowing that you are not necessary to the family is devastating and I believe largely responsible for experiments with religious cults, sexual activity, drugs, and alcohol."

[*Millie Van Wyke,* You're Hired! Insights for Christian Women Who Work outside the Home *(Grand Rapids: Baker, 1983), p. 87.*]

Pain of Children Separating from Parents

One of the most difficult aspects of being a missionary parent is the inevitable separation it brings from children. Sometimes that separation does not come until college years, but it often comes earlier when children are sent away to boarding school for months at a time. Many children adjust quickly to this change. For parents the adjustment is often more difficult—and sometimes impossible if the children are agonizing over the separation.

This pain of separation was so severe for Dorie and Lloyd Van Stone that it brought an end to their missionary careers among the Danis in the Baliem Valley of New Guinea. "As we saw it, we had no alternative," wrote Dorie. "In accepting the missionary call, we had realized we would have to sacrifice. We also believed we must be totally obedient to the mission society. That meant Burney and Darlene *had* to go to school . . . away from their home, or we would have to return to the United States."

In 1959, the Van Stones received a message from the boarding school that Burney had run away. He had been discovered missing that morning, and the school staff and children had searched in vain for him. "Something within us died," wrote Dorie. "Lloyd's knees buckled; he held onto the plane to steady himself. Frightful thoughts flooded our minds." Lloyd immediately flew out to help in the search, and at noon radioed back to Dorie that Burney had been found hiding in an aircraft. "Childish imagination had his escape into the valley all planned: he would hide in the plane, and when the pilot made the next flight, Burney would soon be back in the valley with his father and mother!"

Burney and Darlene were excused from school to return home to the valley with their father to spend a week at home. But at week's end, Burney refused to return. It was an anguishing struggle. "Burney still clung to me, and I had to pry him forcibly away," wrote Dorie. "That was like pulling away a part of my life. Lloyd and I knew that such a decision could not be justified—how could we be separated from our children when they needed us the most? . . . Yet paradoxically, we also knew that God had called us to the Baliem Valley." It was their certainty that God's call had been "unmistakable, direct, clear" that enabled them to send the children away again. "But Burney did not adjust. He would not eat, he did no schoolwork, and he even refused to speak. We decided that I should fly to Sentani to be with Burney for a few days. When I arrived he had been sobbing for two days. . . . The next day . . . sobbing turned into weak grunts."

During that visit Dorie, whose own health was deteriorating again, realized that she could not leave Burney again. "I wanted with all my heart to win Danis. But my first responsibility was to win Burney and Darlene. God had used us to be trailblazers in the Baliem. Someone else would reap the harvest." It was painful to turn back on what had so clearly been the call of God. "Reluctantly, we faced the fact that our days as missionaries in the Baliem might soon be over. Unresolved conflicts churned within us. God had called us, yet now we had to return." Back in the States, the conflict was kept alive by well-meaning supporters. "You've disappointed us," one woman commented. "Why didn't you trust God for healing out there? He'd have taken care of you and your children." Dorie responded, but not with a verbal reply: "I stood in the church lobby and wept." Her response could have been another question, one of Darlene's that she had often pondered, "Why does Jesus ask us to do such hard things?"

[*Doris Van Stone, with Erwin W. Lutzer,* Dorie: The Girl Nobody Loved *(Chicago: Moody, 1979), pp. 131–40.*]

Prayer for Children

Amy Carmichael, a single missionary to India who had no children of her own, gave her life to providing a secure home environment for hundreds of Indian children who had been rescued from temple prostitution. Her love for children was boundless, and that love is illustrated in a prayer that she wrote in poetic form.

> Father, hear us, we are praying,
> Hear the words our hearts are saying,
> We are praying for our children.
>
> Keep them from the powers of evil,
> From the secret, hidden peril,
> From the whirlpool that would suck them,
> From the treacherous quicksand pluck them.
>
> From the worldling's hollow gladness,
> From the sting of faithless sadness,
> Holy Father, save our children.
>
> Through life's troubled waters steer them,
> Through life's bitter battle cheer them,
> Father, Father, be Thou near them.
> Read the language of our longing,
> Read the wordless pleadings thronging,
> Holy Father, for our children
> *And wherever they may bide,*
> *Lead them Home at eventide.*

[*Amy Carmichael,* Toward Jerusalem *(London: S.P.C.K., 1936), p. 106.*]

Treating Children like Adults

In the Middle Ages it was not uncommon for parents to send their children—especially their daughters—to the convent when they were still very young. In some instances, they insisted the decision had been made by the children themselves. Such was the case of Edburga, a tenth-century nun, who was sent to the convent when she was only three years old. When she was only a toddler, her father was determined to let his daughter make the decision that would change the course of her life. On one side of her he set religious objects, including a Bible and chalice, and on the other side worldly objects, including jewels and precious metals. "Without hesitation she reached out for the religious objects, and with that sign, her exuberant father placed her in a convent under the care of Abbess Etheldreda."

[Ruth A. Tucker and Walter L. Liefeld, Daughters of the Church: Women and Ministry from New Testament Times to the Present *(Grand Rapids: Zondervan, 1987), pp. 140–41.]*

Words Children Like to Hear

Most parents would be surprised to know what words and phrases they most frequently use in speaking to their children. Too often they are words of criticism or demands to perform. Such words are indeed necessary at times, but so are words of assurance and praise and offers of kindness. Dolores Curran writes of this need in her book *Traits of a Healthy Family.*

"Recently, for my weekly newspaper column, I invited seventy-five fourth and fifth graders to submit the words they most like to hear from their mothers. Here are the five big winners, repeated over and over by almost all the kids:

I love you.
Yes.
Time to eat.
You can go.
You can stay up late.

Some other Favorites were the following:

I'll help you.
Your friend can spend the night.
You can go out and play.
Sleep in.
How was your day?
You were good tonight.
I'm glad I have you.
I've got a surprise for you.
Let's go for a walk.
You're the best kid in the world.
Do you want to visit Grandma?
I'm sorry."

[Dolores Curran, Traits of a Healthy Family *(Minneapolis: Winston Press, 1983), p. 50.]*

CHRISTIANITY

Effect on Women in Other Cultures

The influence of Christianity on the family and on the role of women in the home has been very significant—especially in some non-Western cultures, where women have had a very low status in society. According to a Hindu observer in India some decades ago, the change was dramatic. "Before these people became Christians they bought and sold wives like we buy and sell buffalos. Now they choose one woman and remain faithful to her as long as she lives." This view was supported by Mrs. Graham Parker, a Presbyterian missionary, who surveyed Indian women on the issue. To the question "Do Christian men treat their wives differently?" 143 responded in the affirmative, and only 20 responded negatively. To the follow-up question "If so, how?" there were a variety of answers. "They don't make us do what we know isn't right. They let us have the money we earn. They help wives in their work. They don't fight. They don't abuse us in words or actions. They are kind and pray for us and our children. They forgive us our faults. They give their wives their rights. In Christian homes husband and wife obey each other."

[*J. Waskom Pickett,* Christian Mass Movements in India *(New York: Abingdon, 1933), p. 193.]*

CHURCH MINISTRIES

Denunciation of Women Missionaries

Despite the remarkable contributions women have made to the foreign-missionary enterprise, some critics have argued that they were doing a disservice to the noble cause of missionary work by their very involvement. One of these critics was John R. Rice, a well-known Bible teacher and radio evangelist of the mid-twentieth century. "The deputation work of great missionary societies has suffered greatly at the hands of women missionaries. If godly, Spirit-filled men, manly men, should go to the churches with the appeal that those whom God has called for His work should come prepared for toil and sweat and blood and tears, it would do infinitely more for the mission cause than the prattle about dress and customs and food, with steropticon slide pictures of quaint heathen groups presented so often by women missionaries, largely to groups of women and children. . . . It certainly violates the command of God for women to speak before mixed audiences of men and women and to take the pulpit in the churches. And we may be sure that the work of the gospel of Christ among the heathen is not prospered by this sin."

[*John R. Rice,* Bobbed Hair, Bossy Wives, and Women Preachers *(Murfreesboro, Tenn.: Sword of the Lord, 1941), pp. 64–65.]*

Opposition to Women Preachers

Opposition to women preachers reached its height with the outspoken writing and preaching of John R. Rice, himself the father of four daughters. "Feminism in the churches is a blight that has grieved

God and made ineffectual His power and it has disillusioned the people and lost their confidence. I have no doubt that millions will go to Hell because of the unscriptural practice of women preachers."

[John R. Rice, Bobbed Hair, Bossy Wives, and Women Preachers *(Murfreesboro, Tenn.: Sword of the Lord, 1941), p. 59.]*

Support of Women Preachers

One of the strongest supporters of women in ministry in the early decades of the twentieth century was Seth Rees, the first president of a tiny denomination known as the Pilgrim Holiness Church. His wife, Hulda, was his ideal of a woman preacher. She started preaching at sixteen, despite the fact that she was "excessively timid." But after she was "sanctified wholly," she began preaching "in the power of the Spirit" and continued her preaching the rest of her life. She became known in holiness circles as the Pentecostal prophetess. Her success was due in part to the strong support she received from her husband, who sometimes offended his fellow pastors with his blunt assessment of the situation. "Nothing but jealousy, prejudice, bigotry, and a stingy love for bossing in men have prevented woman's public recognition by the church. No church that is acquainted with the Holy Ghost will object to the public ministry of women. We know of scores of women who can preach the gospel with a clearness, a power, and an efficiency seldom equaled by men. Sisters, let the Holy Ghost fill, call and anoint you to preach the glorious Gospel of our Lord."

[Seth Cook Rees, The Ideal Pentecostal Church *(Cincinnati: Knapp, 1897), p. 41.]*

CIVIL RIGHTS
Fight against Race Discrimination

One of the most influential individuals in the civil rights movement of the 1950s was an unlikely candidate for greatness. Yet, her name became a symbol of the plight of blacks in America, and her simple protest set off a struggle that drew the nation's attention to the blatant racism being perpetuated in the world's largest democratic society in the mid-twentieth century.

Rosa Parks was not the first black to refuse to give up her seat or to go to the back of the bus, which was designated for "colored" people. She was preceded by an obscure and long-since-forgotten young girl. "Fourteen-year-old Claudette Calvin, the daughter of a day laborer and maid, defied the Montgomery Jim Crow laws shortly before Rosa Parks," but she aroused too little attention to make a significant protest, and the test court case was later dropped. It would be left to Parks to stir the ire of the population, whose deep anger had long been seething beneath the surface. "The indignities encountered daily by Rosa Parks in the course of making a living were hardly unique to her situation as a southern black woman in the 1950s. Each day the Montgomery, Alabama, seamstress rode in the back of a bus to a downtown department store, where she labored in a hot, steamy room and altered clothing for white customers. But one day in December 1955, on her way home from work, this longtime local NAACP member and activist refused to yield her seat to a white passenger; later folks would say that Rosa Parks 'sat down and the world turned around,' for hers was a timely challenge to a historic injustice."

The protest was a peaceful and dignified demonstration against racism that characterized the style of Martin Luther King, Jr. "Drawn to King's emphasis on love and nonviolence, female domestic and service workers refused to ride the Montgomery buses for 381 days and thereby threw white household arrangements into disarray. White women served as reluctant allies when they drove maids to work and back home again rather than watch their own dirty dishes and laundry pile higher." But as deeply as the boycott was felt locally, it took more than the disruption of cheap labor and financial misfortune to rectify the situation. "The boycott ended only with federal intervention in the form of a Supreme Court ruling that outlawed segregated busses; mass direct action could crack but not crumble the southern caste system."

[*Jacqueline Jones,* Labor of Love, Labor of Sorrow: Black Women, Work, and the Family from Slavery to the Present *(New York: Basic Books, 1985), pp. 278, 397.*]

Struggle for Religious Liberty

Religious toleration was not a concept readily adhered to by many of our Colonial forefathers. Although the Puritans had themselves faced harsh persecution for their religious beliefs, they showed no mercy to minority religious groups when they were in power. This was particularly true in Boston, where the punishment of banishment was often used to clear the area of heresy; when that failed, the offenders were hanged. One of those who struggled the hardest to force a change in such brutality perpetrated in the name of religion was Mary Dyer, a Quaker who immigrated to Boston in 1659. Her story, according to historian Daniel Boorstin, is "one of the most impressive in all the annals of martyrdom." She was determined to remain in Boston or to be forever a martyred symbol of Puritan religious bigotry—one that would hopefully force a change in the laws. She was brought to trial only weeks after she arrived in the Bay Colony, and her sentence was hanging, along with two Quaker men. The execution was scheduled for the following week, and on that fateful day she "marched to the gallows between the two young men condemned with her, while drums beat loudly to prevent any words they might preach on the way from being heard by the watching crowd. . . . The two men were executed, and Mary Dyer was mounted on the gallows, her arms and legs bound and her face covered with a handkerchief as the final preparation for hanging. Then, as if by a sudden decision, she was reprieved from the gallows."

The magistrates had no intention of hanging her. Forcing her to go through the terrifying ordeal, however, was an effort to intimidate her and perhaps force her to recant. It only made her more determined to defy her oppressors. "She refused to accept the reprieve unless the law itself was repealed. But the determined judges sent her off on horseback in the direction of Rhode Island. . . . On May 21, 1660, less than a year after her banishment from the colony, the irrepressible Mary Dyer returned to Boston and once more heard her sentence of death. . . . Again there were pleas for her life. And again, as she stood on the ladder of the gallows, she was offered her life if she would just leave the colony. But this time she was not to be thwarted. 'Nay,' she declared, 'I cannot. . . . In obedience to the will of the Lord God I came and in his will I abide faithful to death.' And she was hanged."

[Daniel J. Boorstin, The Americans: The Colonial Experience (New York: Vintage Books, 1964), pp. 39–40.]

CLEANLINESS

Difficult to Maintain in Earlier Generations

Women of previous centuries did not maintain the standard of cleanliness that is common today—and for good reason. The process of washing clothes often took a week to complete, especially during eras when long ruffled gowns were in fashion. In some eighteenth-century American towns there were public washhouses situated near a lake or river, but most women did their washing at home in a large kettle in the yard, where the clothing began the lengthy cycle of soaking, washing, rinsing, and starching before being dried and pressed. Soap was manufactured at home. "To produce a barrel of soap jelly, a household had to collect six bushels of ashes and 24 pounds of grease. A good deal of luck and a tolerant nose were also necessary to the process." Because washing was such an ordeal, it was generally done only once a month, and even less often in the winter months. Washing and maintaining bedding were equally arduous. As such, the common people simply accepted a low standard of cleanliness.

[Annegret S. Ogden, The Great American Housewife: From Helpmate to Wage Earner, 1776–1986 (Westport, Conn.: Greenwood Press, 1986), pp. 21–22.]

COMMUNICATION

Lack of Communication

A parable told by Lee Chang Mon, a Korean pastor, richly describes the problems that can result from lack of communication. "In the village of Chia Lee in Korea lived a not-too-rich young man who was about to be married. On the day before his wedding, his uncle sent him money for a new suit. With great joy he hurried off to the department store in the big city. He selected a suit, tried on the coat (which fit very well), but he did not try on the pants until he reached home late that night. Then to his deep disappointment he discovered that the pants were three inches too long. Since the wedding was to be held the following morning, there seemed to be nothing to do but to wear the pants with the legs rolled up.

"The young man had a very kind grandmother who lived with them in the home. Late that night she rolled and tossed as she thought about her grandson, and the humiliation of having to wear a suit with the pants rolled up. She finally arose from her bed, slipped quietly into the room where the young man had hung his suit. She carefully took the pants from the hanger and with her big scissors she snipped off the extra three inches. She got out her needle and thread and carefully hemmed up the pants and neatly hung them in the closet. Then she went back to bed and slept in peace.

"The mother of the young man had a terrible nightmare that night about her son standing before all those people with his pants rolled up, and so about two in the morning she could endure it no longer. She arose from her bed and went on tiptoe into the room where the suit was hanging. She measured carefully from the bottom of the pants and with her scissors snipped off the pants and then hemmed them neatly and completely.

"Very early the next morning before the sun had begun to rise the older sister of the young lad arose from her bed. Hers had been a troubled night of sleep. Before anyone else was up, she slipped quietly into his room and removed his suit from the hanger. Using her scissors expertly she removed three inches from the bottom of the pants, hemmed them carefully and put them back on the hanger.

"You can well imagine the consternation of the young man as he pulled on this trousers later that morning just before the wedding. They barely covered his knees."

[Allen Finley and Lorry Lutz, Mission: A World-Family Affair (San Jose, Calif.: Christian Nationals Press, 1981), pp. 70–71.]

Language Barriers in Communication

In her novel *No Graven Image*, Elisabeth Elliot tells the story of a single missionary in Ecuador who is struggling with cultural and language barriers with the Indian tribal people whom she had come to serve. Soon after she arrived at her new post, she began her language learning by visiting an Indian woman who knew neither Spanish or English.

" '*Imatai?*' I said, pointing to the sheepskins. She mumbled the answer so that I did not hear. The children repeated it for me. Rosa was not enthralled by the game and was finding it difficult to entertain a visitor whose vocabulary was limited to a single interrogative. I tried a new tactic. I stood up and sat down, using the Spanish word for 'I sit down.' It was clear, from Rosa's expression, that she questioned my sanity. I laughed and tried it again. The children watched mystified and delighted, but offered no information. Rosa was at a loss. She said something to me which I did not understand. Several possibilities came to mind: 'Are you crazy?' 'What is the matter?' or 'When are you leaving?' I thought it most likely that she was trying to tell me she did not understand. Well, enough of this, I decided, and resorted to drawing pictures in the ashes on the ground for the children. Still Rosa did not sit down but busied herself here and there doing nothing. Then she spoke sharply to one of the children and the child went outside, perhaps to get the cow, I thought, or fetch water. Their life must go on, and my intrusion was inhibiting the process. Rosa had done all she knew to make me welcome. Beyond that she was at a loss, and my presence confused her. I could not explain my mission and it would be a very long time before I would be able to. But this was a beginning. A visit to an Indian home, a bare beginning on the language—six or eight nouns and a question form; plus the word for 'yes.' Well, some other day."

[Elisabeth Elliot, No Graven Image *(New York: Harper & Row, 1966), p. 84.]*

Sex Barriers to Communication

Women and men communicate differently, and these differences can prove to be significant barriers in working relationships as well as in personal relationships. Good communication has a powerful impact on job advancement and job success, and yet many women have only male supervisors—a factor that may place them at a serious disadvantage in achieving their goals.

"Talking about her role in the film *Testament,* for which she was nominated for an Academy Award, Jane Alexander noted that it was the first time in 75 roles on screen and stage that she had been directed by a woman. The director/actor relationship was the easiest one she had ever experienced, partly because she could use a 'shortcut in communication' with her director, Lynne Litterman.

"There may have been many reasons for that ease in communication, but one of them almost certainly was that Alexander and Litterman were speaking the same language—which doesn't always happen with men and women. In fact, the sexes differ so greatly in the manner, and sometimes even the substance, of their conversations that each sex can be said to have its own language."

What are these factors that differentiate "boy talk" from "girl talk"? "Males like to talk about things and activity; females prefer to talk about people and feelings. Those distinctions show up at very early ages. Even in preschool, psychologists have found boys are already talking about the physical environment and about activity. . . . They talk about what they're building or the games they're playing. . . . Their talk is auxiliary to activity.

"For little girls, talk often is the activity. Girls tend to play in twos, using shared secrets to establish and maintain friendships."

It is easy to see how these patterns carry over into adulthood and into the workplace and that a woman's style of communication and thus style of management are often entirely different from those of her male counterpart. "Women establish trust with one another through self-disclosure; they share secrets and problems and search for common feelings and experiences. Men, on the other hand, build trust through action. They want to know: Were you with me in the trenches? Will you support me in difficult situations? And they don't find that out through conversation as women do. Only time and experience will tell them what they really want to know about a person. Meanwhile, women who aren't savvy to the ways of men are busy trying to establish trust through disclosure—and men aren't willing to disclose anything until the trust is well established."

[Kathryn Stechert, On Your Own Terms: A Woman's Guide to Working with Men *(New York: Random House, 1986), pp. 19–20, 22–24.]*

COMPASSION

Healing Ministry of Love

Kathryn Kuhlman, the well-known healing evangelist who captured the hearts of her millions of followers for most of three decades from the 1940s to the 1970s, was a woman of deep emotion. Her healing ministry focused not on herself but on others as she compassionately bent over them, seeking to alleviate their pain. Her biographer, Jamie Buckingham, poignantly describes this love that was so evident in her ministry. "I saw her, on dozens of occasions, take a child that was lame, maybe paralyzed from birth, and hug that child to her breast with the love of a mother. I am convinced she would have, at any moment required of her, given her life in exchange for that child's healing. She would hug bleary-eyed alcoholics and mix her tears with theirs. And the prostitutes who came to her meetings, with tears smearing their mascara, knew that if they could but touch her they would have touched the love of God. And those little old women, hobbling along on canes and crutches, some of whom couldn't even speak the English language but were drawn by the universal language of love. No man could have ever loved like that. It took a woman, bereft of the love of a man, her womb barren, to love as she loved. Out of her empti-ness—she gave. To be replenished by the only lover she was allowed to have—the Holy Spirit."

[Jamie Buckingham, Daughter of Destiny: Kathryn Kuhlman . . . Her Story *(Plainfield, N.J.: Logos International, 1976), pp. 259–60.]*

Starving in Order to Feed Others

Charlotte "Lottie" Moon was a Southern Baptist missionary appointed to China in 1873, who was soon accused by the wife of one of her colleagues of being mentally unbalanced because of her "lawless prancing all over the mission lot." Actually, Lottie was involved in church planting, but that ministry was not deemed proper for a woman. Nor was her assertiveness in other matters. But if some of her qualities were not perceived as feminine enough, there should have been no doubt about the motherly compassion she demonstrated during times of famine and hardship in China. She pleaded with the churches back home to share their wealth with the starving and homeless people all around her. Money was contributed, but not nearly enough to alleviate the critical situation that eventually developed. "Outbreaks of the plague and smallpox, followed by famine, and then topped by a local rebellion in 1911 brought mass starvation to the area of Tengchow. . . . Lottie contributed from her personal funds and gave all the help one person could possibly give, but her efforts seemed so trifling in the face of such tragedy." She even gave her own food away. How could she turn away starving children who were begging at her door?

Finally she became ill, and "only then was it discovered that she was starving to death. In hopes of saving her life, her colleagues made arrangements for her to return home in the company of a nurse, but it was too late. She died aboard ship while at port in Kobe, Japan, on Christmas Eve, 1912." The compassion that characterized her life had a deep impact on the women of her church back home, and the following year a Christmas offering in the name of Lottie Moon for needs on the mission field was initiated, which in recent years has netted over twenty million dollars annually.

[Ruth A. Tucker, From Jerusalem to Irian Jaya: A Biographical History of Christian Missions (Grand Rapids: Zondervan, 1983), p. 238.]

CONFESSION

God's Acceptance

One of the great hymns of confession was written by a woman who knew well the release and peace that come in confessing one's sins and failures before God. "Just As I Am," a hymn frequently sung at the close of evangelistic meetings, was written by Charlotte Elliott, who at one time had been very bitter with God about her circumstances in life. She became an invalid as a young woman and deeply resented the constraints that condition placed on her activities. In an emotional outburst, she expressed these feelings to Dr. Cesar Malan, a minister visiting in her home. He listened and empathized with her, but he refused to let her problems divert her attention from what she most needed to hear. He challenged her to turn her life over to God, to come to him just as she was, with all her bitterness and anger. She did so, and her life was changed. Each year on the anniversary of that decision, Dr. Malan wrote her a letter, encouraging her to continue strong in the faith. But even as a Christian she had struggles. At times she almost resented her brother's successful preaching ministry. She longed to be used of God herself, but her health prevented it. Then in 1836, on the fourteenth anniversary of her conversion, while she was alone in the evening, the forty-seven-year-old Charlotte Elliott wrote her spiritual autobiography in verse form. Here, in this prayer of confession, she poured out her feelings to God—feelings that countless individuals have identified with in the generations that followed. The third stanza, perhaps more than the others, described her own pilgrimage.

> Just as I am, though tossed about
> With many a conflict, many a doubt,
> Fightings and fears within, without
> Oh Lamb of God, I come.

In reflecting on the impact his sister made in penning this one hymn, the Reverend Henry Venn Elliott said many years later, "In the course of a long ministry I hope I have been permitted to see some fruit of my labors, but I feel far more has been done by a single hymn of my sister's, 'Just As I Am.' "

[*Robert Harvey*, Best-Loved Hymn Stories *(Grand Rapids: Zondervan, 1963), pp. 79–81.]*

CONSUMER FRAUD

Its Long History

In recent years individuals and watchdog organizations have publicly exposed countless cases of consumer fraud and brought suit in many instances. These cases have been widely reported by news organizations, sometimes giving the impression that such crime is a product of our modern age, when fraud is aided by modern technology. But consumer fraud is as old as humanity itself and has been widely reported since ancient times. In her book *People and Shopping,* Molly Harrison deals with the problem from a broad historical perspective. Merchants in fourteenth-century Europe were guilty of selling thread that was too thin and too loosely woven, and they dampened their spices so as to increase the weight.

"There were other ingenious ways of cheating customers. Bakers put weights into loves or, while making up their customers' own dough, stole a portion of it by means of a little trap door in the kneading board and a boy sitting crouched under the counter. Complaints were made in 1472 about frauds in the upholstery trade: in such articles as feather beds, cushions, and quilts, the buyer 'seeth withoute and knoweth not the stuff within'; down pillows were sometimes 'stuffed with thistill downe and cattes tailles' and 'materas stuffed with haire and flokkes and sold for flokkes'. Cloth was sometimes stretched before being sold, or carefully folded to hide defects; a length of bad cloth might be joined on to a length of better quality; inferior leather was cleaned up to look like the best; pots and pans might be made of poor quality metal which melted when put on the fire, and so on. In Norwich a butcher secretly bought eight drowned sheep and sold the carcasses as good mutton, and in the same town a fishwife mixed herrings with a barrel of oysters and sold it 'to strangers.' "

[Molly Harrison, People and Shopping: A Social Background *(Totowa, N.J.: Rowman & Littlefield, 1975), pp. 17–18.]*

CONVERSION

From Judaism to Christianity

When a Jew becomes a Christian, it is usually a traumatic experience for the family. The immediate suspicion is that the individual is no longer Jewish. To an extent this statement is true because there is a significant change in religious faith, but most Jewish Christians would seek to emphasize their Jewishness. Indeed, many would not use the term *Christian,* but rather *Messianic Jew.* Many observe Jewish holidays and seek to maintain closer cultural bonds than many Jews who would nominally claim to be Jewish in their religious faith.

In his book *Betrayed,* Stan Telchin tells of the anguish he felt when his twenty-one-year-old daughter told the family that she had put her faith in Jesus as the Messiah. It was shocking news that jolted their tranquility, but in the weeks and months that followed, as they observed her newfound happiness and peace, they began to inquire for themselves. Stan's initial study of the Bible was in an effort to refute all that his daughter believed, but as time passed he became a believer, as did his wife and other daughter—all independently of each other.

Did they lose their Jewishness? Stan himself spoke to that issue.

"I am a Jew. I was born a Jew, and I will die a Jew. Even if it were possible for me to reject my Jewish identity and heritage, I would never do so. I am a Jew by birth and by desire. As a matter of fact, I am so comfortable and so secure in my Jewish identity that I am not threatened by the fears and anxieties of some who would question it. My Jewishness was not conferred upon me by public opinion or by government edict. It was not given to me by men, and it cannot be taken away from me by men.

"As a Jew, I am even more sensitive to the teachings of Jesus, who was born a Jew, lived as a Jew, chose other Jews as His disciples and loved the Jewish people. As His disciple today, I know that He is more concerned about the attitudes of our hearts than the actions we perform. . . . In relations with members of my family and friends I am to remain consistent, never turning my back on my heritage, on my ancestry, on Israel or upon them."

[Stan Telchin, Betrayed (Grand Rapids: Zondervan, 1981), pp. 117–18.]

COURAGE

In Opposing Discrimination

Sex discrimination has been rooted in beliefs and traditions that go back thousands of years, and taking a stand against age-old convictions takes courage and sheer boldness in some cases. This was true in the female challenge in the voting issue. The idea of women's voting was utterly ludicrous in the minds of many men. Indeed, when the Fourteenth Amendment, granting blacks citizenship and the franchise, was ratified in 1868, it accorded such privileges to "all persons born or naturalized in the United States and subject to the jurisdiction thereof"—yet, men did not imagine that women might see themselves included in that broad category.

Susan B. Anthony, however, was one such woman. In 1872, when she saw a notice in the Rochester newspaper reminding citizens to register to vote, she immediately contacted her three sisters, and "together the four women headed for the barber shop on West Street, where voters from the Eighth Ward were being registered." She took along a copy of the Fourteenth Amendment, and though shocked by the intrusion, the voting officials permitted them to register. But it did not end with that incident. "If the men in the barber shop thought they were getting rid of a little band of crackpots the easy way, they were wrong. Susan urged all her followers in Rochester to register. The next day, a dozen women invaded the Eighth Ward barber shop, and another thirty-five appeared at registration sites elsewhere in the city."

The following Tuesday the women showed up at the polls to vote but were all denied the opportunity, except for Miss Anthony and those who accompanied her. She was known for her courageous stand, and the inspectors apparently feared her more than they did their superiors. When some of them hesitated, Susan promised them she would take care of their legal costs if that were necessary.

Miss Anthony could not have been surprised three weeks later when a deputy U.S. marshal came to her door to arrest her. All the women who voted were arrested, but only she was brought to trial. She was found guilty, as were the inspectors, but true to her word, she paid the court costs of the men who had permitted her to vote.

[Margaret Truman, Women of Courage: From Revolutionary Times to the Present *(New York: Morrow, 1976), pp. 151–54, 161.]*

COURTESY

Most Evident When Undeserved

Rose Kennedy, the matriarch of the Kennedy family, could be very difficult to deal with at times, and the daughters-in-law, especially, often became very exasperated with her peculiarities. Jackie Kennedy Onassis, though, was more patient than the others, and she accepted her mother-in-law's idiosyncrasies with graciousness. "I was always impressed by Jackie's tactful way of dealing with Mrs. Kennedy," wrote Barbara Gibson, Rose Kennedy's personal secretary. Long after her husband had been assassinated and after she had remarried and been widowed again, she kept in close touch with her mother-in-law, frequently writing notes while she was traveling abroad or away on business. She accepted gifts graciously—even when it became apparent they were not gifts. "During the several years that Mrs. Kennedy was virtually obsessed with cleaning out the attic in Hyannis Port, she kept pressing on Jackie things she found there. Some red glass vases, for example, quite obviously didn't match the cranberry glass that Jackie had painstakingly collected over the years, but Jackie graciously accepted them and thanked Mrs. Kennedy with great courtesy. Later Mrs. Kennedy found a pair of antique tin reflectors, the kind that were once placed behind candles, and wanted to sell them to her daughter-in-law. Jackie quietly paid the $170 Mrs. Kennedy asked for, even though with her connoisseur's eye she had noticed that the reflectors were damaged and thus virtually worthless as antiques."

[Barbara Gibson, with Caroline Latham, Life with Rose Kennedy *(New York: Warner Books, 1986), p. 56.]*

COURTSHIP

Whirlwind

Dr. Susan Forward, a well-known counselor in the field of marriage relationships, warns of the dangers of whirlwind courtships. Some of her advice is no more than basic common sense that has often been repeated by others. Yet, couples continue to ignore the dangers and marry before they have had an adequate opportunity to get to know each other. The result is often devastating. "The danger may actually add to the excitement and stimulation of the affair. When I ride my horse, a trot is very pleasant but not particularly interesting; the thrill lies in the gallop. Part of that thrill is the knowledge that something unexpected might happen—I might get thrown; I might get hurt. It's the same sense of thrill and danger we all experienced as children when we rode the roller-coaster. It's fast, it's exciting, and it feels risky. . . . A whirlwind courtship, thrilling as it may be, tends to provide only pseudo-intimacy, which is then mistaken for genuine closeness."

She goes on to warn of the "romantic blinders" that distort an accurate view of reality, and she cautions lovers to stretch out the development of their relationship. "In order to see who our new partner truly is, the relationship has to move more slowly. It takes time to see others realistically so that we can recognize and accept both their virtues and their shortcomings. In a whirlwind courtship the emotional currents are so swift and strong that they overwhelm both partners' perceptions. Anything that interferes with the picture of the new love as 'ideal' is ignored or blocked out. It's as if both partners are wearing blinders."

[Susan Forward and Joan Torres, Men Who Hate Women and the Women Who Love Them *(New York: Bantam Books, 1976), pp. 20–21.]*

DATING

In Order to Know Opposite Sex

Gary Chapman, a pastor who specializes in counseling engaged and married couples, believes that one of the most important reasons for dating is to get to know and relate to the opposite sex. "Half the world is made up of individuals of the opposite sex. If I fail to learn the art of building wholesome relationships with 'the other half,' immediately I have limited my horizons considerably." Dating, he argues, should be viewed as an opportunity to interact on a personal level in a way that diminishes the tendency to view an individual of the opposite sex as a sex object. He tells about a friend in the military who was stationed on the French Riviera. When he looked out his window at the young women on the beach, "his mind ran wild with lustful fantasies." He shared his problem with a Christian friend, who suggested he go down to the beach and converse with some of the young women. "My friend," writes Chapman, "resisted at first, thinking that not the Christian thing to do but at the insistence of his friend consented. To his amazement, he found that his struggle with lust was not heightened but reduced. As he talked with those girls, he found that they were persons, not things; persons, each with her own unique personality, history, and dreams; persons with whom he could communicate and discuss ideas and who in turn could relate to him as a person."

[Gary Chapman, Toward a Growing Marriage *(Chicago: Moody, 1979), pp. 18–19.]*

DAUGHTER

Conflict with Mother

Serious conflict often develops between mothers and their daughters when the latter reach adolescence. At this time "mothers and daughters may become extremely competitive." This is the time that "marks the beginning of a separation that eventually leads to the daughter's leaving home and her mother's sphere of influence." Then the most stinging conflict sometimes erupts. In her study of mothers and daughters, Signe Hammer found that "there occurred a moment of open confrontation between mother and daughter that marked the point at which their relationship changed, a moment when either a daughter or a mother declared her independence as a separate person, entitled to her own life space, and able to assume responsibility for herself. In doing this, a daughter is asserting her status as her mother's equal." This conflict has become increasingly sharp in recent years, when the daughter's leaving is not to trade her dependence on her mother for her dependence on a husband but rather to declare her own independence. "A confrontation, then, openly establishes a daughter's new sense of herself, and it is up to her mother to decide whether to accept a new relationship based on greater equality."

[Signe Hammer, Daughters and Mothers, Mothers and Daughters (New York: Quadrangle/New York Times Book Co., 1975), pp. 89, 148–49.]

Freedom for a Daughter

In her book *Eighteen, No Time to Waste,* Margaret Johnson tells of her struggles of raising Kathi, her teenage daughter. Just before her high school graduation, Kathi announced to her mother that she was planning to move out and get an apartment with Felicia, a friend whose influence on her had been detrimental—at least in the eyes of her mother. After many tearful arguments and sleepless nights, Mrs. Johnson realized that she had no choice but to let Kathi go—a decision she soon realized was the best for both of them. "The change in Kathi had been so lightning quick. I could scarcely believe that all the years of misunderstanding were over. In letting go of her, I had found her; in letting her grow up to make her own decisions, I had gained a daughter worthy of my trust. Though I had so dreaded her moving away from home in with Felicia, this had actually drawn her closer to her family."

Unfortunately, there was little time for this mother/daughter closeness to develop. On Labor Day weekend following Kathi's high school graduation, she and two of her friends were killed in an automobile accident while returning home from a Christian missions camp. Later her mother wrote, "Tears will always fill my eyes when I think of the skinny dark-haired girl who flew in and out of our home, who filled our lives with havoc, fun, some heartbreak, lots of noise, and finally with a great sense of pride and joy. . . . Coming years will bring other pleasures, other heartaches, and other losses, and as the years pass, the memory of Kathi will fade a little, as it must. But whatever the future holds, Kathi will always have been the one who taught me the most about being a mother, about being a Christian, about being a witness— about being a friend. 'Thank you, Kathi.'"

[Margaret Johnson, Eighteen, No Time to Waste *(Grand Rapids: Zondervan, 1971), pp. 52, 71, 77.]*

Not as Desirable as a Son

Elizabeth Cady Stanton, the most radical of the leading nineteenth-century feminists, began to realize her place as a female when she was yet a young child. She later recalled her father's deep grief when his only son to reach adulthood suddenly died—a tragedy that meant nobody would be left to carry on his name and his career as a judge. "It was easily seen that while my father was kind to us all, the one son filled a larger place in his affections and future plans than the five daughters together." It was during that time of grief that Elizabeth vowed to be to her father all that her brother would have been. "I still recall . . . going into the large, darkened parlor to see my brother and finding the casket, mirrors, and pictures all draped in white, and my father seated by his side, pale and immovable. As he took no notice of me, after standing a long while, I climbed upon his knee, when he mechanically put his arm about me and, with my head resting against his beating heart, we both sat in silence, he thinking of the wreck of all his hopes in the loss of a dear son, and I wondering what could be said or done to fill the void in his breast. At length he heaved and sighed and said: 'Oh, my daughter, I wish you were a boy!' Throwing my arms about his neck I replied, 'I will try to be all my brother was.' "

[Elizabeth Cady Stanton, Eighty Years and More: Reminiscences, 1815–1897, *intro. Gail Parker (New York: Unwin, 1898; reprint, New York: Schocken Books, 1971), pp. 20–21.]*

Oppression from Mother

Growing up as the daughter of one of this nation's most acclaimed actresses is not necessarily a happy and glamorous life, as the book *Mommy Dearest* about Joan Crawford illustrated. The same could be said of B. D. Hyman's book *My Mother's Keeper.* Here Bette Davis is portrayed as an oppressive woman, who perhaps was not even aware that her love for her children had gone beyond the bounds of true love that allows for freedom and individuality. In *Narrow Is the Way,* the sequel to *My Mother's Keeper,* B. D. Hyman describes this oppressive love.

"It is a great tragedy that so many mothers, mine among them, love their children so much that they think they own them. They believe their love for their children transcends even the obligation to acknowledge that those children have rights and freedoms. They believe that nothing must be allowed to distract their children from total and undivided devotion to Mother, the only person in the world who truly loves them and unerringly knows what is best for them."

In this book, B. D. tells of writing her first book, and how she believed that it alone might cause her mother to understand her needs as a daughter and as an individual in her own right. She had tried to communicate with her mother on these issues, but with no success.

"That is why I was writing a book. Once published, it would not go away. Mother would not be able to tear it up, hang it up or run away and wait for it to disappear."

Not surprisingly, the publication of the book outraged her mother and severed their relationship, but B. D. was emotionally prepared to withstand the trauma. Her recent conversion to a deep faith in Christ and the sense of release the book gave her allowed her to free herself from her mother's domination. After not having seen her mother for more than a year, she watched her on a television interview with Rona Barrett.

"Here was this woman who had permeated every facet of my very existence; whose wishes had been my commands long into my adulthood; against whom I'd had to struggle even to keep my husband and children—unto the last dire step of writing a book—and now I was free. I had been healed of my bitterness and resentment long since, but now I was free of the emotional bondage that had dogged my footsteps.

"There she was and, yes, I cared. But she had no more power over me. The rush of freedom was profound. I had no regrets, no guilts; I was truly free. Free to be whom I wanted without having to justify it to my mother. Free to plan holidays without worrying that she might have some conflicting plan. Free from the omnipresent lawyer informing me of my obligations. *free, free, free.* . . .

"With all people like my mother, when the break comes it is like the messiest and most bitter of divorces. It is nasty. That is the only way it can be. If reason and reasonableness were available options, the problem requiring the exercise of those options would not exist.

"The freedom from such oppression can only be appreciated by someone who has been the object of such oppression. . . . I felt like an eagle that had been caged all its life—except when occasionally taken out on a string for short controlled flights—who had finally cut the string. No matter what anyone does to recapture him, he knows he can fly higher and soar longer than any of his pursuers. Even if faced with this previous captor, he knows he has his measure."

[B. D. Hyman and Jeremy Hyman, Narrow Is the Way *(New York: Morrow, 1987), pp. 40–41, 282–83.]*

Resentment of Mother

One of the common reasons for tensions between daughters and mothers is the resentment daughters harbor against their mothers for their imperfections. This is a common attitude that Nancy Friday discovered when she was researching her book *My Mother/My Self.* "I've heard many a grown woman still lament the fact that mother wasn't home when she returned from school in the afternoon. Forget that mother may have been a terrific role model as a professional working woman—the role model the daughter may have patterned her own career upon. Until she accepts that mother didn't have to be perfect, her childish anger will inhibit the full use of the admirable traits her mother did have. Very often for women like these, their very success in work will bring with it associations of the 'bad' mother they do not wish to grow into. They marry suddenly, giving up their career with a sigh of relief. But marriage doesn't work out either: the wife tries to turn her husband into the all-caring, protective mother she never had."

[Nancy Friday, My Mother/My Self: The Daughter's Search for Identity *(New York: Dell, 1978), p. 32.]*

DAY CARE

Not a Tradition in America

One of the factors that makes day care in America seem unnatural is that we lack a historical tradition for early childhood care in this country. In other countries, however, day care has been an accepted part of life for generations. In her book *Women and Children Last,* Ruth Sidel discusses this issue and how it affects cultural values.

"Part of the hostility, or at best ambivalence, toward day care in this country arises from the fact that it has always been perceived as a service for the poor. Day care began in the United States in 1854 with the establishment of the Nursery for Children of Poor Women in New

York City. This and other early day nurseries, as they were called, were modeled after the French crèche, a form of care for the children of working mothers founded in Paris in 1844. The crèche, a response to the increased number of French women working in factories, was also used to improve the health of infants and children and to lower the infant mortality rate. Mothers breastfed their infants in the crèches and were taught methods of hygienic child care. In 1862 crèches received official recognition, and regulations were issued that had to be met in order for the crèches to receive government subsidy.

"Day nurseries in the United States received no such official recognition. Most were sponsored by churches, settlement houses, or voluntary social agencies. Their goals were 'to prevent child neglect during a mother's working hours and to eliminate the need to place children of destitute parents in institutions.' "

[Ruth Sidel, Women and Children Last: The Plight of Poor Women in Affluent America (New York: Penguin Books, 1986), p. 118.]

DEATH

Child's Questions

Children sometimes have very adult questions about death, but they express them more simply. In *Children's Letters to God,* a young boy writes, "Dear God, What is it like when a person dies? Nobody will tell me. I just want to know, I don't want to do it. Your friend, Mike."

[Eric Marshall and Stuart Hample, Children's Letters to God (New York: Simon & Schuster, 1966).]

Consolation

Joyce Landorf, a well-known writer, speaker, and singer in evangelical circles, has written about the deep sorrow she endured when her third child died the day after he was born. There was one elderly minister, known as Pop Warner, who visited her in the hospital and was able to bring comfort as no one else was able to do. His visit was brief, with no unnecessary preliminaries. "That dear man stood and listened as I poured out my anguished heart. He did not offer any advice, lecture, or words, although he was more than capable. He did not busy himself with taking out wilted flowers beside my bed. He simply listened. He looked me directly in the eye and heard my heart as I told him how badly it was going with me. When I'd finally said everything I so desperately needed to say, he bent over my bed and prayed, 'Oh, Lord, You are here and You've heard all that Joyce said. Now, You know the way to heal her heart. Heal her quickly, Lord, and bind up her wounds—we need her.' And then, knowing it was hard for me to believe David was really dead, he gently helped me take my first tottering steps toward acceptance by adding, 'And, dear Lord, take loving care of that precious baby for Joyce.' "

[Joyce Landorf, Mourning Song *(Old Tappan, N.J.: Revell, 1974), p. 40.]*

Definition of Death

Defining death has been one of the most difficult problems the medical profession has faced in recent years. This was not the case in generations past. "For centuries, death was measured by a physician feeling the pulse and putting a mirror under the patient's mouth. If there were no signs of life—no pulse, no breath—death was certified." This was certainly no foolproof method, as horror stories illustrate. "Jean Bruhier, a Paris physician, collected the histories of fifty-two people allegedly buried alive and seventy-two cases mistakenly certified as dead, while in the nineteenth century, forty-six cases of people who recovered while awaiting inhumation were recorded." To avoid the repetition of such errors, doctors devised means of checking on the apparent deceased. One such device was "a bell attached to a pole that rested on the chest of the buried person, whose movement, if he was alive, could trigger the bell to summon rescuers."

These efforts to determine death have become archaic in today's world, which possesses a wealth of modern technology. Two additional factors have made the definition of death more crucial than ever before—the frequency of organ transplants, and the common use of life-support technology in prolonging life. As a result, the definition of death has become a legal matter, and "brain death," rather than respiration and cardiac function, has become the determining factor in defining death. The American Bar Association, in an effort to aid its member attorneys, offered the following definition of death in 1975: "For all legal purposes, a human body with irreversible cessation of total brain function, according to usual and customary standards of medical practice, shall be considered dead." This definition of death has aided those whose loved ones have "died" but whose bodies' breathing and cardiac functions have been continued through artificial means.

[Derek Humphry and Ann Wickett, The Right to Die: Understanding Euthanasia (New York: Harper & Row, 1986), pp. 277–80.]

Delaying of Death by Modern Technology

Prolonging of life has become a controversial issue in the late twentieth century. It used to be that people simply faced death at the end of a terminal illness, but today's technology forces many people to face a limbo that is less than death but that can hardly be defined as life. Richard Taylor, an outspoken critic of the medical profession's needless prolonging of life, has described this process in a hospital intensive-care unit. "Rows of physiological preparations (also known as human beings) lie surrounded by an astounding array of mechanical gadgetry. A tube or catheter of some description violates every natural orifice, and perforations in various parts of the body are made especially for the placement of others. Multicolored fluid is pumped in, similar fluid drains out, respirators sigh, dialysers hum, monitors twitch, oxygen bubbles through humidifiers. The unfortunate hostages, mercifully unresponsive to their environment (either through natural causes or drugs), lie silent while their ritual desecration takes place."

[Richard Taylor, Medicine out of Control: The Anatomy of a Malignant Technology (Melbourne, Australia: Sun Books, 1979), p. 119.]

Effect of Parents' Death on Children

Even when children are adults, the death of a parent is a traumatic experience that affects their own perception of immortality. In addition to the personal grief, it can overturn one's sense of equanimity, as Jane Howard expresses so well in telling of the aftermath of her mother's death. "The death of my own mother made me feel like a deck of cards being shuffled by giant, unseen hands. Parents, however old they and we may grow to be, serve among other things to shield us from a sense of our doom. As long as they are around we can avoid the fact of our mortality; we can still be innocent children. When a parent goes, half of that innocence goes, too. It gets ripped away. Something, someday will replace that innocence, maybe something more useful, but we cannot know what, or how soon, and while we wait, it hurts."

[Jane Howard, A Different Woman (New York: Dutton, 1973), p. 26.]

Fear of Death

The Scripture that is probably most often used at funerals is the beloved Twenty-third Psalm, which comforts the bereaved with the words "Even though I walk through the valley of the shadow of death, I will fear no evil." For those left in grief when a loved one dies, the pain of the loss can be soothed by the assurance that those who have put their faith in the Lord have nothing to fear in death. The truth of this was brought home through a very simple analogy used by a well-known preacher and author of a generation ago.

"Dr. Donald Grey Barnhouse was one of America's great preachers. His first wife died from cancer when she was in her thirties, leaving three children under the age of twelve. Barnhouse chose to preach the funeral sermon himself. What does a father tell his motherless children at a time like that?

"On the way to the service, he was driving with his little family when a large truck passed them on the highway, casting a shadow over their car. Barnhouse turned to his oldest daughter who was staring disconsolately out the window, and asked, 'Tell me, sweetheart, would you rather be run over by that truck or its shadow?'

"The little girl looked curiously at her father and said, 'By the shadow, I guess. It can't hurt you.'

"Dr. Barnhouse said quietly to the three children, 'Your mother has not been overrun by death, but by the shadow of death. That is nothing to fear.' "

[Billy Graham, Facing Death and the Life After *(Waco: Word Books, 1987), pp. 93–94.]*

DECEPTION

Passed Down for Generations

One of the great double deceptions of all times was the reign of Pope Joan in the ninth century. She deceived her contemporaries by disguising herself as a man and studied theology in Rome, where she gained a reputation for scholarship. She went by the name of Hohannas Anglicus and took the name John VIII when she was "elevated to the papal dignity." But her reign as pope came to an abrupt and tragic end. According to some, she died after giving "birth to a child as she was taking part in a procession to the Lateran." Others insist that she was "tied to the hoof of a horse, dragged outside of the city and stoned to death by the people."

The deception of her sex, however, was exceeded only by the deception involved in the whole story. Indeed, most historians regard Pope Joan as mere fiction. Yet, the myth was carried along for centuries and was widely accepted as truth during the late Middle Ages—so much so that a bust of her was displayed with the busts of other popes during the early fifteenth century, and the story was cited as fact at the Council of Constance in a statement against the popes. One churchman, in defense of a pope of low character, argued that, if a woman could be pope, surely it was no worse to have a heretic or a man of low morals.

[Philip Schaff, History of the Christian Church, *vol. 4,* Medieval Christianity, *590–1073 (New York: Scribner's Sons, 1910; reprint, Grand Rapids: Eerdmans, 1979), p. 265.]*

DEMONISM

Reality Demonstrated

Millie Larson, who served for many years with Wycliffe Bible Translators among the Aguaruna tribespeople in Peru, struggled for a long time with the concept of demonism. When she visited a sick woman, the tribespeople had recognized the seriousness of the problem. " 'She's been cursed; she's going to die; it's *tunchi,*' they all said." Yet, Millie felt powerless. "For the first time in my life, I knew that demons were real and powerful. Did I have the courage to cast them out, as Jesus gave his disciples power to do? If I tried and failed, would it do more harm than good? How did I know I could really exorcise a demon?"

Two weeks later Millie received word that the woman had died. In the meantime, she had endured an inner conflict that was the beginning of a turning point in her ministry. She had recognized that she had failed this poor woman because of her own unbelief. She had to confess that she had "always thought of demons as figments of the imagination of primitive peoples, as superstitions learned from their ancestors." She argued with herself, "I am translating Scripture into their language, but do I truly believe it myself?" Yes, she did, but she had been "brainwashed not to take too seriously the battle between Satan and God."

It was a long time before she and her partner were able to come to terms with the whole idea of demonism. "During the years that Jeanne and I had worked among the Aguaruna, we had believed medicine to be the all-powerful force that would overcome superstition and sorcery. If we could prove that all sickness had a natural cause, people would be free from their terrifying fears of it, related to supernatural sources as they considered it to be. Whenever someone claimed to be sick because of *tunchi,* we would try to show how it wasn't actually sorcery. It must be parasites, or some germ—and usually it was.

"We had the all-powerful medicine as our weapon against sorcery. Since it is a figment of the imagination, we reasoned, surely more education and more medical training will lead to its downfall. If pills didn't work, the illness was surely just psychological. Tranquilizers ought to take care of a case like that.

"But in spite of our disbelief, shamans kept healing some people; others died of *tunchi*. People still talked about and acted out revenge against the curser. Even those who claimed to be believers and wanted to obey God went to the shaman as a last resort. He could tell them, as Jeanne and I could not, whether they needed medicine or his own ministrations because they had had a curse placed on them. . . .

"Many times . . . I had seen people that I knew must be possessed."

Through the help of her native language informant, Millie finally came to realize that, through faith in God, she could have power over demons.

[Mildred Larson and Lois Dodds, Treasure in Clay Pots *(Dallas: Person to Person Books, 1985), p. 205.]*

DEPRESSION

Caused by Loss of Love

The most frequent cause of depression among women is that which revolves around loss of love. It may take many different forms, but the common denominator generally is essentially the same—a relationship that has dissolved. Maggie Scarf speaks of this depression in her book *Unfinished Business: Pressure Points in the Lives of Women.* "It is around *losses of love* that the clouds of despair tend to converge, hover, and darken. Important figures leaving or dying; the inability to establish another meaningful bond with a peer-partner; being forced, by a natural transition in life, to relinquish an important love-tie; a marriage that is ruptured, threatening to rupture, or simply growing progressively distant; the splintering of a love affair or recognition that it is souring and will come to nothing."

[Maggie Scarf, Unfinished Business: Pressure Points in the Lives of Women *(Garden City, N.Y.: Doubleday, 1980), pp. 86–87.]*

Depression Must Not Be Nurtured

It is a temptation for people to nurture or "wallow" in their depression. As unpleasant as depression is, it nevertheless has a perverse gratification of its own, and it is difficult for individuals to extricate themselves from its grip and power. In her book *Understanding a Woman's Depression,* Brenda Poinsett writes of this problem. "Depression is a weed, not a flower or a fruit—something that we would want to produce. Part of depression's subtlety is that it makes us want to treat it like a prize rose—nursing it and giving it our undivided attention, causing it to thrive. If given this kind of attention, it can choke out all the other beautiful plants and fruits in our lives. That's why we must increase our understanding of it. We must know its symptoms and its causes. We must know how to destroy it and to live free from it."

[Brenda Poinsett, Understanding a Woman's Depression *(Wheaton: Tyndale, 1984), p. 18.]*

Recovery Rate from Depression Is High

What depressed people often need most is a reason for optimism—something to look forward to in the future. But that is the very aspect of life that so eludes them. Yet, they must take heart in the fact that depression itself is something they will pass through. Though it may seem like a misery that will never pass, it does, as history has so often proved. "The best ammunition we can have in fighting depression," writes Brenda Poinsett, "is the knowledge that we will probably win the fight. For any give case of depression that a woman experiences, there is a 95 percent chance of recovery.

"Depression is a self-lifting illness. Most cases of depression eventually disappear without treatment. If given enough time, things will correct themselves. The miserable feelings, the hopelessness, the agony will be left behind. If this wasn't true, human history might have been very different. Abraham Lincoln, Nathaniel Hawthorne, Winston Churchill, and astronaut Buzz Aldrin are all accomplished people who have had recurrent bouts of depression. They managed to ride through their depressions, and we can, too. No depression lasts forever. Ours will eventually come to an end."

[Brenda Poinsett, Understanding a Woman's Depression *(Wheaton: Tyndale, 1984), p. 115.]*

DETERMINATION
Fulfilling Life's Goals despite Opposition

One of the most heralded missionaries of modern times was Gladys Aylward, who became the subject of Alan Burgess's book *The Small Woman* and of the film "Inn of Six Happinesses," starring Ingrid Bergman. She began her mission career by saving her money and traveling alone to China, after having been turned down by the China Inland Mission. She traveled by rail across Europe, Russia, and Siberia—a harrowing journey that would never have been completed except for relentless determination. In addition to the problems she faced because of language barriers, the train was packed with Russian troops on their way to fight an undeclared border war with China. At one point more than halfway into the journey, Gladys was informed she would have to get off the train. She refused, fearing she would be denied reentry onto the train. Several miles later, the train stopped, the troops were ordered off, and Gladys found herself alone on an empty train in the remote wasteland. She had no choice but to trudge back to the station where she had been ordered to disembark in the first place. Her biographer tells the story.

"The Siberian wind blew the powdered snow around her heels, and she carried a suitcase in each hand, one still decorated ludicrously with kettle and saucepan. Around her shoulders she wore the fur rug. And so she trudged off into the night, a slight lonely figure, dwarfed by the tall, somber trees, the towering mountains, and the black sky, diamond bright with stars. There were wolves near by, but this she did not know. Occasionally in the forest a handful of snow would slither to the ground with a sudden noise, or a branch would crack under the weight of snow, and she would pause and peer uncertainly in that direction, but nothing moved. There was no light, no warmth, nothing but endless loneliness."

Gladys would encounter more frightening episodes before she reached China, but she was determined that nothing would deter her from following God's call to share the gospel with the Chinese people.

[Alan Burgess, The Small Woman *(New York: Dutton, 1957), p. 29.]*

DIETING
Lose Calories While Eating

According to nutritionists, there are so few calories in celery that the number of calories burned up in chewing it exceeds the number consumed. Thus a person can actually lose calories by eating that vegetable.

[Scot Morris, The Book of Strange Facts and Useless Information *(Garden City, N.Y.: Doubleday, 1979), p. 114.]*

DIVORCE
Avoidability of Divorce

James Jauncey, a Christian marriage counselor, has argued that almost any marriage—no matter how badly damaged it is—is salvageable. "I do not think there are wrong marriages—only wrong people. There is nothing final and unchangeable about the wrongness of people. Problems can be made right and when they are, the difficulties in marriage begin to melt away. . . . I've never seen a marriage so desperately ill that it cannot be saved. I have seen plenty that died needlessly because one or both of the partners did not want to pay the price to save their relationship. I've known of cases where couples have retired into such bitterness and hate that all communication has ceased. Yet these couples, in desperation, have begun to let the light through and have gone on to an experience of mutual love so thrilling that they could not have believed it possible."

[James H. Jauncey, Magic in Marriage *(Grand Rapids: Zondervan, 1966), pp. 8–9.]*

Cause of Divorce

When we reflect on the causes for divorce, we do not generally think of lack of romantic love as a legitimate reason for taking such drastic action. Yet, that factor perhaps more than any other is a root cause of marital breakdown, and it is a factor that has been cited as a valid reason to dissolve a marriage—only in the modern era, however. Prior to the eighteenth century, romantic love was not widely considered to be a necessary ingredient in marriage, and thus it is not surprising that it would not be cited in divorce cases. In studying early American life, Ellen Rothman discovered that, while there was evidence that people had an ideal of romantic love, they did not think of it as an expectation in marriage—at least not until the end of the middle decades of the eighteenth century, before the ideal began to turn into an expectation. An investigation of Massachusetts divorce cases showed that, from 1736 to 1765, none of those who petitioned for divorce indicated that loss of romantic love was a factor. But during the decades that followed, there were frequent complaints made by women suing for divorce detailing how their husbands no longer cherished them or that they had lost their affection. Is lack of romantic love a legitimate reason to dissolve a marriage? The study would support the contention that romantic love is not an inherent ingredient in husband/wife relationships but rather "a cultural ideal and an individual expectation" that began taking hold in America in the late eighteenth century.

[Ellen K. Rothman, Hands and Hearts: A History of Courtship in America *(New York: Basic Books, 1984), p. 31.]*

Devastation Caused by Warring Parents

Divorce nearly always has a very negative impact on family life, but parents who truly care for the well-being of their children can make a conscious effort to lessen the detrimental effects of their marital crisis. "It is critical," writes Debbie Barr, "that both parents lay down their weapons, since no one stands to gain anything from prolonging the conflict." Indeed, the devastating effects of warring parents have been described as child abuse.

"Resentment, hatred, bitterness, and an unforgiving spirit are guaranteed to damage at least one person—the person harboring these poisonous emotions. Those next likely to feel their devastating impact are the children. Ironically, the former spouse—the person against whom these weapons are aimed—is least likely to be hurt by them. When both parents fire heavy artillery, the only people sure to be wounded from both directions are the children who must dodge their crossfire."

[*Debbie Barr,* Caught in the Crossfire: Children of Divorce *(Grand Rapids: Zondervan, 1986), p. 267.*]

Effect of Divorce on Wife

Divorce is usually a painful ordeal, even when the marriage has not been satisfying. That was true when Sue and Paul Hubbell divorced after many years of marriage. They had been childhood sweethearts, and they had a child of their own, but they slowly drifted apart. Yet, when the marriage ended, Sue writes, "I had a difficult time sifting through the emotional debris that was left after the framework of an intimate, thirty-year association had broken." The anguish she suffered threw her life into turmoil. "I went through all the usual things: I couldn't sleep or eat, talked feverishly to friends, plunged recklessly into a destructive affair with a man who had more problems than I did but who was convenient, made a series of stupid decisions about my honey business and pretty generally botched up my life for several years running. And for a long, long time, my mind didn't work. I could not listen to the news on the radio with understanding. My attention came unglued when I tried to read anything but the lightest froth. My brain spun in endless, painful loops, and I could neither concentrate nor think with any semblance of order. I had always rather enjoyed having a mind, and I missed mine extravagantly. I was out to lunch for three years."

[Sue Hubbell, A Country Year: Living the Questions (New York: Random House, 1983), pp. 8–9.]

Greater Difficulty for Ministers Who Divorce

A growing problem among ministers and their spouses is marital breakdown. The stress involved in parish ministry often takes its toll on the marriage, and divorce frequently ensues. For the pastoral couple, divorce usually involves far more than a dissolving of the marriage. It often means the end of long-term friendships, of employment, and of spiritual ties. "In most other professions, the collapse of a marriage is now accommodated. Doctors, lawyers, educators, executives—such a thing in their lives causes hardly a murmur. No scorn is heaped upon the politician who must take time out for a divorce court hearing; indeed, he is rather the object of constituents' concern and empathy. In 1980 Americans elected their first divorced President, and returned him with a landslide in 1984. A major bloc of his coalition: conservative Christians." But for the pastor, the situation is entirely different. It is not surprising that, for pastors, "the specter of a marital meltdown is usually their greatest fear. No other tragedy in the ministry holds such a threat." Most evangelical denominations have no place for a divorced pastor, and if the denomination does permit him to continue in the ministry, he finds it difficult to get a call from a local congregation. "The demise of a pastoral marriage—in addition to its bone-deep personal pain, which every divorcing couple experiences—carries immense professional consequences. Thus pastors know they simply *must* make their marriages work, or suffer a double aftermath."

[Dean Merrill, Clergy Couples in Crisis: The Impact of Stress on Pastoral Marriages (Carol Stream, Ill.: Christianity Today, 1985), pp. 9–10.]

Greater Effect of Divorce on the Children

In many ways, children suffer more from divorce than their parents do. This is due in part to the fact that most children of divorce have no past experience of being without both parents. The parents can recall their independent lives prior to marriage and know that a life without a spouse is not an experience that is entirely unknown to them.

"A child, however, has no such assurance. He can recall no time in his life when he lived without father or mother. In fact, just trying to imagine life apart from a parent may be nearly impossible for him to do. One of his greatest natural fears has always been that of being abandoned and left to fend for himself. When separation and divorce breathe life into that fear, an unprecedented crisis can occur. For some, life will never really be the same again."

[Debbie Barr, Caught in the Crossfire: Children of Divorce (Grand Rapids: Zondervan, 1986), p. 23.]

Inequity in New Divorce Laws

In her sociological study of the effects of divorce on women, Terry Arendell found that new laws have put women at a considerable disadvantage. Hailed as laws that free couples from the tyranny of the law and expensive trials, these new laws have had a negative effect on the family and on women. A spouse can walk out and obtain a no-fault divorce, and the remaining parent is often left in dire financial and psychological straits with little or no recourse—especially when the spouse that was left was a wife and mother who was not employed outside the home.

"Both personal testimony and recent research suggest than any equality women have gained within divorce law is largely symbolic. The sixty women interviewed had been repeatedly penalized within the law for having been primarily wives and mothers and not wage earners. Although husbands and wives apparently have equal access to obtaining a legal divorce, in practice even that equality is mythical. In being treated by the law as if they were social and economic equals, these women were put at a profound disadvantage, and the inequalities of the traditional marital arrangement were obscured. They lost the primary source of income and were given nearly total responsibility for their dependent children and themselves. The law's failure to recognize that these women confronted a gender-structured society which puts them at a disadvantage as single-parent providers contributed directly to the extent of the hardship they encountered.

"In other words, our society's promise to honor the role of motherhood proved hollow in divorce; the law, which at least theoretically represents society's values, did not recognize these women's contributions to family life and gave them no protection for carrying on their mothering activities. It simply left them alone, to cope individually with increased responsibilities."

[Terry Arendell, Mothers and Divorce: Legal, Economic, and Social Dilemmas (Berkeley: University of California Press, 1986), pp. 152–53.]

Problem of Bitterness over Divorce

In their anger over the causes and effects of divorce, many women become very angry—a condition that only frustrates their efforts to turn their lives around. Indeed, the pain of marriage breakdown is often magnified by their bitterness, according to Dr. Sonya Friedman. "Bitterness is elevated to such a significant position for some women because it becomes their power, focus, goal and career. Holding fast to bitterness, it is difficult to express much else. It shades all relationships—with a spouse, with children, friends, relatives, co-workers, the corner news dealer. Bitterness drenches us and we become soaked in self-pity. Bitterness will not bring a man back once he's decided to leave. Bitterness does not spite a husband. It only shows him that you cannot care about yourself and for yourself without him. You need not be bitter. Resist the temptation. . . . Divorce is a terrible sadness in our lives. All we can ask of ourselves after a decent period of mourning the death of the marriage is to keep an eye on the road ahead. It's false to believe that husbands all go merrily on to more while you are stuck with less. When he left or when you left him, he didn't take your life along with him. Your life is separate and distinct. You will need time to recover and turn your life around into startlingly new dimensions. Without bitterness."

[*Sonya Friedman,* Smart Cookies Don't Crumble: A Modern Woman's Guide to Living and Loving Her Own Life *(New York: Putnam's Sons, 1985), p. 199.]*

Psychological Stress of Divorce

Some writers and counselors have tried in recent years to put a happy face on divorce—to reassure those who are contemplating divorce or going through the struggles of a painful marriage breakdown that divorce affords opportunity for growth and personal freedom. This is largely a myth—especially for women with children. In her study of divorced women, Terry Arendell found just the opposite to be true. "Most of these women were engaged in an ongoing struggle to make ends meet, to handle simultaneously the tasks of parenting and earning an income, and to cope with the stress brought on by the uncertainties of their lives. Rather than being liberated single women, they were socially and emotionally isolated, as well as overloaded with demands on their time and energy. Additionally, many mothers felt worry and guilt about how their children might be affected by the limited attention they were able to give them. And all agreed that there was a price to be paid for any freedom gained by leaving an unhappy marriage: each of them believed that the economic hardship prompted by divorce had reduced her opportunity to be the kind of mother she had hoped to be.

"For these women, feelings of satisfaction and reward about having coped successfully were reached only by experiencing shaken self-esteem, social and emotional isolation, anxiety and stress, and doubts about their continued ability to manage all the tasks confronting them as single parents."

[*Terry Arendell,* Mothers and Divorce: Legal, Economic, and Social Dilemmas *(Berkeley: University of California Press, 1986), p. 155.]*

Women's Loss in Divorce

Recent studies have shown that men fare far better in divorce settlements than do women. Although alimony is frequently considered a significant aspect of divorce, it is paid in less than 10 percent of divorces. But even more significant is drastic change in life-style for both the husband and wife following the divorce. Men realize a 42 percent increase in their standard of living, while the standard of living declines 73 percent for women. No-fault divorce, once hailed by the feminists as a liberating wave of the future, is now seen as a significant cause of poverty among women. According to Lenore Weitzman, a Stanford sociologist, "Divorce is a financial catastrophe for most women: in just one year they experience a dramatic decline in income and a calamitous drop in their standard of living. It is difficult to imagine how they survive the severe economic deprivation: every single expenditure that one takes for granted—clothing, food, housing, heat—must be cut in one-half or one-third of what one is accustomed to. . . . It is not surprising that divorced women report more stress and less satisfaction with their lives than any other group of Americans."

[Quoted in Sylvia Ann Hewlett, The Myth of Women's Liberation in America *(New York: Morrow, 1986), p. 66.]*

DOMINANCE
Decreases Effectiveness

It is often believed that dominant individuals are more successful because they are able to control others. This is not necessarily true, however, as a scientific study done with monkeys at the University of California at Berkeley would tend to indicate. The researchers were analyzing male power, and they concluded "that the biggest and strongest male monkey does not always get the girl." They had assumed that the dominant male monkey would prevail in mating competition, but they found that the females often shunned him, as did other males. "The dominant monkey, called 'Ta' by the researchers, was indeed able to fight off other males to protect his mating rights. That, in fact, was his trouble. According to the researchers, 'Ta' spent so much time proving he *was* the dominant monkey that he seldom got to enjoy the rewards of his battles—and when he wasn't fighting, he was too *tired* to get the job done. Poor old dominant 'Ta.' He didn't understand how easy it is to make a monkey of yourself when you're behaving like a jackass."

[Linda Ellerbee, And So It Goes: Adventures in Television *(New York: Putnam's Sons, 1986), pp. 117–18.]*

DOUBT

Belief in Spite of Doubt

In the minds of many people, faith and doubt are two opposite extremes. The idea that they can coexist—much less live in harmony—seems utterly preposterous. Yet, many people who believe deeply in God struggle with doubt. They pray the plaintive prayer "Lord, I believe; help thou my unbelief." This is true of Madeleine L'Engle, whose writing reflects a deep faith that is anything but doubt-free. Despite her doubts, she serves actively in the church. "I might be terribly unsure about God," she confessed, "but I was happy working in his house." In answer to a teenager's question about God, she replied, "Oh, Una, I really and truly believe in God with all kinds of doubts." She added, "I base my life on this belief."

When Una probed further, Madeleine gave a fuller response to her and the others in the class. "There are three ways you can live in life. You can live life as though it's all a cosmic accident; we're nothing but an irritating skin disease on the face of the earth. Maybe you can live your life as though everything's a bad joke. I can't. . . .

"Or you can go out at night and look at the stars and think, yes, they were created by a prime mover, and so were you, but he's aloof perfection, impassible, indifferent to his creation. He doesn't care, or, if he cares, he only cares about the ultimate end of his creation, and so what happens to any part of it on the way is really a matter of indifference. You don't matter to him, I don't matter to him, except possibly as a means to an end. I can't live that way, either. . . .

"Then there's a third way: to live as though you believe that the power behind the universe is a power of love, a personal power of love, a love so great that all of us really *do* matter to him. He loves us so much that every single one of our lives has meaning; he really does know about the fall of every sparrow, and the hairs of our head are really counted. That's the only way I can live."

[Madeleine L'Engle, A Circle of Quiet *(San Francisco: Harper & Row, 1972), pp. 57, 63.]*

Guilt Associated with Doubt

Rosalyn Carter's faith was seriously shaken after enduring the sorrow that accompanied her father's death, soon followed by the death of her grandmother. "I had prayed and prayed for him to get better, and because of those prayers, I'd expected him to get better. But he hadn't. And now my grandmother had died too. I felt very sorry for myself and didn't understand why this had to happen to me. Had I been so bad? Didn't God love me anymore? I had doubts about God, and I was afraid because I doubted. That was long before I knew that God is a loving God who cares for us and loves us, who suffers when we suffer and who knows that we are going to have doubts and that we're not always going to do what is right, but He loves us anyway. At that time I thought He was going to punish me more for my thoughts. . . . I believed my doubts were shortcomings, and I didn't want anyone to know about them."

[Rosalyn Carter, First Lady from Plains *(Boston: Houghton Mifflin, 1984), p. 19.]*

Study of Bible Prompted by Doubt

A. Wetherell Johnson, the founder and director of the world's largest Bible study organization, Bible Study Fellowship, struggled with deep doubts as a young British woman who had been educated in France, where "the heavy study left no leisure for thought or emotional introspection." When she returned to England, she realized how much she had changed. "I had time to recognize that when I gave up belief in the Lord Jesus Christ and the Bible, I had no philosophy to fill the vacuum that remained. Life was utterly without meaning." This doubt soon after prompted her to cry out in the night, "God, if there be a God, if You will give me some philosophy that makes reasonable sense to me, I will commit myself to follow it." After that, she testifies, "God met me in a mysterious way which I cannot fully explain." One result of this experience was an intense desire to learn and understand Scripture. She enrolled in five correspondence courses and continued on in a study of the Bible that has influenced women and men all over the world. Indeed, she has been so highly regarded as a Bible scholar that she was invited to be a member of the sixteen-member council of the International Council on Biblical Inerrancy—the only woman so designated.

[A. Wetherell Johnson, Created for Commitment (Wheaton: Tyndale, 1982), pp. 40–43, 308.]

DRUGS

Why We Are Losing the War against Drugs

Despite the tremendous amount of effort and money expended in fighting the war against drugs in our society, there are very few victories and many defeats for law enforcement officials and law-abiding citizens in general. Is it a lost cause? Should Americans surrender and lay down their arms? Arnold S. Trebach argues that this war can be won, but only through a change of strategy that abandons many of the current assumptions about drugs and tactics in combating the problem. Trebach is the founder of the Institute on Drugs, Crime, and Justice of Washington and London, and he is a professor in the School of Justice at the American University in Washington, D.C. He offers the following reasons for our nation's ineffective fight against drugs:

"We are losing the great drug war because our drug laws are irrational, based upon flawed scientific assumptions, and are out of touch with the desires of millions of Americans. . . .

"We are losing the great drug war because we delude one another into thinking that certain dangerous drugs, such as alcohol and tobacco, are less harmful than other dangerous drugs, such as heroin, marijuana, and cocaine. Yet diseases related to alcohol and tobacco kill approximately 500,000 Americans every year. . . .

"We are losing the great drug war because we do not now have, and never had, the capability to manage a successful war on any drug. We should have learned that when we attempted, with the best of motives and for good reasons, alcohol prohibition several generations ago. . . .

"We are losing the great drug war because our leaders, especially those . . . in the Reagan administration, have declared all users of illicit drugs to be 'the enemy.' Thus, they refuse to distinguish between drug use and drug abuse, between responsible drug use and compulsive, addictive use. . . .

"We are losing the great drug war because it does not deal with the most important problems related to drugs: abuse, crime, and corruption. . . . The intensifying war on drugs keeps these substances in the black market, keeps prices high, and creates the conditions in which violent traffickers flourish and criminal addicts feel driven to victimize their innocent neighbors. . . .

"We are losing the great drug war because, as so often happens in wars, hysteria and hate are dominating the public discussion. I have personally felt that hysteria and hate because for years I have been a somewhat lonely dissenter on American drug policy and have pleaded for more tolerance, for new thinking about drugs, and for radical new directions in national strategy, including legalization of some drugs."

[*Arnold S. Trebach,* The Great Drug War, and Radical Proposals That Could Make America Safe Again *(New York: Macmillan, 1987), pp. 3–4.]*

EATING HABITS
Changes over the Centuries

Americans have not always been in the habit of eating three meals a day, plus a bedtime snack. In the Colonial era, only one meal a day was typical. That began to change by the end of the eighteenth century, when two meals became more common. The day began with a big breakfast of griddle cakes, porridge, and tea. The main meal was then served in the early afternoon. "Only those with time to spare and a wealth of food indulged in the European institutions of afternoon teas and late suppers."

[Annegret S. Ogdon, The Great American Housewife: From Helpmate to Wage Earner, 1776–1986 *(Westport, Conn.: Greenwood Press, 1986), pp. 18–19.]*

ECONOMIC OPPRESSION
Opposition to Oppression

Fighting against the giants of industry for the rights of economically oppressed workers has been a formidable task in any era, but during the nineteenth century, when capitalism was on the rise and the financial brokers wielded powers unrestrained by government regulation, it was even more difficult. One of the names most remembered as a champion of the working classes during this period is Mary Harris Jones, simply known as Mother Jones. When she was working in Chicago as a dressmaker, she had a lot of dealings with the wealthy classes. "She saw them in their plush, well-heated mansions while most of her people shivered in unheated, rickety tenements." She became convinced that union organization was the only way to respond to the crass indifference of the industrial bosses. Dressed in a black bonnet, shawl, and long skirt, she became a familiar figure at labor rallies and workers' strikes.

Her main concern was for coal miners, who were forced to work twelve- to fourteen-hour days, six days a week, in unsafe conditions. The workers were virtually slaves of the mine owners, since the housing, the stores, the health care, the schools, and even the churches were controlled by them. "The miners needed a union, but they were too beaten down by their bosses to organize one. Outside organizers who tried to enter the mining districts met with brutal opposition. Company guards, thugs, and hoodlums recruited from the big cities greeted them with guns and clubs, which they had no qualms about using." Mother Jones was not intimidated by such tactics. The physical violence that threatened the miners did not affect her as a woman. On occasion, when the miners were being threatened by strikebreakers, she told the miners to stay home but called on their wives to come out with their dishpans and brooms. The marched to the mineshaft and began beating on their dishpans, frightening the mule teams. Indeed, "the dishpan demonstrations became a favorite technique for discouraging scabs and disrupting mine operations."

At the age of seventy-three, Mother Jones traveled west to Colorado, where, disguised as a peddler, she collected enough data on the oppressive situation to convince the United Mine Workers to call for a strike. But her heart was still in the coalfields of Pennsylvania and West Virginia, and some years later when she heard trouble was brewing, she returned. "The eighty-one-year-old dynamo took charge. She traveled up and down Paint Creek, stopping at every cluster of tents. Her presence renewed the men's sagging spirits. More important, she had a plan. She organized three thousand miners and led them in a march over the hills to Charleston to deliver an ultimatum to West Virginia's Governor. They demanded that he outlaw the coal company's guards and replace them with state militia, who would be responsible to the government of West Virginia and not to the mine operators. The Governor agreed, and the removal of the hated gunmen encouraged the strikers to hold out." Two years later she was arrested on a charge of conspiring to kill a company guard, but she was later pardoned by the governor of West Virginia. Before her pardon was granted, she was permitted to give testimony about the conditions she had seen in the mines.

"Thanks largely to her testimony, many abuses were corrected and the coal companies were forced to recognize their employees' right to join unions."

[Margaret Truman, Women of Courage: From Revolutionary Times to the Present *(New York: Morrow, 1976), pp. 115, 117, 119, 124.]*

ECONOMY

Considering Only the Price

There is hardly anything in the world that someone cannot make a little worse and sell a little cheaper—and the people who consider price alone are this man's lawful prey.

—JOHN RUSKIN

Living within One's Income

This year I shall live within my income, even if I must borrow the money to do it.

—MARK TWAIN

EDUCATION

Not Limited to Formal Schooling

Mothers who stay home to raise a family often feel as though they are vegetating intellectually during those years. That need not be the case. There are many opportunities to participate in adult education programs and to take courses at local colleges, but beyond that, any woman can expand her training and knowledge at home with her own agenda of self-education. Millie Van Wyke, the mother of three children, found educational fulfillment at a time in her life when many other mothers in similar circumstances are convinced their minds are regressing.

"One of the most rewarding things I did during the 'stay-at-home' years was read a great deal. The children and I would troop once a week to our neighborhood library, and while they settled in for 'story time,' I browsed. My reading was undisciplined, unguided, totally free. It was a joyous time. I picked from American history one week, best sellers the next. A religious book might catch my eye on one visit, a how-to book on gardening another. I read psychology, short stories, the women's movement, sociology. I studied maps and read all the magazines.

"The result was a sort of haphazard but delightful education, without ever entering a school door, that has served me surprisingly well. I know *a little bit* about most things (except math or science!). Most important *I* learned how to pursue knowledge. I know where I stand in any given subject and where to find out more when I wish. A side benefit, equally important, was that my children learned also to love books and became excellent readers."

[Millie Van Wyke, You're Hired! Insights for Christian Women Who Work Outside the Home (Grand Rapids: Baker, 1983), p. 24.]

Prayer and Bible Reading in School

Although the issue of prayer and Bible reading in the public schools has recently been in the newspaper headlines and has been the subject of many court cases, it is not a new controversy. Indeed, it was the focus of heated debate in the 1860s in Montana, long before the territory became a state. Alma White, who later founded the "Pillar of Fire" movement, was at the center of the controversy. Immediately after her conversion as a teenager, she felt called by God to minister as a schoolteacher in the Northwest. She packed her belongings and set out on the two-thousand-mile trek from Kentucky to Montana, where teachers were in short supply. Her warm welcome was soon dampened, however, when the school board learned that "for one hour each day she turned the school into a mission; and taught the children to pray, read the Bible, and commit sacred hymns to memory." Although "there was an uprising against her," she refused to back down, and finally with the support of the community, new school board members were elected, and she was permitted to continue her "mission" work.

[Alma White, Looking Back from Beulah *(Bound Brook, N.J.: Pentecostal Union, 1910), pp. 50–51.]*

Sex Discrimination in Education

Catherine Beecher was a strong supporter of female education in the nineteenth century, but even she placed stringent limits on what an educated female could do with her education. "In the kind of world she wanted, right-thinking women stayed at home, and with her seminary she was merely trying to temper the wind for those who could not. Yet there is something puzzling about her ambition to train teachers, since according to her their only object was to train more teachers to train teachers—and so *ad infinitum.*" She did have another important reason, however, for educating women—"so that they might be worthy mothers of men, the achievers."

The first coeducational institutions were in the Midwest. Oberlin initiated the trend in 1833, and Antioch was the second, some two decades later, in 1852. Iowa State University and the University of Wisconsin were the next to make the move for coeducational education, but many schools strongly resisted the trend. "In 1858 and 1859 a dozen girls vainly besieged Michigan, but were fought off each time by the board of regents." Not until 1870 did Michigan finally relent and permit female students to enroll.

[Emily Hahn, Once Upon a Pedestal *(New York: Crowell, 1974), pp. 174–75.]*

EMBARRASSMENT
Most Embarrassing Moment

Everyone has a "most embarrassing moment" story to tell, and Beverly Sills, the great soprano opera star, is no exception. The occasion was a special concert given at the invitation of President and Mrs. Nixon.

"The performance I gave at the White House almost turned into a fiasco. I'd prepared a program of eleven songs, but I don't think I'd gotten through three of them before I popped the zipper on the back of the white silk gown I was wearing. A few minutes later I suddenly realized the back zipper was all the way down to my waist. I grabbed the front of the gown just as gravity was about to turn my recital into a striptease. Without saying anything, I backed out of the East Room, leaving three hundred people wondering if I'd lost my marbles. Moments later I returned wearing a long red velvet evening coat—the only reason I had it with me was because Pat had told me the East Room was drafty. As soon as the concert ended, I was able to joke about what happened, but believe me, for a few seconds there, I knew I had a shot at making a little history of my own in Washington. In front of my mother, yet."

[Beverly Sills and Lawrence Linderman, Beverly: An Autobiography *(New York: Bantam Books, 1987), p. 227.]*

EMOTIONALISM

Female Dependency on Male

Do women have an emotional dependence on men more so than men have on women? Gini Andrews, the author of *Your Half of the Apple,* argues that they do. "You know, when God pronounced Eve's sentence, part of it was: 'Thy desire shall be to thy husband.' I'm wondering if this immense, clinging, psychological dependence on man which is part of us as women is not something we should face as part of our fallenness. You must know by now that I'm very much for men, for love and romance, but it is far too easy to be totally caught up in it. We'll jettison any plans, rearrange our lives or our hair-dos; we'll work our fingers to the first joint, throw up a promising career, and too often even undercut our best friend—all for some man we find compellingly attractive. Isn't this a misuse of one of God's greatest gifts? Moderation, balance—these are not essentially feminine characteristics; we're extremists, and that characteristic can wreck us. We need God to undertake the handling of our rampant emotional natures."

[Gini Andrews, Your Half of the Apple (Grand Rapids: Zondervan, 1972), pp. 51–52.]

Women and Religious Ecstasy

The argument that women are more emotionally inclined than men, and for that reason gravitate to ecstatic religious movements, is not supported by the heavy female involvement in the holiness movement of the late nineteenth century. The movement, at least as it penetrated the urban middle class, was not characterized by ecstatic religion, nor were the female leaders of the movement overzealous emotionally. Hannah Whitall Smith, a well-known Bible teacher and author of the bestseller *The Christian's Secret of a Happy Life,* is an example. Her testimony is particularly interesting in this regard. She had desperately sought for an ecstatic religious experience after her husband experienced great emotion and ecstasy at a camp-meeting revival. She tried hard to achieve the same experience (and even went to the altar with a stack of handkerchiefs, thinking she would be overcome with tears), but nothing happened. For years she sought the experience. Later, she wrote that she believed it was her husband's emotional nature that allowed him to have the experience, and she conceded that she was still "a dry old stick."

As the years passed, she began to question the validity of emotional experiences and actually renounced them. "I have discovered by careful investigation that spiritualists have wonderful emotional experiences quite as often as Christians. I am convinced, too, that there are emotions common to highly exalted mental states, no matter what the cause of this exaltation, whose origin is purely physical or psychical and have nothing to do with God's Spirit. Since such experiences can be of the body and not of the spirit at all, I fear many people are sadly deceived by them into thinking they must necessarily be from God and *must* be tokens of His especial favor, when the individuals concerned know nothing whatever of the reality of being filled with the Spirit."

[Marie Henry, The Secret Life of Hannah Whitall Smith (Grand Rapids: Zondervan, 1984), p. 86; Hannah Whitall Smith, The Christian's Secret of a Happy Life (Grand Rapids: Zondervan, 1984), p. 171.]

ETIQUETTE
Early Standards

Manners and social standards change from one generation to another, a fact that is vividly revealed in etiquette books—especially those from centuries ago. This is illustrated in *De civilitate morum puerilium* (On civility in children), written in 1530 by Desiderius Erasmus, the great Renaissance humanist. Many of the ill manners that he dealt with would not even be included in an etiquette manual today.

On the subject of spitting, he wrote, "Turn away when spitting, lest your saliva fall on someone. If anything purulent falls to the ground, it should be trodden upon, lest it nauseate someone. If you are not at liberty to do this, catch the sputum in a small cloth. It is unmannerly to suck back saliva, as equally are those whom we see spitting at every third word not from necessity but from habit."

He had even stronger admonitions regarding blowing the nose. "To blow your nose on your hat or clothing is rustic, and to do so with the arm or elbow befits a tradesman; nor is it much more polite to use the hand, if you immediately smear the snot on your garment. It is proper to wipe the nostrils with a handkerchief, and to do this while turning away, *if more honorable people are present.*

"If anything falls to the ground when blowing the nose with two fingers, it should immediately be trodden away."

Erasmus also had advice in the area of "bathroom" etiquette. "It is impolite to greet someone who is urinating or defecating. . . .

"A well-bred person should always avoid exposing without necessity the parts to which nature has attached modesty. If necessity compels this, it should be done with decency and reserve, even if no witness is present. For angels are always present, and nothing is more welcome to them in a boy than modesty, the companion and guardian of decency. If it arouses shame to show them to the eyes of others, still less should they be exposed to their touch."

[Quoted in Norbert Elias, The History of Manners: The Civilizing Process, vol. 1, trans. Edmund Jephcott (New York: Pantheon Books, 1978), pp. 129–30, 144, 153–54.]

EUTHANASIA

Cannot Be Condoned

Malcolm Muggeridge, a well-known British antiabortion activist, argues that euthanasia cannot be condoned in any circumstances. The basis for his contention is that life is sacred and thus cannot be terminated until God so chooses. Suffering is part of life that should be accepted for its positive value and should not be used as a reason to end human life. "If there were no God, nor any transcendental purpose in the experience of living in this world," he writes, "then a human being's life [would be] no more intrinsically sacred than is that of a broiler-house chicken, which, if it stops laying eggs, or is otherwise incapacitated, no longer rates its allowance of chicken feed and has its neck wrung." But if we regard life as a gift from God, then, he argues, we have no right to determine when it will end.

[Malcolm Muggeridge and Alan Thornhill, Sentenced to Life (New York: Nelson, 1983), p. 15.]

Mercy Killing Prompted by Suffering

Although few people would ever condone the killing of another individual, there are tragic stories of how people in anguish killed loved ones in order to spare them from painful and prolonged physical suffering. One such incident took place in 1975, when a California housewife tried to take her own life after having endured the torment of killing her husband of thirty-two years. "After she shot her husband,

Mrs. Phillips kept his body hidden under sheets: 'Who would have understood?' she said later. Phillips had been an invalid for more than twelve years, suffering from a painful spinal deterioration. For the last five years of his life, he had been virtually unable to move. He had repeatedly begged his wife to end his misery by killing him." For two months she kept his body hidden, but when she heard relatives were planning to visit, she was convinced she had no choice but to kill herself. Her unsuccessful suicide attempt forced her to tell her story of anguish—the story not of a common criminal or a typical murderer, but the story of a loving wife.

[*Derek Humphry and Ann Wickett,* The Right to Die: Understanding Euthanasia *(New York: Harper & Row, 1986), p. 91.*]

EVANGELISM
Compelling Desire to Share One's Faith

Women throughout church history have been severely restricted in leadership roles in the church. Relatively few women have held high church office or been known as great preachers. But in the area of evangelism—especially personal evangelism—women have excelled. No church council has been so powerful that it was able to silence women in sharing their faith with others. Indeed, many great church leaders credit their conversions to the ministry of women. This compelling desire to share the faith is illustrated in the life of A. Katherine Hankey, a nineteenth-century English woman whose family was active in the evangelical wing of the Anglican church. As a woman, Kate was barred from having an official preaching ministry, but she preached anyway. Her congregation was made up of children in her Sunday schools, located throughout London. So influential was she that many of her pupils went on to become effective Christian leaders. She wrote material for her classes and books of verse, donating the royalties to missions—all the while refusing to allow sex discrimination to slow her ministry. Her view of ministry was summed up in the treasured legacy she left for the church—her testimony in verse that became one of the church's best-loved hymns. The third stanza sums up her philosophy of evangelism.

> I love to tell the story—'Tis pleasant to repeat
>   What seems, each time I tell it, more wonderfully sweet;
> I love to tell the story, for some have never heard
>   The message of salvation from God's own holy Word.

Another hymn she wrote with a similar message, but from the hearer's viewpoint, was her much loved "Tell Me the Old, Old Story." For her, Christian ministry was simply sharing the gospel with others.

[Kenneth W. Osbeck, Singing with Understanding *(Grand Rapids: Kregel, 1979), pp. 143–44.]*

EVOLUTION

Early Fear

When Charles Darwin's *Origin of Species* was published in 1859, most Christians did not know how to react. His research offered a shocking scenario that seemed to contradict totally the widely held belief that the world was created less than six thousand years earlier and that man was created at precisely nine o'clock in the morning of October 23, 4004 B.C. Some churchmen feared that this new scientific theory might have a profoundly negative impact on the church, causing a mass exodus of intellectuals. This fear was reflected in the words of the wife of the bishop of Worcester, "Let us hope it is not true, but if it is, let us pray that it does not become generally known."

[Reay Tannahil, Sex and History *(New York: Stein & Day, 1980), p. 14.]*

Viewed Humorously

"ROOTS"

Great Granddad was a jellyfish;
    his folks were just pure slime.

And Gramps, he was a lizard
  who was on the upward climb.
My Daddy was a monkey,
  and Mom, a chimpanzee.
And here *I* am, a human, with a Ph.D.
            —RUTH A. TUCKER

FAILURE
Does Not Prevent Success Later

During her first term at UCLA, Carol Burnett enrolled in a basic acting class. For her first assignment, she performed a monologue from *The Madwoman of Chaillot,* playing the lead part, the maid. Although she "memorized and crammed like crazy," she was nervous, especially after she had seen her classmates perform so well. "It was my turn. I was the only one left. I didn't feel so okay anymore. The stage in the tiny classroom was about six inches high, and I tripped stepping up on it. I turned around and introduced my presentation. . . . I got it out, and I was word-perfect. My homework had paid off in that respect, and I had added a personal touch to the character of the little maid by making small circles in the air with a clenched fist, so it would look as if she were dusting something. I returned to my seat, with my heart in my ears, thankful to God it was all over. I don't recall any clapping.

"But it wasn't all over. Now came the critiques of each and every scene. . . . She skinned me alive. She wound up giving me a D minus. She explained to the class, 'I'm giving Miss Burnett a D minus, because she at least had the piece memorized. However, it was an F performance.' She dismissed us with 'Now . . . choose new partners for your next scenes.' Everyone left but me. I felt as empty as the classroom. I could quit or stay. It was my choice.

"I decided to stay.

"I had nowhere to go but up."

[Carol Burnett, One More Time *(New York: Random House, 1986), p. 186.]*

FAMILY

Cornerstone of American Society

The family has always been the cornerstone of American society.

Our families nurture, preserve and pass on to each succeeding generation the values we share and cherish, values that are the foundation for our freedoms. In the family, we learn our first lessons of God and man, love and discipline, rights and responsibilities, human dignity and human frailty.

Our families give us daily examples of these lessons being put into practice. In raising and instructing our children, in providing personal and compassionate care for the elderly, in maintaining the spiritual strength of religious commitment among our people—in these and other ways, America's families make immeasurable contributions to America's well-being.

Today more than ever, it is essential that these contributions not be taken for granted and that each of us remember that the strength of our families is vital to the strength of our nation.

——PRES. RONALD REAGAN

[Quoted in Nancy Leigh DeMoss, ed., The Rebirth of America *(Philadelphia: Arthur DeMoss Foundation, 1986), p. 97.]*

Essential Cell of Human Society

"The family, grounded on marriage freely contracted, monogamous and indissoluble, is and must be considered the first and essential cell of human society."

[Pope John XXIII, Pacem in Terris, *April 1963.]*

Family Worship Times

Christian leaders and ministers of the gospel often insist upon the necessity of family worship and devotional times. Yet, in the hustle and bustle of today's world, for many Christian families such times are far more of an ideal than a reality. Sports and music and after-school jobs take precedence over what was once seen as the most important aspect of Christian living. Indeed, family worship was a central feature of the Christian home a century ago, and in this setting lives were molded and futures were built.

"Protestant ministers and writers encouraged families to organize family worship twice a day. Morning worship began before breakfast ('food for the soul before we seek food for the body') and the day's activities. The time for worship should be fixed so that it could not be changed by business or other activities. This regularity promoted 'method and punctuality in domestic affairs, which is the chief ornament of a Christian house.' The father gathered all of the household, including servants and apprentices, together for prayer, hymn singing and scriptural reading. Meeting in the parlor the household started the day 'bowing before the God of mercies.' In 1842, Sarah Hale poetically described the results of morning devotions.

> What a fount of strength, what draught of joy
> That morn's devotion yields!
> It girds the souls with righteousness,
> Or from temptation shields;
> It adds the pearl of priceless worth
> Where Life's rich gifts abound
> And scatters flowers of Paradise
> The lowliest home around.

"The more liturgically minded denominations, such as the Episcopalians, outlined specific prayers for the family. After an opening prayer the household would kneel for a general confession. The father conducted a responsorial prayer with his family answering 'Amen.' A psalm would be recited as well as a verse from the Old Testament. Then all joined together for the Apostle's or Nicene Creed, the Collect from the *Book of Common Prayer,* petitions, and a concluding thanksgiving. If this liturgy was too formal for the family, they could begin with the Lord's Prayer, thank God for preserving them through the night, mention any upcoming family events, and then dedicate the day to the Lord. The service would be concluded with a prayer to keep them from sin, perform the day's duties, and deliver divine guidance."

Recognizing that not all family members were entirely enthusiastic about family worship, "authors warned against over-zealous fathers who burdened their families with long-winded prayers and sermons." One strong advocate of such devotional time admitted that it "was the fault of our forefathers to make it sufferable long," but he went on to insist that "every secular task or amusement . . . be suspended, and absolute silence and quiet . . . be enforced, even in the case of the youngest children."

[Colleen McDannell, The Christian Home in Victorian America, 1840–1900 *(Bloomington: Indiana University Press, 1986), pp. 79–81.]*

Good Times and Bad in Family Relationships

Edith Schaeffer, the wife of the late, internationally known Christian philosopher Dr. Francis Schaeffer, is a prolific writer and widely traveled speaker in her own right, but she is quick to emphasize that her family has been her top priority. She discusses this in her book *What Is a Family?* and she concludes by poignantly answering that question.

"A family—for better or for worse, for richer or for poorer, in sickness and in health! Dirty diapers, chicken pox, measles, mumps, broken dishes, scratched furniture, balls thrown through the windows, fights, croup in the night, arguments, misunderstandings, inconsistencies, lack of logic, unreasonableness, anger, fever, flu, depressions, carelessness, toothpaste tops left off, dishes in the sink, windows open too far, windows closed tight, too many covers, too few covers, always late, always too early, frustration, economics, extravagance, discouragement, fatigue, exhaustion, noise, disappointment, weeping, fears, sorrows, darkness, fog, chaos, clamorings—families!

"A family—for better or for worse, for richer or for poorer, in sickness and in health! Softness, hugs, children on your lap, someone to come home to, someone to bring news to, a telephone that might ring, a letter in the post, someone at the airport or station, excitement in meeting, coming home from the hospital with a new person to add, . . . beloved old people, welcomed babies . . . exchanging ideas, stimulating each other—families!

"A family is a mobile strung together with invisible threads— delicate, easily broken at first, growing stronger through the years, in danger of being worn thin at times, but strengthened again with special care. A family—blended, balanced, growing, changing, never static, moving with a breath of wind—babies, children, young people, mothers, fathers, grandparents, aunts, uncles—held in a balanced framework by the invisible threads of love, memories, trust, loyalty, compassion, kindness, in honor preferring each other, depending on each other, looking to each other for help, giving each other help, picking each other up, suffering long with each other's faults, understanding each other more and more, hoping all things, enduring all things, never failing!"

[Edith Schaeffer, What Is a Family? *(Old Tappan, N.J.: Revell, 1975), pp. 254–55.]*

Importance of Nonverbal Communication

Psychologists and counselors have been telling us for a long time that nonverbal communication is often more important than verbal communication in seeking to understand another person's feelings. Indeed, silence itself often tells another individual more about a person's well-being than speaking does. Parents too frequently fail to pay sufficient attention to this nonverbal communication. "The most common reaction technique of youths in conflict with their families," writes Dolores Curran, "is silence. Often silence is the only reaction acceptable in the family. If youths can't expose what's bothering them for fear of ridicule or censure, or if they aren't allowed to argue, then they will revert to silence. The sad irony discovered by so many family therapists is that parents who seek professional help when their teenager becomes silent have often denied him or her any other route but silence in communicating. . . .

"The healthy families I know recognize positive nonverbal communication as crucial to family life. They use signs, symbols, body language, smiles, and other physical gestures to express their feelings of caring and love. They deal with silence and withdrawal in a positive, open way. Communication to them doesn't mean talking or listening alone. It includes all the clues to a person's feelings—his bearing, her expression, their resignation. Such families have a highly developed form of communication. Members don't have to say 'I'm hurting' or 'I'm in need.' A quick glance tells other members that. And they have developed ways of responding without words—ways that indicate empathy and love, whether or not there's an immediate solution to the pain. And that's what counts in the healthy family."

[Dolores Curran, Traits of a Healthy Family *(Minneapolis: Winston Press, 1983), pp. 44, 46–47.]*

Loyalty in Families

Love and loyalty for family members and friends are not character traits that necessarily have any correlation with moral goodness and virtue. People who demonstrate no inclination to uphold ethical principles in other areas of their lives are sometimes the most loyal and dedicated to their families and loved ones. This was the case with the notorious gangster duo Bonnie and Clyde. As they traversed the South on their murderous rampage, they frequently made risky ventures back to see their families. According to their biographer, "both the fugitives had a strong and continuing need for their home territory and their families—especially Clyde for his sister Nell and Bonnie for her mother." Such conduct was not unusual for people running from the law. "In this respect they were exactly conformed to a traditional pattern of criminal behavior. The outlaw murderers of an earlier generation, such as the James brothers, often took great risks to visit and stay with their families. Even that most formidable and professional of gangsters, John Dillinger, felt strong desires to return to Mooresville, Indiana, to stay with the father to whom he had never been particularly close as a child or a youth."

Bonnie's mother and Clyde's mother each took risks themselves in arranging to meet their children in secluded places in order to spend time with them and provide them with necessary supplies. After their children were gunned down by lawmen, family members spoke out orally and in print in defense of them, hoping somehow to restore the reputation for decency they had long since lost.

[John Treherne, The Strange History of Bonnie and Clyde *(New York: Stein & Day, 1984), p. 36.]*

Problems after Remarriage

Great care must be taken in families brought together by remarriage. This is true when the children all belong to one parent, but even more crucial when there are unrelated children in the new family unit. Blending the two families does not come naturally. It is the result of careful planning and hard work. This is the advice of Tom Frydenger, a family counselor and a man who married a woman with two young girls from a previous marriage.

"If blending, or integration, does not take place in a reconstituted family, its members sound like two bands led by two different conductors, playing two different songs in two different keys. I have counseled blended families where each original family system insisted on playing its own song, and on playing it louder and louder in an attempt to drown the other song out. Eventually the original tune gave way to blasting noise and family discord."

Frydenger gives an example of one such family, where neither parent "was willing to give up old systems and work into a new, unified family system. Both wanted to be sole conductors.

"The lack of blending between the parents in rules, guidelines and expectations made it difficult for both sets of children to accept their stepparents' authority. It also produced fierce competition resulting in jealousy and hostility. . . .

"For blending to take place in a reconstituted family, the new mates must work closely together, analyzing their personal styles, minimizing their weaknesses and maximizing their strengths. With time and lots of practice their blended bands will begin to play a harmonious family melody."

[Tom Frydenger and Adrienne Frydenger, The Blended Family (Old Tappan, N.J.: Revell, 1984), pp. 35–36.]

FASHION
Designed to Please Men

Only in the twentieth century have women's fashions been styled for comfort rather than simply for show. There were valiant attempts to make styles more practical during the nineteenth century, but they were usually very short-lived. One such fashion design was introduced to American culture in the 1850s by Amelia Bloomer. After she printed the pattern for her new dress design in her newspaper, the *Lily,* the subscriptions rapidly escalated, and the costume was referred to as "bloomers." The outfit consisted of a knee-length skirt over loose trousers that were gathered at the ankle. One of the earliest and most vocal advocates of bloomers was Elizabeth Cady Stanton, an early feminist leader who regarded this new design in fashion an important women's issue. "She argued that custom had designed women's clothes to appeal to male passion rather than female necessity. Dependent on men for social status and financial support, women needed to be attractive and ornamental. Wearing five yards of skirt, plus hoops, petticoats, and corsets pleased men but kept women from moving easily, breathing comfortably, or engaging in healthy exercise. . . . Hems dragged in muddy streets promoted disease and increased the time required to care for one's wardrobe."

Many women followed Mrs. Stanton in this noble effort to bring sense into the fashion world, but the crusade was, not surprisingly, strongly opposed by men. When Stanton's husband ran for political office, her bloomers became an election issue. "Some good Democrats," she wrote to a friend, "said they would not vote for a man whose wife wore the Bloomers." Indeed, this flap over fashion became a bitter controversy. "Had I counted the cost of the short dress, I would never have put it on; however, I'll never take it off for now it involves a principle of freedom." After two years of public scorn, however, she gave up and went back to long skirts. The price to be paid was not worth the comfort the bloomers offered, and once again women were defeated in their struggle for freedom.

[Elisabeth Griffith, In Her Own Right: The Life of Elizabeth Cady Stanton (New York: Oxford University Press, 1984), pp. 71–72.]

Economically Priced Fashions

We might assume that an expensive gown would be one of the prerequisites to winning a beauty pageant, but that is not necessarily true. In 1981, Andrea Lund, a high school senior, was crowned Miss Teenage Idaho, dressed in a gown that she purchased at a church second-hand store for $1.48. After pricing expensive dresses and not finding what she wanted, she began going through the racks at Deseret Industries and found one she liked. "She removed the gaudy pink bow, covered a pink sash with delicate white lace, and sewed 'hundreds' of sequins on the dress. Two hours later she was satisfied the outfit would stand up well under the scrutiny of the judges." The price of the gown apparently had little effect on the judges, since the first runner-up spent $450 for hers.

[Grand Rapids Press, July 7, 1981.]

Fashion Forsaken for Spiritual Values

During a spiritual-life conference in England in 1886, Amy Carmichael, who later became a great missionary to India, experienced a deep encounter with God that changed her entire outlook on life. She discovered that her expensive taste in food and clothing had suddenly vanished. Her first realization of this change came when she was invited out to a restaurant by a friend, only to be served very poorly prepared mutton chops. Such an incident would have previously upset the well-brought-up young woman, but she realized that she no longer cared about such trivial things in life.

"If mutton chops didn't matter anymore, neither did clothes. When Amy got back to Belfast, the long mourning period for her father was over and it was time, her mother said, to purchase a few pretty dresses—among them, of course, an evening dress for parties. They went to the shop. The shopman displayed his loveliest things. Suddenly Amy decided she could not have them. She was now, in the language of the apostle Paul . . . 'dead to the world.' To Amy, the world meant fashion, finery, luxury of any sort. She would follow Him who had no home, no earthly possessions beyond the bare minimum. She would be 'dead to the world and its applause, to all its customs, fashions, laws.' For a girl with her eye for beauty, it is the measure of her commitment that she did not hesitate to relinquish all that seemed to her inimical to the true life of discipleship."

[*Elisabeth Elliot,* A Chance to Die: The Life and Legacy of Amy Carmichael *(Old Tappan, N.J.: Revell, 1987), pp. 37–38.*]

FATHER

Neglect of Family in Order to Serve God

Bob Pierce, a man who symbolically became a father to the children of the world, utterly failed as a father to his own children. As the founder of World Vision, Pierce traveled the world feeding and housing hungry and homeless children. He was "a maverick, an innovator, a pioneer, a visionary. The key to his whole ministry was his unhesitating responsiveness to need. If he saw a need that no one else was meeting, he met it." Meeting the needs of his family, however, was more difficult. Marilee Dunker, his daughter, writes of the pain she experienced during his frequent absences. "It was hard for us to believe that Daddy really understood our needs. Although we knew he loved us, he was gone too much to be involved with our everyday lives, and it was impossible to fill him in on a month's worth of life during two dinners and a trip to Disneyland. He was always careful to verbalize his concern and interest, but the life-and-death situations he was constantly dealing with must have made the problems of his healthy, well-fed children difficult to take seriously." One of the problems he did not take seriously was his oldest daughter's depression. Sharon unsuccessfully attempted suicide while he was overseas, when he was too busy to come home, despite her plea for help. A few months later while he was away again, she succeeded in taking her life. Dr. Pierce had once said, "I've made an agreement with God that I'll take care of His little lambs overseas if He'll take care of mine at home." That, according to one acquaintance, was one of "the saddest and most telling" comments he ever made.

[*Marilee Pierce Dunker,* Days of Glory, Seasons of Night *(Grand Rapids: Zondervan, 1984), pp. 121, 133–34.*]

Provider Role of Father

Many women complain that their husbands are workaholics and have little time for the children or for helping around the house. In some cases the husband simply wants any excuse he can have not to be involved with the duties of homemaking, but it may also be due to the fact that society places such high value on the provider role of the husband. Society simply expects men to be successful in their careers, and that expectation often places husbands and fathers under extreme pressure to outperform their coworkers.

"A man validates his maleness by his success as a provider," writes Jessie Bernard. "We have, in fact, specialized the father almost out of the family in any but the provider role. We have defined his role almost exclusively as that of provider, and nearly everything else about him as a human being depends on how well he performs that one function.

If he does well in that role he can get away with almost anything else in the bosom of his family. He can sit uncommunicatively in front of the TV set drinking beer or even leave and go to the local tavern to drink his beer with the boys; no one will hold it against him so long as he is a good provider. But let him cease to be a good provider and no other virtue will compensate for this failure. Everything else collapses, including his manhood. No wonder success as the provider assumes so much importance for men. All their eggs are in that one basket."

A nineteenth-century prototype of what would today be a gold-seal record was a song called "Come Home, Father." It was about a little girl who went to a saloon every night to plead with her father to come home.

> Father, dear father, come home with me now.
> The clock in the steeple strikes one.
> You said you were coming right home from the shop
> As soon as your day's work was done.

"Every hour on the hour she returned. The clock struck two and little Willie was sick and calling for him. The clock struck three and little Willie was worse, coughing and crying. The clock struck four, five, six. The fire went out; the house got cold; mother was waiting. When the clock struck ten in the morning father finally went home. Too late. Willie was dead.

"It was a tear-jerker if ever there was one. In those days it was alcohol that intoxicated fathers. Today it is almost as likely to be work."

[Jessie Bernard, Women, Wives, Mothers: Values and Options *(Chicago: Adline Publishing, 1975), pp. 220–21.]*

FEAR

Employed to Achieve Spiritual Response

Hildegard, a late-medieval German mystic, claimed that she was guided by a divine light that directed her writing and teaching. She recorded the messages and then disseminated them publicly in order that others could benefit from God's direction. Frequently these messages were ones that conjured up fear of the afterlife. Indeed, she pleaded with sinners to repent, lest they suffer the agony that the divine light that she saw in her visionary revelations. "I saw a well deep and broad, full of boiling pitch and sulphur, and around it were wasps and scorpions. . . . Near a pond of clear water I saw a great fire. In this some souls were burned and others were girdled with snakes. . . . And I saw a great fire, black, red, and white, and in it horrible vipers spitting flame; and there the vipers tortured the souls of those who had been slaves of the sin of uncharitableness. . . . And I saw a thickest darkness, in which the souls of the disobedient lay on a fiery pavement and were bitten by sharp-toothed worms." Her visions did generate fear, and people came from far away to speak with her and receive her counsel on spiritual matters.

[Henry Osborn Taylor, The Medieval Mind *(Cambridge: Harvard University Press, 1949), pp. 470–71.]*

FEMININITY

Attractive Quality in Women

In their book *Smart Women, Foolish Choices,* Connell Cowan and Melvyn Kinder, who are both practicing clinical psychologists, give women advice on "finding the right men" and "avoiding the wrong ones." In addressing the issue of how women can make themselves more attractive to men, they broach the subject of femininity—emphasizing its important place in a healthy male-female relationship. It is a quality in a woman that should attract the opposite sex without diminishing the distinctive attributes of her own sex that she cherishes the most. "The traditional definition [of femininity] connoted passivity, weakness, delicacy, and girlishness. It placed fundamental importance upon appearance and presentation and implied coyness, coquettishness, disguises, games, and strategies. Today, femininity is being redefined simply as the quality of being uniquely female or womanly. Specifically, it refers not only to those qualities one traditionally associates more with women than men—tenderness, sensitivity, and nurturance—but also includes behaviors that tradition links more with men—strength, power, and aggressiveness. In fact, this broadened definition of womanliness is already being embraced by increasing numbers of women. These women are learning that being strong and assertive does not detract from feeling womanly, but rather complements such feelings. They also understand that expressions of strength don't rob them of their capacity to be tender and giving."

[Connell Cowan and Melvyn Kinder, Smart Women, Foolish Choices *(New York: Potter, 1985), p. 163.]*

Femininity and Business Careers

In her book *Women like Us,* Liz Gallese studied the women of Harvard Business School, class of 1975, and found that, despite their education and opportunities for advancement, they did not progress up the ladder of corporate success as rapidly as did their male counterparts—in part because they chose a different life-style that reflected their "femininity." She found that "fully two fifths of the group were ambivalent or frankly not ambitious for their careers." Other studies have shown that women are significantly behind equally qualified men in salary scale and position, even though many corporations are eager to promote women. Gallese has concluded that the reason for this involves the psychological and physical make-up of a woman. "The reason for women's tendency to pull back is as fundamental as the difference between women and men, I have come to believe." The women who do succeed, she argues, are those "who choose to live their lives as men in a man's world. . . . In many respects, however, the fact that women pull back is a good sign. For there seems to be, in women's retrenchment, a reluctance to forfeit what is uniquely theirs, their femininity."

When she first began her study, Gallese expected to find women who were very different from ordinary women—women who would do anything to have professional success, but she discovered these were "women like us." "In their reluctance to make themselves into men in a man's world, in their concern about retaining their femininity, however, I could see that they weren't as select a group as I had assumed. Indeed, they had a great deal in common with women in general, that massive pool of women living as wives of men, as mothers of children, as workers of one sort or another, teachers and secretaries as well as professionals and managers."

[Liz Roman Gallese, Women like Us (New York: New American Library, 1985), pp. 313–15.]

Problem of Defining Femininity

Feminism and femininity are sometimes perceived as being incompatible. The qualities that are frequently characterized as being feminine are the very ones that many feminists believe are holding women back and keeping them subservient to men. Opponents of feminism, on the other hand, fear that femininity will be lost as women become liberated. Janet Richards deals with this issue in her book *The Sceptical Feminist.* "The issue of femininity" has aroused "fierce passions . . . on both sides ever since the first stirrings of women's emancipation. The fear that an emancipated woman must necessarily be an unfeminine one has always been the basis of one of the opposition's main objections to feminism, and feminists have never (or at least not recently) made the slightest attempt to allay those fears, since most of them think that the creation of a feminine character is one of the most deeply-rooted and sinister parts of women's oppression, and that until women are free of femininity they will never be free at all."

One of the difficulties in dealing with this issue is that there is no easy or readily agreed-upon definition of femininity. There are lists of supposed feminine characteristics, but they are generally of little value in characterizing particular women. "If it is feminine," writes Richards, "to be illogical, dependent and hysterical, why are countless woman strong, rational and calm without apparently losing any femininity at all? How could Lucy Stone (an early American feminist) arouse public outrage by being unfeminine enough to speak in public, making most unfeminine political suggestions, and yet be found by one surprised member of her audience 'a prototype of womanly grace'? Femininity is very hard to pin down, and that makes it difficult to see precisely what everyone is fighting for or against, and why."

[Janet Radcliffe Richards, The Sceptical Feminist: A Philosophical Enquiry *(Boston: Routledge & Kegan Paul, 1980), pp. 121–22.]*

Trend Away from Femininity

Ruth Peale, the wife of the well-known preacher and apostle of positive thinking, Norman Vincent Peale, is a strong proponent of the traditional role of women in society and in the home. In her book *The Adventure of Being a Wife,* she gives a personal account of her own role as a wife and woman. In it she includes a chapter entitled "A Few Kind Words for Femininity," where she contends that, "unless a woman is willing to look and act and be feminine, she's never going to be a success as a wife or a mother or even as a person." She concedes that "feminists would object to the implication that making a marriage work is primarily the woman's responsibility," but she argues that "on the deepest level it really is." Feminism, she believes, has stripped women of their femininity and has had corresponding negative influences on society. "The trend away from femininity in this country is nothing new; it has been going on for years. Most of the change has come about during my lifetime. I think it really got under way after the first World War, when along with the right to vote women also insisted they had the 'right' to drink, smoke, swear, and put aside standards of sexual conduct that they had maintained for generations. The subsequent appearance of ugly manifestations in our society—the decline of everyday honesty, the increase in crime, the sexual permissiveness, the erosion of discipline, the disrespect for law, the contempt for authority, the increasing reliance on violence as a solution to problems—is something that can't be proved. But to me it seems highly probable that there is a direct connection."

[*Ruth Peale,* The Adventure of Being a Wife *(Englewood Cliffs, N.J.: Prentice-Hall, 1971), pp. 235–37.*]

FEMINISM

Cause of Family Breakdown

Phyllis Schlafly, the founder and head of a conservative political organization, has expressed strong sentiments in speech and writing about working mothers and the detrimental effect their life-style has on the family. She blames feminism for the changes in society that are encouraging women to work. In her book *The Power of the Christian Woman,* she writes about the consequences of feminism as depicted in the movie *Kramer vs. Kramer.* "It tells the unhappy story of a wife walking out on her husband because she wanted to 'know who she is.' She thought she was missing out on something because she was 'only' a wife and mother. She wanted to find 'self-esteem' as a 'whole person.' After consulting with a psychiatrist and landing a job paying more than her hardworking, faithful husband earned, she thought she had found what she was looking for." What was the result of this woman's pilgrimage? According to Schlafly, it was family breakdown, and feminism was to blame. "At the end of the movie, she was unhappy, the husband was unhappy, the child was unhappy. The marriage was irretrievably broken, the custody battle was bitter, and the child had only one parent. None of the usual causes of marriage failure was present: alcohol, adultery, violence, or financial problems. The only cause was the siren call of women's liberation which led the wife down the primrose path seeking her self-fulfillment above every other value. . . . The women's liberation movement disregards, denigrates, and denies the created beginnings of woman and the creative essence of womanhood."

[Phyllis Schlafly, The Power of the Christian Woman (Cincinnati: Standard Publishing, 1981), p. 15.]

Changes in Women Prompted by Feminism

Ginny Foat, who tells of her pilgrimage in life and her move toward feminism in her book *Never Guilty, Never Free,* gives a very telling description of how a woman's personality can change through a commitment to feminism. In her own situation, her marriage was seriously affected by her radical change. Her husband was distressed by the woman his wife was turning into. "What had happened to his princess, the sweet, adoring, submissive woman he'd married? It was as though somebody had snatched her away and left this hard, angry stranger in her place. This new Ginny didn't even look the same. Gone were the false eyelashes and fingernails, the wigs and hairpieces. I got by with my own hair now, though I still dyed it, and my makeup was more subdued. All Ray could do was wait and hope for the return of his original wife. Understandably, he was confused. He was quietly and patiently bewildered at first, but before long he was outright angry."

Foat, unlike some feminists, has since been able to reflect back objectively on those early days in the movement and see herself for what she was. "I became almost a caricature of a feminist. I was going through that phase that most feminists know, the one where you allow yourself to luxuriate in your wonderful newfound anger before the world settles back into a saner perspective. . . . I couldn't discuss my feminism with nonfeminists without yelling and screaming. I was always correcting people, jumping on them for the slightest infractions of my new rules, scorning such useful qualities as humor and tact. I was about as tolerant and diplomatic as Torquemada. I was a royal bitch. Ray, and Ray's golf buddies, and the golf buddies' wives, began to look at me as though I were a lunatic." Feminism, she says, "made me angry and intolerant and bitchy and tired."

[Ginny Foat, Never Guilty, Never Free *(New York: Random House, 1985), pp. 151–53.]*

Cynical Response to Feminism

What is the easiest way for some people to respond to the serious questions that feminists have been asking in recent years? Often it is done with one-liners—cryptic, cynical slogans that do not really speak to the problems women are struggling with in today's world. An example is the verse printed on a church marquee:

ADAMS RIB, PLUS

SATANS FIB EQUALS

WOMANS LIB

[Patricia Gundry, Neither Slave nor Free: Helping Women Answer the Call to Church Leadership *(San Francisco: Harper & Row, 1987), p. 2.]*

Danger of Feminism

In the eyes of many, the church, more than any other institution in society, has the most to lose to feminism. Indeed, feminism is perceived to be a threat to the very core of God-ordained male authority, and women such as Beverly LaHaye of Concerned Women for America are seeking to counteract feminist philosophy in society and the church.

"I believe that one of the greatest dangers facing the Christian church today is women who advocate feminist viewpoints. . . . It grieves me to think that a root of bitterness is growing in our churches because of feminism. I caution 'Christian feminists' against causing divisions in the church. If they have legitimate grievances, they should state their position—once—and commit it to the Lord. Anything more than that is rebellion."

[Beverly LaHaye, The Restless Woman *(Grand Rapids: Zondervan, 1984), p. 121.]*

Failure of Feminism

Sylvia Ann Hewlett, a working mother and one-time supporter of the Equal Rights Amendment, has since written of the failure of the American feminist movement. "American feminists have generally stressed the ways in which men and women should be equal and have therefore tried to put aside differences. This has led them to sidetrack issues of motherhood. When it comes to the special functions of women in the bearing of children, there has been a tendency to focus on reproductive freedom and the right to choose *not* to have a child since that is what would permit women to approximate men. The critical problems of having children or of being a mother are ignored or downplayed."

Hewlett is outspoken in her criticism of the National Organization of Women. "Does NOW realize that women are not men? It is true, only women can have babies; it is both the privilege and the responsibility of the female sex. To ignore this biological difference, as many American feminists choose to do, is to commit a double folly. In the first place, it ensures that most women will become second class citizens in the workplace. For *without public support policies few women can cope with motherhood without hopelessly compromising their career goals.* Secondly, society has to suffer. For a child cannot be compared with a new car or a vacation, some private consumer good that a woman can choose to spend resources on if the fancy strikes her. The decision to have a child is both a private and a public decision, for children are our collective future." Hewlett goes on to make a strong plea not for equal rights but for special privileges for women who have the responsibility of bearing children, and this, she points out, is the philosophy of the European feminists.

[Sylvia Ann Hewlett, A Lesser Life: The Myth of Women's Liberation in America *(New York: Morrow, 1986), pp. 142, 147.]*

Male Opposition to Feminism

"Male opposition to feminism is rigid, deep, and broad, and functions on many levels. One is personal: the equality of women means the eradication of a servant caste. If a caste of people is not born subhuman, is not designed by nature to serve—not programmed, as it were, to perform nonvolitionally—then men must take its grumblings and resentment seriously, must reward services or share them, must credit the responsibility and love that underlie the behavior of those people. This few men are prepared to do. . . . Men as a caste therefore have a huge investment in keeping women subordinate. To accept women as fully human means to accept 'feminine' values as human values appropriate to both sexes."

[Marilyn French, Beyond Power: On Women, Men, and Morals *(New York: Summit Books, 1985), pp. 486–87.]*

Misunderstanding of Feminism

Margaret Forster, who studied many individual feminists of past generations, has concluded that the concept of feminism is very frequently misunderstood—by men and women and by feminists and nonfeminists. "Feminism," she writes, "is full of riddles. One of the most intriguing is why it has not attracted an enormous rank-and-file following among women themselves, why it is still as necessary as it was in the nineteenth century to ask a woman if she *is* a feminist. The plain truth is that not only do large numbers of women feel apathetic but many more actively hate feminism. This is because right from the invention of the word it has been both misrepresented and misunderstood. Undeniably, this was the fault of men, because men controlled the outlets for the spreading of new ideas, but it was also the fault of the feminists themselves. They were too honest, expressed too openly and fully their fears and worries and, most of all, their resentments. The result was that feminism became frightening in its implications.

"But in fact there is nothing to be frightened of. Feminism, both for men and women, is the most attractive and peaceful of doctrines. It is quite wrong to see it as an aggressive, destructive movement which aims at making neuters of us all."

[Margaret Forster, Significant Sisters: The Grassroots of Active Feminism, 1839–1939 *(New York: Knopf, 1985), p. 1.]*

Radical Forms of Feminism

The National Organization for Women (NOW) has changed its style and emphasis over the years, as Ginny Foat, a prominent member, relates. She joined the movement in 1974, and in 1981 was elected president of California NOW. "I joined NOW at a time when the organization itself was undergoing a major upheaval. NOW's founders in the mid-1960s were mostly middle-class and upper-middle class career women, who kept politely to economic issues that were comparatively respectable and safe, and shied away from controversy. But as NOW grew and its membership became more diverse, internal dissent grew as well. For example, a large issue arose over lesbianism, and a number of lesbian women were forced out. A group called the Majority Caucus began pushing for decentralization of the organization, for more input and power from the grass roots, and for involvement in 'radical' issues that affected women on all economic levels. Equal pay for equal work was still important, of course, but the Majority Caucus wanted NOW to act on lesbian rights, abortion, racism, and violence against women. Led by Ellie Smeal, the Majority Caucus was able to take control of NOW in 1975 after a bitter fight. Its slogan was 'Out of the mainstream, into the revolution.'

"As it turned out, it wasn't long before NOW found its way back into the mainstream. But feminism as a revolution was what I believed in when I joined and what I believe in today. I was 'trying to save the world,' my father would have said, and he would have been right. I'm still trying and I suppose I'll die trying, still believing that it's possible."

Some of the revolutionary zeal of the feminists in the 1970s, as Foat admits, backfired. An example was an effort to stage a nationwide women's strike, billed as "Alice Doesn't Day," taken from the movie *Alice Doesn't Live Here Anymore.* The idea was for women in all walks of life to go on strike for a day to show the nation how important women were to the work force. It turned out to be a failure in that many women, threatened by their employers, refused to become involved, and many who did spend the day on strike were fired. Yet, the failure had a profound effect on the movement. "If it failed as a protest, however, the opposition to it succeeded in further radicalizing many of us. We regrouped and looked for new avenues of protest."

[Ginny Foat, Never Guilty, Never Free *(New York: Random House, 1985), pp. 147–48.]*

Shunning of Feminism

Madame Curie, who won the Nobel prize for chemistry in 1911, was a highly motivated woman who impressed upon her daughter, Irène, the same standard of self-sufficiency that she herself maintained. Irène and her husband won the Nobel prize for chemistry in 1935. For Curie, there was no place for woman's rights. She believed that the only way women would make advances was by proving their abilities alongside men. "She never embraced any feminist cause and saw full well that she could only achieve equality by making for herself the conditions under which she could compete with men on equal terms. She must expect no concessions, and be wary of prejudice."

[Robert Reid, Marie Curie *(New York: New American Library, 1974), p. 57.]*

Worst Enemies of Feminism

Harriett Martineau, a nineteenth-century English woman, who was involved in a variety of progressive and radical causes of her day, was critical of some of her fellow feminists. She argued forcefully for higher education for women, but in doing so, she did not scorn the accepted female role as wife and mother. In describing a scholarly woman who was learned in mathematics and the classics, she was careful to point out that she was also "one of the best housekeepers I know." Indeed, Martineau was very critical of women who overstepped their bounds in making a case for feminism. "Nobody can be further than I from being satisfied with the condition of my own sex, under the law and custom of my own country; but I decline all fellowship and co-operation with women of genius or otherwise favourable position who injure the cause by their personal tendencies. When I see an eloquent writer insinuating to everybody who comes across her that she is the victim of her husband's carelessness and cruelty, while he never spoke in his own defense: when I see her violating all good taste by her obtrusiveness in society, and oppressing everybody about her with her Epicurean selfishness every day, . . . I feel to the bottom of my heart that she is the worst enemy of the cause she professes to plead. . . . The best friends of the cause are the happy wives or the busy, cheerful, satisfied single women, who have no injuries of their own to avenge."

[*Harriet Martineau,* Autobiography, *ed. Maria Weston Chapman (1877), quoted in Dee Jepsen,* Women Beyond Equal Rights *(Waco: Word Books, 1984), p. 49.*]

FOOD PREPARATION

Roast Stuffed Camel

One of the most complicated single dishes ever prepared by chefs is roast stuffed camel, which is sometimes served at large Bedouin marriage feasts. "To prepare this delicacy, first take one hundred gutted

Mediterranean trout and stuff them with two hundred hard-boiled eggs, then stuff the trout into fifty cooked chickens, the chickens into a body cavity of a sheep, and the sheep into the carcass of a camel. Roast over a charcoal fire until done: serves three hundred."

[Scot Morris, The Book of Strange Facts and Useless Information *(Garden City, N.Y.: Doubleday, 1979), p. 64.]*

FORGIVENESS

When Humanly Impossible

Corrie ten Boom became famous through the book and film *The Hiding Place,* which tells of her family's efforts to hide Jews in Holland from the Nazis and of her later suffering in a Nazi death camp. In 1947, she returned to visit that death camp in Germany, where she gave a message of forgiveness to a group of German people who had come out to hear her, and it was at that time that she was confronted with the most difficult task she had ever faced.

"The place was Ravensbruck and the man who was making his way forward had been a guard—one of the most cruel guards.

"Now he was in front of me, hand thrust out: 'A fine message, Fraulein! How good it is to know that, as you say, all our sins are at the bottom of the sea!'

"And I, who had spoken so glibly of forgiveness, fumbled in my pocketbook rather than take that hand. He would not remember me, of course—how could he remember one prisoner among those thousands of women?

"But I remembered him and the leather crop swinging from his belt. I was face-to-face with one of my captors and my blood seemed to freeze.

"You mentioned Ravensbruck in your talk,' he was saying. 'I was a guard there.' No, he did not remember me.

" 'But since that time,' he went on, 'I have become a Christian. I know that God has forgiven me for the cruel things I did there, but

I would like to hear it from your lips as well. Fraulein,'—again the hand came out—'will you forgive me?'

"And I stood there—I whose sins had again and again to be forgiven—and could not forgive. Betsie [Corrie's sister] had died in that place—could he erase her slow terrible death simply for the asking?

"It could not have been many seconds that he stood there—hand held out—but to me it seemed hours as I wrestled with the most difficult thing I had ever had to do."

[Corrie ten Boom, with Jamie Buckingham, Tramp for the Lord *(Old Tappan, N.J.: Revell, 1974), p. 56.]*

FRIENDSHIP

Definition

What is a friend? Everyone has their own definition of what friendship really is, but to fine-tune the definition and make it personally meaningful, an individual should reflect on certain questions that get to the heart of friendship. "What do you look for in a friend? How many really good friends do you have, and how often do you see them? What do you do together? Could you live without them? Can you stay friends after a serious fight? Did you ever lose a meaningful friend? Do you keep making new ones? Is there such a thing as having too many friends? Are *you* a good friend to the friends in your life?"

There is a significant difference between friendship and acquaintance—a difference between a friend and a neighbor, or a friend and a coworker. A friend is one with whom a person has a unique and special relationship. That relationship has been reflected on by writers and philosophers from time immemorial. "Audacious as it may seem to use the word 'soul' in connection with friendship, I take my cue from the many thinkers who have already done so," writes Letty Cottin Pogrebin. "As recorded in the Bible: 'The soul of Jonathan was knit with the soul of David, and Jonathan loved him as his own soul.' Aristotle called friendship 'a single soul dwelling in two bodies.' Cicero declared, 'Whoever is in possession of a true friend sees the exact counterpart of his own soul.' Montaigne wrote of himself and his friend, 'Our souls travelled so unitedly together.' Voltaire said, 'Friendship is the marriage of the soul.' And Mahatma Gandhi described true friendship as 'an identity of souls rarely to be found in this world.' "

[Letty Cottin Pogrebin, Among Friends: Who We Like, Why We Like Them, and What We Do with Them (New York: McGraw-Hill, 1987), pp. 3, 21.]

"Don't Be a Bore" to Your Friends

Making new friends and retaining old ones depends to a large extent on conversational proficiency. Some people, because they consider themselves extroverts, assume that they are good conversationalists. They may be sadly mistaken, as Letitia Baldrige points out.

"Don't be a bore. Next to being labeled a malicious gossip, the worst conversational criticism that can be leveled against anyone is to be called a bore. A good conversationalist senses when he or she has begun to bore the audience and does something about it.

"Glance at the checklist below. If you find yourself answering in the affirmative to more than two points, you just might qualify as a bore.

Are You Boring?

—Do you find yourself passionately holding forth on a controversial subject when the other person or people present obviously are not of your opinion?

—Do you interminably drag out a story while people are looking at their watches, fidgeting, demanding another drink, or asking in a joking fashion (they're not really joking) when you're going to get to the point?

—Do you talk too slowly?

—Do you find yourself rambling?

—Do you constantly discuss something technologically complicated when your audience is not as versed in jargon as you are?

—Do you notice the eyes of the person you're talking to glazing over?

—Do you go into lengthy dissertations on your feelings without first determining if your feelings are of interest to others, and without much interest in how others feel?

—Do you have distracting mannerisms, such as constantly brushing your hair back from your forehead or chewing on your eyeglass handles?

—Is your language peppered with cliches? ('Here today, gone tomorrow' . . . 'That's life' . . . 'Let the chips fall where they may' . . . 'I was between a rock and a hard place.')

—Have people ceased even a polite pretense of laughter at your jokes?

—Do the people listening to you start signaling each other with their eyes or stare off into space as you talk?"

Recognizing these problems is the first step to overcoming them. It is important for people to realize that, through conscious efforts, they can change their conversational habits and in doing so strengthen and gain friendships.

[Letitia Baldrige, Letitia Baldrige's Complete Guide to a Great Social Life *(New York: Rawson Associates, 1987), p. 113.]*

Enduring Nature of Friendship

Friendship is very important to women. They seem to need friendship more than men do, and they often put more effort into maintaining friendships. One incredible illustration of this is the friendship that flourished for more than half a century between Elizabeth Cady Stanton and Susan B. Anthony—both pioneers in the nineteenth-century feminist movement, but very different in many ways. Stanton was married and had a large family, while Anthony remained single all her life. Stanton was a radical who thoroughly enjoyed challenging the establishment, while Anthony worked within the system and sought accommodation with conservative elements. Indeed, they frequently locked horns on strategy. They had bitter disputes, and yet their friendship survived.

In 1865, when Anthony was visiting her brother in Kansas, Stanton wrote from New York of her loneliness. "I long to put my arms about you once more and hear you scold me for all my sins and short-comings. . . . Oh Susan, you are very dear to me. I should miss you more than any other living being on this earth. You are entwined with much of my happy and eventful past, and all my future plans are based on you as coadjutor. Yes, our work is one, we are one in aim and sympathy, and should be together. Come home."

In 1888, more than twenty years later, the friendship was still intact, as was evident in another letter from Stanton to Anthony. "We have jogged along pretty well for forty years or more. Perhaps mid the wreck of thrones and the undoing of so many friendships, sects, parties and families, you and I deserve some credit for sticking together through all adverse winds with so few ripples on the surface."

When Stanton published her autobiography, she dedicated it to "Susan B. Anthony, my steadfast friend for half a century." When Stanton died in 1902, Anthony confessed, "I am too crushed to say much . . . it seems impossible—that the voice is hushed that I longed to hear for fifty years—longed to get her opinion of things—before I knew exactly where I stood." Several months later she wrote to a friend, "How lonesome I do feel. . . . It was a great going out of my life when she went."

[*Ida Husted Harper,* The Life and Work of Susan B. Anthony, *2 vols. (Indianapolis: Bowen-Merril, 1899; reprint, Hollenbeck, 1908), 1:244; 2:635; Ida Husted Harper Manuscripts, Henry E. Huntington Library.*]

Importance of Friendship

In her book *Blooming: A Small Town Girlhood,* Susan Allen Toth discusses the importance of female friendship and tells about her early friendships—particularly that of Margie Dwyer, who befriended her in the fifth grade when she had no other friends. But there were many others as well. "Growing up with girls who talked, laughed, and shared together gave me a precious resource I have never lost. When I sprawl in a friend's sunny kitchen, drinking coffee and comparing notes about when and where we'll plant our sugar snow peas; when paring carrots, I cradle a receiver to one ear and ask urgently, 'But what did you say to your mother *then?;* when I'm invited to a friend's for Sunday-night pizza because, she says, 'We haven't seen you for a while' but I know she really means, 'You're sounding blue'; when my college roommate from twenty years ago calls from Vancouver, anxious over the tone of my last letter; when another friend, even busier than I am, yells over the shouts and screams of four children, 'I'm just calling to check in'; I feel a link that goes back to Margie Dwyer. The hand that reached out to me in the fifth grade is still there."

[Susan Allen Toth, Blooming: A Small Town Girlhood (Boston: Little, Brown, 1978), p. 72.]

GOD

Appeasing God

How can an individual influence God? Is simple prayer enough? Or is God's will determined apart from human influence? People answer those questions in many different ways—some of which involve more than words. Indeed, in ages past it was believed by some that only action—drastic action—would get God's attention, and there were various forms of action that were more acceptable than others. During the Black Plague of the fourteenth century, "there developed a maso-chistic urge to accept or divert the divine punishment. The most dramatic expression of this urge was the mania for organized mass flagellation. The flagellants were not a product of the Black Death alone, for they rose to some notoriety in Italy and Germany following a severe famine-pestilence in 1258–9. But in 1348 the movement spread all over Europe and enlisted tens of thousands. The flagellants orga-nized themselves in companies each under a master, wore a special uniform, lived under discipline, and conducted their public and private self-flagellations according to a set ritual. To our minds the flagellants are extraordinary and rather horrible, but the reason for their strange behavior is perfectly logical: the Black Death was a divine chastisement;

the flagellant attempted to divert the divine punishment by chastising himself. Thus it was the rumor rather than the appearance of the plague which induced the exhibition; the flagellant tried to forestall punishment of his fellows by inflicting punishment upon his own body."

[Frederick F. Cartwright, in collaboration with Michael D. Biddiss, Disease and History *(New York: Crowell, 1972), p. 47.]*

Knowing God

Kari Torjesen Malcolm, a missionary herself and a daughter of missionaries, writes of her internment in a Chinese prison camp during World War II. She was a teenager who at times feared she had lost her identity. She was number sixteen, a nameless Westerner, who was given a small space on the bare floor and reminded every day of her lack of freedom by the wall, the moat, and the electric barbed-wire fence that came between her and the outside world. Others there were in the same predicament, and often they managed to get together for a few moments of prayer—prayer for freedom. But as time passed, the enemy loomed larger and larger, and God somehow seemed smaller. In desperation, Kari pleaded with God to reveal himself to her.

"God answered that prayer and spoke to me as I searched the Bible for answers. Gradually it dawned on me that there was just one thing the enemy could not take from me. They had bombed our home, killed my father, and put my mother, brothers and me into prison. But the one thing they could not touch was my relationship to my God.

"With this new discovery, it became more and more difficult to join the gang in prayer at noon. There was more to life than just getting out of prison. One day, I decided I could not climb the bell tower. It was the first time I had missed.

"Debbie looked for me right after the meeting. The spot where we met is riveted in my memory. I cannot even remember trying to defend myself, but Debbie must have surmised something of what had occurred in my thinking. Her reproof ended with the final taunt, 'So we aren't good enough for you anymore, eh? Getting holier than the rest of us, I can see.'

"As I walked away, I felt lonelier than I had ever felt in my life. My last bit of security was peeled off. This was the climax to the peeling process that had been going on through the war years with the loss of my father, my home, my education, my freedom. Now I no longer belonged to my peer group.

"It was only then that I was able to pray the prayer that changed my life: 'Lord, I am willing to stay in this prison for the rest of my life if only I may know You.' At that moment I was free."

[Kari Torjesen Malcolm, Women at the Crossroads (Downers Grove, Ill.: InterVarsity, 1982), pp. 22–23.]

Masculinity of God

Can a woman truly identify with God? Does God fully comprehend her problems and temptations the same as if they were those of a man? Most women would want to respond in the affirmative, believing that God is not to be viewed in only masculine images. There have been strong arguments in the past against this broader conception, however, and these arguments are slow to die. In his book *The Home, Courtship, Marriage, and Children,* John R. Rice made his position on this subject very clear.

"A man is a somebody!

"For the husband is the head of the wife, even as Christ is the head of the church, and he is the saviour of the body. Ephesians 5:23.

"God's inspired Word tells us that the man is the image and glory of God: but the woman is the glory of the man. A man is like God in a sense that a woman is not like God. God is masculine.

"For example: God is always in the Bible called He, never she. He is called Father, never mother. Christ is called the man, not the woman. He is called Bridegroom, not bride, King not queen, Prophet not prophetess, Son not daughter.

"Christ was a man, a masculine man. His body was a man's body. His work was a man's work. His temptations a man's temptations.

"God would not have had the Bible so full of it if He did not want us to notice that Christ was a man, not a woman, and that man is therefore made in the image of God in a sense that cannot be true of woman.

"So in the home, man is the deputy of God."

[John R. Rice, The Home, Courtship, Marriage, and Children *(Wheaton: Sword of the Lord, 1945), pp. 86–87.]*

Motherhood of God

As one whom his mother comforteth, so will I comfort you (Isaiah 66:13).

"In these homely words we have one of the sweetest and tenderest pictures of the character of God. . . .

"The Jews have a sweet saying to the effect that 'God could not be everywhere, so He made mothers.' And this is true, for a loving mother is God's tenderest image in humanity.

> A mother is a mother still,
> The holiest thing alive.

"Mother love on earth, however, is but a pale reflection of the feeling within the heart of God, as with unfailing tenderness He comforts the weary, wounded spirit of His child.

"God combines in Himself all the virtues of a perfect character . . . of the man, and the patient, tender, brooding, comforting, sacrificial love of the woman. John Oxenham expresses this beautifully in his *The Father-Motherhood:*

> Father and mother, Thou
> In Thy full being art—
> Justice with mercy intertwined,
> Judgment exact with love combined,
> Neither complete apart.
> And so we know that when
> Our service is weak and vain,

The Father-justice would condemn,
The Mother-love Thy wrath will stem
And our reprieval gain."

[Herbert Lockyer, All the Women of the Bible (Grand Rapids: Zondervan, 1985), p. 301.]

GOOD WORKS

More Important Than Prayers

Although she might have had an excuse not to be involved in humanitarian service to others, Helen Keller, who was both blind and deaf, was committed to good works. She also challenged others to place the same priority on active ministry. "Sick or well, blind or seeing, bond or free, we are here for a purpose and however we are situated, we please God better with useful deeds than with many prayers or pious resignation."

[Helen Keller, My Religion (New York: Swedenborg Foundation, 1962), p. 185.]

GOSSIP

Harmful Effects

John Wesley, the founder of Methodism, recorded in his *Journal* the account of a woman whose ministry had been destroyed because of malicious gossip that had been passed on from one person to another. "She found peace with God five and thirty years ago, and the pure love of God a few years after. Above twenty years she has been a class and a band leader, and of very eminent use. Ten months since she was accused of drunkenness, and of revealing the secret of her friend. Being informed of this I then wrote to Norwich (as I then believed the charge) that she must be no longer a leader, either of a band or of a class. The preacher told her further that, in his judgement, she was unfit to be a member of the society. Upon this she gave up her ticket. . . . Immediately all her friends (of whom she seemed to have a large number) forsook her at once. . . . On making a more particular inquiry, I found that Mrs. W. (formerly a common woman) had revealed her own secret, to Dr. Hunt and to twenty people besides. So the first accusation vanished into the air. As to the second, I verily believe the drunkenness with which she was charged was, in reality, the falling down in a fit. So we have thrown away one of the most useful leaders we ever had, and for these wonderful reasons."

[*John Wesley,* The Journal of the Rev. John Wesley A.M., *Nehemiah Curnock, ed., 8 vols. Standard Edition (New York: Eaton & Mains, 1909), October 27, 1783.*

Scandalous Behavior for a Minister

The great Colonial New England preacher Jonathan Edwards and his wife, Sarah, had eleven children, which was not uncommon for ministers of that day. What was viewed as somewhat irregular, however, was the day of the week on which six of those children were born. Indeed, it was food for gossip that six out of the eleven were born on Sunday, and it was widely believed that babies were born on the same day of the week on which they had been conceived, which gave many parishioners pause to wonder how their sedate pastor was spending his Sunday afternoons and evenings. So serious was the offense that "some ministers in those days refused to baptize children born on Sunday."

[*Elisabeth D. Dodds,* Marriage to a Difficult Man: The "Uncommon Union" of *Jonathan and Sarah* Edwards *(Philadelphia: Westminster Press, 1971), p. 40.]*

Using Gossip to Harm Others

Anne Hutchinson, the outspoken woman preacher of Colonial Massachusetts, was arrested, brought to trial, sentenced, and banished from the colony because of her "heretical" views of Scripture. She had denounced some of the Puritan ministers from preaching a covenant of works rather than a covenant of grace, and her popularity was perceived as a serious threat to religious unity. But simply banishing her was not enough for some of her most bitter detractors. They sought to ruin her reputation through gossip, spreading scandalous stories that were often too incredible and bizarre to be believed.

Anne Hutchinson was the mother of fifteen children and had become pregnant again and, while under house arrest for her crimes against the colony, had a miscarriage. Of that unfortunate incident a minister wrote that she had not simply had a stillbirth but had "30 monstrous births or thereabouts, at once, some of them bigger, some lesser, some of one shape, some of another; few of any perfect shape, none at all of them (as farre as I could ever learne) of human shape." Only a demonically possessed woman could give birth to monsters, so with that gossip, the minister sought to settle the issue. Some years later when she and a number of her children were massacred by Indians on Long Island, the same minister had a ready response: "The Lord heard our groanes to heaven, and freed us from this great and sore affliction."

[John Winthrop, "Short Story," in The Antinomian Controversy, *ed. David D. Hall (Middletown, Conn.: Wesleyan University Press, 1968), pp. 214, 218.]*

GRACE OF GOD
Brings Out the Best in People

"Amazing Grace," one of America's best-loved hymns, sums up the power of God's grace in changing people's lives. Countless Christians can tell stories of how God turned a wretched life around. Indeed, that is the central theme of Christianity. What is this grace that has such power? Ministers often try to explain grace with other abstract nouns, and the meaning is lost in the process. Lewis B. Smedes tries to explain the meaning of grace by telling a story—a classic familiar to us all.

"Don Quixote, that ridiculous knight who came riding on his silly donkey to conquer his crazy world, is a splendid secular parable of amazing grace. Quixote ended up tilting at windmills, but he had one powerful ability. He was able to make life better for someone by persuading her it was all right when things were really all wrong. He met this tawdry woman in a tawdry tavern in a tawdry little town. She was not a fine woman; in fact, everyone in town knew she was a bad woman. Since they all knew she was bad, they all treated her like a hopelessly dirty sinner. And, since everyone treated her like a bad woman, she felt she must *be* a bad woman. So she acted the part. Then the amazing Don Quixote rode into town. He looked at her through the spectacles of his grace. What he saw was a splendid woman. He broke through the icy judgment of the moral majority and declared her to be a fine and noble person. He said to her: 'It's all right even though everyone says you're all wrong.' And when she was sure that Don Quixote really meant it, when she embraced the grace with which he embraced her, she began to *feel* the *power* of grace. She became what Don Quixote saw."

[*Lewis B. Smedes,* How Can It Be All Right When Everything Is All Wrong? *(New York: Harper & Row, 1982), p. 6.]*

GRANDMOTHER

Child's Description

What's a Grandmother? by a third grader

"A grandmother is a lady who has no children of her own. She likes other people's little girls and boys. A grandfather is a man grandmother. He goes for walks with the boys, and they talk about fishing and stuff like that.

"Grandmothers don't have to do anything except to be there. They're old so they shouldn't play hard or run. It is enough if they drive us to the market where the pretend horse is, and have a lot of dimes ready. Or if they take us for walks, they should slow down past things like pretty leaves and caterpillars. They should never say 'hurry-up.'

"Usually grandmothers are fat, but not too fat to tie your shoes. They wear glasses and funny underwear. They can take their teeth and gums off.

"Grandmothers don't have to be smart, only answer questions like, 'Why isn't God married?' and 'How come dogs chase cats?'

"Grandmothers don't talk baby talk like visitors do, because it is hard to understand. When they read to us they don't skip or mind if it is the same story over again.

"Everybody should try to have a grandmother, especially if you don't have television, because they are the only grown-ups who have time."

[James Dobson, What Wives Wish Their Husbands Knew about Women (Wheaton: Tyndale, 1975), p. 48.]

GUILT
Good and Bad Effects

In dealing with guilt-ridden people, counselors too often focus on the bad effects of guilt without considering the positive side of that emotion. This imbalance is unfortunate because guilt serves as a safeguard against sinful and unacceptable behavior. Much of the guilt people suffer from is legitimate. It is prompted by actions or attitudes that are wrong and should be corrected. "True guilt is a valuable asset for living," writes Brenda Poinsett. "It helps us when we hurt others or betray our own standards and values. God uses guilt to influence us to change our minds about what we are doing, leading us to repentance. If we never felt guilt, we would not follow difficult rules or standards, obey the law, or have good relationships with loved ones.

"But if guilt is so valuable, why does it often lead to depression?

"True guilt can lead to depression when it is unresolved, when we leave it alone and do not take action. Straightening out the wrong is sometimes all that is needed to cure our depression. How simple that sounds, and yet how difficult it is to do. Some of the most difficult words to say are, 'I was wrong.' How hard it is to accept ourselves as people, capable of doing some of the things we do. . . .

"There's another way guilt may cause depression. In this case, the cause is false guilt. False guilt is too much guilt. It is more guilt than is warranted by the circumstances; or persistent guilt out of proportion to the actual transgression; or guilt over something that is not our responsibility or under our control."

[Brenda Poinsett, Understanding a Woman's Depression (Wheaton: Tyndale, 1984), pp. 35–36.]

Guilt Prompts Confession

Carol Burnett tells a story about a shoplifting incident in her youth and how it made an indelible impression on her conscience. After it was over and she had made amends, she writes that she "felt cleansed." Like so many aspects of her life, there was an element of humor in the ordeal, as her retelling of the story indicates. "I stole something once from the dime store, and I made myself take it back. I wasn't as ashamed of myself as I was terrified of getting caught and sent up the river.

"It was a ruby red lipstick from the makeup counter. I ran all the way home with it hidden in my pocket.

"I slammed the door to 102, locked it, and hugged the wall. The apartment was empty, but I checked under the bed anyway.

"I went into the bathroom and closed the door. My hand shook when I reached in my pocket for my loot. I was just about to unscrew the tube when there was a loud knock on the door. It sounded like a gunshot.

" 'Why is this locked?' It was Nanny.

"I shoved the lipstick back in my pocket and opened the door.

" 'I'm sorry!' I cried as I ran right past her, heading back to the store where I had committed the crime. I got there just as it was closing. I banged on the front doors, begging them to let me turn myself in."

Although her guilt was prompted by fear, it was genuine, which is significant, considering the modeling she had from Nanny, her grandmother. She tells about her visits to the diner with Nanny. They would order sodas, "then when no one was looking, she'd put her arm on the counter and in one swift move sweep the knives, forks, and spoons into her purse. Sometimes salt and pepper shakers would go in there, too. She'd quickly tie the four corners of the dishtowel together, so the loot wouldn't rattle around. Then she'd zip the purse closed and safety-pin it again. We'd pay up in a hurry and make a beeline for the exit."

[Carol Burnett, One More Time (New York: Random House, 1986), pp. 74, 91.]

GYNECOLOGY
Early Surgical Methods

In the nineteenth century women—especially childbearing mothers—frequently died young as a result of poor health care. Doctors were perplexed at both the cause and result of female disorders. Women themselves knew even less than their doctors. "Modesty and delicacy kept them prisoners of this ignorance even when they had gained some experience—anything out of the ordinary, anything differing from what their experience had taught them to expect, was worried about and whispered about with their friends, but very rarely discussed with a doctor, until . . . the pain or the bleeding or the swelling grew too great to be hidden."

In many cases they were no doubt far better off by not seeing their physician. "Gynecological surgery was literally murderous. In 1835 a Dr. Sims, who was a pioneer in modern gynecological surgery said that when he began practicing 'doctors were killing their patients.' The ways in which they killed them were various but one of the commonest was to follow surgery by the application *internally* of leeches. The doctor was instructed to count the leeches in case they crept into the uterus itself and stayed there, sucking away. One doctor remarked, 'I have scarcely ever seen more acute pain than that experienced by several of my patients under such circumstances.' Then there was cauterizing the vagina with all manner of poisonous solutions and perhaps worst of all clitoridectomy, performed as a cure for masturbation. It was hardly surprising that women preferred to suffer in silence, or rely on home remedies, nor was it surprising that they came to regard the female parts of their body with fear."

[Margaret Forster, Significant Sisters: The Grassroots of Active Feminism, 1839–1939 *(New York: Knopf, 1985), pp. 64–65.]*

Problems Caused by Victorian Moral Standards

Literature of past centuries abounds with stories of women who suffered from various undisclosed maladies, or "female problems." There was concern for such disorders by the medical profession, but the delicacy of the subject often severely obstructed research. The problem was not just with women, who were too embarrassed to discuss problems and be examined by male physicians, but with the male population, including the physicians themselves. An example is Dr. Charles D. Meigs, a well-known gynecological specialist of the mid-nineteenth century. He was "proud" of women who would "prefer to suffer" rather than compromise their "fine morality."

"It is to be observed that a very current opinion exists as to the difficulty of effectually curing many of the diseases of women; and it is as mortifying as it is true, that we do often see the cases of these disorders going the whole round of the profession in any village, town, or city, and falling, at last, into the hands of the quack; either ending in some surprising cure, or leading the victim, by gradual lapses of health and strength, down to the grave, the last refuge of the incurable, or rather the uncured: I say uncured, for it is a clear and well-known truth, that many of these cases are, in their beginning, of light or trifling importance. . . .

"All these evils of medical practice spring not, in the main, from any want of competency either in medicines or in medical men, but from the delicacy of the relations existing between the sexes . . . and, in a good degree also from want of information among the population in general, as to the import, meaning, and tendency of disorders, manifested by certain trains of symptoms.

"It is, perhaps, best, upon the whole, that this great degree of modesty should exist, even though it go to the extent of putting a bar to special researches, without which no very clear and understandable notions can be obtained of the sexual disorders.

"I confess I am proud to say, that, in this country generally, and particularly in some parts of it, women prefer to suffer the extremity of danger and pain rather than waive those scruples of delicacy which prevent their maladies from being fully explored. I think this is an evidence of the presence of a fine morality in our society; but nevertheless, it is true that a great candor on the part of the patient, and a more resolute and careful inquiry on that of the practitioner, would scarcely fail to bring to light, in their early stages, the curable maladies, which by faults on both sides, are so misunderstood, because concealed and, consequently, mismanaged, and so, rendered at last incurable."

[Charles D. Meigs, M.D., Woman: Her Diseases and Remedies. A Series of Letters to His Class *(Philadelphia: Blanchard & Lea, 1859), pp. 34–35.]*

HANDICAPPED

Concern of Mother for Child

Unless a mother has a handicapped child, it is difficult to comprehend the anguish that is felt. Beverly Sills, the great opera singer and mother of two handicapped children, very poignantly summed up her feelings about her daughter's deafness in relation to her own singing.

"In a sympathetic way, people had often commented on the irony of an opera singer's having a daughter who can't hear her sing. Believe me, that particular concern didn't enter the picture at all. I was a mother whose gorgeous daughter was deaf. My voice was the last thing I worried about Muffy's not being able to hear."

[Beverly Sills and Lawrence Linderman, Beverly: An Autobiography *(New York: Bantam Books, 1987), p. 140.]*

Difference between Disabled and Handicapped

What is the best way to refer to a disabled person? This issue has been a matter of controversy in recent years. No longer is the word *crippled* considered acceptable. But to avoid the social stigma of such a word, others have gone in the other direction and, according to Joni Eareckson Tada, have "coined contemporary phrases to underscore the positive perspective." There are those "who prefer to call us 'handicopeable' or 'handicapable.' We are the 'physically challenged.' . . . To some, we are the 'special people.' To others, we are the 'physically exceptional.' . . . In our great care to do away with prejudice in our semantics, perhaps we end up drawing more attention to the situation than we would have had we stuck with a good old honest word like *disabled* or *handicapped*."

Eareckson, however, points out that there is a difference between the terms *disabled* and *handicapped*. She writes: "Somebody once said that although our bodies may disable us, it is often society which handicaps us. A disease or an impairment—light seizures, loss of vision, the loss of a hand or leg, a progressive condition such as arthritis or MS, mental retardation, or brain or spinal injury—can present problems. Yet many people control or at least manage their disabilities with either therapy, treatment, medication, or adaptive equipment.

"However, these same people, with anything from annoying to chronic disabilities, may be severely handicapped if they lack an attendant or family member who can help with daily care routines. Handicaps occur when these same people are denied access due to steps or curbs, lack of elevators, ramps, Braille signs, or interpreters. One is handicapped by the attitudinal barriers of pity and fear. Even lack of transportation or employment, housing, or finances can present a handicap to the disabled person who desires to live independently."

[Joni Eareckson Tada, "Introduction," in All God's Children: Ministry to the Disabled, *by Gene Newman and Joni Eareckson Tada (Grand Rapids: Zondervan, 1987), pp. 13–15.]*

HAPPINESS

Derived from Christian Service

It is a proven fact that some of the happiest people in this world have the least amount of material wealth. Their happiness comes rather from the joy they derive from giving themselves in service to others who are needy. This is true of Mother Teresa and those who work with her. In a tribute to her and her single missionary sisters, Malcolm Muggeridge writes:

"Their life is tough and austere by worldly standards, certainly: yet I never met such delightful, happy women, or such an atmosphere of joy as they create. Mother Teresa, as she is fond of explaining, attaches the utmost importance to this joyousness. The poor, she says, deserve not just service and dedication, but also the joy that belongs to human love. . . . The Missionaries of Charity . . . are multiplying at a fantastic rate. Their Calcutta house is bursting at the seams, and as each new house is opened, there are volunteers clamouring to go there. As the whole story of Christendom shows, if everything is asked for, everything—and more—will be accorded; if little, then nothing."

[Malcolm Muggeridge, Something Beautiful for God *(Garden City, N.Y.: Image Books, 1971), p. 37.]*

Happiness—A By-product of Helping Others

Too often people think that their unhappiness is caused by a particular individual or set of circumstances, and they seek to change their relationships or circumstances in order to find happiness—but that course so often fails. "Happiness is a unique commodity. *It is never found by the person shopping for it.* You may search the shelves of the whole world for personal happiness and never find it at any price. Lonely men and women in every age have grumbled and complained at the futility of their search for happiness. *Genuine happiness is the by-product of making someone else happy.* Do not the Scriptures say, 'It is more blessed to give than to receive' (Acts 20:35)?"

[*Gary Chapman,* Hope for the Separated *(Chicago: Moody, 1982), p. 66.]*

Happiness amidst Adversity

Helen Keller, who accomplished so much, despite her disabilities of blindness and deafness, was always quick to see the bright side of situations. Optimism ruled her life, and she challenged others by that spirit. She challenged people not to give up in despair when difficulties arise. "When one door of happiness closes, another opens; but often we look so long at the closed door that we do not see the one which has been opened for us."

[The Faith of Helen Keller *(Kansas City, Mo.: Hallmark Editions, Hallmark Cards, 1967), p. 24.]*

Responsibility for Personal Happiness

Happiness is an elusive quality that is often difficult to analyze or understand. Sometimes the happiest people are the ones who seemingly have the least to be happy about. There are some basic factors to keep in mind, however, in the pursuit of happiness. Jo Berry, in her book *Becoming God's Special Woman,* deals with some of these. "The fact that each of us is responsible for our own happiness is difficult for most people to accept because we've been conditioned to believe the opposite. We've been taught that parents are supposed to make their children happy, teachers are supposed to please their students, and husbands or wives are supposed to make their mates happy. So instead of looking for ways to make others happy or taking responsibility for our own well-being, we look for the 'happiness handouts' we've been told to expect in our me-centered society. But we find out too soon that others cannot, or do not, or will not make us happy.

"Not only should we not depend on others for happiness, but we should not depend on our state of being for happiness. Neither should you rely on circumstances to make you happy. Instead, you should be actively involved in whatever happens in your life, however pleasant or unpleasant it may be." Even very distressing situations can be made more tolerable through one's outlook. Jo Berry tells the story of a young woman who was raped. Instead of simply brooding over the details, she became actively involved in journaling her own impressions and reactions. She took positive steps for coping by joining a support group and counseling with her pastor and women at the rape crisis center. She took charge of her own happiness and determined that not even the brutal act of rape would strip her of her happiness.

[Jo Berry, Becoming God's Special Woman *(Old Tappan, N.J.: Revell, 1986), pp. 164–65.]*

HARASSMENT
Against Women Public Speakers

Sexual harassment is usually thought of in terms of a male's making unwanted sexual advances toward a female, but other forms of sexual harassment have been even more demeaning. An example is the physical and psychological abuse women received in the nineteenth century when they sought to lecture in the public arena. Angelina and Sarah Grimké, Quaker sisters who were strong antislavery advocates, were among those who were not only taunted with jeers but were also physically attacked. They had begun their lecture circuit by speaking only to women's audiences, but their appeal was so great that men began attending. The ministers were among their harshest critics, outraged that they were speaking in front of "promiscuous" audiences. Finally, "the Council of Congregational Ministers of Massachusetts issued a pastoral letter warning ministers and their congregations against the danger inherent in 'females who itinerate.' Wherever the sisters spoke, mobs collected to throw rotten eggs and stones."

[Margaret Hope Bacon, Mothers of Feminism: The Story of Quaker Women in America *(San Francisco: Harper & Row, 1986), p. 105.]*

Teacher's Sexual Harassment of a Student

The sexual harassment perpetrated by teachers that often occurs in educational institutions today is not something that has arisen only in the modern era, when sexual promiscuity is more publicized than it was in an earlier age. One of the most celebrated instances of such in all of history is that perpetrated by Peter Abelard, one of the greatest medieval theologians, against Heloise, his brilliant young teenage student, who was in her early teens and half his age. The story is often treated as a romance between two lovers, but it should be seen as a case of sexual harassment. Abelard was employed by Heloise's uncle to be her tutor. "How much tutoring was accomplished is unknown, but apparently more kisses and caresses were given than instruction. Indeed, Heloise became pregnant by Abelard and gave birth to a son." Abelard reluctantly agreed to secretly marry her, but Heloise refused, realizing that his was not true love. "Thy passion drew thee to me rather than thy friendship, and the heat of desire rather than love." She entered a convent, and he became a monk, but not before an enraged uncle avenged the crime by hiring ruffians to attack and castrate him.

[Ruth A. Tucker and Walter L. Liefeld, Daughters of the Church: Women and Ministry from New Testament Times to the Present *(Grand Rapids: Zondervan, 1987), p. 167.]*

HEALING

Testimony Brings Family to Faith in Christ

Yoshikosan Taguchi was one of the "living dead" to survive the infamous atomic bombing of Hiroshima on August 6, 1945. Some seventy thousand people died, and approximately that same number were severely injured—Yoshikosan being one of those. She was fifteen and a student at a Christian school—though she deeply resented the teachings about Jesus, thinking him a god of the Americans, who were the enemy of her people.

On that August morning, she was sitting at her desk when she heard a thunderous blast and the walls began to fall down around her. In her half-conscious state she heard shouts of anguish and confusion, and then realized someone was helping to pull her out of the rubble. Though she did not realize it at the time, more than three hundred students and teachers "died that day in the school, one half mile from the center of the blast.

"That night Yoshikosan huddled with the sick, the dying and the terrified mob along a river on the edge of the city. It was an unforgettable night. The morning, beautiful and hot, revealed the horror of all that had happened, the sickening condition of the half-alive, the city in waste, and all the backwashes of debilitating fear. . . .

"Radiation sickness is a horrible thing. Yoshikosan was hemorrhaging internally and knew she was dying. When it seemed unbearable, she would vacillate between wishing she could die and terror that she might. . . .

"One day when the fear of death was particularly acute, a hymn she had sung at the Christian school came to her mind. . . .

> God is our refuge,
> Our refuge, and our strength
> In trouble, in trouble, a very present help."

That song prompted her to reflect on Jesus and what she had heard about him and his ministry of healing. She began to pray "in the name of Jesus." "A peace came over her instantaneously; the fear was gone. She knew He had heard and that He cared about her.

"Slowly her wounds began to heal, the hemorrhaging stopped; the vomiting, the nausea were gone. All around others continued to die, but in two months' time Yoshikosan was healed. She knew Jesus had healed her. . . .

"One by one she began convincing her family that Jesus was a *living* God who heard prayers. Japanese families don't change their beliefs easily, but Yoshikosan was living proof of His reality. Her older sister believed first . . . and one by one others in family came to trust Christ. Yoshikosan herself went on to reach out to students through a campus Christian ministry."

[Gladys Hunt, Does Anyone Here Know God? *(Grand Rapids: Zondervan, 1967), pp. 137–42.]*

HERESY
Questionable Charges

Heresy is defined by one's view of the truth, and thus one person's orthodoxy may be another person's unorthodoxy. That was true in the medieval church when many people, including women, were accused of heresy. One group of women that was condemned by the Synod of Cologne in 1260 and by the Council of Vienna in 1312 was the Beguines. They were charged with refusing to confess their sins to priests and to give proper respect to the elements in communion. They were also accused of antinomianism—that they allegedly believed they could commit immoral acts without committing sin. The gravest of their sinful vices, however, was their translation of the Bible into the Gallic vernacular. Indeed, they had gone further and were reading commentaries on the Bible, not only in private meetings, but also in public places. At a time when the Catholic church did not permit lay people to read the Bible, it was considered a serious heresy when women not only read but interpreted and preached it.

[Robert E. Lerner, The Heresy of the Free Spirit in the Later Middle Ages *(Berkeley: University of California Press, 1972), pp. 45–46.]*

HOME ENVIRONMENT
Influence on Next Generation

The importance of creating a congenial atmosphere in the home was one of the many concepts Pearl S. Buck stressed in her writings. The abilities to live an orderly life and to interact harmoniously with others are character traits, she believed, that are formed in the family environment. "Seldom indeed do men and women rise above the atmosphere of their childhood homes. They may become rich and powerful, they may build houses very different from the one they first knew, but they carry within themselves the atmosphere of the first home. If that home was a place of order and beauty, however simple, then they are tranquil and able to cope with life's problems. If there was neither order nor beauty in the home, the lack follows them all their lives. They may not know what is the matter with them or why they are eternally restless and seeking, but they know they live in uncertainty and inner confusion."

[*Pearl S. Buck,* To My Daughters, with Love *(New York: Day, 1967), p. 186.*]

HOMEMAKING

Importance of Homemaking

Pearl S. Buck, known for her earthy and outspoken writings, had an amazing appreciation for homemaking. In her book *To My Daughters, with Love,* she wrote: "Do I, who am a professional writer, believe that homemaking is the most important work in the world for a woman? Yes I do, and not only for others but for myself. As a writer, I know that it is essential for a woman to be a homemaker, and this is true whatever else she is. Man and woman, we have our separate but cooperating functions to fulfill for our own completion, as well as for the human beings we serve because we are responsible for them.

"Woman, the housewife and homemaker, creates more than she knows. While she sweeps and cleans and makes beds, while she cooks and washes and puts away, she is creating human beings. She is shaping dispositions and building character and making harmony."

[*Pearl S. Buck,* To My Daughters, with Love *(New York: Day, 1967), pp. 184–85.*]

Value of Homemaking

The monetary value of the services of a housewife is far more than most husbands could ever afford to pay. Attorney Michael Minton made an economic study of value based on the duties an average housewife performs. "They included: chauffeur, gardener, family counselor, maintenance worker, cleaning woman, housekeeper, cook, errand runner, bookkeeper/budget manager, interior decorator, caterer, dietitian, secretary, and public relations woman/hostess." If outside help were employed to carry out those tasks, Minton estimated the cost would be approximately $785 per week, for a total of more than $40,000 per year.

[Daily Bread, August 7, 1981.]

HOMOPHOBIA
Greater among Men Than among Women

Homophobia, the fear of homosexuals, is not an uncommon attitude expressed in everyday life—particularly among boys and men. It begins when children are young, and the fear is expressed in jokes and ridicule, but the fear often becomes exaggerated in adolescence and adulthood, when males are more conscious of their sexuality. In recent years, homophobia has been more pronounced with the increasing incidence of AIDS. Why do not women experience homophobia to the same extent that men do? "First, little girls are largely spared the indoctrination that equates affection with sexual orientation, propaganda that squelches boys' expressiveness. Second, masculinity is more prized than femininity and is more rigorously standardized and guarded. Thus, the fear of being thought 'unmanly' coerces men into harsher anti-gay attitudes and allows the expletive 'sissy' to wound far more deeply than 'tomboy.' (Tomboy may even carry implicit admiration for a girl.) Third, there is less female homophobia because the women's movement has emphasized common female needs and raised the consciousness of straight women about lesbian reality."

[Letty Cottin Pogrebin, Among Friends: Who We Like, Why We Like Them, and What We Do with Them (New York: McGraw-Hill, 1987), pp. 213–14.]

HOSPITALITY

Entertainment versus Hospitality

In her book *Open Heart, Open Home,* Karen Mains talks about the differences between entertaining and hospitality. As an inner-city pastor's wife, her home became a refuge for many people, and she became consciously aware of the gift of hospitality that she as a Christian woman possessed.

"Hospitality is more than just a human talent, it is a gift of the Holy Spirit. It is a supernatural ministry which, when combined with righteous living, bathed in prayer, and dedicated to the Lord, can be used by God far beyond anything we ask or think. . . .

"Secular entertaining is a terrible bondage. Its source is human pride. Demanding perfection, fostering the urge to impress, it is a rigorous taskmaster which enslaves. In contrast, Scriptural hospitality is a freedom which liberates.

"Entertaining says, 'I want to impress you with my beautiful home, my clever decorating, my gourmet cooking.' Hospitality, however, seeks to minister. It says, 'This home is not mine. It is truly a gift from my Master. I am his servant and I use it as He desires. Hospitality does not try to impress, but to *serve.*

"Entertaining always puts things before people. 'As soon as I get the house finished, the living room decorated, my place settings complete, my housecleaning done—then I will start having people in.' 'The So-and-so's are coming. I must buy that new such-and-such before they come.' Hospitality, however, puts people before things. 'We have no furniture; we'll eat on the floor.' 'The decorating may never get done. Please come just the same.' 'The house is a mess—but these people are friends. We never get to see them. Let's have this time together anyway.' . . .

"The model for entertaining is found in the slick pages of women's magazines with their appealing pictures of foods and rooms. The model for hospitality is found in the Word of God."

[Karen Mains, Open Heart, Open Home *(Elgin, Ill.: Cook, 1976), pp. 24–26.]*

HOUSEWORK

Distaste for Housework

Frances Willard, a leader in the nineteenth-century Women's Christian Temperance Union, swam against the current in many areas of her life. She resented the established role for women that society mandated, and that feeling was seen in her attitude toward housework. "Mother did not talk to us as girls, but simply as human beings, and it never occurred to me that I ought to 'know house-work' and do it. Mary took to it kindly by nature; I did not, and each one had her way. Mother never said, 'You must cook, you must sweep, you must sew,' but she studied what we liked to do and kept us at it with no trying at all. There never was a busier girl than I and what I did was mostly useful. I knew all the carpenter's tools and handled them: made carts and sleds, cross-guns and whip-handles; indeed, all the toys that were used at Forest Home we children manufactured. But a needle and a dishcloth I could not abide—chiefly, perhaps, because I was bound to live out-of-doors."

[*Frances E. Willard,* Glimpses of Fifty Years: The Autobiography of an American Woman *(Chicago: Smith, 1889; reprint, New York: Source Book Press, 1970), pp. 25–26.]*

Housework as Enjoyment

Housework can become a reprieve for women who have more difficult work to do, as writers who work at home often find to be true. How much easier to dust the furniture or even scrub the toilet than to form sentences and paragraphs that make sense and meet the editor's approval. Elisabeth Elliot, who loved housework, had to force herself to do the much more difficult work she was committed to.

"When I was both a writer and a wife I was sorely tempted to do nothing but housework because I love housework and I especially love doing it in order to make a home for a husband, but there were times when I had to tear myself away from the kitchen and get down to the study to do the harder job first, to 'eat my spinach before I could have my dessert.' "

[Elisabeth Elliot, Let Me Be a Woman *(Wheaton: Tyndale, 1976), p. 114.]*

Role Reversal in the Home

The difficulty of housework and male aversion to it are illustrated in *The Marvelous Land of Oz.* "As they passed the rows of houses they saw through the open doors that men were sweeping and dusting and washing dishes, while the women sat around in groups, gossiping and laughing.

" 'What has happened?' The Scarecrow asked a sad-looking man with a bushy beard, who wore an apron and was wheeling a baby-carriage along the sidewalk.

" 'Why, we've had a revolution, your Majesty—as you ought to know very well,' replied the man, 'and since you went away the women have been running things to suit themselves. I'm glad you have decided to come back and restore order, for doing housework and minding children is wearing out the strength of every man in the Emerald City.'

" 'Hm!' said the Scarecrow, thoughtfully. 'If it is such hard work as you say, how did the women manage it so easily?'

" 'I really do not know,' replied the man, with a deep sigh. 'Perhaps the women are made of cast-iron.' "

[L. Frank Baum, The Marvelous Land of Oz *(New York: Dover Publications, 1969), pp. 171–72.)*

Shared Duties in the Home

Surveys have shown that working women do as much as twenty hours more housework per week than do men. In their book *American Couples,* Philip Blumstein and Pepper Schwartz write: "Working wives do less housework than homemakers but they still do the vast bulk of what needs to be done . . . even if a husband is unemployed he does much less housework than a wife who puts in a 40 hour week. . . . This is the case even among couples who profess egalitarian social ideals. . . . While husbands might say they should share responsibility, when they break it down to time actually spent and chores actually done, the idea of shared responsibility turns out to be a myth."

[*Philip Blumstein and Pepper Schwartz,* American Couples: Money, Work, and Sex *(New York: Morrow, 1983), p. 145.*]

Shared Responsibilities in the Home

One of the reasons so many women complain about being overburdened with housework is that they do work they should not be doing. "Any woman who cleans up after a husband or a kid over two years old," writes Don Aslett, "deserves the garbage cans she has to lug out everyday!" Aslett, who heads a large house-cleaning corporation and gives seminars on housework, has some blunt admonition for mothers. "Refuse to be the janitor for the kids' and husband's messes. Picking up after them is bad for everyone involved. You teach irresponsibility perfectly by assuming responsibility for someone else, except those who don't know any better or can't help themselves." He also suggests that jobs that need to be done be written down and assigned to the various family members.

[*Don Aslett,* Is There Life after Housework? *(Cincinnati: Writer's Digest Books, 1981), p. 34.*]

Slave of Housework

Although some women regard housework as fulfilling, others come to realize that many wasted years have gone into nonessential cleaning and dusting. This was true of Mira, a women of whom Marilyn French writes in her book *The Women's Room.* So consumed was Mira with housework that she "bought herself a small file box and some packages of 2 × 3 cards. On each card she wrote one task that had to be performed and filed them in sections. The section headed WINDOW WASHING would contain cards for each one in the house. Whenever she washed the windows in one room, she would mark the date down on the card, and place it at the end of the section. The same was true for FURNITURE POLISHING, RUG SHAMPOO-ING, and CHINA. . . . She did not make cards for ordinary, daily cleaning, only for the large special tasks. . . . Mira would feel tremendously satisfied when she finished her mornings' work. . . . She would walk through the house, dressed to go out, relishing the silence, the order, the shine of polished wood in the sun." Not until her husband of fifteen years left her did she realize what a waste of time and energy all her excess housework had been. After that she returned to college to prepare for a teaching career.

[Marilyn French, The Women's Room (London: Jove, 1978), pp. 209–10.]

HUMILIATION
Most Persistent Emotion

It is very easy to fall into the false impression that we are the only ones who experience humiliation. Yes, of course we grieve for our friends and laugh at our adversaries when they face humiliation, but the only humiliation that we harbor and refuse to forget is our own. Nancy Friday, in her book My Mother/My Self, gives valuable insight on this common emotion. "Humiliation is perhaps the most persistent of all emotions. In time we forget feelings of passion, the faces of people we've loved. We laugh at old angers and rages, time heals the memory of even physical pain. But old humiliations stay with us for life. They wake us out of the deepest sleep and flush our face with shame and anger even when we are alone. 'Patients with problems of humiliation,' says Dr. Robertiello, 'are the most difficult to treat.' Humiliation is so powerful it can make us wish for our own annihilation: our very ego shrinks and wills itself for the moment no longer to exist. 'I felt as if I wanted the ground to open up and swallow me.' " How can we best respond to humiliation? As difficult as it is, it is essential to remember that we are not alone in experiencing this emotion and that, while our humiliation is consuming us (and we might naively assume it is consuming others), others may be entirely oblivious to it.

[Nancy Friday, My Mother/My Self: The Daughter's Search for Identity *(New York: Dell, 1978), pp. 151–52.]*

HUSBAND

Attitude toward Wife

Although John Chrysostom, the fourth-century bishop of Constantinople, is often quoted in reference to his negative views on women and their leadership in the church and society, he took a very adamant position on how a wife should be treated by her husband. "You see the rule of obedience? Well, hear also the rule of love. Do you wish your wife to obey you, as the Church obeys Christ? Then take care for her, as Christ did for the Church; and even if you must give your life for her, or be cut in a thousand pieces, or whatever you must undergo and suffer, shrink not from it; and even if you suffer all this, you have not yet done anything that Christ did; for you do this being already joined in marriage to her, but He suffered for a Bride who rejected and hated Him. As then He brought to His feet her who rejected Him . . . with wonderful care and affection, not with terror, nor with threats . . . so do you toward your wife. . . . A slave a man may perhaps bind by terror . . . but the partner of your life, the mother of your children, the subject of all your joy, you ought to bind not by terror and threats, but by love and gentle considerations."

[Quoted in Henry Alford, The New Testament for English Readers *(Chicago: Moody, n.d.), p. 1244.]*

Domineering Husband

Before she developed her Total Woman program, Marabel Morgan struggled through difficult marital problems with a noncommunicative, domineering husband—similar to many of the husbands the Total Woman course was designed to cope with. The problems began developing soon after their marriage. "As the months passed," she wrote, "our lives became more complicated, and we gradually changed. I was amazed to realize that Charlie had stopped talking. He had become distant and preoccupied. Instead of talking heart-to-heart, we never seemed to talk at all. In answer to my questions about his work and the events of the day, I received an indecipherable grunt. . . . As the years wore on, things got worse. Those barriers became insurmountable. I didn't know what caused them, and I certainly didn't know how to make them go away. Sometimes they lasted for days, or weeks, or even months. I was helpless and unhappy."

Finally the situation came to a head on the evening of a dinner party. It came to light that they had made conflicting plans for the following evening. In front of the guests he said, "From now on when I plan for us to go somewhere, I will tell you twenty minutes ahead of time. You'll have time to get ready, and we'll do it without all this arguing." Needless to say, she was devastated. "My beautiful dinner was ruined. I ran upstairs and cried. . . . When he didn't come upstairs to comfort me, I had to stop crying. . . . Something drastic had to be done. . . . That night I made a decision to change the collision course I was on." It was then that she began to formulate what became her Total Woman course and book, which had the basic philosophy, "Your husband is what he is. Accept him as that." The wife was to become the "total woman" by accepting him, admiring him, adapting to him, and appreciating him—a virtual guarantee for salvaging a bad marriage.

[*Marabel Morgan,* The Total Woman *(Old Tappan, N.J.: Revell, 1973), p. 53.*]

Husband Enslaved by Wife

In his book *The Hazards of Being Male,* Herb Goldberg reflects the resentment of many men toward the feminist movement and women in general. One individual he interviewed was bitter about the unfairness he perceived in the marriage relationship. "The famous male chauvinistic pigs who neglect their wives, underpay their women employees and rule the world—are literally slaves. They're out there picking the cotton, sweating, swearing, taking lashes from the boss, working 50 hours a week to support themselves and the plantation, only then to come home to do another 20 hours a week of rinsing dishes, toting trash bags, writing checks, and acting as butlers at the parties."

[Herb Goldberg, The Hazards of Being Male (New York: Signet Books, 1977), p. 67.]

Husband's Failure to Assume Responsibilities

In evangelical circles where the husband is expected to be dominant and the wife submissive, there is often severe criticism of a wife who takes the dominant position in the family. It is generally assumed that she is the one who is to blame. According to Raymond C. Stedman, that is not usually the case. He writes, "I know it is popular to make jokes about bossy wives and henpecked husbands, but having observed the marriage scene for a considerable time and having personal involvement in it, I would say the problem is not so much due to the demand of wives to assert leadership as it is the refusal of husbands to assume their responsibilities."

[Raymond C. Stedman, "Man, the Initiator," in The Marriage Affair, *ed. J. Allan Petersen (Wheaton: Tyndale, 1971), pp. 78–79; used by permission of* Eternity *magazine, copyright 1969 by Evangelical Foundation.]*

Husband's Support of Wife

Some husbands are threatened by their wives' success, but others are their wives' chief supporters. This has been true of Beverly Sills's husband, Peter. Her operatic career suffered a severe blow after the discovery that both of their children were handicapped—Muffy being deaf, and Bucky autistic. Beverly was "deeply depressed and despondent," and by her own testimony, "rarely wandered out of my nineteen-room cocoon." It was her husband who sparked the turning point in her life. "On my thirty-third birthday he gave me fifty-two round-trip tickets for the Boston–New York shuttle. He wanted me to resume my weekly lessons with Miss Liebling, to start seeing my mother in New York, to get back into opera again—and to stop feeling sorry for the kids and for myself."

[Beverly Sills and Lawrence Linderman, Beverly: An Autobiography *(New York: Bantam Books, 1987), p. 144.]*

INCEST

Minimizing Its Appalling Effects

It is difficult to imagine, but some people would seek to justify or minimize the evils of incest. In 1981, it was reported that Wardell Pomeroy, who coauthored the first Kinsey reports, argued that incest can at times have beneficial effects. Although such rash statements are rare, the horrors of incest have been minimized in other ways. An example is the new term that has been employed to define the problem: intrafamily child sexual abuse, or ICSA. "While the meaning is the same as incest, a great number of incest victims (including myself)," writes Katherine Edwards, "will find it offensive. It is clearly an attempt to make an ugly word more socially acceptable. In 'civilizing' the word that describes the act, we make the act itself less shocking."

[Katherine Edwards, A House Divided *(Grand Rapids: Zondervan, 1984), pp. 15, 112.]*

Pain—and Value—of Disclosure of Incest

Almost as agonizing as the incest itself is the pain of disclosure for many of the victims. Yet, in the end, most will feel that they did what was right, and the wound will begin to heal.

"The results of disclosure will vary according to the status of the affair. If the incest is ongoing, discovery of the fact may create what appears to be a holocaust. Every family member can emotionally 'explode' in a different direction, and all at the same time. Pain, fear, humiliation, and anger do not combine for reasonable discussion. Accusations, both true and false, may be made; accusation of lying or of seduction, accusations that attempt to place the blame on others' shoulders, accusations involving the complicity of other family members. Painful details will have to be communicated, and it may be necessary for the family to be separated for a while. Even if the incest has ceased before the disclosure, the results may not be less chaotic if the victim is still living at home.

"If the victim is no longer at home, the psychological pain of disclosure will still, undoubtedly, be tremendous. Painful decisions will have to be made in order to determine the proper action. The perpetrator will not seek help on his own, and there may be others in the home who might be spared victimization if disclosure is made. Gratitude for such action will not be soon apparent. . . . However, the temporary pain can be the forerunner of health; it can be the corrective surgery for incest. At times it will seem that anaesthetic is in short supply, but the results can be well worth the price. They may well turn a house divided into a house reunited in an atmosphere of safety and love."

[Katherine Edwards, A House Divided *(Grand Rapids: Zondervan, 1984), pp. 144–45.]*

Typical Perpetrator of Incest

Like the husband that physically abuses his wife, the adult perpetrator of incest rarely gives hints of his true self to the outside world. He is often the very last person anyone would suspect of committing such a heinous crime. This is what Katherine Edwards, an incest victim herself, found in her research on the subject.

"The person seen in public often proves to be quite different in private, in the context of his own home. Frequently seen as a 'good provider' for his family, the perpetrator of incest is many times viewed by the community as one of its 'pillars.' Many of these men have been abused or deprived as children themselves; their public appearance masks the insecurity and depression that has followed them through the years.

"Some are physically abusive, others exploit their power through verbal attacks. Most are characterized by poor impulse control. They are not sex perverts or 'dirty old men.' Rather, the average is somewhere in his late 30's and . . . many have experienced sexual alienation from their wives. The abusive father-figure is lonely, frustrated, out of control, with a distorted view of reality.

"Afraid, confused, unhappy, and desperately disgusted with himself, the man who commits incest is most likely searching for a love and acceptance long denied him. He is unable to define what it is that he really wants. Most likely, he would have preferred being a good father. He is miserable in his failure."

[*Katherine Edwards*, A House Divided *(Grand Rapids: Zondervan, 1984), pp. 116–17.*]

INCOMPATIBILITY

In Marriage

Charles Dickens, one of the most popular writers in nineteenth-century England, did not have a happy home life, which was due largely to what he perceived to be the incompatibility between him and his wife, Catherine. After twenty-three years of marriage he filed for a separation, whereby he would continue to support her while she lived in a separate residence. This type of arrangement was not common in Victorian England, and Dickens was very conscious that he would face criticism. He sought to justify his decision and his poor treatment of her by claiming irreconcilable differences. He explained the situation from his perspective to a John Forster, a close friend. "Poor Catherine and I are not made for each other, and there is no help for it. It is not only that she makes me uneasy and unhappy, but that I make her so too—and much more so. She is exactly what you know, in the way of being amiable and complying; but we are strangely ill-assorted for the bond there is between us. God knows she would have been a thousand times happier if she had married another kind of man. . . . I am often cut to the heart by thinking what a pity it is, for her sake, that I ever fell in her way; and if I were sick or disabled tomorrow, I know how sorry she would be, and how deeply grieved myself, to think how we had lost each other. But exactly the same incompatibility would arise, the moment I was well again; and nothing on earth could make her understand me, or suit us to each other."

[John Forster, The Life of Charles Dickens, 2 vols. (London: Dent, 1872), 2:198–99.]

INDEPENDENCE

Necessity for Women

Some women find themselves almost incapable of thinking and functioning for themselves after they are widowed or divorced. They had become so used to depending on someone else's brain that their own was out of condition. "No woman can establish self-identity," writes Jo Berry, "unless she learns to think for herself. When you let others tell you what to believe, you reflect their taste and ideas and you get lost in the process. It is my personal opinion that women in general have not been taught or encouraged to think for themselves or to develop their own system of beliefs. Instead, we've been conditioned not to question authority but to accept secondhand opinions as our own. In the Christian community women are told that disagreeing with their husbands, or pastor, or anyone who is in authority, is being 'nonsubmissive.' "

[Jo Berry, Becoming God's Special Woman (Old Tappan, N.J.: Revell, 1986), p. 173.]

INDIVIDUALITY

Importance for Wives in Marriage

In her book *Men Are Just Desserts,* Sonya Friedman tells of "listening to a well-intentioned minister sermonizing to a young couple about to take their marital vows." The minister focused his comments primarily on the bride, whom he admonished to forsake her individual self and become one with her husband. "By assuming her husband's name, she would be subsumed into another identity. These two would share one name, one bedroom, one purpose in life, and cleave unto each other in this exalted 'oneness.'"

Friedman warns women to beware of "this ideology of oneness" that depreciates self-identity. "Give a man top priority in your life—make him the main course—and chances are you will lose not only your self but your self-esteem. Worship a man just because he *is* one, and you will subjugate yourself to him and wait, like a child, for his praise. Decide that you are nothing without a man, and this will become a self-fulfilling prophecy. . . . Every woman has an obligation to make herself economically and emotionally independent before she chooses a mate. . . . The woman who has learned to care for herself may then seek out a man who will be the *reward* for the completion of her mission—that is, the dessert. Such a man will be an enrichment, an addition, and will provide a lovely place to lie at night, but he won't be the main course. No man is going to make you happy or give you a purpose in life—you are."

[*Sonya Friedman,* Men Are Just Desserts *(New York: Warner Books, 1983), pp. 6–7.*]

INDUSTRIOUSNESS

Keeps Life Meaningful

Abigail Adams, who maintained a very busy life as the nation's second First Lady, was also busy with domestic concerns. She raised five children while her husband was consumed in government service. Yet, her fifty-four-year marriage to John Adams was happy and fulfilling. She credited that largely to her industriousness. "I have frequently said to my friends, when they thought me overburdened with care, I would rather have too much [to do] than too little. Life stagnates without action. I could never bear merely to vegetate."

[Charles Francis Adams, Letters of Mrs. Adams, the Wife of John Adams, 4th ed. (Boston: Wilkins, Carter, 1848), p. 402.]

INFANTICIDE
Practiced in Many Cultures

Some opponents of abortion argue that the practice of abortion leads to the practice of infanticide and point to a long history of infanticide in various cultures. In ancient Greece and Rome, babies were disposed of in many instances in order to slow population growth. Plato and Aristotle defended infanticide in cases of deformity, and these babies were sometimes thrown from cliffs. "Unnatural progeny we destroy," said Seneca; "we drown even children who at birth are weakly and abnormal." Many modern-day "primitive" cultures also practice infanticide. The Netsilik Eskimos "revealed that 38 out of 96 infants had been killed, either because food was scarce or in order to maintain a population balance of male and female."

[Peter Leithart, "Infanticide in History," Eternity, September 1986, p. 24.]

INFERTILITY
Facing the Issue with Courage

How does a couple who desperately want a baby cope? They have tried so hard and nothing works. This is the final issue that Lynda Stephenson deals with in her book *Give Us a Child: Coping with the Personal Crisis of Infertility*. The book is full of helpful information that offers an infertile couple ideas and alternatives, but in the end, there is no guarantee that pregnancy will occur. What then? The couple, whether they choose to adopt children or remain childless, must determine to go on living their lives to the fullest. It often requires a conscious decision on the part of the grieving couple, as Stephenson testifies.

"So can I grieve for a part of my life that may never be? I think so. But I believe that it will be almost impossible for me to come to this point without a change in attitude—and with the realization that I will now and then still feel the grief of my years of infertility—no matter what my choice.

"But it will be up to me—to us—to take the focus off our infertility, and off children, and once again put it back where it was when we first married—on our relationship and our future.

"We all can do that. First, we can allow ourselves to ask 'What if never?' Then we all have the capacity to choose. And whether we believe it or not at this moment, we have the capacity to answer yes *and* no to all that goes with the rock-hard question. We have the capacity to say *yes,* we want to parent, or *no,* adoption is not for us. We have the capacity to say *yes,* I married you for you, and infertility doesn't change that. But most of all, we can say *no,* I will not allow this one part of our lives to take any more from our life together. And if we cannot make the choice for the future today, then we can tomorrow. Or the next day—because we're willing to face the tensions of the choices, mind clear and eyes open—taking control once again."

[*Lynda Rutledge Stephenson,* Give Us a Child: Coping with the Personal Crisis of Infertility *(San Francisco: Harper & Row, 1987), pp. 223–24.]*

A Woman's Desperate Plea for a Baby

I am in pain
Someone just died.
Who you say?
Someone who never was.

I am infertile
My period just came.
I hurt so much.

My own body
Keeps reminding me
That I am incomplete,
I don't function properly.

Why? Why? Why?
Oh, my baby,
Why can't you be?

—ANONYMOUS

[Quoted in John Van Regenmorter, Sylvia Van Regenmorter, and Joe S. McIlhaney, Jr., Dear God, Why Can't We Have a Baby? *(Grand Rapids: Baker, 1986), p. 59.]*

Reminders of Infertility Everywhere

For some women infertility becomes a grief that manifests itself in almost every situation. The longing for a baby becomes so all-consuming that virtually anything reminds her of her inability to bear a child. Kaye Halverson describes this pain in her book *The Wedded Unmother.*

"I cried uncontrollably at almost anything: a pregnant woman walking down the street, a friend announcing her pregnancy. Baby showers became impossible for me to attend. I felt pitied, atypical, and extremely vulnerable. . . . Mother's Days and holidays, formerly happy times, became difficult. Birthdays just made me feel older, without any progress toward set goals.

"Magazine articles were either geared at parenting or homemaking. Although I loved being a homemaker, I felt unsuccessful because we had no children. I pictured myself a failure, an inadequate, unfulfilled woman. I began to dislike teaching and became irritable with the children. Now I was a failure at my job, too. I lost all confidence in myself and went in and out of deep depressions. I coped publicly, but privately I fell apart."

[Kaye Halverson and K. M. Hess, The Wedded Unmother *(Minneapolis: Augsburg, 1980), pp. 60–61.]*

INFIDELITY

Avoiding the Potential

In her book *Seasons of Friendship,* Ruth Senter tells how a friendship developed between her and a fellow graduate student. Although they both were married and had good relationships with their spouses, they found an attractiveness in each other. Ruth found appealing qualities in Rick that her husband, Mark, did not possess. The friendship continued, and it became apparent to both Ruth and Rick that their attraction for each other could lead to an intimate relationship. Ruth knew what she had to do. It was a painful decision, but it was the only right course of action. "The courage to do it didn't come overnight. But one day I sat down at my typewriter and typed the letter. I typed it on blue monogrammed notepaper and addressed it to his home. 'Friendship is always going somewhere unless it's dead.' I'd said it to him before, but I said it again. 'You and I both know where ours is going. When a relationship threatens the stability of commitments we've made to the people we value the most, it can no longer be.' I folded the letter and watched it disappear down the mailbox chute. There was no way I could get it back now."

It had been a very difficult move to make, as Ruth so poignantly confessed. "I felt that final ripping apart with every part of my body. My hands shook as I typed the letter. My eyes stung. My insides felt like lead. But I also felt the load shift—from my shoulders to God's. I'd obeyed that inner voice. I'd done what I knew I had to do. I would trust God to heal the wounds. The ultimate triumph belonged to Him. I knew myself too well to think otherwise."

[Ruth Senter, Seasons of Friendship: A Search for Intimacy *(Grand Rapids: Zondervan, 1982), p. 72.]*

Viewed Humorously

My wife ran off with my best friend . . . and I sure do miss him.

—ANONYMOUS

INJUSTICE

Influenced by Antifeminism

In her book *Never Guilty, Never Free,* Ginny Foat tells about the prison terms she served because her vengeful former husband accused her of being an accomplice in two murders in Nevada and Louisiana that he had been convicted for. "There were no other witnesses against me and there was no other evidence. There was only Jack's word, the uncorroborated word of a co-principal, an alcoholic, suicidal, self-confessed thief and murderer."

Countless other people have been arrested and incarcerated for crimes they did not commit, but when Foat reflects on her circumstances, she sees sex discrimination. She was a well-known feminist, a factor that may have influenced her case. Indeed, had the sexes been reversed, as Foat traces the scenario, the arrests would probably never have occurred. "Suppose that some man who came from fairly humble beginnings and made some mistakes early in his life managed to work his way up to a position of some respect in his community. He became, say, the president of a state chamber of commerce, as well as a political activist, a man whose support was courted by well-known public figures. And suppose that out of the blue, this man's ex-wife, now a derelict, a mentally disturbed, suicidal ex-convict, a chronic alcoholic and confessed multiple murderer, telephoned the police one night with a story about how this prominent man had helped her commit murders years before. Would the man be locked up and indicted and brought to trial? Would there be the remotest chance that he'd be convicted and sentenced? . . . A far more likely outcome would be that his ex-wife would be put away in some institution and never heard from again."

[Ginny Foat, Never Guilty, Never Free *(New York: Random House, 1985), pp. 185, 249.]*

Legal Injustice

In instances of domestic violence women often confront unsympathetic jurors, judges, and even attorneys who are willing to tolerate inhumane treatment if it is perpetrated by the spouse or former spouse. "In Seattle, Gloria Timmons at nineteen had been raped, beaten, and burned with scalding water by her estranged husband. In January 1973 while she was hospitalized with injuries sustained when he threw her down a flight of stairs, he came to the hospital and beat her up again. Restrained by hospital personnel, he was arrested and released to await trial; he came after her again with a screwdriver and she shot him once with a .22 pistol. She was charged with murder, and despite ample evidence of self-defense, her attorney convinced her to plead guilty to manslaughter. She served five and a half years of a one to twenty-year sentence for a 'crime' that never should have been brought to trial."

[Ann Jones, Women Who Kill *(New York: Holt, Rinehart & Winston, 1980), pp. 313–14.]*

Political Injustice

Frances Willard, who fought for female suffrage so that women could promote temperance through the political process, wrote of the pain she experienced when her brother first voted—a privilege she was denied because of her sex. "This is election day and my brother is twenty-one years old. How proud he seemed as he dressed up in his best Sunday clothes and drove off in the big wagon with father and the hired men to vote for John C. Fremont, like the sensible 'Free-soiler' that he is. My sister and I stood at the window and looked out after them. Somehow, I felt a lump in my throat, and then I couldn't see their wagon any more, things got so blurred. I turned to Mary, and she, dear little innocent, seemed wonderfully sober, too. I said, 'Wouldn't you like to vote as well as Oliver? Don't you and I love the country just as well as he, and doesn't the country need our ballots?' Then she looked scared, but answered, in a minute, ' 'Course we do, and 'course we ought,—but don't you go ahead and say so, for then we would be called strong-minded.' "

[*Frances E. Willard,* Glimpses of Fifty Years: The Autobiography of an American Woman *(Chicago: Smith, 1889; reprint, New York: Source Book Press, 1970), pp. 69–70.*]

IN-LAWS

Problems

In her book *The Adventure of Being a Wife,* Mrs. Norman Vincent Peale discusses the frequent tensions married couples have in resolving in-law problems. She knew from experience the trauma of in-law interference. Her own in-laws accompanied her and her bridegroom on their honeymoon. Yet, she showed little bitterness about such experiences in her advice to others. "The best single rule for anyone facing an in-law problem is this: stop thinking of your marriage partner's relatives as a special breed known as in-laws (a term with faintly unpleasant connotations) and think of them simply as human beings with flaws and imperfections but also lovable qualities. Just discard the in-law label in your mind. Think of them as people. Treat them like people!"

In counseling a young wife, whose mother-in-law came into her home and took over the housework, she advised, "Instead of resenting this, why don't you turn it to your advantage? Which aspects of housekeeping do you dislike? Ironing? Sewing? Why not plan to have a small mountain of ironing on hand and ask your mother-in-law to do it for you? Do you need curtains made, or slip covers? Get the material and leave it in her room. And while she does the work, get out of the house and do something with your husband. If she insists on taking over, let her take over tasks that you'd rather avoid anyway!"

To a mother-in-law, she counseled: "Look for something to praise in your daughter-in-law every time you're with her. If your son hears you speak well of the girl he has chosen, it makes him feel proud and happy, and strengthens the ties he still has with you." And regarding grandchildren, she writes: "Love them and admire them, but don't make suggestions about how they should be brought up. You may have your doubts, but it's better to keep them to yourself. I'm startled, myself, at the way *my* children seem to neglect *their* children's table manners. They seem to me to be extremely messy eaters. But theirs is a new generation, with new standards and new points of view. Who am I to say that I am right and they are wrong?"

[Ruth Peale, The Adventure of Being a Wife (Englewood Cliffs, N.J.: Prentice-Hall, 1971), pp. 95–97.]

INTELLECTUAL DEVELOPMENT

Necessity of Reading

Television and busy schedules are two primary reasons that people fail to broaden themselves adequately through reading. Indeed, reading is often viewed as a luxury that can be enjoyed during a two-week summer vacation at a cottage. But reading is not a luxury. It is a necessity for anyone who wants to interact with others in thought-provoking discussions. This was the view of John D. Snider, who wrote *I Love Books,* before television soap operas, sit-coms, and sports programing had begun to take up so much of the average American's "free" time.

"The first step toward becoming an original thinker is to become familiar with the thoughts of others. . . . The man who never learns how to read will never become much of a thinker. When left alone, his mind is empty because he has not filled it with useful knowledge and can make no comparisons of ideas. When cast upon his own resources, he finds no reservoirs of thought within him to refresh his soul. Wide reading is the very foundation of ideas and constructive thinking, and the happiest person is one who thinks the most interesting thoughts."

[John D. Snider, I Love Books (Washington, D.C.: Review & Herald, 1942), pp. 347–48.]

INTELLIGENCE
Are IQ Tests Biased?

The Stanford-Binet IQ test, which was formulated by Lewis H. Terman, was introduced in 1916. "When it was administered to the student population, it showed females at all levels outscoring males of the same ages by 2 to 4 percent. So Terman and his colleagues *changed* the test, removing the questions on which girls did especially well; they thus created boys and girls equal. One wonders what would have been done if the first results had shown boys outstripping girls: Would the test have been changed? Would it have been used as proof that boys were more intelligent than girls?"

[Marilyn French, Beyond Power: On Women, Men, and Morals *(New York: Summit Books, 1985), p. 385.]*

LEADERSHIP
Assumed by Unlikely Individuals

Sometimes the least likely candidates for leadership prove to be most capable for the task at hand. That was true of Harriet Tubman, whose work with the Underground Railroad in the 1850s was legendary. "Easily the most outstanding Negro conductor on the Underground Railroad was Harriet Tubman. Although frail of body and suffering from recurrent spells of dizziness, she not only escaped from slavery herself, but conveyed many others to freedom, including her sister, her two children, and her aged mother and father. She is said to have gone South nineteen times to have emancipated more than 300 slaves. Unable to read or to write, she nevertheless displayed remarkable ingenuity in the management of her runaway caravans. She preferred to start the journey on Saturday night, so that she could be well on her way before the owners had an opportunity the following Monday to advertise the escape of their slaves. She tolerated no cowardice and threatened to kill any slave who wished to turn back. Well known in Philadelphia, New York, and Boston, where she frequently delivered the escaped slaves, she preferred to carry them all the way to Canada after the passage of the Fugitive Slave Law in 1850, explaining that she could not trust Uncle Sam with her people any longer."

[John Hope Franklin, From Slavery to Freedom: A History of Negro Americans, *3d ed. (New York: Random House, 1969), pp. 259–60.]*

LEGALISM

Sabbath Restrictions

Various forms of legalism have always been a significant part of Protestantism, though the specifics have differed from generation to generation. The Puritans and their descendants were particularly concerned about Sabbath keeping, and according to Colleen McDannell, "By the nineteenth century the New England Calvinist Sabbath had reached almost mythical proportions and stood for all forms of unreasonable, harsh religious devotion. The Puritan, who hung his cat on Monday for killing a mouse on Sunday, became a symbol for New England rigidity and old fashioned attitudes. Even writers within the Reformed tradition commented that previous generations had been too extreme in their demands for a sacred Sabbath. And yet, the Sabbath continued to be a day devoted to God, devoid of work, amusements, and secular activities. Few Protestant writers would challenge the Sabbath's religious nature."

[Colleen McDannell, The Christian Home in Victorian America, 1840–1900 *(Bloomington: Indiana University Press, 1986), pp. 91–92.]*

LEISURE

Curtailed by the Accumulation of Junk

A subtle problem that deprives people of happiness and often curtails their leisure time is what Don Aslett describes as the "burden of junk." Many people do not realize the restrictions junk places on them, and they simply accept the "Law of the Packrat," which says, "Junk will accumulate proportionately to the storage room available for it." But disposing of junk is an essential part of maintaining a comfortable life that allows for leisure. "It is a job that you cannot palm off on anyone else, or postpone too long, because there is no escape from the toll that junk takes on your life. Everything stashed away or hidden discreetly or indiscreetly is also stashed away in your mind and is subconsciously draining your mental energy. Once discarded, it is discarded from your mind, and you are free from keeping mental tabs on it. . . . Why spend a valuable part of yourself polishing, washing, dusting, and thinking about it? YOU CAN'T AFFORD JUNK. It will rob you physically, emotionally, and spiritually. Freeing yourself from junk will automatically free you from housework. . . . If you'll just 'dejunk' your home, the time you have left over in the course of a year will be enough to complete and pay for three credit hours in that college class you've always wanted to take."

[Don Aslett, Is There Life after Housework? *(Cincinnati: Writer's Digest Books, 1981), pp. 24–26.]*

LESBIANISM

As a Feminist Ideology

Many lesbians are not feminists, and countless feminists are not lesbians, but for some women the two are intricately bound together, and lesbianism becomes the ultimate expression of feminism. For them, it is far more than having a sexual preference for another woman; it is a political declaration of freedom from the male sex. In ministering to lesbians, as is true of any group, it is important to understand their backgrounds and perspectives. In her book *What's Right with Feminism?* Elaine Storkey, a Christian writer, seeks to explain some of the motivations for lesbianism.

"Being a lesbian is . . . for many the logical outcome of a woman-centered ideology. Lesbianism draws together so many different strands. It attacks again the idea of the 'natural'. If a woman really can find deeper sexual fulfillment with another woman, how can anyone maintain the naturalness of heterosexual relations? It challenges again the dependence of women on men. It flouts the patriarchal masculinity where it will hurt the most. The message is clear: men are irrelevant. Patriarchy does not have the last word. An alternative woman-centered culture is workable in every way."

Lesbianism is certainly not confined to those women who wish to make a political statement. Storkey goes on to point out that many other factors influence lesbianism and, for those women, serve as a justification for the life-style. Many of these women have been deeply hurt by men, and they thus turn to women for their deepest and most intimate relationships.

"But lesbianism is not merely a defiance towards male domination, the 'rage of all women condensed to the point of explosion'. It is also a belief that only women can give to each other a real sense of self, of personal identity. It is seen by those involved as a process of healing, of emotional growth and tenderness which is impossible within heterosexual relations. Put simply, heterosexuality means 'men first'. Through this recovery of personal worth and growth, a woman is now better able to reach out to others."

[Elaine Storkey, What's Right with Feminism? (Grand Rapids: Eerdmans, 1985), pp. 105–6.]

LONELINESS
Remedy

In her book *Lifelines,* Lynn Caine, a widow who struggled with loneliness and isolation, seeks to offer solutions to others in similar situations. She identifies with those who are wallowing in self-pity, and with those who are trying too hard to find someone to fill the vacuum in their lives. She offers a simple prescription to loneliness that helped alleviate her own depression. "The only solution is to strengthen oneself. And here is where those courses and committees, sports and crafts can play an important role. They can help a woman grow. If you join a tennis club or study accounting or go on early-morning bird walks because you think you will meet a man or make a friend, the chances are you won't. But if you have always wanted to understand the stock market, have dreamed of being a real estate agent, then go to it. Enroll in a class; join a club; follow your interests. If you are passionate about saving the whales, building dollhouses, running for political office, working for women's rights, get going. Get involved. You may meet like-minded souls and make lifetime friends, or you may not. But you will be less lonely because you will be more interesting—and stronger."

[Lynn Caine, Lifelines *(Garden City, N.Y.: Doubleday, 1978), p. 56.]*

LOVE
Addiction to Love

In his book *Love and Addiction,* Stanton Peele maintains that love, like alcohol and drugs, can be addictive. As a social psychologist, he has studied human relationships and various addictions, and his observations and findings are thought provoking and original in many respects.

"Love is an ideal vehicle for addiction because it can so exclusively claim a person's consciousness. If, to serve as an addiction, something

must be both reassuring and consuming, then a sexual or love relationship is perfectly suited for the task. If it must also be patterned,
predictable, and isolated, then in these respects, too, a relationship can
be ideally tailored to the addictive purpose. Someone who is dissatisfied
with himself or his situation can discover in such a relationship the most
encompassing substitute for self-contentment and the effort required to
attain it."

Peele distinguishes true love from addictive love. "Love is the opposite of interpersonal addiction. A love relationship is based on a desire
to grow and to expand oneself through living, and a desire for one's
partner to do the same. Anything which contributes positively to a
loved one's experience is welcomed, partly because it enriches the loved
one for his own sake, and partly because it makes him a more stimulating companion in life. If a person is self-completed, he can even accept
experiences which cause a lover to grow away from him if that is the
direction in which the lover's fulfillment must take her. If two people
hope to realize fully their potential as human beings—both together
and apart—then they create an intimacy which includes, along with
trust and sharing, hope, independence, openness, adventurousness, and
love."

An almost sure mark of an addictive relationship, according to Peele,
is the vindictive manner in which it generally terminates. "Because the
involvement has been so total, its ending must be violent. Thus it is
possible for two people who have been the most intimate of friends
suddenly to turn around and hate each other, because they have been
thinking more of themselves than each other all along. The exploitation
that has been going on throughout the relationship simply becomes
more overt when the breakup occurs; then the two ex-lovers withdraw
emotionally, perhaps to the point of trying to hurt each other."

[Stanton Peele, with Archie Brodsky, Love and Addiction *(New York: New American Library, 1975),
pp. 70, 80, 88.]*

Differentiating Love from Addiction

Many psychologists have now concluded that love can be addictive,
and this addiction most commonly affects women. "Love addicts,"

according to psychologists Connell Cowan and Melvyn Kinder, "are people who feel they can't live without the person who nourishes them." Such addiction should not be confused with real love, and in some cases the addiction goes on even after the pleasure is gone. "In the beginning phase of love addiction, women are convinced that the excitement they experience with men is the reason they continue the behavior. But in the later phases, even the love addict admits she is hooked. Few are actually aware of the lack of pleasure in their repetitive experiences. . . . Love addicts are most frequently women for whom the world seems bleak, empty, and fraught with perils. . . . Relief from these deep feelings of insecurity is found in the thoughts, feelings, and fantasies these women have about men. This 'relief,' however, is both fleeting and illusory and exists only as a temporary state of excitement and promise of contentment. What better feeling than the euphoria of falling in love?"

[Connell Cowan and Melvyn Kinder, Smart Women, Foolish Choices *(New York: Potter, 1985), pp. 127–28.]*

Differentiating Love from Romance

Sonya Friedman, a clinical psychologist who is known for her television and radio programs and her writing, advises women to beware of romantic love that often has a suffocating effect on one's individuality. "Romance," she writes, "may not necessarily have anything to do with love, but it certainly looks and sounds as though it does." Romance, however, "is marked, most notably, by a temporary detachment from ordinary life. It is a couple's indulgence in illusions about each other, and even an ennobling of each other."

She points out some significant distinguishing features of the two emotions. "While romance has a lot of fantasy going for it, love is grounded in reality. And when people love and care about each other, there is no need for the constant breathlessness that romance is known to inspire. People who really care about each other can maintain that mutual caring without a great deal of gushiness, neediness, or dramatically teary entreaties." There is a difference in language as well. "The romantic says: 'I couldn't bear it if you didn't love me. Tell me you love me again.' The loving person says: 'I love the fact that you're alive. It does something important to my life, knowing you're in this world and that you care about me.'

"The romantic: 'You're everything to me. Am I everything to you?' The loving person: 'I'm happy being with you.'

"The romantic: 'You never loved me! If you leave me, you'll be sorry!' The loving person: 'Let's talk about what's gone wrong with us. I don't want this relationship to end.' "

[*Sonya Friedman,* Men Are Just Desserts *(New York: Warner Books, 1983), pp. 19–20.]*

Effect of Love on Health

How do love and affection influence an individual's physical well-being? This question has been pondered for centuries, with many variations in the response. In 1817, Prof. O. S. Fowler wrote that "health is controlled by love," and that "its value exceeds all earthly values." He was particularly interested in negative and positive marriage relationships and was not adverse to giving sweeping statements about the dire consequence of the former or the panacea of the latter.

"Love controls the health . . . as if by magic. A pure hearty Love state will regenerate anybody's health; while vitiated Love will break down everybody's. Ninety-nine hundredths of our strong constitutional men in physical ruin, wrecked themselves on the breakers of abnormal Love. . . . Let all fairly happily married men think back how much their health improved within two years from the beginning of their courtship; and those who have lost a loved wife, how much poorer after her loss; while, per contra, many improve their health by losing an uncongenial wife. And let all men note how much better they feel for 'going a-courting,' provided they court purely. Yet nothing tears the life right out of any, all men, as does lust."

[*O. S. Fowler,* Creative and Sexual Science; or, Manhood, Womanhood, and Their Mutual Interrelations *(Chicago: Follett, 1870), p. 91.]*

Love at First Sight

Many people profess to have begun their road to marital bliss on the romantic surge of "love at first sight." James Dobson, well-known family counselor, takes issue with such claims.

"Though some readers will disagree with me, love at first sight is a physical and emotional impossibility. Why? Because love is not simply a feeling of romantic excitement; it is more than a desire to marry a potential partner; it goes beyond intense sexual attraction; it exceeds the thrill of having 'captured' a highly desirable social prize. These are emotions that are unleashed at first sight, but they *do not constitute love.* I wish the whole world knew that fact. These temporary feelings differ from love in that they place the spotlight on the one experiencing them. 'What is happening to *me?!* This is the most fantastic thing *I've* ever been through! *I* think *I* am in love!' You see, these emotions are selfish in the sense that they are motivated by our gratification. They have little to do with the new lover. Such a person has not fallen in love with another person; *he has fallen in love with love!* And there is an enormous difference between the two."

[James Dobson, What Wives Wish Their Husbands Knew about Women *(Wheaton: Tyndale, 1975), pp. 88–89.]*

Pain of a Love Affair

John Wesley, who endured more than one painful love affair, received a letter from his sister Emilia, who herself was struggling through a period of frustrated love. Among other things she advised him, "Never engage your affections before your worldly affairs are in such a posture that you may marry very soon. . . . Were I to live my time over again and had the same experience I have now, were it for the best man in England I would not wait one year. I know you are a young man encompassed with difficulties that has passed through many hardships already . . . but believe me if you ever come to suffer the torment of a hopeless love all other afflictions will seem small in comparison of it."

[*Quoted in Robert G. Tuttle, Jr.,* John Wesley: His Life and Theology *(Grand Rapids: Zondervan, 1978), p. 65.*]

Parents' Love of Child

Many observers of human behavior have suggested that the loss that generates the greatest stress is the loss of a child. One of the reasons for this is the unique love that a parent has for a child. Indeed, it may surpass the love that is felt in any other relationship. Dr. Marianne Neifert captures the essence of this love in descriptive terms. "Unconditional love, parental love, is unearned and unending. It has no strings attached, no conditions that must be met. Many of our other relationships in life depend on reciprocal benefits, but parental love is given freely to both gifted and retarded child, beautiful and blemished child, precocious and handicapped child, planned and unplanned child, boy and girl child. When delightful or obnoxious, we continue to love our child. It's the most selfless thing we ever do, sometimes the bravest thing we ever do. We love simply because it comes so naturally and because someone once did it for us."

[*Marianne E. Neifert, with Anne Price and Nancy Dana,* Dr. Mom: A Guide to Baby and Child Care *(New York: Putnam's Sons, 1986), p. 11.*]

Viewing Love in Humorous Vein

Do you love me,
Or do you not?
I used to know,
But I forgot.
—ANONYMOUS

Best country song title of the week: "Why did you leave me when I said I didn't love you when you know I've been a liar all my life?"

—"PAUL HARVEY NEWS," JANUARY 9, 1986

LUST

Origin of Lust

The Cathars, a heretical sectarian group in southern France during the late-medieval period, had an oral tradition that explained to them how lust first came to this world. Historian Philip Schaff tells the story. Although women among the Cathers were given positions of authority involving ministry, they were seen as the instigators of sin, and normal husband-wife sexual relationships were prohibited.

"A strange account of the fall of the angels was current in Southern France. Satan ascended to heaven and waited in vain thirty-two years for admittance. He was then noticed and admitted by the porter. Hidden from the Father, he remained among the angels a year before he began to use his art to deceive. He asked them whether they had no other glory or pleasure besides what he saw. When they replied they had not, he asked whether they would not like to descend to his world and kingdom, promising to give them gifts, fields, vineyards, springs, meadows, fruits, gold, silver, and women. Then he began to praise woman and the pleasures of the flesh. When they inquired more particularly about the women, the devil said he would descend and bring one back with him. This he did. The woman was decked in jewels and gold and beautiful of form. The angels were inflamed with passion, and Satan seeing this, took her and left heaven. The angels followed. The exodus continued for nine days and nights, when God closed up the fissure which had been made."

[Philip Schaff, History of the Christian Church, *vol. 5,* The Middle Ages, 1049–1294 *(New York: Scribner's Sons, 1907; reprint, Grand Rapids: Eerdmans, 1979), p. 476.]*

MALE TRAITS

Predisposed toward Numbers Rather Than Individuals

In her book *Women's Reality,* Anne Wilson Schaef discusses the enormous impact the "White Male System" has had on modern society. "It makes our laws, runs our economy, sets our salaries, and decides when and if we will go to war or remain at home. It decides what *is* knowledge and how it is to be taught." She contrasts this system with the "Emerging Female System," which has different values and ways of thinking. She illustrates this difference in many ways, one of which comes from her own personal experience.

"Our society is engulfed in numbers. Many of us feel as if we are sacrificing our own identity to them. We are lost without our social security numbers, credit card numbers, and telephone numbers, *ad nauseam.* Many more work hours are spent with numbers than they are in production or with people.

"I once attended a church service in a small Midwestern town. Afterward, I told the minister how pleased I had been with the prayer and sermon meditation. He nodded and immediately launched into a discussion of church attendance and how few people were there on communion Sundays during summer. I had commented on the quality and content of the service—and he had responded with numbers!

"The White Male System believes in the reality of numbers. It has to in order to support its own mythology. If numbers are not real—if they are merely symbols which are open to subjective interpretation—then they can not be used to measure, predict, and control."

[*Anne Wilson Schaef,* Women's Reality: An Emerging Female System in a White Male Society *(San Francisco: Harper & Row, 1985), pp. 2, 19.]*

MANAGEMENT
Female Advantage

After working as a newspaper and television reporter for many years, Linda Ellerbee developed convictions on management style, and one related to the sex differences that are often strikingly different. "I have come to appreciate the value of letting women run things: not all things and not all the time, but some things, sometimes." Her experience in working with the late night news program "Overnight" led her to this conclusion. "Before *Overnight,* I had never worked around or for so many women, and neither had any of the men on the program. We learned, for the most part, that everything and everyone worked easier. Fewer power games were played. Perhaps it was because women, having had little real power in our business, didn't know the games. . . . On *Overnight,* women made coffee *and* policy. If there was a production meeting, and someone walked in with tears in her eyes and told us her husband or boyfriend had left her, someone got that woman a cup of tea, someone gave her a squeeze, someone said a kind word—*and then the meeting continued."* The style of management apparently paid off. Although the program had "just about the worst shift in NBC in terms of lousy hours," it "had the lowest absentee rate of *any* shift in the company."

[Linda Ellerbee, And So It Goes: Adventures in Television *(New York: Putnam's Sons, 1986), pp. 118–20.]*

MARITAL ADVICE
Viewing Husband as Jesus

Ruth Carter Stapleton, the late sister of President Jimmy Carter, experienced such troubling marital problems that she attempted suicide, soon after the birth of her fourth child. In her book *The Gift of Inner Healing,* she told the story of how her life was changed by surrendering her life to Jesus. She advised a woman in circumstances similar to hers to do what she had done to solve her problems. "Try to spend a little time each day visualizing Jesus coming in the door from work. Then see yourself walking up to Him, embracing Him. Say to Jesus, 'It's good to have you home Nick.'"

[Ruth Carter Stapleton, The Gift of Inner Healing *(Waco: Word Books, 1976), p. 32.]*

MARRIAGE
Bickering and Fighting

What effect do continual bickering and fighting have on a marriage? Most would think that it would be very detrimental, but apparently some people thrive on it. Carol Tavris, in her book *Anger: The Misunderstood Emotion,* tells a story that illustrates this.

"My father once reluctantly agreed to be the best man at a friend's wedding. He was reluctant because he feared that the marriage would end in three months or in murder, whichever came first. Still, friendship prevailed. As he drove the bridal couple to the judge's chambers, they bickered incessantly in the back seat about her choice of judge. As he drove them to the train station after the ceremony, they quarreled violently about the groom's choice of honeymoon hotel. My father predicted that the marriage would never last beyond the first night. In fact, the couple stayed together happily, fighting and cooing all the while, until the husband's death, of natural causes, thirty-five years later."

This couple was similar to the parents of Janet, a friend of Carol's, whose father enjoyed telling about his apparent ability to thrive on the bickering of his wife. "My father read in the paper one day about an unhappy hippo in a zoo. Somebody got the brilliant idea of putting a goat in with the hippo to keep it company. The goat, in the manner of goats, would butt the hippo all day long. And of course the hippo, in the manner of hippos, didn't feel a thing. It was the perfect marriage. The hippo went from lethargy and torpor into bliss. Finally he was getting some attention.

"My father was very fond of that story. To him my mother was the goat, and he was the hippo who protested."

Carol emphasizes that, although this is an amusing story, in many instances the outcome is not so pleasant. "Usually the hippo complains to you of being nagged and attacked all day long ('Never a moment's peace! Never a tranquil meal!'), and the goat gets you in a corner to grumble of the hippo's thick-skinned intransigence ('I might as well be a stone for all the attention I get! No one in this house ever does what I want!')."

[*Carol Tavris,* Anger: The Misunderstood Emotion *(New York: Simon & Schuster, 1982), pp. 203–4.]*

Constructive Criticism of Spouse

Dr. M. Scott Peck, a nationally known psychiatrist, believes it is essential for husbands and wives to confront each other when differences arise between them. Indeed, he insists that "loving spouses must repeatedly confront each other if the marriage relationship is to serve the function of promoting the spiritual growth of the partners. No marriage can be judged truly successful unless husband and wife are each other's best critics. The same holds true for friendship. There is a traditional concept that friendship should be a conflict-free relationship, a 'you scratch my back, I'll scratch yours' arrangement, relying solely on a mutual exchange of favors and compliments as prescribed by good manners. Such relationships are superficial and intimacy-avoiding and do not deserve the name of friendship which is so commonly applied to them."

[*M. Scott Peck,* The Road Less Traveled: A New Psychology of Love, Traditional Values, and Spiritual Growth *(New York: Simon & Schuster, 1978), p. 153.]*

Desirability of Marriage

Although many people in recent years have suggested that marriage is going out of style, the statistics do not support such a conclusion.

While marriages do not last as long on the average as they once did, the popularity of marriage has not diminished. Americans hold strongly to traditional values, and a recent survey showed that some 90 percent of unmarried young adults expect to marry. The choices are wider than they were some decades ago. "Interracial marriages have more than doubled since 1970, and 21 percent of women marry younger men." Remarriage has rapidly increased as well. "If the marriage doesn't work out, singlehood of one or both ex-spouses doesn't last long—seven out of ten divorced people decide to remarry within five years of the divorce. . . . Divorce has quadrupled since 1960, with the average marriage lasting 6.8 years. While only 68.8 percent of formerly married women remarry, their ex-spouses go to the altar again at the rate of 78.3 percent."

Why does marriage, with all its problems, continue to have such a high appeal? "Marriage," writes Sonya Friedman, "is the deepest form of connection between two people. Intimacy, true intimacy, is bliss. But we are human—bliss is not a consistent state of mind. Our differences do turn up, and then life isn't quite so blissful when issues become powder kegs. And guess what? We blame *marriage*—marriage as a thing apart from us, as if it were something that could come alive and be nice to us, not a unique interaction between two people.

"So marriage got a bad name years back. The news of its fall from grace was shocking—much like the disclosure that a clergyman is corrupt. And so we must ask: Dare we commit ourselves to this institution or will we be made fools of?"

That may be a difficult question for some people to resolve, but for the vast majority of Americans, marriage will continue to be viewed as the most desirable course of living for adult life. Indeed, statistics show that married people—especially married men—are the happiest subgroup in society.

[*Sonya Friedman*, Smart Cookies Don't Crumble: A Modern Woman's Guide to Living and Loving Her Own Life *(New York: Putnam's Sons, 1985), p. 158.]*

Disclosing Secrets before Wedding

How much personal information and how many dark secrets should be revealed during a dating relationship or following an engagement? Marriage counselors differ on this subject, but most would agree that withholding information that eventually will come to light can have a very harmful effect on a marriage relationship. This is the position Prof. O. S. Fowler took in the advice book he wrote in 1870, a volume that has relevance today—though sometimes in a humorous vein. He cautioned young men not to claim they neither smoked nor chewed tobacco when, in fact, they did. He likewise admonished both men and women to avoid trying to hide their physical flaws, which would become obvious after marriage.

"Making your beau think by millinery appearances that you have a splendid form, when marriage reveals only padded shams, throws a 'wet blanket' over his Love, the more fatal the more he is thus enamored. So equally of false teeth, making believe younger by dyeing hair or whiskers, etc. The age should never be concealed. . . .

"A splendid young man, whose Love was quite personal, on marrying a supposed beauty, found she had a slight umbilical blemish; which so disgusted him of her that he abandoned her, though enamored of her otherwise; which agonized both beyond description; yet would have been prevented by its mere mention."

[O. S. Fowler, Creative and Sexual Science; or, Manhood, Womanhood, and Their Mutual Interrelations *(Chicago: Follett, 1870), pp. 144–45.]*

Domestic Happiness

B. T. Roberts, who founded the Free Methodist denomination in the late nineteenth century, was a strong supporter of women in ministry. He also was a strong advocate of egalitarian marriages. In his book *Ordaining Women,* he wrote a prescription for domestic happiness. "The greatest domestic happiness always exists where husband and wife live together on terms of equality. Two men, having individual interests, united only by business ties, daily associate as partners for years, without either of them being in subjection to the other. They consider each other as equals. Then, cannot a man and woman, united in conjugal love, the strongest tie that can unite two human beings having the *same* interests, live together in the same manner?"

[B. T. Roberts, Ordaining Women *(Rochester: Earnest Christian, 1891), p. 52.]*

Engagement

Jim Elliot, who later became famous through his death at the hands of the Auca Indians in Ecuador, had initially intended to serve God as a single missionary. That resolve changed, however, after years of correspondence with Elisabeth Howard, whom he had known at Wheaton College and who also was serving as a missionary to the Indians in South America. Prior to his proposal for marriage, he wrote in his journal how their engagement would change his actions and philosophy. "Engagement for us, as I understand it now, would mean. (1) we would kiss (how I've refrained from this so long I'll never know); (2) she would give me further liberty with her body; (3) she would be free to be aggressive in embrace; (4) I would give her this to read, and she would let me see her diary; (5) she could say what she really feels for me, rather than just having to whisper, 'Jim . . . !' and remarking, 'If you only knew'; (6) we would throw off our public distance; (7) for my part a more responsible care for her, a sense of divine obligation, first, to protect her from any social inconvenience; second, to preserve my own health and body for *her* (as contrasted with my present attitude of expendability of my powers); more time spent with her to align attitudes; (8) a definite idea of 'when' for marriage; (9) fairly clear guidance about the nature of our future work, as, for instance, I now have with Pete."

[Elisabeth Elliot, ed., The Journals of Jim Elliot *(Old Tappan, N.J.: Revell, 1978), pp. 390–91.]*

Equality in Quaker Marriages

Quakers have had a long history of insisting that the husband and wife are fully equal in the marriage partnership. They take each other on equal terms, neither one promising to obey the other. This was true of Lucretia Mott, the well-known nineteenth-century abolitionist, and her husband, James. He was a strong advocate of woman's rights, and he supported his wife in her public activities. "Less articulate than his gifted wife, he found great satisfaction in accompanying her on her travels and listening to her talks. When she spoke, she expressed his feelings. It was a symbiotic relationship. She leaned on him for support when she was under attack; he, in turn, chaired many antislavery, women's rights, and peace meetings. The two were inseparable."

Mrs. Mott advocated an equal partnership for others as well, and at weddings she often admonished the bride and groom with her own self-styled maxim. "In the true marriage relationship, the independence of the husband and wife is equal, their dependence mutual, and their obligations reciprocal."

[Margaret Hope Bacon, Mothers of Feminism (San Francisco: Harper & Row, 1986), pp. 56, 112.]

Equal Partnership in Marriage

Must marriage change to reflect societal changes? This is often hotly debated, and yet most people would agree that the institution of marriage has not remained static over the centuries. Feminism has had an impact on society, and whether one agrees with its philosophy or not, it will no doubt influence the marriage relationship significantly.

"If workable marriages are to exist in this latter part of the twentieth century, the artificially determined roles of male and female . . . structure . . . cannot function in today's environment. Neither can the extreme feminist dream of female domination. Modern marriage requires equality, just as world history indicates a trend toward equality among people regardless of sex, race, or creed."

[William J. Lederer and Don D. Jackson, The Mirages of Marriage *(New York: Norton, 1968), p. 18.]*

Failure to Safeguard Marriage

The crucial importance of caring for and preserving a marriage is related in an interesting analogy by Patti Roberts, whose marriage breakdown with Richard Roberts and the entire Oral Roberts empire is related in her book *Ashes to Gold.* She compares the care she took in preserving her wedding gown with the care she took in preserving the marriage itself.

"My dress had an empire waist with a tight bodice and a pretty little high neck with lots of seed pearls on it. Seed pearl flowers covered the skirt and ran down the long train. I paid $120 for it and thought that was a tremendous amount of money for a dress you'd only wear once.

"Little did I know I'd have that dress forever. As I have moved from house to house from city to city, I've always carefully kept it. I don't know what you do with a dress from a marriage that didn't work. It seems almost a sacrilege to throw it away, but the marriage turned out to be disposable. The dress is all packed away in huge gold boxes, free from dust and guaranteed not to yellow. When I look at it, it hurts that all that care is taken to preserve a dress when so little care was taken to preserve a family, but I guess it's easier to store a dress than to make a marriage work."

[Patti Roberts, with Sherry Andrews, Ashes to Gold *(Waco: Word Books, 1983), pp. 66–67.]*

Female Dominance in Marriage

The tradition of the Kikuyu tribe in Kenya includes the belief that long ago the women were powerful warriors who practiced polyandry and treated men cruelly—sentencing them to death for committing adultery and other crimes. "The women were physically stronger than the men, and better warriors. The men decided on a plan for rebellion. On a selected day, all the men copulated with their wives (they seem to have had the power to initiate sex): six months later, all the women were pregnant, and the men took over, established polygamy and prohibited polyandry, and dominated the tribe."

[Marilyn French, Beyond Power: On Women, Men, and Morals *(New York: Summit Books, 1985), p. 53.]*

Female Urge for Marriage

Ruth Benedict, a renowned social scientist of the early twentieth century, would have given up all her success for a happy marriage with children. Her own childless marriage ended in divorce, and she longed for what had been deprived her. In 1912, she wrote in her journal, "To me it seems a very terrible thing to be a woman. There is one crown which perhaps is worth it all—a great love, a quiet home, and children. We all know that is all that is worthwhile, and we must peg away, showing off our wares on the market if we have money, or manufacturing careers for ourselves if we haven't. We have not the motive to prepare ourselves for a 'lifework' of teaching, of social work—we know that we would lay it down with hallelujah in the height of our success, to make a home for the right man. And all the time in the background of our consciousness rings the warning that perhaps the right man will never come. A great love is given to very few. Perhaps this makeshift time-filler of a job is our lifework after all."

[Quoted in Elisabeth Elliot, Let Me Be a Woman *(Wheaton: Tyndale, 1976), pp. 52–53.]*

Futility in Trying to Change Marriage Partner

Sometimes through pressure and nagging it is possible to change a marriage partner to one's liking, but often this approach proves to be futile. This was true of Tom Frydenger, who married Adrienne, who had two daughters from her previous marriage. One of the big issues that arose soon after the wedding was that of "the early riser versus the night owl." Tom gives his somewhat exaggerated description of the situation. "Adrienne expected me to jump out of bed, fling the window open, crow with the roosters and still be able to function the rest of the day. Much to her chagrin, I have never viewed getting up in the morning as a high point in my day. I made it a practice to never get out of bed until the last possible minute.

"Adrienne did everything she could think of to get me up. On her more subdued mornings she left the door open for me to hear any and every sound she, the girls, or Fred [the dog] would make. I woke up but we all wound up grouchy.

"The more she insisted I needed to get out of bed earlier, the later I would sleep, until finally she gave up. With one grand statement she acquiesced. 'Tom, you sleep as late as you want. Far be it from me to stop you from sleeping your life away if that's what you really want to do.'

"The next morning when the girls woke up, Adrienne fed them breakfast and told them to play quietly downstairs. She didn't come back to the bedroom every five minutes to see if I was up. As a matter of fact, she didn't come back to wake me at all and I loved it. And once she stopped trying to force me to be an early bird, something very strange began to happen. I started wanting to get up earlier. And even stranger, I did. When Adrienne quit trying to change me, I had the motivation to change myself. And the turmoil between us, which caught the girls in the crossfire, ended."

[Tom Frydenger and Adrienne Frydenger, The Blended Family *(Old Tappan, N.J.: Revell, 1984), pp. 45–46.]*

God's Leading or Human Error?

It is often very dangerous to claim God's direction in a matter that can be so emotional as that of romantic love and marriage. The heart can tell the brain many things that are not necessarily true, and when a person claims that God has divinely shown that a particular individual is the right one to marry—without the other usual signs of marriage readiness—the alarm should sound to warn of impending danger. James Dobson has found this to be true in his counseling experience.

"A young man whom I was counseling once told me that he awoke in the middle of the night with the strong impression that God wanted him to marry a young lady whom he had only dated casually a few times. They were not even going together at that moment and hardly knew each other. The next morning he called her and relayed the message which God had supposedly sent him during the night. The girl figured she shouldn't argue with God, and she accepted the proposal. They have now been married for seven years and have struggled for survival since their wedding day!

"Anyone who believes that God guarantees a successful marriage to every Christian is in for a shock. This is not to say that he is disinterested in the choice of a mate, or that he will not answer a specific request for guidance on this all-important decision. Certainly, his will should be sought in such a critical matter, and I consulted him repeatedly before proposing to my wife. However, I do not believe that God performs a routine match-making service for everyone who worships him. He has given us judgment, common sense, and discretionary powers, and he expects us to exercise these abilities in matters matrimonial. Those who believe otherwise are likely to enter marriage glibly, thinking, 'God would have blocked this development if he didn't approve of it.' To such confident people I can only say, 'Lotsa luck.' "

[James Dobson, What Wives Wish Their Husbands Knew about Women *(Wheaton: Tyndale, 1975), pp. 94–95.]*

Growing Apart in Marriage

Young couples marry with the assumption that their love and devotion to each other will grow with the years, but often the very opposite occurs. Pearl S. Buck tells about the differences in personality that characterized her parents, and how these differences slowly pulled them apart. They were missionaries in China and devoted to their work, but as time passed, they drifted further and further away from each other. "Alone together in the house, alone on the junks, alone plodding side by side through the dusty country roads or along the crowded cobbled streets of cities, there was no talk to be made between them." Their personalities and manners of expressing themselves were entirely different. "Carie, whose cheerful, humorous, running conversation was a delight to so many others, found that to Andrew her racy comments on what she saw were often only a weariness and unwarranted audacities."

[Pearl S. Buck, The Exile *(New York: Reynal & Hitchcock, 1936), pp. 251, 278.]*

Importance of Marriage Vows

Marriage vows are often taken lightly, but for many people they are the staying power of the relationship. Madeleine L'Engle testifies to this in reflecting on her own marriage. "When we were married we made promises, and we took them seriously. No relationship between two people which is worth anything is static. If a man and wife tell me they've never had a quarrel, I suspect that something is festering under the skin. There've been a number of times in my marriage when—if I hadn't made promises—I'd have quit. I'm sure this is equally true of Hugh; I'm not an easy person to live with.

"I'm quite sure that Hugh and I would never have reached the relationship we have today if we hadn't made promises. Perhaps we made them youthfully, and blindly, not knowing all that was implied; but the very promises have been a saving grace."

[Madeleine L'Engle, A Circle of Quiet *(San Francisco: Harper & Row, 1972), p. 107.]*

Individuality in Marriage

In her book *Heirs Together,* Patricia Gundry strongly emphasizes the importance of viewing marriage as an institution that is not bound by age-old formulas and traditions. While the Bible gives principles and patterns, it does not outline every specific detail for a good marriage because marriages are what the marriage partners are, and each partner must be free to grow and expand within the institution of marriage. This need for individuality struck her in a new way through a cartoon.

" *'I now pronounce you person and person,'* read the cartoon caption. My first thought was—what a witty commentary on the kind of contemporary marriage that is so open as to be almost empty!

"I put the magazine down and went about my work. Then another thought came to me. . . . *To still be whole persons after marriage . . . to be affirmed as individuals by marriage instead of having your individuality stamped out or stamped upon. How fine it would be to expand marriage to fit the people instead of shrinking the people to fit an institution.* And I realized I had identified a central problem couples face today in marriage.

"Many people now feel marriage demands that they give up their own personalities and dreams. They fear it will destroy the very uniqueness each brought to the union and, eventually, bring on an oppressive stagnation. They fear marriage will even destroy their love. . . .

"A marriage based on the principle of mutual submission goes beyond roles and formulas and makes them unnecessary. It becomes a marriage of equal persons and makes possible the intimacy so many people are longing for today."

[Patricia Gundry, Heirs Together: Mutual Submission in Marriage *(Grand Rapids: Zondervan, 1980), pp. 19, 22–23.]*

Loving Spouse in Spite of Imperfections

The love required to sustain a marriage is quite different from the love that initially stimulates the marriage. Ruby Johnson writes of this regarding her own marriage. She discovered that the love that she and her fiancé had for each other before they were married, which was stimulated by their respective positive qualities, was not enough to carry them through the trials of married life. They had loved each other *because* they met each other's qualifications, not *in spite of* each other's imperfections.

"After our honeymoon, we discovered traits in one another that disturbed us. Icebergs in our sea of matrimony began to surface, chilling our voyage. Not only that, but we realized that colliding with any one of them could have wrecked our precious craft and destroyed our cargo. A collision such as that must be avoided.

"In answer to prayer, we learned how to change our course. We discovered that marriage needed another kind of love—*in-spite-of love.* That kind of love is unselfish.

"*Because love* is selfish. It says: he is handsome, therefore he makes me feel proud; he is kind, therefore he will comfort me; he is reliable, therefore he will give me security.

"*In-spite-of love* is different. It says: he is careless, therefore, even though it will make more work for me, I will try to compensate for his weakness and patiently endure; he is moody, and that disturbs my peace of mind, but I will do my best to help him cultivate a better mood; he is a spendthrift and that makes me feel insecure, but I will try to understand his generous spirit and charitable nature."

[Ruby E. Johnson, From the Heart of a Mother *(Chicago: Moody, 1982), pp. 46–47.]*

Need for Space in Marriage

In his book *The Prophet,* Kahlil Gibran eloquently reflects on the deep human need for space:

But let there be spaces in your togetherness,
And let the winds of the heavens dance between you.

Love one another, but make not a bond of love:
Let it rather be a moving sea between the shores of your souls.
Fill each other's cup but drink not from one cup.
Give one another of your bread but eat not from the same loaf.
Sing and dance together and be joyous, but let each one of you be alone,
Even as the strings of a lute are alone though they quiver with the same
    music.

Give your hearts, but not into each other's keeping.
For only the hand of Life can contain your hearts.
And stand together yet not too near together:
For the pillars of the temple stand apart,
And the oak tree and the cypress grow not in each other's shadow.

[Kahlil Gibran, The Prophet *(New York: Knopf, 1969), pp. 15–16.]*

Negative Views of Marriage

Charles Darwin agonized over whether or not to marry, and what effect that would have on his career. At one point he made a list of the pros and cons, and among the advantages of marriage were the following factors: "Children—(if it please God)—constant companion, (friend in old age) who will feel interested in one, object to be beloved and played with—better than a dog anyhow—Home, and someone to take care of house—Charms of music and female chit-chat. These things good for one's health. Forced to visit and receive relations *but terrible loss of time."*

When considering a life of singleness, however, Darwin became more emotional and added further reasons to buttress his case. "My God, it is intolerable to think of spending one's whole life, like a neuter bee, working, working and nothing after all.—No, no it won't do. . . . Imagine living all one's days solitary in smoky dirty London House.—Only picture to yourself a nice soft wife on a sofa with a good fire and books and music perhaps—compare this vision with the dingy reality of Grt Marlboro St." The specter of such a life apparently was too awful, for he concluded his list of advantages by scrawling at the bottom, "Marry—Marry—Marry."

[Peter Brent, Charles Darwin: "A Man of Enlarged Curiosity" *(New York: Harper & Row, 1981), p. 247.]*

Optimism about Marriage

Bolstered by statistics, many contemporary writers and speakers decry the decay in American family life and in marriage in particular.

The divorce rate in this country is indeed higher than that of any other Western nation, but there are also some factors that indicate that marriage is still an honored institution, despite the battering it has endured in recent decades. "Ninety percent of Americans marry," writes Cecil Osborne, "and the divorce rate is less disturbing when we remember that only a small fraction are repeat divorces. . . . The statistical evidence is still less disturbing when we remind ourselves that no other human relationship is fraught with so many possibilities of failure. There are no perfect marriages for the simple reason that there are no perfect people, and no one person can satisfy *all* of one's needs. The difficulty of achieving a workable marriage is compounded enormously by genetic differences between any two persons. Their environmental backgrounds are different, as are their personalities, needs, goals, drives, and emotional responses."

[Cecil Osborne, The Art of Understanding Your Mate *(Grand Rapids: Zondervan, 1970), pp. 9–10.]*

Positive Role of Problems in Marriage

Ruth Peale, the wife of Norman Vincent Peale, the well-known pastor of Riverside Church in New York City, writes openly of the marital problems and tensions she and her husband have experienced during their marriage of more than a half century. She believes that marital tensions are an inevitable part of the husband/wife relationship, and that they should not always be seen in a negative light. Indeed, she is suspect of those who live in marital bliss. "Countless times, talking with a married couple I've just met, I've had them say to me, 'Oh, yes, we've been married fifteen years (or twenty, or thirty) and we've never had a cross word between us.' I always smile and nod happily, but what I'm really thinking is, 'How dull! How boring! What a drag a marriage like that would be!" She goes on to say that bitter quarrels can be very destructive but that "disagreement between married partners can actually be constructive and useful."

[Ruth Peale, The Adventure of Being a Wife *(Englewood Cliffs, N.J.: Prentice-Hall, 1971), p. 155.]*

Sharing Pain and Suffering in Marriage

It is very difficult for starry-eyed lovers to consider the reality of a truly shared life together once they are married. Too often they are oblivious to the problems and pain that lie ahead of them and are not prepared to accept the fact that marriage, by its very nature of bringing two people together, increases the number of problems a person must face. His problems become hers, and vice versa. "Anybody's marriage is a harvest of suffering," writes Lewis B. Smedes. "Romantic lotus-eaters may tell you marriage was designed to be a pleasure-dome for erotic spirits to frolic in self-fulfilling relations. But they play you false. Your marriage vow was a promise to suffer. Yes, to suffer; I will not take it back. You promised to suffer, only to suffer *with,* however. You get your share of suffering *from,* will-nilly, thrown at you. You *promised* to suffer *with.* It made sense, because the person you married was likely to get hurt along the route, sooner or later, more or less, but hurt he or she was bound to get. And you promised to hurt *with* your spouse. A marriage is a life of shared pain.

"(Mind you, now, you did not vow to suffer *from* your spouse. If some clod of a husband hurts you by bashing you about bodily or spiritually, put a stop to it, now. Jesus does not want you to be a conjugal door-mat.)

"But a woman who is living inside a husband's pain while he is slowly, surely, devoured by cancer knows what suffering *with* can be like. Maybe it hurts her worse than it hurts him. Maybe she wants it to go away more than he does. . . .

"God's own answer to suffering is to join it, feel it, hurt with it. . . . This is why: When I get inside the life of another person, and feel her pain with her, I am on track with the ultimate meaning and power of the universe. Never mind that I do it poorly. Never mind that I don't like doing it at all. When I stick with the outrage of another's pain, I have joined Jesus. And that makes it all right with me. I have begun to be saved. I am an heir of God. It is all right with me, even though everything may be all wrong."

[Lewis B. Smedes, How Can It Be All Right When Everything Is All Wrong? (New York: Harper & Row, 1982), pp. 61, 68.]

MARRIAGE COUNSELING
Need for Counseling

Many people shun the idea of seeking help when their marriages are breaking down. They would not hesitate seeing a doctor for a physical illness or calling a plumber or auto mechanic when the need arose, but marriage is something that often goes without fixing—very frequently because the husband balks at the suggestion. Husbands, writes Cecil Osborne, will employ the services of other specialists, "but when his wife suggests they see a counselor about a marital problem, the typical response is 'No! We're adults; we'll work this out, ourselves. What can one of those head shrinkers tell us that we don't know already?' The human personality is roughly a hundred thousand times as complex as a television set, and the marriage relationship is much more complex than any other. It is a totally unrealistic, fear-ridden response on the part of the husband which causes him to reject professional help."

[*Cecil G. Osborne,* The Art of Understanding Your Mate *(Grand Rapids: Zondervan, 1970), p. 66.]*

MASCULINITY
Shunning Exclusive Masculinity

Mahatma Gandhi prided himself in being half man and half woman and "blatantly aspired to be more motherly than women born to the job." His biographer maintains that "he undoubtedly saw a kind of sublimated maternalism as part of the positive identity of a whole man, and certainly of a *homo religiosus.*" Indeed, Gandhi came close to renouncing his maleness physically. "All overt phallicism had become an expendable, if not a detestable matter to him." Not surprisingly, the reaction was not generally one of admiration. "Most men, of course, consider it not only unnecessary, but in a way, indecent, and even irreverent, to disavow a god-given organ of such singular potentials;

and they remain deeply suspicious of a sick element in such sexual self-disarmament. And needless to say, the suspicion of psychological self-castration becomes easily linked with the age-old male propensity for considering the renunciation of armament an abandonment of malehood."

[Erik H. Erikson, Gandhi's Truth: On the Origins of Militant Nonviolence (New York: Norton, 1969), pp. 402–3.]

MASTURBATION

A Problem to Be Avoided

Gini Andrews, a well-known Christian author, takes issue with modern-day psychologists who view masturbation as a harmless practice that can be an effective release of sexual tension. She admonishes single women to avoid falling into that trap if at all possible. "Self-love, loneliness, frustration, physical desire—these can all be strong motivations for the practice of masturbation, but God wants something better for His cherished ones. . . . In practicing masturbation you may find some consolation and release, but I think you'll like yourself better in the bright light of day if you've won through with God's help. Don't be discouraged: if you find you've been succumbing four or five times a week and reduce it to one or two, rejoice! This is progress. Rome, I've heard somewhere, wasn't built in a day, and God does know our weaknesses and will continue to aid. He may not wave a wand and deliver us instantly from every vestige of our habits; often there are trials and some heartbreaking failures—one step forward and two backward—but God is a God of victory, and He is concerned in *all* that enslaves you. He wants you to be a truly emancipated woman."

[Gini Andrews, Your Half of the Apple (Grand Rapids: Zondervan, 1972), pp. 96–97.]

Terrifying Consequences of Masturbation

During the nineteenth century ominous warnings were given to young people, especially boys, about the terrifying consequences of masturbation. Some of these dire effects were listed in William Alcott's book, entitled *Young Man's Guide*, in which he wrote, "The Young ought at least to know, briefly, to what a formidable host of maladies secret vice is exposed.

1. *Insanity.* The records of hospitals show that insanity, from solitary indulgence, is common. . . .
2. *Chorea Sancti Viti,* or *St. Vitus's dance.* . . .
3. *Epilepsy.* Epileptic or *falling sickness fits,* as they are sometimes denominated, are another very common scourge of secret vice. . . .
4. *Idiotism.* . . .
5. *Paralysis* or *Palsy,* is no uncommon punishment of this transgression. . . .
6. *Apoplexy.* This has occasionally happened; though more rarely.
7. *Blindness,* in some of its forms. . . . Indeed a weakness of sight is among the first symptoms that supervene on these occasions.
8. *Hypochondria.* This is as much a disease by itself as the small pox, though many regard it otherwise. The mind is diseased, and the individual has many imaginary sufferings. . . . [It] is a very common result of secret vice.
9. *Phthisis,* or consumption, is still more frequently produced by the cause we are considering, than any other disease I have mentioned. . . . Is it not madness to expose ourselves to its attacks for the shortlived gratifications of a moment?"

[*William A. Alcott,* The Young Man's Guide *(Boston: Marvin, 1846), pp. 337–40.*]

MATURITY

Moving from One Stage in Life to Another

One of the causes of discontent in life is the inability to cope with the aging process. This is true of children as well as adults. Moving from one stage of life to another is often accompanied by feelings of insecurity and stress. A mark of maturity is how gracefully an individual eases into a new and uncharted stage of life. Charles Swindoll, in his book *Growing Strong in the Seasons of Life,* discusses this maturing process in a spiritual context. "As each three-monthly segment of every year holds its own mysteries and plays its own melodies, offering sights and smells, feelings and fantasies altogether distinct, so it is in the seasons of life. The Master is neither mute nor careless as He alters our times and changes our seasons. How wrong to trudge blindly and routinely through a lifetime of changing seasons without discovering answers to the new mysteries and learning to sing the new melodies! Seasons are designed to deepen us, to instruct us in the wisdom and ways of our God. To help us grow strong . . . like a tree planted by the rivers of water."

[*Charles R. Swindoll,* Growing Strong in the Seasons of Life *(Portland: Multnomah Press, 1983), p. 13.*]

MEDICINE

For Women

It is not without significance that the first female medical doctor in the United States was prompted to make her career in the field of medicine in order to seek to alleviate some of the common physical ills suffered by those of her own sex. Concern for female disorders was not a top priority for most physicians, and she was convinced that more attention should be given to curing these common ailments. Her name was Elizabeth Blackwell, and in 1845, when she was in her early twenties, it was unthinkable that a woman should be a medical doctor. Indeed, the thought had not occurred to her until one day when she was visiting a friend who had a serious uterine disorder. She confessed that she had been suffering for a long time but had been too embarrassed to give the details of her problem to a male doctor. Knowing Elizabeth had a keen mind and was an avid reader, she suggested that she study medicine so that she could help women with maladies of such a personal nature. Like countless other women of this period, the woman died without proper medical treatment—a tragedy that made a powerful impression on Elizabeth. That women should be embarrassed about talking about gynecological problems was not simply due to their own prudishness. When the male-authored book *Female Physiology* came out in 1854, there was an outcry against it. It was considered indecent and offensive, and the public was strongly discouraged from reading it.

Elizabeth Blackwell applied to many different schools over a long period of time before she was finally accepted at the Geneva Medical College in New York. She graduated in 1849, "the acknowledged leader of the class," and she spent most of the remaining sixty years of her life working for the cause of understanding and treating female physical disorders.

[Margaret Forster, Significant Sisters: The Grassroots of Active Feminism, 1839–1939 *(New York: Knopf, 1985), pp. 63–70, 85.]*

MEN

Men's Lack of Friendships

It is interesting that male friendships have historically been idealized in literature and viewed as the deepest and truest of relationships. Indeed, "for centuries, friendship between men was the paradigm of human comradeship, mutual trust, loyalty, compatibility, and selfless love." At the same time, friendship between women was denigrated. "Hundreds if not thousands of writers and social scientists from Homer to Freud have shared the view that women are incapable of deep, enduring friendship for various reasons, ranging from their supposed solipsism and superficiality to their competition for husbands and their inferior psychosexual development." In fact, according to recent studies, the very opposite is true. Interviews with large numbers of men have indicated that most have no real friends at all, though many spoke of casual acquaintances as such. Men were found to value friendship less than women and to be far less interested in sharing intimate concerns with other men.

[Letty Gottin Pogrebin, Among Friends: Who We Like, Why We Like Them, and What We Do with Them *(New York: McGraw-Hill, 1987), pp. 252–53.]*

"Pseudo-Liberated Male"

Many women are highly attracted to what they perceive to be the liberated male—what psychologists Connell Cowan and Melvyn Kinder call the "Pseudo-Liberated Male." This type of man "seems gentle and sensitive, vulnerable, expressive, revealing—a real dream come true! But it's a dream that frequently turns into a nightmare." Too often this man sees his newfound liberation as opportunity to "express endless fears and personal insecurities, often to the point of utter distraction." Women are often enticed by such men, because they are being led to believe that such qualities are the real mark of a caring man. But too often it is the woman who becomes the victim. "This man hides the fact that he is an emotional drain, that he's a taker. He is so happy and relieved to have a chance to legitimize his insecurity and neediness that he doesn't realize that he is taking without giving. He sincerely believes that his emotional diarrhea is a gift. He hides his fears and passivity beneath a deceptive costume of gentleness and sensitivity—and hopes that the woman won't see through his disguises. . . . These men are sensitive, and that can be a refreshing experience. The problem is that, as time goes by, it becomes increasingly apparent that their sensitivity is one-sided, directed consistently toward themselves."

[Connell Cowan and Melvyn Kinder, Smart Women, Foolish Choices *(New York: Potter, 1985), pp. 91–93.]*

MENSTRUATION

A Cause of Insanity?

The female "sickness" was at one time widely believed to be the cause of mental illness among women. Henry Putnam Stearns, the nineteenth-century author of *Insanity: Its Causes and Prevention,* was a lecturer at Yale and the director of a Connecticut insane asylum. On the basis of his study and observations, he concluded that "in a general way the sexual system in the female exerts a much larger influence on the whole physical and mental economy, than in the male. A very intimate sympathy exists between it and both the stomach and the brain. This becomes especially manifest at the period of puberty, and continues until after the cessation of menstruation. The whole moral nature appears to come into existence and activity when the child becomes a woman, and thereafter, for thirty or thirty-five years, the whole person is largely affected one fourth of the time by the functional activity of the pelvic organ." The mental problems were generally most severe among unmarried women who were often found to be "nervous, capricious, irritable, and hysterical" because of "uterine derangement of one kind or another."

[*Henry Putnam Stearns,* Insanity: Its Causes and Prevention *(New York: Putnam's, 1883), pp. 188–91.*]

"If Men Did"

The monthly menstrual period that women endure is generally viewed as a nuisance, and it is difficult to imagine its being a facet of life that could bring any stature or dignity, but Gloria Steinem suggests that it would be entirely different if men menstruated instead of women.

"So what would happen if suddenly, magically, men could menstruate and women could not?

"Clearly, menstruation would become an enviable, boast-worthy, masculine event:

"Men would brag about how long and how much.

"Young boys would talk about it as the envied beginning of manhood. Gifts, religious ceremonies, family dinners, and stag parties would mark the day.

"To prevent monthly work loss among the powerful, Congress would fund a National Institute of Dysmenorrhea. Doctors would research little about heart attacks, from which men were hormonally protected, but everything about cramps.

"Sanitary supplies would be federally funded and free. Of course, some men would still pay for the prestige of such commercial brands as Paul Newman Tampons, Muhammad Ali's Rope-a-Dope Pads, John Wayne Maxi Pads, and Joe Namath Jock Shields—'For Those Light Bachelor Days.'

"Statistical surveys would show that men did better in sports and won more Olympic medals during their periods.

"Generals, right-wing politicians, and religious fundamentalists would cite menstruation (*'men-struation'*) as proof that only men could serve God and country in combat ('You have to give blood to take blood'), occupy high political office ('Can women be properly fierce without a monthly cycle governed by the planet Mars?'), be priests, ministers, God Himself ('He gave this blood for our sins'), or rabbis ('Without a monthly purge of impurities, women are unclean')."

[Gloria Steinem, Outrageous Acts and Everyday Rebellions *(New York: Holt, Reinhart & Winston, 1983), p. 338.]*

Myths about Menstruation

Through the centuries there have been many myths and customs relating to the woman's menstrual period. The ancient manuscript *Natural History of Pliny* blames crop blight, metal rust, and other problems and natural disasters on the close proximity of menstruating women. In certain cultures women were not permitted to prepare food during their monthly period for fear the food would spoil or the milk would sour, and in other cultures menstruation was associated with demonic activity.

[Letha Scanzoni and Nancy Hardesty, All We're Meant to Be *(Waco: Word Books, 1974), p. 126.]*

Religious Restrictions Regarding Menstruation

It was customary for many medieval churchmen to place restrictions on women during the menstrual period and immediately following childbirth. The restrictions took many forms but were most commonly related to the sacraments. In 601, Augustine of Canterbury (who had been sent to England as a missionary some years earlier) wrote to Pope Gregory I, inquiring about these very restrictions. The true character of Gregory is indicated by his response. He argued that it would make no sense to refuse baptism to a pregnant woman—denying her the gift of grace through baptism to one whose very condition was evidence of God's gift of fertility. As to whether an "unclean" woman could enter a church and partake of the sacrament, Gregory reminded Augustine of the women (with an apparent menstrual problem) who touched the hem of Christ's garment. Thus it was not sin for such women to partake.

Gregory's pronouncement did not settle the matter, however. Several decades later Theodore, who was then bishop of Canterbury, reverted to the old practice of restricting women following pregnancy and while menstruating, and such restrictions continued during the medieval period in England and on the Continent as well.

[Joan Morris, The Lady Was a Bishop: The Hidden History of Women with Clerical Ordination and the Jurisdiction of Bishops *(New York: Macmillan, 1973), pp. 110–11.]*

MENTAL ILLNESS
Difficult to Treat

Very often the individuals who most need treatment by a psychologist or psychiatrist are the very ones who most defiantly reject it. This is what M. Scott Peck has discovered in his many years as a practicing psychiatrist. "It is a sad state of affairs, but the fact of the matter is that the healthiest people—the most honest, whose patterns of thinking are least distorted—are the very ones easiest to treat with psychotherapy and most likely to benefit from it. Conversely, the sicker the patients—the more dishonest in their behavior and distorted in their thinking—the less able we are to help them with any degree of success. When they are very distorted and dishonest, it seems impossible."

[M. Scott Peck, People of the Lie: The Hope for Healing Human Evil *(New York: Simon & Schuster, 1983), p. 63.]*

MINISTRY
Fulfilling Impossible Dreams

Jo Berry, a widely traveled women's speaker and workshop leader, challenges women to have high aspirations and "think creatively" as they reflect on the gifts God has given them for ministry. "God plants those dreams, wants, wishes, visions, and 'if only I could's' in us if we are delighting Him. Why is it that we think that if something appeals to us, it must be wrong? How many times have we quenched our Spirit-planted desires?" Jo relates her own experience of dreaming big and her accompanying sense of guilt.

"The first time I was aware of a Spirit-planted desire, I thought I was sinning. My dear friend Georgia Lee, who is a Christian actress and speaker, was standing in the podium at a large conference center, speaking to about eight hundred women. As I watched her I remember thinking, 'Someday I want to do what she is doing. I want to talk to huge groups of women about the Lord.'

"When I realized what I was thinking, I guiltily looked around to see if anyone had sensed my 'envy.' I was ashamed and asked God to forgive me for coveting my friend's position. But that desire did not go away; rather, it grew in intensity. And several years later, when I was standing at that same podium, teaching about eight hundred women, I recounted the story with tears in my eyes. I knew by then I wasn't covetous, because I in no way wanted to detract or interfere with Georgia Lee's ministry. I knew that the Holy Spirit of God had planted that desire in my heart and then had brought it to pass."

[Jo Berry, Growing, Sharing, Serving (Elgin, Ill.: Cook, 1979), pp. 66–67.]

Marriage Problems and Christian Ministry

People who are involved in Christian ministry often are afraid to admit they are struggling with deep personal problems—fearing the knowledge of such would damage the ministry. This is particularly true with marriage problems. Marriage breakdowns frequently occur because there was no treatment sought after in the early stages of the difficulty. Patti Roberts writes of this in relation to her own marriage to Oral Roberts's son Richard and to other people she has talked with.

"It is not unusual for me to receive a phone call in the middle of the night from a well-known Christian and hear him say, 'I am living in hell, but I can't do anything about it, because I'll let the cat out of the bag if I admit it. And I've got to keep up my work; I've got to keep up my ministry. It would present a fragmented front to the public if I sought counseling. Besides, I'd be too embarrassed to talk to a counselor. Everyone expects me to have my life together.'

"Sadly, these people often feel owned by, and responsible to, the ministry even more than they feel responsible to God. God forgives, but institutions do not. People can't take the time or the risk of seeking healing, because if the healing process in any way impinges on the operation of the institution, the institution immediately speaks out and demands loyalty. . . . So, rather than risk angering the institution, some Christians continue to live fragmented, destructive lives. But holding a marriage together for the sake of the ministry rather than the sanctity of their scriptural vows does not please God. God places tremendous importance on truth in human relationships, and when two people are living a lie in order to protect a ministry, they are violating God's definition of marriage."

[Patti Roberts, with Sherry Andrews, Ashes to Gold (Waco: Word Books, 1983), pp. 112–13.]

Ministry without Ministering

In her book *Ms. Means Myself,* Gladys Hunt talks about women who are gifted for ministries but fail to appropriate those gifts properly to maximize the ministry. "The challenge in exercising a gift in the ministry is to do for others rather than for self-gratification. The musician who wants to minister to others will keep the needs of her audience in mind. Otherwise she may show excellent voice control and a marvelous range, but there will be no ministry. Teachers do not teach subjects, they teach people, if they want to minister. . . .

"I think of a diligent woman who volunteered to be in charge of the visual aid materials for a small school. She wanted a ministry. She became obsessed with the perfection of the materials and their arrangement. She worked very hard, and did an excellent job. But she became possessive. Procedures for the use of materials became so complicated that people stopped using them. She had a perfect department with no ministry. People are the point of any ministry, and we do well to remind ourselves of this."

[Gladys Hunt, Ms. Means Myself (Grand Rapids: Zondervan, 1972), p. 120.]

No Room for Women in Ministry

The Christian church throughout history has closed the door to strong women who have felt called into leadership roles. This has been a monumental loss to the outreach of the church, a fact that was recognized more than a half century ago by Lee Anna Starr, a Greek scholar and an ordained minister in the Methodist Protestant church.

"The Church of England afforded no room for the talent and energy of Catherine Booth, 'The Mother of the Salvation Army,' so she took her stand by the side of her husband, William Booth, in the work of evangelizing the degraded classes in London. She became a preacher and turned many to righteousness. She was the mother of eight children, seven of whom became preachers. . . .

"The church had no room for the ministries of Maud Ballington Booth, so she wended her way to jails and penitentiaries, with God's word in her hand, and His love in her heart, and today an army inside prison walls, and thousands who have served their term and been released revere her as 'The Little Mother.'

"Clara Barton found scant encouragement for her God appointed task within the courts of His sanctuary, so stepped outside and founded the ever alert, ever prepared organization—The American Red Cross—an organization that may be characterized as Christianity in action.

"We might extend this list indefinitely. We might add the name of Miss Robart of London, who, in 1839, organized the Young Woman's Christian Association; Elizabeth Fry, whose consecrated efforts tamed 'the savages of Newgate prison'; Florence Nightingale, 'The Angel of the Crimea,' who was in deed and truth, the forerunner of the Red Cross; Anna Wittenmyer, whose great work in the Christian Commission during the Civil War, was the means of saving thousands of lives and the restoring of invalided soldiers to health and usefulness. . . . Jane Addams, the Shepherdess of the Hull House Settlement; and a host of others whose names might well be inscribed high on the scroll of the world's benefactors.

"The church afforded these women of ten talents no tasks commensurate with their ability, so they lifted their eyes and looked on the fields outside, and lo! they were 'white already unto the harvest,' and the laborers few. In the need, they read God's call to the larger service.

The church lost, but the world gained when they responded: 'Here am I: send me.' Who can charge them with dereliction?"

[Lee Anna Starr, The Bible Status of Woman (Zarephath, N.J.: Pillar of Fire, 1926), pp. 386–87.]

Pitfalls of Women's Ministries

It is not an easy task to organize a women's ministries program in a local church or simply to plan meetings for women to attend, but even those who imagine they are successful are often missing the mark in offering effective ministry to women. Daisy Hepburn deals with this issue in her book *How to Grow a Women's Minis-Tree.*

"One of the greatest pitfalls of ministry is to choose the path of least resistance by hiring a speaker, sending out publicity and even notices, arranging for some special music and gathering a crowd. Depending upon the size of the response you no doubt will feel that your ministry, as a whole, is a success or failure.

"But above and beyond this immediate experience, this kind of approach to ministry excludes the opportunity of ever *really* coming to grips with the specific need women have in your community. Putting on a program and *hoping* someone will come or giving women the opportunity to hear yet another speaker is missing the mark. It is a far more productive ministry that (1) catches sight of what the real needs of the women are and (2) plans programs that really touch and affect lives. May we stop congregating people who will meet anonymously and come away with information that they find 'interesting' or 'thought-provoking.' The Lord Jesus calls us to be life-changers."

[Daisy Hepburn, How to Grow a Women's Minis-Tree: Harvesting the Power of God's Woman (Ventura, Calif.: Regal Books, 1986), pp. 22–23.]

Service-Oriented Ministry

There has been a great deal of debate in recent years as to the nature of Christian ministry—a debate that has focused to a large extent on whether or not women ought to be permitted certain roles in Christian ministry. If the true nature of Christian ministry is viewed as servanthood, few would deny women opportunities to serve. But if the nature of ministry is viewed as authority or power, then women are often restricted from upper levels of the power structure. Patricia Gundry, a well-known Christian feminist, speaks to this issue.

"I, being a Baptist in background, think of ministry always in terms of service, mutual service. I never think, regarding the Church, in terms of authority, office, or ruling. To me, a leader is someone who goes where others want to follow. He or she has no superiority in essence or in position. And I think that my orientation has much to recommend it both biblically and practically.

"If I am right, and ministry *is* service, then we do not need anyone human to validate it for us. We do not need an ecclesiastical body to give us a special item of clothing to validate our ministry, or a special service that passes us into a fraternal group, an initiation by ordeal and touch (ordination seems that way to me). If we are led by God and our own inclination to minister, then we do it. The question is *how*, not *if*."

To Patricia Gundry, D. L. Moody is a role model for both women and men for this type of ministry. "In a day when the clergy were the intellectual upper crust, he was an uneducated man who dared to believe that he could serve God by simply doing the obvious to the best of his ability. He noticed that the poor people of Chicago were not present in the rented pews for the clean and starched, moneyed churchgoers. So he started his work among the slums. His ability to reach people by 'just talking to them,' a startling contrast to the stuffy orations of most preachers of that time, caused people to crowd in to hear him. He never sought ordination, believing it would restrict his ability to reach a wide range of people. He thought he did not need it. And, of course, he didn't.

"Moody . . . began small with what he could do. He did that well. That was his ministry. That's what I think ministry is. If you find your ministry that way, the restrictions of form and structure will not stop you or shrink your possibilities."

[Patricia Gundry, Neither Slave nor Free: Helping Women Answer the Call to Church Leadership *(San Francisco: Harper & Row, 1987), pp. 71–72.]*

MIRACLES

Multiplying Drops of Medicine

During their imprisonment at the Nazi death camp of Ravensbruck, Corrie ten Boom and her sister Betsie agonized under the ill-treatment and privations accorded them by their captors. Yet, amid all the hardship they credited God with miraculous protection in the times of their deepest need. During one very difficult period when Betsie was very ill, Corrie realized that the tiny bottle of Davitamon was down to the very last drops. "My instinct," she wrote, "was always to hoard it— Betsie was growing so very weak! But others were ill as well. It was hard to say no to eyes that burned with fever, hands that shook with chill. I tried to save it for the very weakest—but even these soon numbered fifteen, twenty, twenty-five. . . ."

Betsie reminded Corrie of the biblical account of the poor widow of Zarephath who ministered to Elijah and whose handful of meal and small amount of oil lasted as long as there was need, but Corrie initially discounted the possibility of such a miracle in modern times. "And still, every time I tilted the little bottle, a drop appeared at the tip of the glass stopper. It just couldn't be! I held it up to the light, trying to see how much was left, but the dark brown glass was too thick to see through."

Each day she continued to dispense the drops, until one day when a female guard, who had shown kindness to the prisoners before, sneaked a small sack of vitamins into the barracks for them. Corrie was elated, but she determined that they would first finish the drops in the bottle. "But that night, no matter how long I held it upside down, or how hard I shook it, not another drop appeared."

[Corrie ten Boom, with John Sherrill and Elizabeth Sherrill, The Hiding Place (Old Tappan, N.J.: Revell, 1971), pp. 202–3.]

MISCARRIAGE

Grieving as for a Fully Formed Child

In the book *Free to Grieve,* Maureen Rank tells the story of visiting with a pregnant friend who referred matter-of-factly to the death of her unborn child, "The baby wasn't stillborn—it was just a miscarriage."

"Beverly's apology revealed the fact that she had accepted a myth of mourning which our society holds onto very tightly. It assumes that the more days you've had with a person, the more attached you become; therefore, the harder it is to lose him or her in death. It's the belief in this theory that causes people to say, 'How good that the baby didn't live any longer than a few hours, or you could have become so attached.' Or 'At least you'd only been pregnant three months when you miscarried. Imagine how much harder it would have been to carry to term, and then lose it.'

"Sometimes this theory holds true; sometimes it doesn't. Of course, the loss of a friend in which you've invested twenty years of yourself will tear the fabric of your heart so that it will never be the same again. But not everyone you've known twenty years has touched you in the same way. And haven't there been those you've been with but a short time, who have so deeply affected your life that the pain of separation from them never quite heals?

"So it can be with these babies of ours. Even if your child died so early that his tiny body was barely formed, the loss of who that little one was to you may be mourned deeply, and rightly so."

[Maureen Rank, Free to Grieve (Minneapolis: Bethany House, 1985), pp. 27–28.]

"Is It Proper to Cry?"

Is it proper to cry
For a baby too small
For a coffin?
Yes, I think it is.
Does Jesus have
My too-small baby
In His tender arms?
Yes, I think He does.
There is so much I do not know
About you, my child—
He, she? quiet or restless?
Will I recognize
Someone I knew so little about
Yet loved so much?
Yes, I think I will.
Can we say
Your life was worth nothing
Because your stay was so short?
Can we say
We loved you any less
Because we never held you?
No, I think not.
Ah, sweet, small child.
Can I say
That loving you is like loving God?
    Loving—yet not seeing
    Holding—yet not touching
    Caressing—yet separated by the chasm of time.
No tombstone marks your sojourn
And only God recorded your name.
I had neither opportunity
Nor capability
To say good-bye.
Not saying good-bye
Is just as hard
As saying good-bye.

The preparations are halted,
The royal guest was called away.
The banquet was canceled.
Just moved. Just moved.
Yet a tear remains
Where baby should have been.
    Dedicated to my baby
    this September 17, 1983
    Age: — 6 months
    Sex: unknown
    Weight: unknown
    Color of eyes: unknown
    Loved: by the Father, Son and
        Holy Spirit and by Mommy
        and Daddy

—BOB NEUDORF

[Alliance Life, *September 16, 1987, p. 14.*]

MISSIONARY SERVICE

Desire for Service

Ann Hasseltine, who was converted in a New England revival in the early nineteenth century, had a strong desire to join the foreign missionary crusade that was just beginning on this side of the Atlantic. She married Adoniram Judson, who would become one of America's most renowned missionaries, but she considered herself much more than simply a missionary wife. She testified of a "call" that prompted her to go abroad despite the dangers, and after she arrived in Burma, she wrote of her desire to have a fruitful ministry. "I desire to no higher enjoyment in this life, than to be instrumental of leading some poor, ignorant females to the knowledge of the Saviour. To have a female praying society, consisting of those who were once in heathen darkness, is what my heart earnestly pants after, and makes a constant subject of prayer. [I am] resolved to keep this in view; as one principal object of my life."

[James D. Knowles, Memoir of Mrs. Ann H. Judson (Boston: Lincoln & Edmands, 1829), p. 58.]

Fear of Missionary Service

Although Ann Hasseltine Judson later developed a great compassion for women "in heathen darkness" and was one of the most dedicated women missionaries of all time, her initial reaction to going overseas as the first female missionary from the United States was one of fear. Indeed, for weeks she agonized over the decision. "For several weeks past, my mind has been greatly agitated. An opportunity has been presented to me, of spending my days among the heathen, in attempting to persuade them to receive the Gospel. . . . I have felt ready to sink, being distressed with fears about my spiritual state, and appalled at the prospect of pain and suffering, to which my nature is so adverse, and apprehensive, that when assailed by temptation, or exposed to danger and death, I should not be able to endure, as seeing Him who is invisible." Finally after many weeks of indecision, she felt peace about going. "Yes, I think I would rather go to India, among the heathen, notwithstanding the almost insurmountable difficulties in the way, than to stay at home and enjoy the comforts and luxuries of life. Faith in Christ will enable me to bear trials, however severe."

[James D. Knowles, Memoir of Mrs. Ann H. Judson (Boston: Lincoln & Edmands, 1829), pp. 37–41.]

Need for Missionaries

Ruth Hitchcock, a missionary to China, tells in her autobiography how God first impressed upon her the need for missionary service when she was only ten years old. Horace Houlding, a missionary from China, was staying in her home, and he told a story that she would never forget. "On the great plains near the Yellow River, the peasants sow their wheat at the beginning of winter and then wait for the snow to cover it. During those snowy winter months they are shut up in their houses, busy with indoor things such as shoe-making, spinning, weaving, and sewing. One winter a man came two days' journey by cart to the Houldings' mission station. He asked for a missionary to go back with him to his village during this quiet winter time to tell the people the good news which they had heard was available from these foreigners. Later on, the farmers would be too busy in their fields to listen, but now they were free. The missionaries thought this a wonderful opportunity. Who could return with the messenger? To their dismay, everyone was busy with the work they already had at the mission station. No one could be freed to go. Though the man begged them to find someone, he finally had to return alone with his cart to that village where they wanted to hear the Gospel. At the beginning of the next winter he appeared again—and again the bleak decision was reached. No one could go. The cart crept slowly back across the miles." After hearing that, Ruth writes, "In my heart the resolve grew: 'Lord, when I grow up, I'll go.'"

[*Ruth Hitchcock*, The Good Hand of Our God *(Elgin, Ill.: Cook, 1975), pp. 14–15.*]

Support of Missionaries

Throughout the nineteenth century, evangelical women provided the support base for foreign missions. The women's "mite societies" sent out the first missionaries from American shores, and after they arrived on the field, they wrote back to their churches imploring women to do even more. "Adoniram Judson enjoined American women to forsake 'the demon vanity' for the amelioration of their sisters in the East," and he suggested they form "Plain Dress Societies." Church publications supporting missions made similar requests of the women in their denominations. "American Christian women were perceived as having a special responsibility to practice 'proper economy' within the home and in terms of their personal attire. The mites they saved by eschewing necklaces, ear ornaments, and the seductions of creative millinery were to be set aside for their heathen sisters."

[Joan Jacobs Brumberg, Mission for Life *(New York: Free Press, 1980), p. 88.]*

MODESTY

Standards in Ancient Times

Plutarch, a Greek biographer and essayist who lived at the time of the close of the New Testament, had a very high standard of modesty for women. He spoke of one woman in particular, but then applied the illustration to all women in general. "Theano, in putting her cloak about her exposed her arm. Somebody exclaimed, 'A Lovely arm.' 'But not for the public,' she said. Not only the arm of the virtuous woman, but her speech as well, ought to be not for the public, and she ought to be modest and guarded about saying anything in the hearing of outsiders, since it is an exposure of herself; for in her talk can be seen her feelings, character, and disposition."

[Livy, History of Rome *34.1–8; quoted in Ruth A. Tucker and Walter L. Liefeld,* Daughters of the Church: Women and Ministry from New Testament Times to the Present *(Grand Rapids: Zondervan, 1987), p. 76.]*

Victorian Prudishness

There are many examples of Victorian prudishness in both England and America, many of which are amusing to the modern reader. "Edward Livingston, a pioneer judicial reformer, omitted certain sexual offenses from a model law code he drafted for the new state of Louisiana, reasoning that a body of laws should be open to the public and 'as every crime must be defined, the details of such a definition would inflict a lasting wound on the morals of the people.' To talk about sexual transgressions, even for the sake of punishing them, would, in Livingston's view, encourage depravity."

Of even greater concern during the Victorian age was personal modesty. Capt. Frederick Marryat, a sailor and novelist, found American standards curious at best. That Americans could not permit any nudity or other forms of immodesty in their statues should not have surprised him, but he "further cited the example of a girl whose modesty was so highly developed that she was deeply offended when he used the word 'leg' to refer to the 'limb' she injured in a fall. He later discovered Americans who, to his astonishment, felt that legs were risqué even on musical instruments. In a seminary for young ladies he happened upon a piano, the four 'limbs' of which were concealed 'in modest little trousers, with frills at the bottom of them.' "

[Ronald G. Walters, Primers for Prudery: Sexual Advice to Victorian America *(Englewood Cliffs, N.J.: Prentice-Hall, 1974), pp. 1–2.]*

MONEY

Miserliness

Despite her great wealth, Mrs. Rose Kennedy was very tight with money. She was a very religious woman who attended mass daily and always left an offering. "Every morning she put one dollar in the collection box, never more and never less." Because the large residence in Palm Beach had been willed to the children (with the provision that she could live in it as long as she desired), Mrs. Kennedy objected to the use of her funds for upkeep. The home was shabby, with tiles falling off the roof, worn linoleum floors, and curtains hanging in shreds, but she held on to her millions, not wanting to spend money on what would only increase the value of her children's inheritance. But it was not just major repair jobs that concerned her. Indeed, after her husband died, "Mrs. Kennedy often ended up worrying most about the smallest expenses. She would become obsessed with the idea that she was spending too much money for phone service and decide to take out some of the extensions—a convenience that cost only $6.50 a month in a house worth millions. Or she would get all fired up about making a donation to the local thrift shop, and she and I [her personal secretary] would spend hours sorting through old clothes and household goods. . . . Many of the things she donated weren't even salable. The funniest example I remember was when she gave the Hyannis thrift shop *one* of Teddy's old sneakers."

She was excessively frugal in her eating habits as well. For lunch on one occasion, she insisted on having a left-over baked potato from the previous day. Her secretary had thrown it out, but rather than confess that to her boss, she dutifully went through the trash and retrieved it.

Even when it came to her grandchildren, it was impossible for Mrs. Kennedy to show any extravagance. "Each of the twenty-nine grandchildren, even the ones who were then in their teens, got just fifteen dollars on their birthday. Exceptions to this rule were rare. One year Pat Lawford suggested that it would be nice for Mrs. Kennedy to give her godchild Victoria Lawford a portable electric typewriter for her birthday. Mrs. Kennedy responded to this suggestion with a very funny letter about the impossibility of spending such a large amount as $125."

[*Barbara Gibson, with Caroline Latham,* Life with Rose Kennedy *(New York: Warner Books, 1986), pp. 78–79, 124–25.]*

MORALITY

Evident in Words More Than Deeds

In an age when the issue of morality is front-page headlines in the news and an organization named "Moral Majority" can wield powerful influence in political circles, the whole concept of morality is being redefined and challenged. Marilyn French offers one of these definitions.

"Morality is a neutral term: it has no specific content. It refers to the set of values by which we judge, which guide our behavior and even our emotions. Morals are our real values—not qualities we claim to revere, to which we give lip service and not much more. Our moral system is a system of priorities, or rather, a texture, an interlocking set of shifting, ambivalent, and conditional goods and ills. Our morality manifests itself in our choices—how we live, to what we devote our time and money, the kinds of friends we make, the way we spend our leisure, and above all, the kind of person we become, the kind of person we want to be. The morality of a society also manifests itself in its choices: how much it spends on what; its language and art; its mode of production and what it produces; its mode of ordering itself and the kind of order deemed desirable."

[Marilyn French, Beyond Power: On Women, Men, and Morals *(New York: Summit Books, 1985), p. 16.]*

MOTHER

Blame for Children's Behavior

Psychologists of the twentieth century have been notorious for blaming the mother for everything that goes wrong with the children in society. Juvenile delinquency grew considerably during the early decades of the century, and there were many efforts to reverse the trend. "One thing was clear: Mother was to blame. And as the juvenile-justice system grew, so did the charges against 'Mom.' By mid-century psychiatrist Marynia Farnham and writer Ferdinand Lundberg, warning readers that Hitler was his mother's son, could identify four kinds of bad mothers: the rejecting, the overprotective, the dominating, and the overaffectionate. All of them ruined their sons. (The experts were never much concerned with the fate of the daughters.) The overaffectionate mother produced 'sissies' or 'passive-homosexual males,' while the rejecting, overprotective, and dominating mothers 'produced the delinquents, the difficult behavior problem children' and 'some substantial percentage of criminals.' 'Momism' had become a major social problem, and Mom, when not a criminal herself, the mother of criminals."

[Ann Jones, Women Who Kill *(New York: Holt, Rinehart & Winston, 1980), p. 249.]*

Memorial to Mother

Linda Ellerbee, who has attracted national attention for her fresh style in television news, confessed that she was much indebted to her mother, who lived in a different era and never had the opportunities to excel that she herself had had. She made this known publicly shortly after her mother's death. "For me, the most personal thing I ever said on the air had to do with my mother, who had recently died. I said that she'd wanted to go to college but there was no money, that she'd wanted to work but her husband wouldn't let her, that she'd wanted to go into politics but she knew no other women in politics. She'd said it wasn't her time. Instead, she'd pushed me to read, to stretch, even when she didn't agree with what I read or where I stretched. She said it was my time, and so I pointed out on the air that this two minutes at the end of a television show was indeed my time and I wanted to use it to say a public and sincere thank you, from my time to hers, from me to her. It was hard for me to write, harder to say. I'd buried her only two weeks before. It was also hard for me to open up that way on television; it was contrary to everything I'd been taught about television and our role in it. One is not supposed to use the medium for personal statements and one is not supposed to let the audience get that close, but I did not do it for television, I did it for my mom."

[Linda Ellerbee, And So It Goes: Adventures in Television (New York: Putnam's Sons, 1986), pp. 181–82.]

Overmothering

Sue Hubbell, the mother of one child, a son, tells of the struggle she had with being overprotective of him. Initially, she was almost uncaring and aloof, but that quickly changed. "When I was pregnant with Brian, I was pleased, curious and interested, but somehow detached and objective about the baby I was carrying. I was young, and had no notion of what he would mean to me." After she held him for the first time, however, the mother love suddenly manifested itself. "There was a fierceness to the love that was born the instant I saw him that startled and bewildered me. It was uncivilized, crude, unquestioning, unreasoning." She did not fully comprehend that love until some years later when she and her family were awakened one night while camping by "an old sow bear who had wandered into our campsite with her cub. Her baby had strayed to the other side of our tent. She was frantic, fierce, angry, and would have become dangerous had not the cub waddled back to his mother of his own accord."

From this incident, Sue made analogies in her own life. "In order to become an adequate mother, I had to learn to keep the old sow bear under control. Sow-bear love is a dark, hairy sort of thing. It wants to hold, to protect; it is all emotion and conservatism. Raising up a man child in the middle of twentieth-century America to be independent, strong, capable and free to use his wit, intellect and abilities required other kinds of love. Keeping the sow bear from making a nuisance of herself may be the hardest thing there is to being a mother. Over the years she snuffed about when he learned to walk and explored the edges of high places, whenever he was unhappy, when he went off to boarding school, when he started driving a car. It was the sow bear who fifteen years ago pushed me into organizing a chapter of a peace group, and to become a draft counselor on the Brown University campus where I was working. It seemed just possible in those days that Brian might turn eighteen with a war still in progress. Even if I had to organize a whole peace movement to keep it from happening, no government was going to be allowed to send my son off to war."

Sue eventually came to terms with her overmothering instincts. "I did learn to live with the old bear. Fortunately, so did Brian; he and I understand one another pretty well."

[Sue Hubbell, A Country Year: Living the Questions (New York: Random House, 1983), pp. 89–91.]

Reflection of God's Character in Motherhood

It is important for mothers (as well as fathers) to realize that their children's understanding of God can be deeply influenced by the relationship they have with their parents while growing up. To some people God is an absentee landlord who intervenes when a payment is due, or perhaps he is someone who is called on only during a serious crisis.

"How different in turning to God as our Mother," writes Herbert Lockyer, reflecting on Isaiah 66:13. "And mark, the prophet is not thinking of a little child, but of a grown man heartsore and broken, fleeing back for the comfort of his mother's presence. 'As a man whom his mother comforteth, so I will comfort you.' Many a man weary and broken by a pitiless world, with things against him, and fortunes ruined, or with dear ones gone, or faith almost giving way, or entangled in the net of sin, has retreated in such dark, lone hours to the mother who gave him being. Many a man has crept back home like a wounded animal and has cast himself upon the mother love that warmed his heart in childhood days.

"And here is God, the source of our being, the ancient home to which all belong, offering Himself to us as the divine, eternal Mother.

> The watchful mother tarries nigh
> Though sleep has closed her infant's eye;
> For should he wake, and find her gone,
> She knows she could not bear his moan.
> But I am weaker than a child,
> And Thou are more than mother dear;
> Without Thee, heaven were but a wild;
> Without Thee, earth a desert drear.

[Herbert Lockyer, All the Women of the Bible *(Grand Rapids: Zondervan, 1985), p. 302.]*

Regrets after a Mother's Death

Jane Howard, a journalist who grew up in the Midwest in the 1950s, has looked back on her life with some regrets—one of the most poignant being her lack of closeness and communication with her mother. She and her mother failed to talk woman-to-woman as she wished later they had, and since then she has traveled across the country talking to women, asking their insights on issues they care about. "Maybe it is to atone for my own pretense, my own evasions," she writes, "that I have been preoccupied since my mother's death with what I hope has been honest talk with surviving women." Of her own mother she speaks with remorse. "Quite often I wish that we had talked to her, and she to us, less guardedly. Now and then I see some woman on the street or in a store who from a distance, for a split second, looks like her. If it were, I would go talk with her, with fewer evasions and nervous silences than we had when she was around. What, I wonder, were we all afraid of? Why was there so much pretense on both sides?"

[Jane Howard, A Different Woman *(New York: Dutton, 1973), p. 28.]*

Relationship of Mother with Son

How can a mother have a healthy, nurturing, and positive influence on her son that will prepare him adequately for life? Sonya Friedman, a nationally known clinical psychologist, paints a portrait of this kind of mother. "Such a woman tells her son that women are to be loved, considered, and respected. . . . A mother's demonstration of affection will show her son that, in fact, affection is natural, important, and not necessarily a prelude to sex. A good mother prepares her son to take care of someone else. She gives him a sense of worth, a clear idea of his place in the world—neither exalted nor debased. She will be instrumental, as well, in determining the nature and level of his ambitions. Finally, his understanding of a woman's desires and needs will come from her.

"It is easy to be a healthy mother to a son, but you must be a healthy woman first. If you are not, you can come to hate him, clutch at him, haunt him, and bind him to you for the rest of your lives."

[Sonya Friedman, Men Are Just Desserts *(New York: Warner Books, 1983), pp. 145–46.]*

Unaffectionate Mother

Winston Churchill cared deeply for his mother, but not because they had a close, warm relationship. She was typical of many highborn women of her day who had very little close contact with their children. Of her, he wrote, "My mother always seemed to me a fairy princess: a radiant being possessed of limitless riches and power. . . . She shone for me like the evening star. I loved her dearly—but at a distance. My nurse was my confidante."

[*Winston Churchill*, My Early Life: A Roving Commission *(New York: Scribner & Sons, 1930), pp. 4–5.*]

MOTHERHOOD

Highest of All Professions

The agony of not attaining a most cherished dream sometimes inspires the deepest appreciation for that which is unattainable. More than anything else, Adele Fielde longed to be a wife and mother. She fell in love with a Baptist missionary candidate to Siam (Thailand), and in 1865 she set sail to join him in marriage and ministry. When she arrived at port, his missionary colleagues met her with the tragic news that her fiancé had died some months earlier—just after she had set sail. "To Miss Fielde the death of Cyrus Chilcott was the greatest misfortune that could have possibly occurred. She was disappointed beyond measure. She was naturally domestic and it was simply out of the question for her to conceive of a successful life for herself that was not based upon conjugal love, the care of a home and the rearing of children." Yet, despite the bitter anguish, Adele stayed in Siam and later served in China as one of the most effective female missionaries of all time. She was referred to as the "Mother of the Bible Women" because of her pioneer work in training hundreds of national women to evangelize their own people in China. Yet, through all her success, she had never attained her highest dream of motherhood as she had envisioned it. She did attain motherhood, however, by taking a "State as her brood," as she penned in a tribute to motherhood.

> Whatever else women may do in the
> world, their chief and enduring hold on
> the esteem of the human family is attained
> by their excellence as mothers.
> She goes into the valley of the shadow
>   of death three or four times in the course
>   of her existence and returns there each
>   time, bringing a new life with her, does
> more for humanity than the writer of books,
> the opera singer, the fine artist, the skill-
> ful physician, the wise voter or the woman in
>   public life, useful and necessary as they all are.
> The spirit of the pioneer mother should
> abide in all women. Sometimes a woman who has
> no progeny, has to take a State as her brood
> and that is Motherhood, too.

[*Helen Norton Stevens,* Memorial Biography of Adele M. Fielde *(New York: Fielde Memorial Committee, 1918), p. 80, frontpiece.]*

OBESITY

Displeases God

Many people are afraid to speak out openly against overeating and its resulting condition obesity because it is a problem that has so long been accepted as a natural part of American society. In recent years, however, an organization has been founded that blatantly calls overeating a sin. Overeaters Victorious was the brainchild of Neva Coyle, who developed her convictions through biblical principles, her own personal experience, and extensive research. In *Free to Be Thin,* Marie Chapian and Neva Coyle bluntly state the philosophy of the organization.

"Overeating isn't something that affects the body only. It is intricately involved and intertwined with the emotions. It is the personality that produces the fat, in fact. Psychologists tell us that overweight is an indication of a maladjusted personality. Overeating, especially overeating of sweets, is often a response to feelings of inadequacy, depression, anger, fear, loneliness, fear of failure, anxiety and other debilitating emotions. . . .

"Gorging on food wounds more than our bodies. Our souls are hurt, too. Unfortunately, it has been acceptable to be obese. If there's a drug addict or an alcoholic among the members of the church, everybody can plainly see someone with a serious problem. But the obese person, addicted to gluttony, is regarded as normal.

"Is obesity normal in the eyes of the Lord? Compulsive acts without evidence of disease fall under the category of psychoneurosis. Overeating is a compulsive act. Jesus went to the cross so that His people no longer need be the victims of compulsive acts. We need to ask ourselves, then, *is overeating sin?*

" 'Ouch!' you say. 'I've never considered my overweight a *sin!* I mean, I'm free to be who I am in the Lord. He loves me just the way I am! Fat or thin, I'm his and he loves me.' . . .

"Lust for food will never be satisfied. Unbridled lust is sinful, and lust for food is as sinful as unbridled physical lust for someone's body."

[Marie Chapian and Neva Coyle, Free to Be Thin *(Minneapolis: Bethany House, 1979), pp. 13–14.]*

Perceived as a Sin against God

The definition of sin often reflects current culture as much as it does biblical admonitions. This has been particularly true of social sins—that which is characterized as "worldliness." In her book *Close to Home,* columnist Ellen Goodman speaks to this issue and how it relates to obesity.

"It occurred to me about two years ago that eating had become the last bona fide sin left in America. That was the year an imaginative sex therapist came out with a book on dieting which contained the memorable line: 'Reach for your Mate instead of your Plate.' "

Goodman goes on to cite recent attempts to convince Americans that overeating is sinful. "At Oral Roberts University, for example, fundamentalists are so sure that leanness is next to godliness, that they cast out of the covenant (and the school) anyone who couldn't get rid of the excessive body fat. Half-a-dozen former students are bringing suit. At the very least they should rule that the university's first name constitutes false advertising.

"There are several other groups trying to persuade fat people to repent of their sins. They all seem convinced that the weight on our bodies may keep our souls from soaring, and they preach How to Find God and Lose Weight. . . .

"Among these get-thin evangelists is Frances Hunter, who has written a book called *God's Answer to Fat*. No one knows exactly what Fat asked God, but apparently His answer was 'Cut calories!'

"Another book, by Joan Cavanaugh, is called *More of Jesus and Less of Me*. Ms. Cavanaugh's nonfattening truths read like this: 'I can't imagine Jesus coming out of the supermarket with twelve bags of chips, one for each apostle.' The lady is tough to argue with.

"In Minneapolis this week a group called Overeaters Victorious, Inc., is forming a statewide network of revivalist diet workshops under the motto 'He must increase, but I must decrease' (John 3:30).

"The Calorie Conscience Movement has all kinds of ramifications for religion. You can kiss the church cake sale good-bye. Passing the plate is going to have a very different connotation. The notion that the devil lies within is still OK, but he's hiding in all those fat cells, and the work of a good preacher is to starve him out.

"All in all, Sinners of America, it appears that the current stairway to heaven is lined with celery sticks.

[Ellen Goodman, Close to Home *(New York: Fawcett Crest, 1980), pp. 40–42.]*

ORDINATION
Prayer for Ordaining a Woman

In the early church the office of deacon was important, and in the early centuries women deacons (or deaconesses), like men deacons, were often consecrated or "ordained" by prayer and the laying on of hands in the presence of other clergy. This was not accomplished without hearing a justification of female ministry. Indeed, the ordination prayer that was commonly used may have been worded purposely to counteract those who would object to a woman's leadership role in the church.

"Eternal God, Father of our Lord Jesus Christ, Creator of man and woman, who didst fill Miriam and Deborah and Hannah and Huldah with the Spirit, and didst not disdain to suffer thine only-begotten Son to be born of a woman; who also in the tabernacle and the temple didst appoint women keepers of thine holy gates: look down now upon this thine handmaid who is designated to the office of deacon, and grant her the Holy Ghost, and cleanse her from all filthiness of the flesh and of the spirit, that she may worthily execute the work intrusted to her, to thine honor and to the praise of thine Anointed; to whom with thee and the Holy Ghost be honor and adoration forever. Amen."

[Philip Schaff, History of the Christian Church, *vol 3,* Nicene and Post-Nicene Christianity, *311–600 (New York: Scribner's Sons, 1910; reprint, Grand Rapids: Eerdmans, 1979), pp. 260–61.]*

ORGANIZATION
Lack of Organization

I work as hard as anyone
    and yet I get so little done;
The morning goes and noon is here,
    before I know it night is near;

> And all around me I regret
> the things I haven't finished yet.
> If I could just get organized!
>
> —ANONYMOUS

Myths about Organization

In his book *Is There Life after Housework?* Don Aslett, who is an expert on the subject of housecleaning, argues that the so-called foolproof organizational methods generally do not work in practical situations. The experts often suggest that people list the things they wish to accomplish in order of priority and then do them one at a time until the list of tasks is completed. "I can't imagine anyone being able to exist (let alone succeed)," writes Aslett, "following that kind of organizational concept. It is grossly inefficient, non-creative, inflexible—not to mention no fun. I know many housewives who have been trying desperately to organize their lives and housework to fit this ridiculous concept, and they are paying dearly for it. They suffer endless frustrations because they can't make it work for them. If I followed that style of organization in my business or personal activities, I'd be 20 years behind!"

Aslett prescribes a "multiple tract" concept of organization—doing several tasks at once to minimize time and make them more tolerable. The secret of the multiple-tract system is to start the first job right away, and once it is going, start the second, and then go on to the third. "By then the second one is done, so pounce on the fourth, fifth, and sixth, and if the third isn't done, start on the seventh. Don't start and finish any two tasks at the same time. Don't start one thing when you are finishing another. Start another project while you are in the middle of three or four. . . . The success of this system is amazingly exhilarating, and once you get it down, you'll use it beneficially in every area of your life."

[Don Aslett, Is There Life after Housework? (Cincinnati: Writer's Digest Books, 1981), pp. 16–17.]

Overabundance of Benevolent Organizations

At one period during the nineteenth century, England went through what some have described as a society craze. It seemed everyone, especially women, wanted to be a part of some benevolent organization, as societies were formed to aid virtually every imaginable group of people that might need help. Ford Brown has humorously detailed this craze.

"There were societies for putting down gin-mills and Sunday fairs and closing cook-shops on Sundays, for sending Bibles, homilies and Prayer Books everywhere and for keeping country girls at home. There were societies for educating infants, and adults, and juveniles, and orphans, and female orphans, and adult orphans, and nearly everybody else, according to the formularies of the Established Church or not according to them but always according to some religious formulary. There were societies for the deaf and dumb, for the insane, for the blind, for the ruptured, for the scrofulous, for the club-footed, for the penitent syphilitic and for the impenitent syphilitic, for legitimate children and illegitimate children, for chimney sweepers' apprentices and against Tom Paine and Shelley, in aid of juvenile prostitutes and against juvenile mendicants, for distressed respectable widows, for poor pious clergymen in the country, for poor females in the maritime districts, for distressed foreigners, for small debtors, for prisoners, for female émigrés, for the deserving poor, for respectable married women and disreputable unmarried women, for sick people in hospitals and sick people out of hospitals and for simple ordinary sick strangers."

[Ford Brown, Fathers of the Victorians *(New York: Cambridge University Press, 1961), pp. 327–28.]*

PARENTING
Male/Female Differences

In her discussion of the differences between what she calls the White Male System and the Female System, Anne Wilson Schaef identifies different styles of parenting often seen in individual fathers and mothers. "In the White Male System, parenting is primarily focused on teaching the child rules so she or he can live comfortably in the System and contribute to it. The mother is usually delegated to do the teaching, but she is expected to restrict her training efforts to White Male System values and goals. As a result, the child is overprotected and constrained from exploring other alternatives.

"In the Female System, parenting means facilitating a child's development and unfolding. The emphasis is not on *making* a child into something, but on *participating* in the child's gradual discovery of who she or he is. Parent and child are seen as working together in this process. It is assumed that the child will have to learn to live in the world and therefore develop some coping skills. If the child is overprotected, then she or he will never learn the skills necessary for survival.

"The Female System emphasizes the *process* of growing and becoming. The White Male System emphasizes the *content* of being a White Male System person."

[Anne Wilson Schaef, Women's Reality: An Emerging Female System in a White Male Society (San Francisco: Harper & Row, 1985), pp. 122–23.]

Need for Corporal Punishment by Parents

In an era when many child psychologists and family counselors are cautioning against or vehemently denouncing corporal punishment of children, James Dobson stands out as one who advocates corporal punishment for the benefit of the child. He gives the following guidelines and rationale for this form of punishment.

"First, the parent should decide whether an undesirable behavior represents a direct challenge to his authority—to his position as the father or mother. Punishment should depend on that evaluation. . . . In my opinion, spankings should be reserved for the moment a child (age ten or less) expresses a defiant 'I will not!' or 'You shut up!' When a youngster tries this kind of stiff-necked rebellion, you had better take it out of him, and pain is a marvelous purifier. When nose-to-nose confrontation occurs between you and your child, it is not the time to have a discussion about the virtues of obedience. It is not the occasion to send him in his room to pout. It is not appropriate to wait until poor, tired old dad comes plodding in from work, just in time to handle the conflicts of the day. You have drawn a line in the dirt, and the child has deliberately flopped his big hairy toe across it. Who is going to win? Who has the most courage? Who is in charge here?"

[James Dobson, Dare to Discipline *(New York: Bantam Book, 1981), pp. 15–16.]*

Parents' Influence on Image of God

It is a sobering thought to reflect on one's influence over children. Children look up to parents far more than the parents often realize, and they form lasting images of life and of God as they daily interact with their parents. Indeed, parents are in some ways role models for God, according to Richard Strauss, who asks parents some very pointed questions in this regard.

"What kind of God-concept is our child cultivating by his relationship with us? Is he learning that God is loving, kind, patient, and forgiving? Or are we unintentionally building a false image of God into his life, implying by our actions that God is harsh, short-tempered, and critical, that He nags us, yells at us, or knocks us around when we get out of line? Our children's entire spiritual life is at stake here. It is imperative that we learn what kind of parent God is, then follow His example in order that our children may see a living object lesson of the kind of God we have."

[Richard Strauss, Confident Children and How They Grow *(Wheaton: Tyndale, 1975), pp. 23–24.]*

Personal Parental Attention to Children

Susanna Wesley is remembered as the Mother of Methodism, the woman who reared that movement's two founding leaders—John the preacher and organizer, and Charles the hymn writer. With nineteen children, Susanna had to make a special effort to spend quality time with each child that was old enough to have meaningful conversation and that was still living at home. To do this she scheduled daily appointments. "On Monday, I talk with Molly; on Tuesday with Hetty; Wednesday with Nancy; Thursday with Jacky; Friday with Patty; Saturday with Charles; and with Emily and Suky together on Sunday." This was a meaningful time for the children, and years later when he was away in school, John (Jacky) remembered fondly those Thursday nights with his mother.

[John Drakeford, Take Her, Mr. Wesley *(Waco: Word Books, 1973), p. 19.]*

Raising Givers instead of Takers

Kevin Leman, an internationally known psychologist and author, focuses much of his attention on childrearing. In his view, one of the most important aspects of raising children is to help them to become givers instead of takers. He summarizes some of the differences and offers advice on how parents can help their children become givers. "Givers understand reality and human need," while "takers prefer fantasy and meeting their own needs." "Givers realize they may have to wait to get what they want or even do without," while "takers live by the law of instant gratification." "Givers look out for their families," while "takers look out for themselves." Through positive family and community experiences, children can develop the traits of givers.

"All parents like to recall situations or events that were good learning experiences for their children. One of my own favorites is the time my oldest child, Holly, and her fifth-grade classmates provided food and other practical gifts to needy people right in our community.

"What made the project so valuable, however, was their 'hands-on approach.' Instead of just collecting money and having the teacher send the check to some agency that could in turn help these less-fortunate people, Holly and her friends took the food and other things to their homes and handed it to them, eyeball-to-eyeball, so to speak. Holly will never forget standing in the kitchen of a grateful mother who seemed to have at least a dozen kids. The floor was clean, but it wasn't made of tile, hardwood, or linoleum. It was *bare dirt,* and as Holly visited that modest dwelling she got an education in cultural differences and sociology that no textbook could ever provide.

"I believe experiences like that are what produce a child who is a giver, not a taker."

[*Kevin Leman,* Bonkers: Why Women Get Stressed Out and What They Can Do about It *(Old Tappan, N.J.: Revell, 1987), pp. 104–5.]*

PEACE

Peace of God

Henri Nouwen, a widely acclaimed author, educator, and Roman Catholic priest, tells how he came to a deeper understanding of peace—especially that peace which comes from God. In the 1980s, after having lived and taught at Harvard University, he moved to a community near Toronto called Daybreak—a "family" comprised of six mentally handicapped individuals and four who were not, all seeking to live by the beatitudes of Jesus.

In this life of mutual sharing, it has been Adam who has had the deepest impact on Nouwen. "He is a 25-year-old man who cannot speak, cannot dress or undress himself, cannot walk alone, cannot eat without much help. He does not cry or laugh. . . . He suffers from severe epilepsy and, despite heavy medication, sees few days without grand mal seizures."

To many people Adam is a virtual "vegetable," but not to Nouwen. "As my fears gradually lessened, a love emerged in me so full of tender affection that most of my other tasks seemed boring and superficial compared with the hours spent with Adam. Out of his broken body and broken mind emerged a most beautiful human being offering me a greater gift than I would ever offer him."

Adam gave him the gift of peace—"a peace rooted in being." Nouwen had been caught up in his prestigious career—one "so marked by rivalry and competition, so pervaded with compulsion and obsession, so spotted with moments of suspicion, jealousy, resentment and revenge." But with Adam he discovered there was more to life and ministry. "Adam's peace, while rooted more in being than in doing, and more in the heart than in the mind, is a peace that calls forth community. . . . Adam in his total vulnerability calls us together as a family."

[Henri Nouwen, "Adam's Peace," World Vision (August/September 1988), pp. 4–7.]

PHYSICAL DISABILITIES

Triumphing over Disabilities

In many instances people have overcome physical handicaps to accomplish great things, and in some cases the disabilities seem even to have enhanced the individual's creativity. This seems to have been true of hymn writers. One of the most prolific hymnists of all times was Fanny Crosby, who was blind from early childhood. She began writing lyrics as a youngster and went on to write more than eight thousand hymns altogether. Some of these, such as "Blessed Assurance," "All the Way My Savior Leads Me," "My Savior First of All," and "Rescue the Perishing," have become beloved favorites of the church. Other great hymns were written by invalid and sickly women. Charlotte Elliott, who was bedridden nearly all of her eighty-two years, wrote "Just As I Am" and more than one hundred other hymns. Frances Havergal was frail and sickly and died at forty-three—after bequeathing to the church many hymns, including "Take My Life and Let It Be" and "I Gave My Life for Thee." Elizabeth C. Clephane, who penned "Beneath the Cross of Jesus" and "The Ninety and Nine," was handicapped by many physical problems and died before she reached forty; and A. Katherine Hankey wrote "Tell Me the Old, Old Story" and "I Love to Tell the Story" during a period of serious illness.

[Kenneth W. Osbeck, Singing with Understanding (Grand Rapids: Kregel, 1979), pp. 60, 74, 76, 135, 182, 200, 245, 273, 284.]

PHYSICAL STRENGTH
Exhibited by Women

During the Middle Ages the warlike Celtic peoples of western Europe were proud of the strength of their women. Women had important positions in society, some directing military training schools and some serving as military queens, the most famous of whom was Boudicca. "She was huge of frame, terrifying of aspect, and with a harsh voice. A great mass of bright red hair fell to her knees: she wore a great twisted golden torc, and a tunic of many colors, over which was a thick mantle fastened by a broach. Now she grasped a spear, to strike fear into all who watched her." Her daughters followed in her footsteps and fought alongside her in the front lines of battle. When her army was defeated, she took her own life rather than to be taken captive by the Romans. The Romans feared the Celts (also known as Gauls), and especially their women, and they were convinced that "a whole troop of foreigners would not be able to withstand a single Gaul if he called his wife to his assistance who is usually very strong and with blue eyes; especially when, swelling her neck, gnashing her teeth, and brandishing her sallow arms of enormous size, she begins to strike blows mingled with kicks, as if they were so many missiles sent from the string of a catapult."

[Nora Chadwick, The Celts (London: Cox & Wyman, 1970), p. 50.]

PLANNED PARENTHOOD
Delaying Family to Enhance Romance

Birth control, once frowned upon by Christians, is now recommended by many Christian marriage counselors. Charlie Shedd, in his book *Letters to Karen,* encourages couples to delay having children so that they can give themselves entirely to each other for the first few years of marriage. "Most young men come into marriage with a large reservoir of sexual frustration which has accumulated through their growing years. This is one reason it is important for you to keep from having babies too soon. . . . It is good for you both if you can thoroughly clear your systems of the things you had to backlog before it was legal. . . . But the child will have a better mother and father if they have spent plenty of time learning each other and pouring out their love to each other with no competition for the first few years."

[Charlie W. Shedd, Letters to Karen *(Nashville: Abingdon, 1965), p. 106.]*

Superior Offspring through Planning

The concept of planned parenthood for the specific purpose of producing a superior offspring is not of recent origin. Though such modern innovations as sperm banks did not exist centuries ago, there were incredible attempts to breed more perfect specimens of humanity. One such effort was made by an eleventh-century emperor of China, who had more than a hundred wives and concubines. Because astrological destinies of individuals were determined at the time of conception, the emperor employed professional calendrical timekeepers, who calculated when particular wives and concubines should sleep with him. Their sex schedule was delineated in the Record of the Rites of the Chou dynasty. "The lower-ranking [women] come first, the higher-ranking come last. The assistant concubines, eighty-one in number, share the imperial couch nine nights in groups of nine. The concubines, twenty-seven in number, are allotted three nights in groups of nine. The nine spouses and the three consorts are allotted one night to each group, and the empress also alone one night. On the fifteenth day of every month the sequence is complete, after which it repeats in reverse order."

There was an apparent method to this madness, for "by this arrangement, the women of highest rank would lie with the Emperor on the nights nearest to the full moon, when the Yin, or female, influence would be most potent, and so best able to match the potent Yang, or male, force of the Son of Heaven. So timely a combination, it was believed, would assure the strongest virtues in the children then conceived. The main function of the women of lower ranks was to nourish the Emperor's Yang with their Yin."

[*Daniel J. Boorstin,* The Discoverers *(New York: Random House, 1983), p. 76.*]

POLITICS

Female Involvement

American women did not acquire the right to vote until the ratification of the Nineteenth Amendment in 1920, but long before that they were involved in political endeavors. One of the most bizarre instances of such involvement was the presidential candidacy of Victoria Woodhull. She ran against Ulysses S. Grant and Horace Greeley in 1872, with the financial help of Cornelius Vanderbilt. Among other things she was a stockbroker, a newspaper publisher, a spiritualist, and a prostitute. "Her platform supported free love, short skirts, abolition of the death penalty, vegetarianism, excess-profit taxes, female orgasm, world government, better public housing, birth control, magnetic healing, and easier divorce laws." In her newspaper she published the *Communist Manifesto* in its entirety, which had never before been done in English, and she published how-to articles on abortion.

She received the most public attention from her disclosure of one of the most talked-about scandals of the nineteenth century—the adulterous affair between the well-known minister Henry Ward Beecher and one of his parishioners, Elizabeth Tilton. She publicized details of the scandal and was sued for sending obscene materials through the mails, for which she was found guilty. Although it gave her national notoriety, "the scandal she had brought to light had done little to aid her in her bid for the Presidency. She was behind bars in the Ludlow Street Jail on November 5, 1872, when General Ulysses S. Grant soundly defeated Horace Greeley to win reelection to the Presidency. Victoria received no electoral votes and but 'few scattered popular ones.' "

[*Irving Wallace,* The Nympho and Other Maniacs *(New York: Simon & Schuster, 1971), pp. 204, 388–421.*]

PORNOGRAPHY
Denies the Soul of Women

Pornography has harmful effects that most people would never even recognize. What impact does it have in society on the image of women and on a woman's own perception of herself? These questions will never be fully answered, but they are being explored today. In her book *Pornography and Silence,* Susan Griffin maintains that the pornographic mind-set places the very soul of woman in jeopardy. In the prologue she writes:

"As we explore the images from the pornographer's mind we will begin to decipher his iconography. We will see that the bodies of women in pornography, mastered, bound, silenced, beaten, and even murdered, are symbols for natural feeling and the power of nature, which the pornographic mind hates and fears. And above all, we will come to see that 'the woman' in pornography, like 'the Jew' in anti-Semitism and 'the black' in racism, is simply a lost part of the soul, that region of being the pornographic or the racist mind would forget and deny."

Griffin expands this thesis later in the book. "Over and over, pornography depicts acts of terrible violence to women's bodies. Yet even as part of these images of women beaten and dying and always as a ghost image behind these sufferings, a more silent and invisible death takes place. For pornography is violent to a woman's soul. In the wake of pornographic images, a woman ceases to know herself."

[*Susan Griffin,* Pornography and Silence: Culture's Revenge against Nature *(New York: Harper & Row, 1981), pp. 2, 202.*]

POSTERITY

Offering Our Lives to Future Generations

As human beings who have a choice of what we do with our lives, we should ever realize that we have contributions to make that will affect more than our own generation. What can we do to make life better for future generations? Marilyn French reflects on this issue in her book *Beyond Power: On Women, Men, and Morals.*

"The past had its moment; we have ours. After a moment all life dies and is transformed, transubstantiated. The end of life is the continuation of life; the means we use to attain that end is the mode in which we live it. All of us, victors and victims, and we are all both, are transitory. Like the world, we are passing. We are like soldier ants, moving from a depleted area to seek food beyond, in an unexplored terrain. We have encountered a river that separates us from sight of the future; we have a choice only to die where we stand, or to enter it. The ants always enter: and drown. They drown by the millions, and in their death add their bodies to a bridge on which the survivors can cross over to what they hope will be richer ground, as the devoured terrain behind them regenerates itself."

[Marilyn French, Beyond Power: On Women, Men, and Morals *(New York: Summit Books, 1985), p. 545.]*

POVERTY

Caused by Capitalistic Greed

Poverty in America is a stark reality. It is painfully evident in the inner cities and no less disguised in many rural areas. The situation in Southern Appalachia is an example. Kathy Kahn has vividly described the hardships. "I'll never forget the day Myra Watson got indoor plumbing in her house and the pride she felt because she had finally saved up enough money to have it installed. Why did she have to wait sixty-four years for indoor plumbing? Why did Granny Hager have to walk mile after mile in the rain and snow from her house to the Social Security office before she was granted the benefits she was due? Why do the women in Goose Creek, Kentucky, have to pick over clothes rejected by the Salvation Army when they and their families need something to wear? . . . I remember a six-week-old baby girl who died of malnutrition because local doctors refused to treat her. The mother was too poor to pay a doctor and too weak from malnutrition herself to nurse the baby. When the baby died, they had to bury her in a wooden box out in the back yard of their tenant farmer's shack. They couldn't afford a funeral."

Kahn has made a convincing argument that poverty has certainly not been due to laziness, as some people have suggested. The people of Southern Appalachia, as she described them, are hard-working people—people who are denied the dignity of a decent standard of living by a sometimes heartless capitalistic economic system. She told of a family "whose house was burned to the ground by company-hired nightriders because the woman and her husband were organizing a union in a local factory." And that incident was only one of many. "People who fight for safe living conditions are murdered en masse like the people in Buffalo Creek, West Virginia. Miners who fight for safe working conditions are punished by death in the mines, or, like Jock Yoblanski, his wife and daughter, are murdered while they sleep. These are not accidents; they are the direct result of the greed of the wealthy and powerful people who control American Society."

[*Kathy Kahn*, Hillbilly Women *(Garden City, N.Y.: Doubleday, 1973), pp. 213–15.*]

Making the Best of It

In her book *Labor of Love, Labor of Sorrow,* Jacqueline Jones tells of the struggles of black women in America since the time of slavery. Poverty was a way of life for most of these women, but the most striking aspect of their wretched condition was the effort they made to make the best of their lives and to put a cheerful face on their privation. Even in temporary housing, when blacks migrated from place to place, women sought to bring a personal touch to their surroundings. "When sharecropping families in Georgia's Black Belt moved to a new plantation at the end of the year, the wife 'puts up new clothes lines and clears the path to the spring or well and chops the weeds from the back door.' Women who snatched some time from their daily round of chores to plant flowers around their cabins might have had to tend them at night, after the children fell asleep, but they could 'be seen standing idle for a moment during the busiest part of the day to gaze across the even rows to where gaily colored zinnias flame among the white cotton.' City dwellers prided themselves on their window boxes, and many women in the North and South sewed curtains, hung photographs of the champion black boxer Joe Louis on the walls, and arranged their simple furniture in the most pleasing and practical manner possible."

[Jacqueline Jones, Labor of Love, Labor of Sorrow: Black Women, Work, and the Family from Slavery to the Present *(New York: Basic Books, 1985), p. 226.]*

POWER
Attained through Selfless Service

We sometimes think that power comes only through assertive self-promotion, but Dee Jepsen, who served as an assistant to her husband, a U.S. senator, found that this was not always true. Sometimes those who had the greatest influence were among the weakest and most unassuming members of society. "The unimportance of sophistication was brought home to me," she writes, "at a Capitol Hill luncheon for Mother Teresa. . . . In came this tiny woman, even smaller than I had expected, wearing that familiar blue and white habit, over it a gray sweater that had seen many better days, which she wore again to the White House the next day. As that little woman walked into the room, her bare feet in worn sandals, I saw some of the most powerful leaders in this country stand to their feet with tears in their eyes just to be in her presence. . . . As I listened that afternoon, I thought, 'Don't forget this, Dee. Here in this little woman, who doesn't want a thing, never asked for anything for herself, never demanded anything, or shook her fist in anger, here's *real* power.' It was a paradox. She has reached down into the gutter and loved and given. She has loved those the world sees as unlovable—the desolate, the dying—because they are created in the image of the God she serves. Ironically, seeking nothing for herself, she has been raised to the pinnacle of world recognition, received the Nobel Peace Prize, and is a figure known to most people, at least in the Western world, and revered by many. She has nothing, yet in a strange way, she has everything. Is she so unlike what womanhood should be?"

[*Dee Jepsen,* Women beyond Equal Rights *(Waco: Word Books, 1984), pp. 52–53.*]

Power of the Christian Gospel

John Sung, the great evangelist of China, has an amazing testimony of how the power of the gospel changed his life. He was born into a Christian family in China, the son of a Methodist minister. As a youth he traveled with his father and became known as a boy preacher with exceptional talent. He was a brilliant scholar and won scholarships that entirely paid for his college and graduate education in American universities. He won honors in physics and chemistry, and in 1926 received his doctorate from Ohio State University. But with all this prestige, he was not happy. He could not forget his Christian background and the feeling he had that God was calling him into the ministry. He sought the advice of a minister, who urged him to enroll at Union Theological Seminary—a decision that might have been fatal for his struggling faith. "The spirit of skepticism which was prevalent at the time began to shake the foundations of his Christian faith." While at Union, "he began to turn to the ancient religions of the East for solace. He read many volumes on Buddhism and Taoism. He even resorted to chanting the Buddhist scriptures in the secret of his room."

It was a depressing time for him, as he later recalled. "My soul wandered in a wilderness. I could neither sleep nor eat. My faith was like a leaking, storm-driven ship without captain or compass. My heart was filled with the deepest unhappiness." Then very suddenly, John's life began to change.

"Shortly before Christmas, John Sung accompanied some fellow students to a special evangelistic campaign at the First Baptist Church. He expected to hear Dr. Haldeman, an eloquent and learned preacher, but instead, the speaker was a fifteen-year-old girl! She spoke simply and yet powerfully. The proud, skeptical heart of the Ph.D. scientist was moved to the depths. So impressed was he, that he went back for four consecutive evenings, and each time the tremendous power in the young evangelist's preaching gripped him. He determined to discover for himself the secret of such spiritual power."

He began reading Christian biographies "to investigate the secret of the effective ministry of great Christians of the past" and "soon discovered that in each case it was the power of the Holy Spirit that made the difference." After that the "light broke on his darkened soul" and he became a different man. Turning down opportunities to teach science in America and China, he decided rather to give his life to preaching the gospel.

[John T. Seamands, Pioneers of the Younger Churches (Nashville: Abingdon, 1967), pp. 88–89.]

Power Wielded by Men

It is obvious, when looking through lists of names of leaders in industry, politics, commerce, media, religion, education, publishing, and almost any other field, that men wield the vast majority of power. But the full extent of this power worldwide can perhaps best be summed up in a few well-chosen statistics. According to figures from the International Labor Organization, "men own 99 percent of the world's property and earn 90 percent of its wages, while producing only 55 percent of the world's food and performing only one-third of the world's work."

[Marilyn French, Beyond Power: On Women, Men, and Morals (New York: Summit Books, 1985), pp. 530–31.]

Power Wielded by the Pen

The power of the pen is often mightier than the power of political officials or of military forces. That was demonstrated in one of the most widely read books of the nineteenth century—*Uncle Tom's Cabin,* by Harriet Beecher Stowe. Dramatic sales of over 300,000 in its first year indicated its popularity. It was quickly turned into a stage play, and Northern theaters drew crowds wherever it played. "Its story of abject cruelty on the part of masters and overseers, its description of the privations and sufferings of slaves, and its complete condemnation of Southern civilization won countless thousands over to abolition and left southern leaders busy denying the truth of the novel. The damage had been done, however, and when Southerners counted their losses from this one blow, they found them to be staggering indeed."

[John Hope Franklin, From Slavery to Freedom: A History of Negro Americans, *3d ed. (New York: Random House, 1969), pp. 266–67.]*

PRAYER

How to Pray with Simplicity

Susan Stanford, a psychologist and well-known speaker and workshop leader, tells about a very difficult time in her life when she was suffering deep depression and physical back pain and was contemplating suicide. Though not a Christian herself, she had taken a short vacation with a Christian friend, who was sensitive to Susan's hesitancy to share her problems. In seeking to minister to Susan, her friend offered to pray, and her prayer style is a model of simplicity and sincerity.

"Upstairs, I sprawled on top of my sleeping bag. Jeanie came in, knelt down beside me on the floor, and started to knead the painful knots around my lower and middle back.

" 'Susan,' she said, a little timidly, 'would you mind if I said a prayer for you?'

"I was surprised. Accusations ricocheted inside me. *Don't you know, Jeanie? I'm lower than dirt. What God would listen to a prayer for a sinner like me?* But I replied, 'Sure, if you want.'

"Clearing her throat as her hands continued to knead, Jeanie started to speak in a soft voice.

" 'Dear Jesus, I'm not sure of what to say. But I come to You in prayer for my friend Susan.'

"As I lay there listening I was amazed at the simplicity of her words. Even more amazing was her childlike confidence that God was actually listening to her prayers. . . . Jeanie's prayer went on for five or ten minutes, interspersed with times of silence while she continually rubbed my back. There was such gentleness, depth of spirit.

"As I grew drowsy I heard her conclude: 'Susan is hurting badly, Lord. Reach down and touch her. Let her know that *You* are the solution. Let her not despair. She is my good friend, and I care about her so much. I know that You are the Almighty. You can do all things. And You can help her.'

"Then she leaned forward, gave me a hug, and said goodnight. Switching off the light, she quietly slipped from the room."

[Susan Stanford, with David Hazard, Will I Cry Tomorrow? Healing Post-Abortion Trauma *(Old Tappan, N.J.: Revell, 1986), pp. 93–94.]*

Little Time for Prayer

In her book *The Exile,* Pearl S. Buck contrasts the prayer life of her mother and father, who were missionaries in China. She relates an incident when she asked her mother one morning after breakfast, "What makes the red marks on Father's forehead?

"They are marks from his fingers where he leans his head on his hand to pray," Carie answered soberly. 'Your father prays for a whole hour every morning when he gets up.'

"Such holiness was awe inspiring. The children looked for like marks of it on their mother's forehead, and one asked, 'Why don't you pray, too, Mother?'

"Carie answered—was it with a trifle of sharpness?—'If I did, who would dress you all and get breakfast and clean house and teach you your lessons? Some have to work, I suppose, while some pray.'

"Andrew came out of his habitual abstraction long enough to over-hear this, and to remark gently, 'If you took a little more time for prayer, Carie, perhaps the work would go better.'

"To which Carie replied with considerable obstinacy, 'There isn't but so much time and the Lord will just have to understand that a mother with little children has to condense her prayers.'

"The truth of it was that Carie was not very good at long prayers. She prayed hard and swiftly at times, but she prayed as she worked, and she was always perhaps a little conscious against her will that her voice seemed to go up and come back to her without surety of reply."

[Pearl S. Buck, The Exile *(New York: Reynal & Hitchcock, 1936), pp. 191–92, 264.]*

Prayer instead of Action

It is often easier to pray for a person in difficult circumstances than actually to expend the effort to help solve the problem. Indeed, prayer can be misused in an effort to absolve us of responsibilities that belong to us as Christians.

"Prayer can be a wonderful excuse for not doing God's will. 'Let's pray about it,' we say, and settle for words instead of work. As God said to Joshua, 'Get up off your face and go and do what I've told you to do. There is sin in the camp, and you know my principle about that. Go and put it right, and then come and pray' (Josh. 7:10, 11, author's paraphrase)."

[Jill Briscoe, There's a Snake in My Garden *(Grand Rapids: Zondervan, 1975), p. 43.]*

Prayer of a Child

E. Stanley Jones often repeated the prayer of a little girl who was the daughter of missionary friends of his in India: "God bless mamma and papa, my brothers and sisters, and all my friends. And now, God, do take care of yourself, for if anything should happen to you, we'd be in the soup."

[E. Stanley Jones, A Song of Ascents: A Spiritual Autobiography (Nashville: Abingdon, 1968), pp. 346–47.]

Prayer with Children before School

In an era when many parents are protesting against laws that prohibit prayer in school, it would be revealing to survey those very parents to find out how many take time themselves to have prayer with their children before they go to school. Evelyn Christenson, who has long been a prayer "activist," encourages parents to do this by relating her own experience. "Since our first child was in kindergarten, we have made a practice in our home of praying individually with each of our children just as they left for school. This to me has been a very precious experience. It's been more than a time to pray! We have been able to put our arms around our children, assuring them of the security of their home, and then to send them out into the big, often overwhelming world with God watching over them, whatever they will face that day.

"Every once in a while I'm told by my son, 'Hurry up, Mom, make it short. The school bus is coming,' and out the door he goes! Sometimes it's only one or two sentences. But meeting God with our family before we separate is a very vital part of our day."

[Evelyn Christenson, with Viola Blake, What Happens When Women Pray (Wheaton: Victor Books, 1975), pp. 93–94.]

Telling God What to Do

Prayer, for many Christians, is a time to tell God what to do. They work out possible solutions to their problems and then ask God to carry out their plans. This is what Ruby Johnson refers to as "pea soup prayers."

"Curt taught us about 'pea soup prayers.'

"When he was in grade school, he walked home for lunch every day. As he walked, he would pray something like, 'Please, Lord, don't let Mom fix pea soup today.'

"Why did he pray like that? The answer probably is obvious: he hated pea soup. No matter how hungry he was, a bowl of that 'green goop' just didn't appeal to him at all. He knew it was nutritious and good for him, but that did not change his view in the least. Nutritious or not, he wanted no part of pea soup.

"This is what I call a 'pea soup prayer': it's a prayer in which we acknowledge that we have a problem needing God's help. Instead of allowing Him to intervene and solve the problem in His own way, however, we tell Him how to provide the solution.

"When Curt prayed he was really saying, 'God, I have a need. I'm hungry. Supply that need, but not with pea soup. Give me something I like (apple pie, for instance).' In more concise terms, 'This is my need, and this is my solution.'

"On one hand, in effect he recognized God's superior abilities, but on the other hand he played the superior role by advising God. Absurd, isn't it? But we are like that."

[*Ruby E. Johnson,* From the Heart of a Mother *(Chicago: Moody, 1982), pp. 103–4.*]

PREGNANCY

Early Testing

In recent years more and more tests have become available for pregnant women to determine everything from the sex of the child to genetic defects. Pregnancy testing, however, is not a new development. Its value and accuracy have increased significantly in recent decades, but it was commonly done in ancient times—if for no other reason than to seek somehow to explore the mysteries and wonder of birth and to make some effort to thwart adverse conditions, particularly that of not bearing male children.

"The Near Eastern preoccupation with sons meant that the problems of conception merited special study. Pregnancy testing was as commonplace 4,000 years ago as it is today, even if the results may not always have been as reliable. It was recommended to the Egyptian doctor that he put wheat and barley seeds into separate cloth purses and then tell the woman to 'pass her water on it every day. . . . If both sprout she will give birth. . . . If they do not sprout, she will not give birth at all.' Assuming the test was positive, would the child be a boy or a girl? If the wheat sprouted first, it would be a boy, if the barley, a girl. (Wheat was a more valued grain than barley.) Mesopotamian medical men argued, less persuasively, that 'if the forehead of the mother-to-be is heavily freckled, the child she is carrying is a boy.' But they did have a sure test for permanent sterility. 'To know a woman who will bear from a woman who will not bear: Water-melon, pounded and bottled with the milk of a woman who has born a male child; make it into a dose. To be swallowed by the woman. If she vomits, she will bear. If she belches, she will never bear.' "

[Reay Tannahill, Sex in History (New York: Stein & Day, 1980), pp. 65–66.]

PROBLEMS

Value of Problems

In his book *The Road Less Traveled,* M. Scott Peck, a well-known psychiatrist, maintains that problems are the very basis on which individuals develop and mature. "Problems are the cutting edge that distinguishes between success and failure. Problems call forth our courage and our wisdom; indeed, they create our courage and our wisdom. It is only because of problems that we grow mentally and spiritually. When we desire to encourage the growth of the human spirit, we challenge and encourage the human capacity to solve problems, just as in school we deliberately set problems for our children to solve. It is through the pain of confronting and resolving problems that we learn. As Benjamin Franklin said, 'Those things that hurt, instruct.' It is for this reason that wise people learn not to dread but actually to welcome problems and actually to welcome the pain of problems.

"Most of us are not so wise. Fearing the pain involved, almost all of us, to a greater or lesser degree, attempt to avoid problems. We procrastinate, hoping that they will go away. We ignore them, forget them, pretend they do not exist. We even take drugs to assist us in ignoring them, so that by deadening ourselves to the pain we can forget the problems that cause the pain. We attempt to skirt around problems rather than meet them head on. We attempt to get out of them rather than suffer through them."

[M. Scott Peck, The Road Less Traveled: A New Psychology of Love, Traditional Values, and Spiritual Growth *(New York: Simon & Schuster, 1978), p. 16.]*

PROSTITUTION
Condoned by Church Leaders

Church leaders are typically among those who most vehemently oppose prostitution and the vices that accompany it, but throughout the centuries of church history and particularly during the Middle Ages, some in the church believed it had a function in society.

"The leading fathers of the Christian Church were at times inclined to tolerate and even to sanction prostitution, and some Christian emperors were not at all reluctant to accept tax money from prostitutes and brothels. On the other hand, the concept of original sin and the condemnation of all erotic pleasures (even in the marriage bed, which was to serve procreation only), had its start in the same Christian Church that had adopted a large portion of its antisexual outlook from older Hebrew codes.

"Saint Augustine, at the dawn of the Middle Ages, had believed prostitution essential. 'Suppress prostitution,' he warned, 'and capricious lusts will overthrow society.' (Or, as he is otherwise quoted, 'the world will be convulsed with lust.') In the Thirteenth Century, another and equally formidable Catholic theologian, Saint Thomas Aquinas, would take a similar position, arguing in his *Summa Theologica* that prostitution is a necessary evil, preventing seductions and rapes. Elsewhere he remarked that 'Prostitution in the towns is like the cesspool in the palace. Do away with the cesspool, and the palace will become an unclean and stinking place.'

"Ecclesiastical debates centered around such vital matters as whether women engaged in prostitution should be allowed to attend church, whether prostitutes should be permitted to marry Christians, and whether, if they did, they should be admitted to communion. At the Council of Elvira, in the Fifth Century, all whores were excommunicated; while at the Council of Basle, in the Fifteenth Century, a priest presented a paper arguing that prostitution is essential to the preservation of good morals. . . .

"Whatever the official attitudes of the moment in any given locality, prostitution was well-nigh omnipresent throughout the Middle Ages. . . . Special religious orders were established for ex-harlots, and asylums and other institutions were established for rehabilitation. The results were those with which we are familiar from our own similar efforts today: some harlots perished of boredom, some seduced their keepers, lesbianism was rampant, and almost all survivors went back to whoring just as soon as they could gain their freedom."

[*Harry Benjamin,* Prostitution and Morality *(New York: Julian Press, 1964), pp. 51–52.]*

Prostitution a Product of Sinful Nature

Prostitution has always existed and will continue to exist, despite laws making it illegal. It is a product of a sinful society made up of sinful individuals. This is unmistakably clear in Irving Wallace's description of it, though he seems to downplay the degrading nature of it. "Prostitutes are as old as the Bible. A harlot watched the walls of Jericho tumble down. And whores long ago peddled their bodies on the crooked streets of ancient Egypt, of Persia, and of Greece. Largely a city phenomenon in modern times, they exist by the thousands in New York, London, Paris, Rome, and Berlin. They are there because men need them. Just as monogamy created the mistress in general, so the chivalric concept of love has fostered and maintained the prostitute in particular. The romantic restrictions of the act of love in many marriages—the obligations to be gentle, kind, diplomatic, persuasive, and unselfish—thwart man's selfish, irrational, brutally primitive sexual urge. The act of love, in prostitution, does not throw up such barriers. Man may, for his hour, be an animal, coarse, unrestrained, utterly self-gratifying. And after his hour, he may depart without obligations, emotional, economic, or social."

[Irving Wallace, The Nympho and Other Maniacs (New York: Simon & Schuster, 1971), p. 32.]

PSYCHIATRY

Limitations

It is popular in some circles today to place a great deal of faith in psychiatry, but a wary consumer should be acutely aware of the limitations of that field of specialty. Even though the "experts" are highly educated, there are still many unknowns, and unlike other medical specialties, there are extreme differences in prescriptions for cures for almost any abnormality. Indeed, according to Madeleine L'Engle, more harm than good may result from visiting a psychiatrist.

"I have been accused by several friends and acquaintances of being . . . 'against psychiatrists.' I don't really think I am. That would be as silly as being 'against dentists' or 'against barbers.' I do think that psychiatry is still a very young science, not unlike surgery when the surgeons were barbers. If you absolutely had to have a leg amputated in the seventeenth century, you went to a barber; you didn't rush to him for a scratch. I've seen psychiatry save and redeem. I've also seen people going year after year to psychiatrists or therapists and growing steadily more self-centered. Most of us like being the center of the universe; no wonder these people don't want to give up their bi-weekly sessions. I've also seen them regress in their work and deteriorate in personal relationships. But, my friends tell me, that means it's a bad psychiatrist. True perhaps."

[Madeleine L'Engle, A Circle of Quiet (San Francisco: Harper & Row, 1972), pp. 46–47.]

PUBERTY
A Chaotic Time in One's Life

In his book *Junior High Ministry,* Wayne Rice talks about the difficult time of transition that children face as they approach their teen years. "The years between eleven and fourteen are without a doubt the most unsettling in a person's life. This is when puberty occurs; a person changes physically, and in every other way, from a child to an adult. During this period there is a tremendous amount of upheaval, which takes many different forms. A once-in-a-lifetime metamorphosis is taking place.

"Puberty is not a disease that a person catches, so it doesn't need a cure. Everyone experiences it, and so it's perfectly normal, even though it results in what appears to be rather abnormal behavior."

Youngsters in this age bracket can go from giggles to tears in an instant, or from romping energy to lethargy, or from optimism to pessimism. Mood swings are erratic and dramatic. When working with this age group, Rice cautions that "it is a good idea to keep in mind that the abnormal *is* the normal most of the time."

[Wayne Rice, Junior High Ministry: A Guidebook for the Leading and Teaching of Early Adolescents *(Grand Rapids: Zondervan, 1978), p. 18.]*

PUBLIC SPEAKING
Overwhelming Fear

Although Rosalyn Carter would become one of the most active and outspoken political wives to be involved in a presidential campaign, her fear of public speaking was at first almost overwhelming. She shares this terrifying aspect of her life in her biography *First Lady from Plains.* "Then it happened. I was at a luncheon in Gainesville, Georgia, and was very pleased by the large crowd that had turned out. I was talking with my luncheon partner when suddenly I heard someone saying,

'And now Mrs. Carter will say a few words.' I couldn't believe it. I knew it had to come sooner or later, but I'd never thought about being called on to speak on the spur of the moment. Stand up, I ordered myself. Just tell them about Jimmy and his qualifications. But all I could think of standing there was how scared I was and what they were going to think of me. All of my poised calm and self-confidence left me. I finally stammered out something about my husband running for governor and needing their help, then sat down, trembling. I was miserable, not only about the speech but about the realization that it was going to happen again and again.

"I spent that night with friends in a neighboring town, and as soon as I could get away, I went straight to my room to sit down and write a speech—something, anything—to say the next time I was called on. I wrote and wrote and cried, fearful of humiliating Jimmy and also myself in public. I finally got something down on paper and went to bed. But I couldn't sleep. The words kept whirling around in my head and I felt so alone. I couldn't even call Jimmy because I didn't know where he was. I wanted to see Amy and cuddle her and feel necessary and competent again. I had always managed to do what I had set as a goal, but this seemed beyond me. I couldn't do it. But I had to.

"I started practicing at small coffees and receptions, making a deliberate decision to say a few words at each. I always arrived very nervous and headed straight for the bathroom, locked myself in, and said my lines (which couldn't have been more than two minutes long) over and over. Then I would reappear, supposedly refreshed, glad to see everyone and eager to speak to them. For a long time it was torture for me. I never knew when I opened my mouth whether any words would come out or not. My knees shook. I was always afraid I would go blank in the middle of my remarks and not know what I was going to say next."

[Rosalyn Carter, First Lady from Plains (Boston: Houghton Mifflin, 1984), p. 70.]

PURITY

Characterizes Women More Than Men

The "cult of true womanhood" that arose in the Victorian age manifested itself in many ways. Women were placed on a pedestal and viewed as the keepers of the home, the family, and religion. But the ideal of female purity arose even prior to the Victorian period. As the keepers of the home and of religion, women were held "responsible for maintaining the sexual boundaries in a relationship with a man. . . . What was new in the late eighteenth century was the proposition that women had the inclination as well as the obligation to control sexuality." That concept did not fade with the passing of generations, and a double standard of morality has persisted well into the twentieth century.

In past generations, the concept was defended more systematically, however. "Evangelical writers of the 1790s attributed to women 'quick feeling of native delicacy and a stronger sense of shame' than men and argued that the female sex was 'naturally attached to purity.' The message of the evangelical clergy, who after 1790 preached to an increasingly female audience, was that women could, through obedience to God, replace their traditional sexual power with moral influence over men and male society. Joseph Buckminster's 1910 sermon to the members of the Boston Female Asylum called upon them 'to raise the standard of character' of the male sex: 'We look upon you, to guard and fortify those barriers, which still exist in society, against the encroachments of impudence and licentiousness.' In statements such as this, the clergy 'renewed and generalized the ideal that women under God's grace were more pure than men.' . . . For their part, men were assumed to be carnal creatures."

[Ellen K. Rothman, Hands and Hearts: A History of Courtship in America *(New York: Basic Books, 1984), pp. 50–51.]*

RACISM

In the Church

While white Christians in the pews are admonished to support and become involved in missionary work in Africa, blacks next door to the church are often ignored. This is the testimony of Michael Haynes, a black pastor who has served the Twelfth Baptist Church in Boston.

"My entire lifetime was spent just a few yards from a great evangelical church. I had lived two-thirds of my life before I ever received an invitation to come in. As a child whose family had just moved into a fast-changing white neighborhood on the edge of a Negro ghetto, I sat on the stairs of this church and played. I looked into the downstairs window as white face upon white face sat around tables at church suppers. I can vividly recall one day that I, a poor black child whose family was on welfare, yelled into the window of this church, 'We're hungry. Give us something to eat!' only to have a beautiful white lady come out and tell my brother and me how rude we were.

"Nevertheless, thank God, His love found me. And . . . it was not through the church that I was lifted from sinking sands of misdirection and degradation. It was through a . . . settlement house that I was lifted high enough to be able to catch a breath of air in this society.' "

[Michael Haynes, "Three Minutes to Midnight: The Evangelical and Racism," Evangelical Missions Quarterly, Fall 1968, pp. 2–3.]

Overcoming the Effects of Racism

Despite almost insurmountable obstacles, Mary McLeod Bethune, who was raised on a poor five-acre cotton patch in South Carolina, made some remarkable accomplishments during her eighty-year-long life. "She built a college and hospital for blacks in Daytona Beach, Florida. She mothered the influential National Council of Negro Women," and she "advised presidents, had a hand in shaping the

Charter of the United Nations, and worked for voting rights for all American women." She was the fifteenth of seventeen children, born of parents who had been freed from slavery by Lincoln's Emancipation Proclamation. But though she was free, "she encountered Jim Crow laws, racial bigotry of the heart, and endless social obstacles." She was deeply religious and enrolled at Moody Bible Institute to become a missionary to Africa, "but upon graduating from Moody in the mid-1890s was told there were no openings for black missionaries in Africa." Barred from serving as a missionary overseas, Mrs. Bethune turned to education, social service, and civic affairs and made outstanding contributions to the secular world that might have been made to Christian ministry, but for racial prejudice.

[*Elliott Wright,* Holy Company: Christian Heroes and Heroines *(New York: Macmillan, 1980), pp. 93–94.*]

Victim of Racism Who Refused to Strike Back

It is a temptation for an individual who has been viciously discriminated against to strike back, especially if the individual is a celebrity who has the encouragement and support of others to do so. Such was not the case, however, with Marian Anderson, one of the truly great vocalists of the twentieth century. Long before her voice was regarded a national treasure, she had confronted blatant racism, but because of her mother's plea for her to shun vengeance she did not seek to strike back even after waiting in line all day to apply to a music school, only to be told, "We don't take colored." Her mother was a department store cleaning woman who was widowed and raising her three daughters by herself. She encouraged Marian to concentrate her energies, instead, on finding other options. Marian took voice lessons and began touring small towns in the South giving concerts. But as she traveled she was compelled to ride in the Jim Crow section of the train, and she and her accompanist "had to sit at the end of the dining car and eat behind drawn curtains as if they were lepers or two-headed freaks." In Europe Marian was first recognized as an outstanding singer, and she was invited to sing before heads of state.

Yet, even after such acclaim, she faced racial bigotry when she returned to her homeland. "When she appeared at Carnegie Hall, for instance, not a single hotel in midtown Manhattan would rent her a room. In another city, the local concert manager did not meet her at the train or call on her at her hotel. He did not see her, in fact, until he appeared backstage minutes before curtain time and pointedly declined to shake hands. Marian said nothing. She just went out and sang. That was her rule. Not to fight but to perform."

Marian did become involved in a highly publicized controversy—but it certainly was not of her own doing. In 1939, she was invited by Howard University to be a guest artist. When the university sought to reserve Constitution Hall for the occasion, however, the request was denied. The rental contract prohibited black artists from performing there—a contract drawn up by the Daughters of the American Revolution, who owned the tax-free property. When this incident came to light, many people were enraged, not the least of whom was the First Lady, Eleanor Roosevelt, who promptly resigned her membership from that organization.

Once again Marian remained in the background and refused to become involved, but other well-known figures joined Mrs. Roosevelt in her protest, and Marian was brought to the nation's capital on Easter Sunday of 1939 to sing at the Lincoln Memorial. It was a historic occasion as more than seventy-five thousand people, black and white, came to hear her sing.

[*Margaret Truman,* Women of Courage: From Revolutionary Times to the Present *(New York: Morrow, 1976), pp. 164–70.*]

RAPE

Early Opinions on Rape

It is not surprising that women who have been raped face so much difficulty with the law and the court system today when one considers that, only a generation or so ago, it was widely believed that women either were to blame for that violent crime or they could have resisted it had they tried. This view was explained and defended by William J. Robinson, in his book *Woman: Her Sex and Love Life,* published in 1929. What is significant about Robinson is that he was not otherwise antiquated in his views relating to sexual matters. Indeed, he was in many ways ahead of his time on the issue of birth control, and he often supported the practice because he believed it would give women more options for a fulfilling life. But in the matter of rape, his views were more typical of his time and may have had the unfortunate effect of escalating the problem. Unlike many of his colleagues, however, he did concede that rape was rape, even if the woman failed to resist to the point of preventing it. In his assertion that most accusations of rape were false, it is interesting that he—a physician—went out of his way to defend physicians.

"It is not my intention to go into an exhaustive discussion of this painful subject. In this brief chapter I merely wish to bring out two facts.

"First, that it is the almost unanimous opinion of all experts that it is practically impossible for a man to commit rape on a normal adult girl or woman if she really offers all the resistance of which she is capable. Of course, if the man knocks the woman down with a blow, rendering her unconscious, that is a different matter. But where no brutality is used by the man, and the woman offers all the resistance she is capable of, rape is practically impossible. It is, however, possible that is some cases the girl may be so paralyzed by fear as to be incapable of offering any resistance. When the man threatens her with death or severe bodily injury, then it is rape even if she offers no resistance.

"The second point is that it has been established that of the many accusations of rape brought before the courts *most* are false. Out of a hundred cases only about ten are true. The rest are false. This false accusation of rape is due to a peculiar perversion with which some women suffer. Some of the cases are due to hysteria, to imagination, the women really believing that rape or an attempt at rape was committed on them, while investigation shows the accusation to be entirely false. Many accusations of rape are due to a desire for revenge or merely to motives of blackmail.

"Careful doctors and dentists will refuse to give laughing gas or another anesthetic to women except in the presence of others, because, as is well known, an anesthetic often causes in women erotic dreams and sensations and makes them believe that the doctor was committing or about to commit an indecent assault on them, and when they came out of the anesthetic they may be so sure of the reality of their dream that they will bring a complaint against the doctor. Many men have suffered disgrace and imprisonment and have had their lives ruined or even paid the death penalty on account of false accusations against them by either pervert, hysterical, revengeful or blackmailing women."

[William J. Robinson, Woman: Her Sex and Love Life *(New York: Eugenics Publishing, 1929), pp. 309–10.]*

Effect of Rape on Plantation Slaves

The awful humiliation of rape that slave women endured at the hands of their white masters was matched only by the vile debasement suffered by their husbands. Indeed, some odious slaveowners enjoyed tormenting their slave men in this fashion. "Regardless of the circumstances under which their womenfolk were sexually abused, black men reacted with deep humiliation and outrage, a reaction that at least some slaveholders intended to provoke. One Louisiana white man would enter a slave cabin and tell the husband 'to go outside and wait 'til he do what he want to do.' The black man 'had to do it and he couldn't do nothing 'bout it.' (This master 'had chillen by his own chillen.') Other husbands ran away rather than witness such horrors. Recalled one elderly former slave, 'What we saw, couldn't do nothing 'bout it. My blood is bilin' now at the thoughts of dem times.' It would be naive to assume that the rape of a black wife by a white man did not adversely affect the woman's relationship with her husband; her innocence in initiating or sustaining a sexual encounter might not have shielded her from her husband's wrath. The fact that in some slave quarters mulatto children were scorned as the master's offspring indicates that the community in general hardly regarded this form of abuse with equanimity."

[Jacqueline Jones, Labor of Love, Labor of Sorrow: Black Women, Work, and the Family from Slavery to the Present (New York: Basic Books, 1985), pp. 37–38.]

Experience of Rape as a Source of Counsel

After Helen Roseveare, the noted missionary doctor to the Congo, was raped by Simba rebels in 1964, she drew on that experience to minister to Roman Catholic nuns who had endured similar sexual brutality. One young nun, Sister Dominique, was particularly distressed. She had been paraded naked before the mocking soldiers before she was violently deprived of her virginity. She was convinced she had lost her purity before God and that there was no purpose in going on living. Helen, having suffered so deeply herself, reassured her of God's love and understanding. "If you know of Christ living in you, no one can touch your inner purity," she counseled. "No living man can touch or destroy or harm that real purity inside you. . . . You have not lost your purity. If anything, you have gained purity in the eyes of God."

[Alan Burgess, Daylight Must Come (Minneapolis: Bethany Fellowship, 1975), p. 33.]

Misconceptions about Rape

In her book *Raped,* Deborah Roberts tells the story of her brutal rape that took place one summer when she was serving in an inner-city church ministry program in Chicago. She describes in detail the horror of the attack and the humiliation she endured at the hands of hospital attendants and police officials and how she finally came to terms with the trauma that lingered for years. She is now helping others deal with the effects of rape by sharing her story and by offering information that helps women overcome feelings of guilt on their own part. In doing so, she seeks to correct misconceptions about rape.

"Rape is *not* a sexual act of passion. Rape is a crime of violence and power using sex as the weapon. The rapist chooses to feel powerful by humiliating and degrading his victim.

"Not just young, attractive women are victimized by rapists. Persons of all ages, all physical appearances, all income levels, and all educational backgrounds are victims of sexual assaults. . . .

"Rapists are generally *not* sexually sick, psychotic individuals. Many rapists have access to a willing sexual partner. Sex is not the primary motivation for a rapist. The convicted rapist is found to have a normal sexual personality. He differs from a normal person in having a greater tendency to express violence.

"An unwilling woman can be raped. In at least 85 percent of all rapes, physical force and threats are used. Anyone can become immobilized by fear, verbal threats, or weapons. . . .

"More than half of all rapes are planned, and statistics show that assailants tend to rape more than once.

"The incestuous rapist is also a repeater. Incest is usually an established pattern in a family, with several children being victimized.

"Rape is not primarily an interracial crime. Over 90 percent of all rapes involve persons of the same race.

"Over half of all reported assaults occur in a residence, often in a victim's own home. Even more frightening is the fact that 85 percent of rapists are known to their victims. (Warning children about strangers will not necessarily keep them safe from sexual abuse.)"

[*Deborah Roberts,* Raped *(Grand Rapids: Zondervan, 1981), pp. 149–50.*]

Self-defense against Rape

Although television images of rape often imply there is very little a woman can do to prevent or minimize the violence, the opposite is true in real life. After working for six years on a rape hotline in California, Gail Groves realized that "one of the most surprising aspects of these calls was the fact that so many women got away without being raped."

How did these women defend themselves? It is important to realize that "the body is a collection of potentially lethal weapons and vulnerable targets. When police and other 'authorities' warn women against resisting assault, they often talk about women's lack of bodily strength relative to men. . . . But every male human body has vulnerable areas . . . and every female body has powerful weapons to use against those targets.

"For instance, women are not often told that they have especially strong legs, or that it takes only fifteen pounds of kicking pressure to break a kneecap. An elbow to the solar plexus, a foot smashing an instep, a knee to the face or the groin, a scream against an eardrum— these acts are not beyond the scope of women. There are so many possible combinations of techniques, some more lethal than others, but all capable of, at the least, buying time, loosening a hold, or opening the way for another strategy."

What can women do to increase their expertise in self-defense? One obvious response is to enroll in courses and read books on self-defense and assertiveness. But also helpful is to simply keep in shape physically and to imagine violent situations and appropriate responses. "When you make a situation real in your mind, there are always options for the defender—ways she can damage the attacker, verbal points she can gain through negotiation, strategies that will work. Self-defense means looking for these openings, having the faith that there will be one at some point, and then trying something, and not giving up."

[Denise Caignon and Gail Groves, eds., Her Wits About Her: Self-Defense Success Stories by Women *(San Francisco: Harper & Row, 1987), pp. xv, xix, xx, xxxi, 255–61.]*

REJECTION

Learning to Accept It

Often rejection is perceived to be associated with some form of defectiveness, with the latter causing the former. But that is frequently not the case. What might appear to be rejection might be simply oversight or might be a reaction motivated by envy or resentment that has nothing to do with the character of the individual or the quality of her work. Madeleine L'Engle made this discovery during a time when she was entirely unrecognized for her extraordinary gifts as a writer. "When I accepted myself as Madeleine on my fortieth birthday," she writes, "not a computer's punch-out, or my social-security number, or the post-office date on the latest rejection slip, it had nothing to do with the degree of talent. I could, during the long years of failure, console myself with the fact that van Gogh sold precisely one picture while he lived, and that he was considered an impossible painter. I could try to reassure my agent when he was concerned about the damaging effect on me of so much failure; he was afraid it would kill my talent. . . .

"During that dreadful decade I pinned on my workroom wall a cartoon in which a writer, bearing a rejected manuscript, is dejectedly leaving a publisher's office; the caption says, 'We're very sorry, Mr. Tolstoy, but we aren't in the market for a war story right now.' That cartoon got me through some bad hours. It didn't mean that I was setting myself beside Tolstoy."

[Madeleine L'Engle, A Circle of Quiet *(San Francisco: Harper & Row, 1972), pp. 37–39.]*

RELIGION

Must Be Functional

Helen Barrett Montgomery, who was the first woman to translate the New Testament from the Greek and the first woman to serve as the head of a major Protestant denomination (American Baptist), was a well-known missions and ecumenical leader of the early twentieth century. During her youth and college years, she was a doctrinaire Baptist, but that slowly changed as she began to see the value of other points of view and the futility of arguing over minor points of doctrine. She expressed her feelings on this after she had been in the company of a dogmatic Baptist who was convinced he was orthodox on every doctrinal point. In reflecting on him, she was philosophical about her own religion. "I tell you this Christian faith of ours is all shop-worn being handled over the counter and mussed and creased and discussed. We want to get it off the counter and cut into coats to cover the naked. My own soul is sick with theory—I'm getting so I don't care how or when or where or whether the Pentateuch wrote Moses or Moses, the Pentateuch. There is good news, the gospel, the love of God, the life of Jesus, and here am I, sinful and selfish and blind as a bat—for the secret of the Lord is with them that fear him. I know enough things now to make me a saint if I lived 'em. I'm going to live more and talk less."

[*Helen Barrett Montgomery,* Helen Barrett Montgomery: From Campus to World Citizenship *(London: Revell, 1940), p. 78.*]

RETIREMENT
Accepting New Roles in Retirement

After a long and successful career it is often very difficult to retire gracefully—especially when the work is never far away. Ida Scudder, the great missionary medical doctor to India, found this to be true. She turned over the reins of the Vellore medical complex to one of her students and retired in 1946 at the age of seventy-five. It was a hard adjustment, but she graciously accepted her new role. "She who had been all her life a leader—some had called it dictator—now found it possible to be a follower." She remained active for another decade, teaching her weekly Bible class and serving as a consultant at the medical center. She remained active physically as well, and at the age of eighty-three, "was still serving a wicked tennis ball."

[*Dorothy Clarke Wilson,* Dr. Ida: The Story of Dr. Ida Scudder of Vellore *(New York: McGraw-Hill, 1959), pp. 243, 321.*]

REVENGE

Poor Results

Nathaniel Hawthorne is known for his great works of literature, but not all his works were successful. His novel *Blithedale Romance* was, according to critics, "the feeblest" and "the poorest" of his writings—a novel written in part to discredit a woman he intensely disliked and to avenge that woman's brother-in-law, Ellery Channing, who had written a poem that made ugly insinuations against Hawthorne's wife. Zenobia, the main character in the novel, was modeled after Margaret Fuller, a brash and outspoken woman's rights advocate. In Hawthorne's view, she "had a strong and coarse nature" and was "a great humbug" who had "stuck herself full of borrowed qualities" in an effort to "make herself the greatest, wisest, best woman of the age." He took detailed notes on her manners, "which he hoarded for his future fiction against the day of Miss Fuller's death." That time came in 1850, when she was only forty. She was on board a ship from Rome to New York, and as it approached its destination in stormy seas, it hit a sandbar. The hull broke, allowing the water to gush in, and she and many others drowned.

When the book appeared two years later, Margaret Fuller's friends harshly criticized Hawthorne for his portrait of her (although some tried to claim there was no resemblance), but the vengeance had been accomplished, and the damage was done. "In death," writes Irving Wallace, "that shocking and talkative female, Margaret Fuller, had lost her tongue, and Nathaniel Hawthorne had his wish—but it was to be Margaret Fuller's victory, finally. For, because of her tongue, Hawthorne had been driven to write one of the least successful of all his books. He would have been forewarned, had he known an old Japanese proverb: A woman's tongue is only three inches long, but it can kill a man six feet high."

[Irving Wallace, The Nympho and Other Maniacs *(New York: Simon & Schuster, 1971), pp. 273–82.]*

ROLE MODEL
Found through Reading

Elisabeth Elliot, in the preface to her biography of Amy Carmichael, tells how this single missionary woman of a generation earlier influenced her life. She found in this self-sacrificing servant of God a model that she could follow during her own struggles as a single missionary.

"To Amy Carmichael I owe . . . as great a debt as one can owe another. I cannot pay it. But I hope that this biography will introduce its subject to a generation which has not had the privilege that was mine. I 'met' her when I was fourteen. Mrs. P. W. DuBose, headmistress of a small boarding school in Florida, used to quote often in school vespers from Carmichael books. I was captivated, and told her so. She lent me the books.

"Dohnavur became a familiar place. I knew its bungalows, its paths, its people; I breathed its air. Amy Carmichael became for me what some now call a role model. She was far more than that. She was my first spiritual mother. She showed me the shape of godliness. For a time, I suppose, I thought she must have been perfect, and that was good enough for me. As I grew up I knew she could not have been perfect, and that was better, for it meant that I might possibly walk in her footprints. If we demand perfect models we will have, except for the Son of man Himself, none at all."

[*Elisabeth Elliot,* A Chance to Die: The Life and Legacy of Amy Carmichael *(Old Tappan, N.J.: Revell, 1987), p. 15.*]

ROLE REVERSAL
Satisfying in Some Cultures

On the small remote island of Cheju, off the coast of Korea in the Yellow Sea, the men do housework and care for the children, while the women go out to work to support the family. This arrangement has apparently gone on for centuries, and both sexes have been satisfied with the arrangement, until recent years when outsiders began coming to the island.

[*Virginia Ramey Mollenkott,* Women, Men, and the Bible *(Nashville: Abingdon, 1977), p. 78.*]

ROMANCE
In the Sunset Years of Life

When Adoniram Judson, the great Baptist missionary to Burma, was fifty-seven, he began courting Emily, who was half his age and soon to become his third wife. She wrote to him that she vowed to "do all I can to make the autumn of your days brighter than their summer has been, that their winter may be glorious."

[*A. C. Kendrick,* The Life and Letters of Mrs. Emily C. Judson *(New York, 1860), p. 189.*]

SCANDAL
Disgraced an Evangelist's Ministry

Aimee Semple McPherson, the most noted female evangelist of the early twentieth century, became embroiled in scandal at the very height of her career. She was known for her dramatized sermons, in which she would dress up in football togs and carry the ball for Jesus or ride a motorcycle onto the stage and play the part of a traffic cop stopping people from going to hell. But the most dramatic event in her life was her kidnapping—or her *alleged* kidnapping, as her critics would charge. On May 18, 1926, the headlines of a Los Angeles paper read, "Evangelist McPherson Believed Drowned!" For weeks the newspapers all over the country were filled with rumor and conjecture about her sudden disappearance. Then, nearly six weeks after her disappearance, Aimee appeared from out of nowhere in the tiny desert town of Douglas,

Arizona, claiming she had been kidnapped. Many reporters initially accepted her story at face value. The *Los Angeles Times* headlined the incident with "Aimee Tortured for Huge Ransom." But others were more skeptical, claiming she had been spotted in a hideaway with Kenneth Ormiston, her radio announcer.

So serious were the accusations against her that she was brought to trial on the charge that the kidnapping story was a hoax, but she was acquitted and soon returned to her ministry. The scandal lingered, but Aimee managed somehow to rise above it and continue on with her ministry and build the church she founded, the International Church of the Foursquare Gospel. Although her most recent biographer rejects outright the kidnapping story, church officials continue to maintain that her story was not fabricated.

[Robert Barr, Least of All Saints: The Story of Aimee Semple McPherson *(Englewood Cliffs, N.J.: Prentice-Hall, 1979), pp. 212–16.]*

SECURITY

Calm in the Midst of Storm

Where do we find our security when the world is crashing in around us? Joyce Landorf tells an interesting story of a little boy who found peace in the midst of strife. She encountered a mother and two little boys in a grocery store, at which time the boys were creating more than a minor upheaval—which small boys in grocery aisles are prone to do. Hoping to escape them, Joyce tried to move on ahead but was not successful until nearly the end of her shopping—and then, who should she find in front of her in the check-out lane but this fractious trio. All of a sudden, she writes, "The store sort of blew up all around me. . . . It seems the younger boy in that cart ahead of me had run out of wonderful things to do, so he reached up, grabbed the gum and candy rack, and gave it a healthy yank.

"As it toppled over it connected its wires with another rack, a large one filled with a jillion candy bars, and the two meshed together and sprayed the front of the store with all kinds of gum, lifesavers, cough drops, and giant Peter Paul Almond Joy bars.

"One sixteenth of a second later, the volcano I mentioned earlier erupted into a hot, molten mass of hysterical screaming. All of which was directed, of course at her two little boys. Everyone was immediately called on duty for a 'red alert.' . . . Manager, assistants, meat men, clerks and box boys flew into a flurry of action. . . .

"By now the volcano was pouring a screaming hot torrent of big words, dirty words, and threatening words into the four little ears below her. She didn't think she was getting through to them so she reached down, grabbed one by his sweater collar, the other by one shoulder, swooped them up to eye level, and then really let them have it!

"She shook those boys . . . and let everyone else in the store know that they were to *'shut up and not move!'*

"They froze in ramrod positions. I think they even stopped breathing.

"Bedlam was still taking place, so she started helping the pick-up crew. I was about to come out of shock and begin to help, too, when the younger boy *moved.*

"I was fascinated. He was deliberately disobeying his mother, and I wondered what could motivate such a dangerous action.

"To avoid his mother's eyes, he moved like a cautious snake in slow motion toward his mother's large straw purse and, with deliberate, smooth movements, reached into its depths and inched out a small, faded blue blanket. All the time he was pulling it out of the purse, he never took his eyes from his mother.

"Finally he had the blanket tucked under his chin and when he was sure it was there, his tense little shoulders relaxed, he breathed quite a loud sigh and color returned to his face. Tranquility, as I have rarely seen it, erased the fear from his eyes, and as he began to sway from side to side he ever so gently hummed a little tune. I was completely captivated by this peaceful scene."

This incident caused Joyce to realize that God was speaking to her about being the kind of person that could be a source of security and peace to other people. "I didn't want to leave that work to some synthetic blue blanket, and I thanked God for the gift of gentleness that I knew He was about to give me."

[Joyce Landorf, The Richest Lady in Town *(Grand Rapids: Zondervan, 1973), pp. 38–42.]*

SELF-ACCEPTANCE

Can Excuse Evil

We hear so much about the benefits of self-acceptance that we often fail to realize the potential for evil when immoral or sinister behavior is tolerated and sometimes encouraged under the guise of "self-acceptance." Ellen Goodman, a widely syndicated columnist who is recognized for her perceptiveness, speaks to this issue in her book *Close to Home.*

"I knew a man who went into therapy about three years ago because, as he put it, he couldn't live with himself any longer. I didn't blame him. The guy was a bigot, a tyrant and a creep.

"In any case, I ran into him again after he'd finished therapy. He was still a bigot, a tyrant and a creep, *but . . .* he had learned to live with himself.

"Now, I suppose this was an accomplishment of sorts. I mean, nobody else could live with him. But it seems to me that there are an awful lot of people running around and writing around these days encouraging us to feel good about what we should feel terrible about, and to accept in ourselves what we should change.

"The only thing they seem to disapprove of is disapproval. The only judgment they make is against being judgmental, and they assure us that we have nothing to feel guilty about except guilt itself. It seems to me that they are all intent on proving that I'm OK and You're OK, when in fact, I may be perfectly dreadful and you may be unforgivably dreary, and it may be—gasp!—*wrong."*

[Ellen Goodman, Close to Home *(New York: Fawcett Crest, 1980), p. 28.]*

SELF-ANALYSIS

One's Own Worst Enemy

I have never met a man who has given me as much trouble as myself.

—D. L. MOODY

Unhealthy Focus

It can be very unproductive for people to consume an excessive amount of time analyzing themselves. This is the thesis of Eugenia Price's book, which is summed up in the title: *Leave Your Self Alone: Set Yourself Free from the Paralysis of Analysis.*

"The 'wave' now is to focus on ourselves—on our weaknesses, our strengths, our idiosyncrasies, our failures, our successes, our marriage expectations, our friendship and career expectations. Self-enlightenment is good. We need to know ourselves. We need to accept ourselves. But wait. Here comes the key again: What gets our attention (for too long) gets us.

"What gets our attention *gets us.*

"I have read many of the 'wave' books, and I have found some to be helpful, insightful as far as they go. But I tire of them because they keep me focused on *me.* Happily, healthily, after a time I tire of thinking about Eugenia Price. I begin to want some fresh air. Some 'native air.' The air in the kingdom of God is always fresh, and it is outside air—outside ourselves."

[*Eugenia Price,* Leave Your Self Alone: Set Yourself Free from the Paralysis of Analysis *(Grand Rapids: Zondervan, 1979), p. 28.*]

SELF-DENIAL
Extreme Religious Asceticism

Catherine of Siena, the famous fourteenth-century mystic and canonized saint, was known for a life of self-denial. From her early childhood, she sensed that God had a special ministry for her. At the age of seven she made a vow of virginity, and when her parents tried to match her with a young man when she was twelve, she cut off her long flowing hair in order to make herself less attractive. During her teenage years she practiced extreme asceticism that included shunning food and sleep, long periods of silence, severe flagellation, and wearing painfully course undergarments and an iron chain.

Her adult life was characterized by a public ministry that included service to the poor and imprisoned. There are many stories of her self-sacrificing service during this period—the most gruesome of which have been the most publicized. One of these stories depicts her with a dying woman—Catherine gently swabbing the pus-filled sores but nearly overcome by the sickening stench. But then in an instant, she is guilt-stricken by her revulsion. In a demonstration of love and identity with this wretched creature, she picks up the bowl of pus she has drained from the foul sores and drinks it, later claiming that it delighted her taste buds as nothing else ever had.

[Michael De La Bedoyerre, Catherine: Saint of Siena *(London: Hollis & Carter, 1947), p. 46.]*

SELF-ESTEEM
Low among Women

Historically women have suffered from low self-esteem to a greater degree than have men. In 1940, a survey indicated that only 11 percent of women could affirm the statement "I am an important person." That figure rose to a remarkable 66 percent in 1984, and yet, many women were still denigrating their own worth. The physical abuse women endure is closely tied to their self-esteem. "The assumption that she is worthless affects all areas of a woman's life," writes Jo Berry. "Statistics show that women who are physically abused by their husbands think they are only getting what they deserve, so they stay and are continually brutalized rather than trying to get help." Low self-esteem affects the way people treat themselves. "Many people treat themselves badly. They say unkind things about themselves, judge themselves unfairly, are supercritical of themselves, and feel guilty if they do something nice for themselves."

[Jo Berry, Becoming God's Special Woman (Old Tappan, N.J.: Revell, 1986), pp. 54, 68.]

People View Themselves above Average

Do most people suffer from a low self-image, as many psychologists and therapists would claim? In their book, *Psychology Through the Eyes of Faith,* David Myers and Malcolm Jeeves offer evidence that would suggest they do not.

"In virtually any area that is both subjective and socially desirable, most people see themselves as better than average. Most business people see themselves as more ethical than the average business person. Most community residents see themselves as less prejudiced than their neighbors. Most people see themselves as more intelligent and as healthier than most other people. When the College Board asked high school seniors to compare themselves with others their own ages, 60 percent reported themselves better than average in athletic ability, only 6 percent below average. In leadership ability, 70 percent rated themselves above average, 2 percent below average. In ability to get along with others, *zero* percent of the 829,000 students who responded rated themselves below average while 60 percent saw themselves in the top 10 percent and 25 percent put themselves in the top 1 percent."

[David G. Myers and Malcolm A. Jeeves, Psychology Through the Eyes of Faith (San Francisco: Harper & Row, 1987), p. 130.]

Signs of Low Self-Esteem

How would you paint a word picture of a woman with low self-esteem? A poor single mother in a ghetto eating on food stamps with her five barefoot children? More likely it would be a middle-class women with not enough to occupy her time. In his book *What Wives Wish Their Husbands Knew about Women,* James Dobson paints just such a picture. "It is sitting alone in a house during the quiet afternoon hours, wondering why the phone doesn't ring . . . wondering why you have no 'real' friends. It is longing for someone to talk to, soul to soul, but knowing there is no such person worthy of your trust. It is feeling that 'they wouldn't like me if they knew the real me.' It is becoming terrified when speaking to a group of your peers, and feeling like a fool when you get home. It is wondering why other people have so much more talent and ability than you do. It is feeling incredibly ugly and sexually unattractive. It is admitting that you have become a failure as a wife and mother. It is disliking everything about yourself and wishing, constantly wishing, you could be someone else. It is feeling unloved and unlovable and lonely and sad. It is lying in bed after the family is asleep, pondering the vast emptiness inside and longing for unconditional love. It is intense self-pity. It is reaching up in the darkness to remove a tear from the corner of your eye. *It is depression!*"

[James Dobson, What Wives Wish Their Husbands Knew about Women *(Wheaton: Tyndale, 1975), pp. 22–23.]*

SELF-FULFILLMENT
New Emphasis in Women's Ministries

The post 1960s era that some pop philosophers refer to as the "Me Generation" has influenced the church as well as secular society. Indeed, the church has followed the emphasis on self-fulfillment that is so current in society. That trend has been particularly evident in women's ministries. Women have had a long history of sacrificial service in the

church, and until recently that service has been characterized by humanitarian and evangelistic outreach. Countless nineteenth-century urban
missions were founded by women, and women have been at the fore-
front of the missionary advance for most of a century.

In recent years, however, women's ministries have been far more
self-centered. The focus has been more on self-help programs rather
than on helping others. This is illustrated by the significant increase of
organizations in the 1960s and 1970s focused on marriage enrichment,
health and exercise, and political activism. "Overeaters Anonymous"
and "Overeaters Victorious" are examples, as are Marabel Morgan's
"Total Woman" groups, Phyllis Schlafly's "Eagle Forum," Beverly
LaHaye's "Concerned Women for America," and feminist-oriented
organizations such as the "Evangelical Women's Caucus" and "Daughters of Sarah." Even the home Bible studies that have grown by leaps
and bounds in the past decades are often more focused on self-help than
on Christian outreach. Indeed, the massive army of women volunteers
who were characterized by sacrificial service to others has all but
vanished from the American scene.

—RUTH A. TUCKER

SELF-PRESERVATION

An Escape against All Odds

"By 1698 the most famous woman in New England was Hannah
Duston"—and with good reason. She had responded to violence with
violence in a manner that few, if any, men could ever equal. Indians
had fallen on her little town of Haverhill and had killed or captured
some forty of its residents. But Hannah survived to become a celebrity.
It was a time when the emotions of fear and hatred of Indians were
at an all-time high, and killing them, especially to protect oneself, no
matter how vicious it might be, was praised. "Hannah Duston's deed
was spectacular," writes historian Laurel Ulrich. "Five days out of
childbed, she had marched a hundred miles into the wilderness and with

the help of her companion, Mary Neff, and a boy named Samuel Lennardson had not only killed her captors and escaped but had brought home ten scalps to prove it. Little matter that six of those scalps were of children. Boston acclaimed her a heroine. . . . Her name and her significance were to extend beyond her own time and place. Canonized in 1702 in Mather's monumental *Magnalia Christi Americana,* she became an American amazon, a defender of Israel, and an archetypal heroine of the New World frontier."

[Laurel Thatcher Ulrich, Good Wives: Image and Reality in the Lives of Women in Northern New England, 1650–1750 *(New York: Knopf, 1982), pp. 167–68.]*

SELF-RELIANCE
Demonstrated by Frontier Women

Frontier life was only for the heartiest individuals—for those who could endure long periods of privation and loneliness. Although western movies and novels often depict men as their lead characters, a great many of those hearty pioneers were women, who were often forced to fend for themselves against the harsh elements of nature and the dangers of the unpoliced wilderness. Joanna L. Stratton writes of this self-reliance in her book *Pioneer Women.* "To the pioneer women, the day-to-day uncertainties of wilderness life proved especially harrowing. During the working hours of the day, her husband was frequently too far out of range to respond to any call for assistance. Furthermore, circumstances often required him to leave his family for days or weeks at a time. Setting off on trading or hunting expeditions, the frontiersman left his family unguarded with only the hope of his safe return.

"Such long absences were wearing for the waiting mother. Burdened with both the maintenance and the protection of the family homestead, she could rely on no one but herself. In these lonely circumstances, she fought the wilderness with her own imagination, skill, and common sense and determination."

[Joanna L. Stratton, Pioneer Women: Voices from the Kansas Frontier *(New York: Simon & Schuster, 1981), p. 79.]*

SENILITY

Learning to Accept It

In his book *Growing Up,* Pulitzer-prize-winning journalist Russell Baker writes of his difficulty in initially accepting his mother's senility. "At the age of eighty my mother had her last bad fall, and after that her mind wandered free through time. Some days she went to weddings and funerals that had taken place half a century earlier. On others she presided over family dinners cooked on Sunday afternoons for children who were not gray with age. Through all this she lay in bed but moved across time, traveling among the dead decades with a speed and ease beyond the gift of physical science. . . .

"The doctors diagnosed a hopeless senility. Not unusual, they said. 'Hardening of the arteries' was the explanation for laymen. I thought it was more complicated than that. For ten years or more the ferocity with which she had once attacked life had been turning into rage against the weakness, the boredom, and the absence of love that too much age had brought her. Now, after the last bad fall, she seemed to have broken chains that imprisoned her in a life she had come to hate and to return to a time inhabited by people who loved her, a time in which she was needed. Gradually I understood. It was the first time in years I had seen her happy.

"She had written a letter three years earlier . . . : 'If I seemed unhappy to you at times, I am, but there's really nothing anyone can do about it, because I'm just so very tired and lonely that I'll just go to sleep and forget it.' She was seventy-eight then.

"Now, three years later, after the last bad fall, she had managed to forget the fatigue and loneliness and, in these free-wheeling excursions back through time, to recapture happiness. I soon stopped trying to wrest her back to what I considered the real world and tried to travel along with her on those fantastic swoops into the past."

[*Russell Baker,* Growing Up *(New York: New American Library, 1982), pp. 1–5.]*

SENSITIVITY
Characteristic of Women More Than Men

Although many researchers and counselors would argue that it is a simplistic stereotype to characterize women as more sensitive than men, a great deal of evidence nevertheless indicates that such is the case. Some researchers believe that this difference between men and women is due in part to "differences in the brains of men and women that are genetically determined." They "have found some interesting indications that men and women do not perceive the world in the same way. They feel it differently, hear it differently, and puzzle out its problems in different areas of their brains. . . . Men are right hemisphere oriented. That's why men have an advantage at visual-spacial tasks. Women are left-hemisphere oriented and consequently have an advantage at verbal skills."

Some researchers also believe that a man's brain is more specialized than a woman's. He uses the right side for spatial problems and the left for verbal. This is not the case with women. "She can work on a problem with both hemispheres, making her potentially more perceptive than men. . . . A woman's perception may make her hearing superior to man's. She is sensitive to tones of voice and intensities of expression. She is extremely sensitive to the presence and variation of sound.

"Women are at an advantage in reading the emotional content of faces. Women can sense the difference between what people say and what they mean. They are good at picking up expressions that reveal another person's true feelings. Women can pick up unspoken thoughts, often understanding how another person feels. The perception of women is the result of both left and right hemispheres coming to bear on a single subject or person or statement."

[*Brenda Poinsett,* Understanding a Woman's Depression *(Wheaton: Tyndale, 1984), pp. 49–51.*]

Sensitivity Related to Creativity

Frequently the most creative people are also the most sensitive. That was evident in the life of Gustave Flaubert, the author of the great novel *Madame Bovary*. It appeared in 1857, and although it sold only fifteen copies in the first two months, it later went on to become a classic in literature. It was a book that Flaubert anguished over, but the end result was something that his readers could relate to, and for that reason it was a lasting success. The words came slowly, sentence by sentence, seven hours a day, seven days a week, for fifty-five months. "At times, his work made him ill. He recalled: 'When I was describing the poisoning of Emma Bovary, I had such a taste of arsenic in my mouth and was poisoned so effectively myself, that I had two attacks of indigestion, one after the other—two very real attacks, for I vomited my entire dinner.' Other times, he was emotionally upset by his own creation. 'Last Wednesday I was obliged to get up and look for my handkerchief; tears were streaming down my face. I had moved myself deeply as I wrote.' "

[Irving Wallace, The Nympho and Other Maniacs *(New York: Simon & Schuster, 1971), pp. 207, 214–15.]*

SERENITY

God's Peace

> Drop Thy still dew of quietness
> Till all our strivings cease.
> Take from our souls the strain and stress,
> And let our ordered lives confess
> The beauty of Thy peace.
> —JOHN GREENLEAF WHITTIER

SERVICE
Functional for God

One reason so many people fail to be truly effective in ministry is that they are not flexible or functional enough. They have preconceived ideas on how they should serve and are not open to being freely used by God. Lewis B. Smedes discusses this in light of the biblical injunction for Christians to be clay in the potter's hands.

"Most clay jars are made to be of some use. I go to a museum and wonder about those vases that have survived the furies of volcanoes and tides of time; what were they for? The potter in his shop in a back alley of Athens three thousand years ago was not making a vase to be a collector's item to reveal the glories of Greek culture to museum buffs of the twentieth century. He was making a jar for a slave to carry water to his master's garden, or maybe a jug for wine to be served at a wedding. Most of the time, an earthen vessel is functional. It becomes a piece of art as a secondary matter. It is made mostly to carry and pour whatever someone puts in it. Earthen vessels of God function as pourers out of what God fills in. What God fills them with is himself.

"Earthen vessels must be fillable in order to be functional. Somehow, in his subtle way, he has to get inside us; he has to come with his spirit, work his way into our consciousness, and become God in us. . . . We may be ornamental, but he does not invest his treasure in bookshelf ornaments. *Fragile,* we are, and *fallible,* but *fillable and functional* we can be, earthen vessels containing God's finest gift."

[Lewis B. Smedes, How Can It Be All Right When Everything Is All Wrong? (New York: Harper & Row, 1982), p. 75.]

Service Given Freely to Others

Serving others joyfully and without obligation is one of the most gratifying aspects of life, and yet this type of service is often a rarity among family members. There are ways to encourage loving service in the family, as Judith Lechman points out. "In my home, we have what we've dubbed The Reciprocity Jar, which is filled with slips of paper listing our names and the jobs we heartily dislike doing around the house and yard. Sitting in full view in the kitchen, the jar gives family members the opportunity to serve one another whenever we choose to open the lid and draw out one of the unpopular jobs."

[Judith C. Lechman, The Spirituality of Gentleness: Growing toward Christian Wholeness *(San Francisco: Harper & Row, 1987), p. 87.]*

SEX DIFFERENCES

Babies' Responsiveness

Some researchers would argue that there are significant personality differences observable in babies from the time of birth and that these differences are often determined by sex. Indeed, there are indications that the sensitivity that often characterizes women more than men is something that develops from infancy.

"From birth, females are more tuned in to other people than men are. Studies have shown that a female baby is more reactive and responsive to other human beings than a baby boy. Baby girls smile more. They are more responsive to the cries of other babies in the nursery. They start crying along with another baby more readily than baby boys do.

"Baby girls babble more in response to the sight of a human face. At the age of three months, girl babies show great interest in and pay attention to photographs of human faces. Male babies, at the same age, can't quite distinguish between photos and simple line drawings of both normal and distorted faces. All stimuli are equally acceptable to male infants, while girls prefer photos of human faces. There's an innately stronger 'other people' bias in even the smallest female."

[Brenda Poinsett, Understanding a Woman's Depression *(Wheaton: Tyndale, 1984), p. 51.]*

Childbearing

Of all the First Ladies in our nation's history, Eleanor Roosevelt stands out as one of the most independent and outspoken. Yet, she shunned any association with feminism and emphasized the differences between men and women. "Women are different than men," she wrote; "their physical functions are different, and the future of the race depends upon their ability to produce healthy children." She was an ardent opponent of the Equal Rights Amendment because she feared the loss of benefits given to women in the workplace that in some cases exempted them from night shifts as well as dangerous and exceptionally arduous labor.

[Sylvia Ann Hewlett, A Lesser Life: The Myth of Women's Liberation *(New York: Morrow, 1986), p. 147.]*

Physical Sex Differences

Although Martin Luther was in many ways ahead of his time in his attitude toward women, he demonstrated many of the typical biases of his day in his conversations about women with friends and colleagues. "Men have broad and large chests, and small narrow hips, and more understanding than women, who have but small and narrow chests, and broad hips, to the end they should remain at home, sit still, keep house, and bear and bring up children."

[Will Durant, The Reformation: A History of European Civilization from Wycliffe to Calvin, 1300–1564 *(New York: Simon & Schuster, 1957), p. 416. Originally appeared in Martin Luther,* Table-Talk, *725, 1569.]*

Psychological Sex Differences

In her book *Let Me Be a Woman,* Elisabeth Elliot maintains that there are inherent differences between the sexes that prepare men and women for different roles in society. "It was God who made us different, and

He did it on purpose. Recent scientific research is illuminating, and as has happened before, corroborates ancient truth which mankind has always recognized. God created male and female, the male to call forth, to lead, initiate and rule, and the female to respond, follow, adapt, submit. Even if we held to a different theory of origin the physical structure of the female would tell us that woman was made to receive, to bear, to be acted upon, to complement, to nourish."

[Elisabeth Elliot, Let Me Be a Woman (Wheaton: Tyndale, 1976), p. 59.]

Speech Patterns in Men and Women

Although it is a popular myth that women spend more time talking about themselves and gossiping than men do, research has disputed that conclusion. Elizabeth Aries, a social psychologist, recorded single-sex and mixed-sex conversations and discovered that women in all-female groups were less likely than men in all-male groups to talk about themselves. "Men were also more likely to use self-mentions to demonstrate superiority or aggressiveness, while women used them to share an emotional reaction to what was being said by others."

A similar conclusion was drawn by Phil Donahue, who summarized the difference between male and female conversation succinctly. "If you're in a social situation, and women are talking to each other, and one woman says, 'I was hit by a car today,' all the other women will say, 'You're kidding! What happened? Where? Are you all right?' In the same situation with males, one male says, 'I was hit by a car today.' I guarantee you that there will be another male in the group who will say, 'Wait till I tell you what happened to *me.*' "

[Gloria Steinem, Outrageous Acts and Everyday Rebellions (New York: Holt, Rinehart & Winston, 1983), p. 182.]

Vocational Differences between Sexes

Man for the field, and woman for the hearth;
Man for the sword, and for the needle she;

Man with the head, and woman with the heart;
Man to command, and woman to obey;
All else confusion.

—ALFRED LORD TENNYSON, *The Princess,* Part 5

SEX DISCRIMINATION

Church Ministry

As a young woman, Florence Nightingale longed to be involved in Christian ministry, but all she encountered was roadblocks. "I would have given her [the church] my head, my hand, my heart. She would not have them. She did not know what to do with them. She told me to go back and do crochet in my mother's drawing-room. 'You may go to Sunday school if you like,' she said, but she gave me no training even for that. She gave me neither work to do for her, nor education for it.' "

[Marlys Taege, And God Gave Women Talents! *(St. Louis: Concordia, 1978), p. 90.]*

Female Inferiority

Ancient as well as modern literature contains frequent strains of strong antifemale bias. Plato, in *Timaeus,* warns those who live wickedly that they will become women in their reincarnation. Aristotle, recognized as an authority in natural sciences, wrote in *The Generation of Animals* that "the female is, as it were, a mutilated male." In modern times the philosopher Schopenhauer belittled women, saying they were "childish, frivolous, and short-sighted and existed solely for the propagation of the species." Nietzsche scorned them for their "pedantry, superficiality, presumption, petty licentiousness and immodesty." Charles Darwin regarded women inferior to men in everything "requiring deep thought, reason or imagination, or merely the use of the senses or the hands."

[Paul K. Jewett, Man as Male and Female *(Grand Rapids: Eerdmans, 1975), pp. 151–52.]*

Male Authority over Women

The view that, by nature, men are leaders and women are followers has been espoused by many church leaders throughout history, but none have spoken so forcefully in recent decades as John R. Rice. "There are women doctors, and any woman who can pass the medical course is permitted to be a doctor; yet how few men will call a woman doctor! How few business men on a board of directors would elect a woman as general manager of a big company. How few men would hire a woman boss over other men. The truth is that men know that which is so plain in all nature, that God did not intend a woman to be in authority over men. It is unnatural and inefficient. Then do you wonder that in the modern sissyfied churches the average he-man will have no part? There was never any lack of men to hear the gospel under the bold, strong preaching of Spurgeon, Wesley, Finney, Moody, Torrey and Billy Sunday. And plain, solid, masculine preachers with holy boldness and a John the Baptist type of ministry, have no trouble getting a hearing among men today."

[John R. Rice, Bobbed Hair, Bossy Wives, and Women Preachers *(Murfreesboro, Tenn.: Sword of the Lord, 1941), p. 65.]*

Missionary Service and Sex Discrimination

During the early decades of the modern missionary movement, single women were not granted overseas assignments. The only way a woman could be a missionary was to marry one, and even then she was regarded only as an "assistant." But even getting overseas as a missionary wife was often difficult, as was true with Mrs. John Scudder, the mother of the famous Dr. Ida Scudder, who was a pioneer in women's medical work in India. When Ida's parents first made plans to go to India, her mother was denied mission-board support because she was regarded a poor health risk. The rigors of missionary life and the tropical disease-ridden climate were judged to be too severe for a frail woman. She went despite the board's rejection of her (her husband accepted the responsibility for her support) and conducted a fruitful ministry for sixty-three years, outliving her husband by a quarter of a century.

[Dorothy Clarke Wilson, Dr. Ida: The Story of Dr. Ida Scudder of Vellore *(New York: McGraw-Hill, 1959), p. 221.]*

Sex Discrimination Not Recognized by Women

One of the reasons that sex discrimination is so easily perpetuated is that it is often unrecognized by the very people against whom it is directed. This can also be true of other forms of discrimination, but in the case of sex discrimination, many women believe it is deserved or that it represents an ideal perspective. "The first step a woman must take toward getting parity with men," writes Kathryn Stechert, "is to recognize when she's discriminated against—and surprisingly enough that's not as easy as it sounds." She cites a study done by Faye Crosby, a professor of psychology at Yale University, which showed that "women seemed unable to see discrimination against themselves, even though they thought *other* women were discriminated against. Paradoxically, women said they felt satisfied by conditions that were obviously unsatisfactory.

"The study involved a group of 163 women and 182 men who were matched in background, job status, motivation, and job satisfaction. In the groups of men and women there were equal proportions of people in high-status jobs, like doctors, lawyers, and business consultants, and low-status jobs, such as clerks. The men, however, earned an average of $8,000 to $10,000 more than the women. And yet the women, like the men, reported they were satisfied and fairly treated in all aspects of their jobs, *including pay.* The women said they thought sex discrimination in the American labor force was strong and that men and women received unequal pay for equal work; they simply didn't think they specifically were suffering from discrimination. Crosby says that women in her study seemed to follow an unspoken syllogism. It starts with the major premise: 'Women are discriminated against.' It continues with the minor premise: 'I am a woman.' And in a burst of psychologic it concludes: 'Phew, that was a close call.' "

[Kathryn Stechert, On Your Own Terms: A Woman's Guide to Working with Men (New York: Random House, 1986), pp. 234–35.]

Sex Discrimination and the Church

The Roman Catholic church, of all the large denominations, has been the least inclined to make changes in its stance on women and their place in the church. Indeed, some of its pronouncements in the twentieth century have sounded more like they were made during the Middle Ages, when the church found very little that was positive to say about women. "Are the souls of women equal to the souls of men? This issue actually made its way into the 1913 edition of the *Catholic Encyclopedia.*" The author of one of the articles maintained that "the female sex is in some respects inferior to the male sex, both as regards body and soul." Can women sing in church choirs? In 1927, the bishop of Providence called for priests to abide by the teachings of Pope Pius X. "In *Motu Proping,* issued in 1903, the Pope had affirmed that church singers filled a 'real liturgical office' and that 'women, being incapable of exercising such office, cannot be admitted to form part of the choir'; soprano and contralto parts must be sung by boys." In 1977, the Vatican issued the *Declaration on the Question of the Admission of Women to the Ministerial Priesthood,* in which it stated that women were equal with men, but because of the significance of Christ's maleness, they were unsuited to be priests. A Gallup poll taken after that declaration showed that 41 percent of American Catholics supported women as priests.

[Ruth A. Tucker and Walter L. Liefeld, Daughters of the Church: Women and Ministry from New Testament Times to the Present (Grand Rapids: Zondervan, 1987), p. 377.]

"Women's Work"

It is well known that some types of employment command lesser salaries because the jobs are considered "women's work." A century ago, when most clerical office workers were men, their incomes were nearly double that of blue-collar employees. The same was true of bank tellers. Prior to World War II they were predominantly male, and their profession was well paid. In the modern era women have largely filled these positions, and with that change the real incomes these jobs command have dropped dramatically. "Today 80 percent of all clerical jobs are held by women, and the average wage is far below that of blue-collar work. In fact, in the modern economy a secretary with eighteen years' experience earns less than a parking lot attendant."

[Sylvia Ann Hewlett, A Lesser Life: The Myth of Women's Liberation in America (New York: Morrow, 1986), p. 75.]

SEX EDUCATION

Early Support

Although much controversy surrounds sex education in public schools, advocates of sex education have been sounding their voices for generations. They did not arise as a response to the sexual revolution of the 1960s, as some might suppose. Opposition to their viewpoint, however, was much stronger in generations past, and the extreme care taken not to offend delicate moral standards was plainly evident in writings and lectures. One such advocate of sex education was Sylvester Graham, a one-time clergyman who became a health reformer. A lecture he delivered in 1834 shows his prudence and his foresight in matters as controversial as sex education. His concern was primarily for young men, a factor in itself which allowed him more latitude than if he had been suggesting the same for young women. He deplored any effort to tantalize the sexual urge, but ignorance of the subject was not the solution either. In many ways his advice has as much merit today as it did a century and a half ago.

"I am fully aware of the delicacy and difficulty attending the discussion of the subject of the following Lecture, and have seriously and solemnly considered all the objections which can be made against its publication; but I am also aware of the immense importance that young men should be correctly and properly instructed on this subject. He who in any manner endeavours to excite the sensual appetites, and arouse the unchaste passions of youth, is one of the most heinous offenders against the welfare of mankind. . . . There is no point of morality of more importance; and none that is intrinsically connected with so much difficulty. Through a fear of contaminating the minds of youth, it has long been considered the wisest measure to keep them in ignorance; and too generally, in order to sustain this measure, the natural inquisitiveness of the young mind has been met by misrepresentation and falsehood, on the part of those who would preserve their purity; while, on the other hand, the basest of human cupidity has eagerly catered to the restless and prying curiosity, which has thus been exceedingly augmented. So that, while parents have been resting securely in the idea of the ignorance and purity of their children, these have been clandestinely drinking in the most corrupt and depraving knowledge from mercenary and polluted hands.

"I am fully convinced that mankind have erred in judgment and in practice on this point. Truth, properly inculcated, can never be injurious. The only questions are, When and How? As to the *when,* I am decidedly of the opinion that it should be as early as the young mind can be made to understand the subject accurately; and in regard to the manner or the *how,* I am satisfied that it should at first be as purely scientific as possible. Anatomy and Physiology must become common branches of education, and fundamental principles in all our systems of instruction and government, and all our domestic and social customs, before society reaches its highest good. And this kind of knowledge can never be corrupting in its effects nor tendencies. The more perfectly scientific the young mind becomes in anatomy and physiology, the more strongly is it secured against the undue influence of lewd associations; and it learns to think even of the sexual organs with as little lasciviousness as it does the stomach and lungs. But all this requires great wisdom and prudence."

[*Sylvester Graham,* Chastity, in a Course of Lectures to Young Men: Intended Also for the Serious Consideration of Parents and Guardians *(New York: Fowler & Wells, n.d.), pp. i–ii.]*

SEXUAL INTERCOURSE
Abstinence

Mahatma Gandhi believed that sexual intercourse was for procreation and not for pleasure, and he publicly took a vow of celibacy some years after he was married. He believed that "the physical and mental states of the parents at the time of conception are reproduced in the baby" and thus intercourse should be regarded as serious business and be practiced only when the husband and wife "desire issue." He summed up his position by saying, "I think it is the height of ignorance to believe that the sexual act is an independent function necessary like sleeping or eating. The world depends for its existence on the act of generation, and as the world is the play-ground of God and a reflection of His glory, the act of generation should be controlled for the ordered growth of the world. He who realizes this will control his lust at any cost, equip himself with the knowledge necessary for the physical, mental and spiritual well-being of his progeny, and give the benefit of that knowledge to posterity."

[Erik H. Erikson, Gandhi's Truth: On the Origins of Militant Nonviolence *(New York: Norton, 1969), p. 193.]*

Diminishes Physical and Mental Powers

Ellen G. White, the nineteenth-century prophetess of Seventh-day Adventism, wrote a lot about what she believed to be sexual immorality. She did not limit the scope of such to be just those sins outside marriage, but was convinced that "the marriage covenant covers sins of the darkest hue." She admonished wives to avoid at all costs such immorality. "Let the Christian wife refrain, both in word and act, from exciting the animal passions of her husband. Many have no strength at all to waste in this direction. From their youth up they have weakened the brain and sapped the constitution by the gratification of animal passions. Self-denial and temperance should be the watchword in their married life; then the children born to them will not be so liable to have the moral and intellectual organs weak, and the animal strong. Vice in children is almost universal. Is there not a cause? Who have given them the stamp of character? May the Lord open the eyes of all to see that they are standing in slippery places."

[Ellen G. White, Testimony for the Church *(Oakland: Pacific Press, n.d.), 2:472, 477, 478.]*

Orgasm

Some women have become very concerned in recent years by the stories they frequently hear on talk shows or in print of other women experiencing the ultimate pleasure of sexual orgasm, while they themselves experience no such comparable pleasure. Dr. Ruth Westheimer maintains that such women should not be overly concerned about their situation.

"Women who do not have orgasms from intercourse are in the majority. Is this a gloomy fact? Look at it this way—if you have orgasms from intercourse, fabulous. If not, you are with the majority and not singled out by a cruel fate through some fault of your own.

"Statistics in this area are not up to date, and are constantly changing anyway. Suffice it to say that some women have orgasms through intercourse, some only through masturbation or other direct stimulation of the clitoris and some report having never had an orgasm.

"There is also a small percentage so orgasmic that they can *think* themselves into an orgasm and a small percentage who may be physically incapable of orgasm.

"Whatever the numbers, and whatever category you fall into, sex should still be a cherished and special part of your life."

[Ruth Westheimer, Dr. Ruth's Guide for Married Lovers *(New York: Warner Books, 1986), p. 219.]*

Passive Role of Women in Sex

In her book *The Power of Sexual-Surrender,* Marie Robinson maintains that the woman must be passive in sexual intercourse in order to have complete fulfillment. "The ability to achieve normal orgasm can be called the physical counterpart of psychological surrender. . . . For a woman orgasm requires a trust in one's partner that is absolute. . . . As we know, in sexual intercourse, as in life, man is the actor, woman the passive one, the receiver, the acted upon. . . . There must be a sensual eagerness to surrender; in the woman's orgasm *the excitement comes from the act of surrender.* There is a tremendous surging physical ecstasy in the yielding itself, in the feeling of being the passive instrument of another person, of being stretched out supinely beneath him, taken up will-lessly by his passion as leaves are swept up before a wind."

[Marie N. Robinson, The Power of Sexual-Surrender *(New York: New American Library, 1962), pp. 157–58.]*

Puritanical Views of Sex

Puritanical (or prudish) views of sex and pleasure in the Protestant tradition developed through the teaching and preaching of John Calvin, who sought to bring a new moral standard to the worldly city of Geneva in the sixteenth century. He not only rebuked public social amusements such as the theater, but he sought to regulate the private sexual pleasures of married couples. Unlike Martin Luther, who "held that in marriage a child of God could and should enjoy the full pleasure of sexual relations," Calvin "advised a husband to approach his wife 'with delicacy and propriety' and held that it was inexcusable for a wife to touch or even look at her husband's genitals. As a matter of fact, Calvin seemed to be afraid that enjoying one's self too much in marriage was wrong."

[Oscar E. Feucht, ed., Sex and the Church *(St. Louis: Concordia, 1961), p. 86.]*

Victorian Limitations on Sex

Advice books in the nineteenth century frequently warned people—married couples in particular—about the harmful effects of overindulging in sexual intercourse. They also warned of the dangers of having sex at certain times of the day. Sometimes this advice was given by nonprofessional moral reformers of the day; other times by medical specialists. An example of the latter is Dr. Frederick Hollick, who wrote *The Male Generative Organs in Health and Disease.*

"The *time* for sexual indulgence should be so chosen that the temporary excitement and after-exhaustion resulting from it, may not interfere with any of the bodily or mental functions, nor distress the system by necessitating too much effort during any needful exertion. Ignorance of this important rule, and consequent neglect of it, very often leads to great inconvenience, and even serious mischief. Sexual indulgence just after eating is nearly certain to be followed by indigestion, even if it does not cause immediate vomiting, owing to the temporary loss of nervous power thereby produced, which arrests the action of the stomach. Just *before* eating also the same evils may follow, from the stomach being made so weak that digestion cannot properly commence, and the food consequently ferments. . . . It is true that most men experience *stronger desire* for indulgence *immediately after* a full meal, particularly when stimulating drinks have been used, but this does not prove that they choose the best time. . . . Nor should the licentious furor produced by wine be in any way considered as the promptings of nature.

"Upon the same principles it is obviously injudicious to seek indulgence just previous to any mental effort being made, because the vital energy will be too much exhausted to allow of such effort being made with advantage. Nor is it advisable immediately *after* any great mental effort, because it is injurious to have *two* causes of exhaustion in action at the same time. The same remarks also apply to *muscular exercise,* which should neither immediately follow nor closely precede sexual indulgence, for the same reasons above given. In short the period chosen should be one when both body and mind can enjoy repose, at least for a short period, both before and after, and when none of the functions are like to be disturbed."

[*Frederick Hollick,* The Male Generative Organs in Health and Disease *(New York: Strong, n.d.), pp. 357–59.*]

Viewing Sex as Sin

Because sexual intercourse has often been associated with sin in the Christian tradition—especially the original sin in the Garden of Eden—some theologians and sectarian leaders have invented extreme restrictions to curb the sexual appetite. A number of groups condemned marriage and the sexual act altogether, and some, such as the Cathari of the Middle Ages, went as far as to avoid eating anything that could be associated with the sexual process, including such foods as eggs, milk, butter, and cheese. But extreme views regarding sex were not limited to the so-called heretical movements. "Catholic writers admit that during the Middle Ages the church itself went to great extremes in attempting to belittle the sexual side of marriage. Complete abstinence from sex relations had to be maintained on no less than five days out of seven, on Thursdays in memory of the arrest of our Lord, on Fridays in commemoration of His death, on Saturdays in honor of the Blessed Virgin, on Sundays in honor of the resurrection, and on Mondays in honor of the faithful departed."

[*Oscar E. Feucht, ed.,* Sex and the Church *(St. Louis: Concordia, 1961), p. 61.*]

What Women Want from Sex

Kevin Leman, a well-known psychologist who has effectively counseled hundreds of women, has learned in some ways to think like a woman. This learning process has been aided by his wife, and he confesses that he is far better equipped to counsel women after having endured difficult struggles with his wife. Women have different perspectives on life than men do, and unless these differences can be resolved, serious problems develop.

"One obvious difference between men and women centers around sexuality. I see men constantly ignoring this difference, usually out of ignorance. I sympathize with a man who is baffled by his wife's lack of enthusiasm for sex when *he* wants it, because I was very naive myself during the first years of our marriage.

"I thought the greatest thing we could share together was *copulating.* Sande taught me that the greatest thing we could share together was *communicating.* She taught me that a woman likes to be held and loved but not pawed and used. And she taught me that sex is a beautiful experience to share together as a natural result of communicating and loving each other. Sex is not to be simply the gratification of a natural urge."

[*Kevin Leman,* Bonkers: Why Women Get Stressed Out and What They Can Do about It *(Old Tappan, N.J.: Revell, 1987), pp. 15–16.*]

SEXUALITY

Cause of Embarrassment

Even before the Victorian age, when it was considered a disgrace for a woman's ankle to be seen, anything related to one's anatomy or sexual makeup was viewed by some as improper for discussion—especially in the presence of girls or women. When Emma Willard opened the Troy Female Seminary in 1821, she was determined to teach her students more than the traditional domestic skills. The girls were taught "mathematics, geography, history, and the 'natural sciences,' which included physiology, a staggering innovation for female students. Any mention of the human body was considered the height of indelicacy." This attitude was seen when some of the students' mothers visited the classroom. They were so appalled at their daughters' outlining the circulatory system on the blackboard that they walked out in horror.

To help alleviate such distress, Mrs. Willard had paper pasted over any textbook illustrations of the body or its organs.

[Emily Hahn, Once Upon a Pedestal *(New York: Crowell, 1974), p. 34.]*

SHYNESS

How to Overcome It

Shyness can be overcome if an individual recognizes the problem and is committed to changing certain behavioral patterns that perpetuate it. Indeed, an individual can prepare herself ahead of time to deal with shyness in difficult situations. In *Letitia Baldrige's Complete Guide to a Great Social Life,* Baldrige offers some helpful suggestions.

"Keep using images to help you along and to ease your discomfort. Imagine you have a big, handsome treasure chest in your mind, chock full of conversational tidbits about *other* people and other subjects, not about yourself. Imagine that these conversational gambits are all neatly laid away in the drawers of that chest. When you need to start up a conversation, visualize yourself opening one of the drawers and pulling out a topic, statement, or question to ask of the other person. Once you have put the topic in front of the other person, it is his or her responsibility to make the response, and for you then to make a further response. When you find there is nothing left in the drawer on that particular topic, open another drawer and launch a fresh topic. And remember: If you choose topics relevant to the other person, he or she will be pleased and flattered."

Baldrige strongly emphasizes the point that shy people must focus on other people, not themselves. "One way of combatting your shyness, quite apart from learning how to make conversation with strangers, is to convince yourself that you are *not* one of those selfish, self-centered people who don't care about anyone other than themselves. Extreme shyness is extreme introversion that shuts out thoughts of others. It is a most unattractive trait, and you should prove to yourself and everyone else that you are not like that. In actual fact, once you start caring and thinking about others, you won't be turned inward. You can't be two places at the same time—inside yourself and outside in the world! So think 'outside,' and you *will* be outside—out in the wonderful world that has so much to offer you."

[Letitia Baldrige, Letitia Baldrige's Complete Guide to a Great Social Life *(New York: Rawson Associates, 1987), pp. 71–72.]*

SINGLENESS

Appreciation

> When I think of my single bliss
>   which is doomed to be my lot,
> I make a list of all the men
>   whose wives I'm glad I'm not.
>   —ANONYMOUS

Contentment in Being Single

Mary Slessor, the much-revered Presbyterian missionary to Calabar in West Africa, knew well the anguish of a difficult marriage. Her father was an alcoholic without steady employment, and there were nights after she came home from long hours in the mill earning money to support the family that he threw her out in the street in one of his drunken rages. She escaped the mills to become a pioneer missionary in Africa, working alone—except for her adopted African children and friends. On one occasion she almost married. She had fallen in love with a visiting missionary who was eighteen years her junior. In fact, she accepted his marriage proposal and wore an engagement ring. But the marriage never took place. His health was not suitable for tropical Africa, and Mary refused to give up her ministry.

Experience indicated that she was not really suited for marriage anyway. Her living habits and daily routine were so haphazard that she was better off by herself. Single women had tried to live with her, but usually without success. Indeed, her life-style was far more suited to the Africans than to her European colleagues. She labored for nearly forty years in the unhealthy African climate and heartily testified that she was "a witness to the perfect joy and satisfaction of a single life."

[Carol Christian and Gladys Plummer, God and One Red Head: Mary Slessor of Calabar (Grand Rapids: Zondervan, 1970), pp. 34, 177.]

Lack of Male Companionship

An attractive feature of singleness is the independence that it offers, but along with independence there are sometimes loneliness and the yearning for male companionship. Audrey Lee Sands, who served for twelve years as a missionary in Europe, writes of this problem in her book Single and Satisfied.

"By the end of my first year on the field, though still very happy in the work, I began to feel deep depression resulting from lack of companionship and friendship with the opposite sex. It was a feeling of inadequacy, a feeling that no man would ever really want me anyhow. . . .

"Another year passed and then came a jolt. I suddenly realized that what I craved was not marriage. The Lord had indeed helped me to lay that aside. There was something else. Except for brief exchanges of conversation over our work, I was completely cut off from masculine minds. Frantically I wondered if I would ever be able to communicate with a man again.

"At the time I was the only single girl living with several families, all of them fairly young. All the men with whom I worked were married. That meant I was rightfully cut off from real fellowship with them. I shall never forget the day this realization hit me. I went to my apartment and cried for hours. Finally, on my knees, I said another big 'yes' to the Lord. 'All right, Lord, you've taken me this far. Now if you want me to be forever barred from a conversation with a man about anything except work and weather, all right. Take that too. I want you to be in my life.' Was that a ridiculously extreme commitment? When the Lord asks, he asks for all. When we have said 'yes' to all, then he can in his wisdom and grace and love give back the portion he knows will not hurt us. And of course, that is exactly what he has done for me. There has been abundant opportunity for stimulating fellowship with follow laborers and others.

"From time to time the whole issue of masculine companionship has to be recommitted. Sometimes there comes a temptation to feel sorry for yourself. An overwhelming emotion sweeps over you as you look out on a breathtaking scene. There's a surge of desire to have a masculine hand in yours—someone with whom to share the beauty. How many fresh commitments I have made to God as I watched the moon make a golden path across the sea, a scene I could see often from my apartment.

"Sometimes the whole issue arises all over again when you are presented with a physically difficult situation which under normal conditions a man would handle. Perhaps it is when you're alone in a dangerous spot at night with a flat tire. . . .

"It is times like these that the Lord can be the most precious. Do not sink into self-pity. The only way to handle such experiences is to lift your heart instantly in adoration and praise to your Lord. Tell him once more that you love him and that is all you need. . . .

"If you wish, there's a method guaranteed to shatter your contentment in the Lord. Build air castles over a man you used to know or one you would like to know. Dream a little. Indulge in a few moments of self-pity. . . .

"The enemy longs to take our minds off the Lord. He knows that the Lord alone can supply the very thing we most desire."

[Audrey Lee Sands, Single and Satisfied (Wheaton: Tyndale, 1971), pp. 27–30.]

SMOKING

Help in Quitting

In her book *Caught with My Mouth Open,* Winnie Christensen tells how she teamed up with Nena, an acquaintance at church, to start a neighborhood Bible study. Nena was enthusiastic and "such an effective leader and good teacher"—but she was a smoker, and Winnie feared that habit would "hinder the scope of her outreach." Yet, Winnie was hesitant to confront her directly on the issue. "If I had told her she couldn't lead and smoke at the same time, one of two things might have resulted—she could have become resentful and closed herself to usefulness, or she might have tried to stop to please me. This would have been such a shallow reason that it wouldn't have lasted. By waiting for the Lord to do the work, the job was done far better. And it was permanent."

Nena did stop smoking after being convicted about her habit during a Bible study session. That afternoon, she later testified, "while cleaning the bedroom, I gave up the fight. I knelt down and turned my life, without reservation, over to God." That commitment was only the beginning of a very difficult struggle, but with the help of friends, Nena carried out her vow. Another member of the Bible study who had herself struggled with a smoking habit came to the rescue. "She prepared a 'survival kit' with beautifully wrapped packages of toothpicks, life savers, gum, aspirin, all marked to be opened right after breakfast, 10 A.M., after lunch, after dinner, bedtime, or 'when you think you can't last another minute!' " Others phoned her to give encouragement, and most of all, writes Winnie, "we prayed." In the end, Nena confessed that she had been freed. God—not cigarettes—was in control of her life.

[Winnie Christensen, Caught with My Mouth Open *(Wheaton: Shaw, 1969), pp. 66–67.]*

SOLITUDE

Love of Aloneness

"I find it wholesome to be alone the greater part of the time. To be in company, even with the best, is soon wearisome and dissipating. I love to be alone. I never found the companion that was so companionable as solitude. We are for the most part more lonely when we go abroad among men than when we stay in our chambers."

[Henry David Thoreau, Walden *(New York: New American Library, 1960), p. 95.]*

Value of Solitude

Anne Morrow Lindbergh, the widow of Charles Lindbergh, who endured the agonizing sorrow that dragged on after the kidnapping of her small child, was strengthened through times of solitude. "How wonderful are islands! Islands in space . . . ringed about by miles of water, linked by no bridges, no cables, no telephones. . . . People, too, become like islands, not intruding on their shores, standing back in reverence before the miracle of another individual. . . . We seem so frightened today of being alone that we never let it happen. Even if family, friends, and movies should fail, there is still the radio or television to fill up the void. Women, who used to complain of loneliness, need never be alone any more. We can do our housework with soap-opera heroes at our side. Even day-dreaming was more creative than this; it demanded something of oneself and it fed the inner life. Now, instead of planting our solitude with our own dream blossoms, we choke the space with continuous music, chatter, and companionship to which we do not even listen. It is simply there to fill the vacuum. When the noise stops there is no inner music to take its place. We must re-learn to be alone."

[*Anne Morrow Lindbergh,* Gift from the Sea *(New York: Vintage Books, 1978), pp. 41–42.]*

SORROW

Hidden from Others

Sorrow comes in a variety of forms, but according to Elisabeth Dodds, the most painful sorrow is frequently that which is kept secret because of the disgrace connected with it. "The sharpest sorrow is the one we dare not confide to any other. A death or obvious disaster is at least evident to others, and friends can comfort us with casseroles and kindly notes. But the shadow we must carry in secret forces us to listen to admonitions about why we should perk up. We must maintain the facade of poise when we really want to screech: 'My husband is having an affair ... My son has become a surly stranger ... I love to distraction someone I dare not even name ... I'm afraid my daughter is beginning to steal things ... Today is my birthday—and where has my life gone?"

[Elisabeth D. Dodds, Marriage to a Difficult Man: The "Uncommon Union" of Jonathan and Sarah Edwards (Philadelphia: Westminster Press, 1971), p. 82.]

SOVEREIGNTY OF GOD
Seen in the Course of Human Life

My life is but a weaving, between my God and me,
I do not choose the colors, He worketh steadily,
Oftimes He weaveth sorrow, and I in foolish pride,
Forget He sees the upper side, and I the underside.
Not till the loom is silent, and shuttle cease to fly,
Will God unroll the canvas and explain the reason why.
The dark threads are as needful in the skillful Weaver's hand
As the threads of gold and silver in the pattern He has planned.

—ANONYMOUS

[Quoted in Corrie ten Boom, with Jamie Buckingham, Tramp for the Lord (Old Tappan, N.J.: Revell, 1974), p. 12.]

SPIRITUAL GIFTS
Used to Serve the Handicapped

Joni Eareckson Tada illustrates how people can utilize various spiritual gifts to serve handicapped people—and these illustrations could apply equally to hurting or needy people who may not be handicapped. "The *gift of mercy* is one of those behind-the-scenes gifts, often administered away from the public eye. It's the lady armed not only with her Bible, but with a box of Kleenex, ready to console the lonely or comfort the hurting. It's that person who will touch or share a hug— someone who will sit and listen and pray.

"During those lonely, fresh-out-of-the-hospital days of early adjustment, I remember one girlfriend who, during visits, would occasionally lie next to me in bed, hold my hand, and sing hymns to me. She didn't give me advice or a grocery list of Bible verses. My merciful friend simply used her spiritual gift.

"Does somebody in your church have the *gift of service?* . . . When I was first injured, neighbors would often call my mother and say, 'Look, I'm on my way to the market. Have your list ready, and I'll be glad to pick up your items.'

"People who have the *gift of administration* have the ability to envision success for those who are often too weak to envision it for themselves. They break down big goals into small tasks and, in the final analysis, enjoy seeing all the pieces come together.

"For instance, I never dared to dream of going to college. . . . Thankfully, another friend of mine used her managing skills to arrange for transportation to and from campus, volunteers to assist with note-taking, and . . . someone to feed me at the school cafeteria.

"The disabled community can be benefited greatly just by people using their spiritual *gift of giving.* Adaptive equipment—new parts for wheelchairs, braces and crutches, seat cushions, arm splints, Braille typewriters, TTY telephones for the deaf, hearing aids, canes—is very expensive. Federal and state cutbacks in programs which assist the disabled population have brought these special needs to the attention of the private sector. By pooling free-will offerings, the church can demonstrate God's love in action by meeting special financial needs of certain disabled persons."

[Joni Eareckson Tada, "The Role of the Volunteer" in All God's Children: Ministry to the Disabled, *by Gene Newman and Joni Eareckson Tada (Grand Rapids: Zondervan, 1987), pp. 35–37.]*

SPIRITUALITY

Among Common People

The Reformation brought spiritual renewal to many parts of Europe, but in the century that followed, the church in many areas was cold, and the church leaders often showed little evidence of spirituality. This was not always true among the common people, as Madame Jeanne Guyon found when she traveled around. She was a widow and a self-appointed Catholic evangelist who went from village to village challenging people to renew their faith in Christ. Sometimes she was amazed at the spiritual hunger she encountered, as was the situation in the town of Thonon. "I have never in my life had so much consolation as in seeing in that little town so many good souls who vied with each other in giving themselves to God with their whole heart. There were young girls of twelve and thirteen years of age, who worked all day in silence in order to converse with God, and who had acquired a great habit of it. As they were poor girls, they joined in couples and those who knew how to read, read out something to those who could not read. It was revival of the innocence of the early Christians."

[Jeanne Guyon, The Autobiography of Madame Guyon, *trans. Thomas Allen (New Canaan, Conn.: Deats, 1980), p. 231.]*

Daily Devotions

Gary Chapman, a pastor who has counseled many troubled people and written books on the subject of broken relationships, maintains that the first step in healing a relationship with another individual is to heal or develop one's relationship with God. He challenges his counselees and readers to set aside time each day to be with God, and he relates his own experiences as an example of a very specific way to do this.

"For many years I have followed the practice of daily sitting down with God, opening the Bible, and beginning the conversation with these words: 'Father, this is Your day in my life. I want to hear Your voice. I need Your instructions. I want to know what You would say to me this day. As I read this chapter, bring to my mind the things You want me to hear.' Then I read the chapter silently or aloud with pen in hand, marking those things that stand out as I read. Sometimes I read the chapter a second time, saying, 'Lord, I'm not sure I understood what You were saying; I want to read again. I want You to clarify what's on Your mind for me.' I may underline additional lines or phrases.

"Having completed the chapter, I then go back and talk to God about what I've underlined, for if that is what God is saying to me I want to respond to God. Many people simply read the Bible, close it, and then begin praying about something totally unrelated to what they have read. Nothing could be more discourteous. We would not treat a friend like that. If a friend asks a question, we give an answer. If a friend makes a statement, we have a response, so if God speaks to us through the Bible we should respond to what God is saying."

[Gary Chapman, Hope for the Separated *(Chicago: Moody, 1982), p. 46.]*

Women Compared with Men

Women have been found to be more spiritually oriented than men. A Gallup survey showed that 62 percent of "evangelical Christians" were women. A study done by Connecticut Mutual reported that "women are more inclined than men to be highly religious (34 percent to 19 percent)."

[Beverly LaHaye, The Restless Woman *(Grand Rapids: Zondervan, 1984), p. 115.]*

SPORTS

Female Perspective on Football

Despite the growing equality of the sexes in American life, the differences between the two sexes still remain, and one of those differences lies in how women perceive contact sports. Although the numbers of female spectators are growing, a large percentage of women remain uninterested in or rankled by the lengthening football season each year. Gloria Emerson, who writes about American men, offers her perspective on this popular male sport. "A brutish and dull game, nonsensical or murderous at times. The tackled halfback jumped on by so many other players his body cannot be seen, the incessant interruptions and delays, the fumbling or incompleted passes, the broken runs, the crudity of blocking, makes football a tedious and clumsy game to watch. But not to all: every November a sweet suspense stirs the country and lasts, scores are sought, television sets stay on, people drive great distances to see The Game. Defeat does not discourage, hopes are always high, the power of the game eases something clenched and dulled, men are free to jump, scream, roar, beseech, plead. Football lets them be playful when little else does.

"Some women love football but most, like me, do not care or are suspicious and haughty about it. Only the sight of one man alone, poised to kick the ball over the crossbar, rising on his toes, is of the faintest interest."

[*Gloria Emerson,* Some American Men *(New York: Simon & Schuster, 1985), p. 286.]*

STILLBIRTH
Guilt and Pain of the Mother

The guilt, pain, and sorrow that a mother endures from a miscarriage or stillbirth are told by Sylvia Ann Hewlett, who became pregnant with twins while she was teaching at Barnard College, Columbia University. It was a difficult pregnancy, but one she expected to go to full term until one evening, while she was still in her office after a long tension-filled day, she suddenly "realized in horror that my waters had broken." It was only the sixth month of her pregnancy, and she feared for the worst. "I stumbled out into the corridor and, discovering that no one was in the building except me, made my way, dripping, shivering, and sobbing, across the cold dark campus to Broadway. I hailed a cab and asked to be driven to Lenox Hill Hospital."

After three days in the hospital and many hours of agonizing labor, the second of her twins was born dead. "Afterward, for quite a long time, life was truly hard to bear. First, there were the physical ironies. My breasts swelled up hard and hurtful, full of milk for my dead babies. Several weeks later my breasts were still leaking milk, providing a constant reminder of my loss. But I needed no reminder. I mourned my children with an intensity that frightened me. In addition to my grief, I was coping with an overwhelming sense of responsibility. Night after night I lay awake going through various scenarios in my head. I found at least four or five ways in which I thought I might be directly to blame. If only I had given up work, I would not have miscarried. If I had sought a third medical opinion, I might have found a doctor who could have saved the pregnancy. Or if I had chosen an obstetrician attached to a teaching hospital, perhaps one of the babies could have been saved by access to a 'state of the art' neonatal unit. I was riddled with guilt; I had failed to protect my babies and therefore had no pity on myself. For a while I believed that I was living proof of the conservative wisdom that women could not have both careers and babies."

[*Sylvia Ann Hewlett,* A Lesser Life: The Myth of Women's Liberation in America *(New York: Morrow, 1986), pp. 26–27.]*

STRESS

Learning to Live with It

Some people react poorly to stressful situations because they have failed to learn how to live with stress in their lives. Until they do so, they will fail to utilize stress in a way that can actually bring growth in their character. "You need to accept stress as an inevitable part of life," writes Jo Berry. "Peace is not due to the absence of stress in our lives but to the ability to handle it properly. . . . Generally, stress factors are neutral. What stresses one person doesn't affect another. For example, I can speak to large groups and never get nervous, but I wouldn't be able to utter a note if I were asked to sing before that same crowd. Conversely, my friend Sue can pour out her heart in song in front of a large audience but clutches if she has to pray aloud in a small group. It's your personal reaction to stress, based on your own personality, beliefs, strengths, weaknesses, and attitudes, that causes you to react negatively. . . . When faced with a stressful situation, we have two alternatives: do something about it if we can or accept it if we can't. Christ cautioned Martha not to be worried and bothered about so many things; He stressed that 'each day has enough trouble of its own' (Matthew 6:34)."

[Jo Berry, Becoming God's Special Woman *(Old Tappan, N.J.: Revell, 1986), pp. 100–101.]*

Not Determined by Outward Circumstances

Most people blame the stress they encounter on their marriage, their children, their financial situation, their job, or some other set of circumstances. But the primary cause of stress is how people perceive their circumstances. Kevin Leman, a psychologist, gives a typical example that bears this out. "When a boss gets on your case every morning, you can perceive it as a problem or you can realize the boss has arthritis and is never very human until after a three-martini lunch.

"Unfortunately, in your case, the boss's crabby attitude really bothers you and you are just about ready to quit. Why is it that Marge, whose desk is next to yours, just brushes off his tirades and even seems to curry his favor? The answer lies in perception. You perceive the boss one way; Marge perceives him another way. Your perception causes you great stress. Marge sails through without a qualm."

[Kevin Leman, Bonkers: Why Women Get Stressed Out and What They Can Do about It *(Old Tappan, N.J.: Revell, 1987), pp. 34–35.]*

STUBBORNNESS
An Asset and a Liability

Clara Barton, one of the greatest humanitarians of the nineteenth century, could not sit idly by when she saw Civil War soldiers suffering for want of supplies for medical care and in some cases needlessly sacrificing their lives when they could have gone on to contribute further to the war effort. She began collecting supplies and opened a warehouse for distribution. So successful was she that the surgeon-general permitted her free travel to the front lines to carry out her service. Following the war she traveled abroad and learned about the International Red Cross, located in Geneva, and was determined to have it started in America. She wrote and lectured on the topic at a time when many people were far more interested in getting their lives back together and earning money. But her stubborn persistence paid off. Despite bouts of sickness, "she continued campaigning in this one-woman struggle until at last, in 1882, she won. The American Red Cross came into being, with Clara Barton as its president."

But the stubborn persistence that was an asset in founding the organization was a liability in keeping it going. "Miss Barton, still determined to be boss, insisted on managing everything in the organization." Problems developed, and those under her complained about her management. At the age of eighty-three, after an investigation by a special commission, "she was forced to resign, and she departed still fully convinced that she was in the right and everyone else was wrong. During the seven years that followed, her friends found difficulty in persuading her not to cross the border into Mexico, to set up another Red Cross there." She was a woman who gave so much to society, but in the end she failed by stubbornly refusing to step aside and allow others to do the things she was unable to do.

[Emily Hahn, Once Upon a Pedestal (New York: Crowell, 1974), pp. 160–61.]

SUBMISSION

Demanded by Husband

Susanna Wesley, the mother of nineteen children, among whom were John and Charles, is known for her domestic qualities. She was a well-organized minister's wife who had many responsibilities besides those of her own children. Less is known about her relationship with her husband, Samuel. She had been an independent thinker since she was a teenager, when she determined she would not follow her father's footsteps into nonconformity but rather would place her loyalties with the Church of England.

Samuel, her husband, was a domineering man who had difficulty getting along with his parishioners. They resented his strict discipline and sought revenge for it. "They burned his flax corp, taunted the Wesley children, pried the hinges off the rectory doors. They stabbed his cows so that they gave no milk and once even tried to cut off the legs of the house dog." Soon after that he was arrested for failure to pay his debts and sent to debtors' prison.

Even before this humiliating incident, though, Samuel had been away from the parish for an extended period. The cause was Susanna's alleged insubordination—occasioned by a political disagreement. Susanna believed the Stuarts were the only legitimate line of royalty and considered William of Orange a usurper of the throne. This personal political conviction suddenly became ensnarled with the issue of wifely submission when Susanna refused one evening to say "Amen" to her husband's prayer for King William III. In Samuel's mind, his wife had overstepped her bounds—a defiance that required drastic action. "We must part," he insisted, "for if we have two Kings, we must have two beds."

Samuel went through with his threat and left home. Susanna was convinced that she was not to blame. "Since I am willing to let him quietly enjoy his opinions, he ought not to deprive me of my little liberty of conscience." He returned after King William died, who was succeeded by Queen Anne, a Stuart whom they could both support. Shortly after his return Susanna became pregnant with John, who was later referred to as the child of their reconciliation.

[Rebecca L. Harmon, Susanna: Mother of the Wesleys *(Nashville: Abingdon, 1968), pp. 20, 47–49.]*

Submission Initiated by Wife

In discussing Puritan marriage, which has often been characterized by the husband's leadership and authority, Leland Ryken points out that wifely submission was seen as a high priority, but not at the expense of the wife's freedom. "Submission, of course, is something that a wife must yield at her own initiative. If a husband has to force it, the battle has already been lost. Perhaps this accounts for the frequency with which Puritan preachers appealed to the wife to submit to her husband. Their way of phrasing the appeal varied. John Winthrop said that a Christian wife's submission was 'her honor and freedom. . . . Such is the liberty of the church under the authority of Christ.' Gataker admonished the wife 'in holy wisdom and godly discretion . . . to acknowledge her husband . . . her head.' The emphasis in all such Puritan statements was on the attitude of the wife as the crucial element."

[Leland Ryken, Worldly Saints: The Puritans As They Really Were *(Grand Rapids: Zondervan, 1986), pp. 76–77.]*

Lack of Submission in Marriage

In her book *Pioneer Women: Voices from the Kansas Frontier,* Joanna Stratton tells the stories of many rugged and self-reliant women who had the courage to endure the hazards of the stark Kansas environment in the late nineteenth and early twentieth centuries. Although most of these women were married, they manifested an independence in business affairs and in their marriages that was uncommon elsewhere during this period. "Men and women worked together as partners, combining their strengths and talents to provide food and clothing for themselves and their children. As a result, women found themselves on a far more equal footing with their spouses."

One of these pioneer brides later recalled her personal declaration of independence. "I already had ideas of my own about the husband being the head of the family. I had taken the precaution to sound him on 'obey' in the marriage pact and found he did not approve of the term. Approval or no approval, that word 'obey' would have to be left out. I had served my time of tutelage to my parents as all children are supposed to. I was a woman now and capable of being the other half of the head of the family. His word and my word would have equal strength. God had endowed me with reason and understanding and a sense of responsibility. I was going west to try out as a wife and homemaker. How well I have succeeded I leave to those who know me best to tell."

[Joanna L. Stratton, Pioneer Women: Voices from the Kansas Frontier *(New York: Simon & Schuster, 1981), pp. 57–58.]*

Treating Husband like Jesus

How literally should a wife seek to follow Scripture in submitting to her husband? The husband is commanded to love his wife "as Christ loved also the church," but few would ever deem him capable of that kind of perfect love. But is the wife capable of perfect submission to her husband? Judith Miles, in her book *The Feminine Principle,* writes that wives ought to submit to their husbands as though he were God incarnate.

"One day this familiar verse acquired a heightened meaning for me, 'Wives be subject to your husbands, as to the Lord' (Eph. 5:22). . . . I was to treat my own human husband as though he were the Lord, resident in our own humble home. . . . Would I ask Jesus a basically maternal question such as 'How are things at the office?' Would I suggest to Jesus that He finish some tasks around the house? Would I remind the Lord that He was not driving prudently? Would I ever be in judgment over my Lord, over His taste, His opinions, or His actions? I was stunned—stunned into a new kind of submission."

[Judith Miles, The Feminine Principle: A Woman's Discovery of the Key to Total Fulfillment *(Minneapolis: Bethany Fellowship, 1975), p. 44.]*

SUCCESS

Combined Efforts in Christian Ministry

One of the great success stories of the Christian church involves that of the Women's Missionary Movement, which began in 1860. Despite the opposition the pioneers of this movement confronted, they pressed forward, and by 1915 there were over three million women involved in professional and volunteer capacities. Helen Barrett Montgomery, the most visible spokeswoman for the movement, related its accomplishments after a half century of ministry.

"It is indeed a wonderful story. . . . We began in weakness, we stand in power. In 1861 there was a single missionary in the field, Miss Marston, in Burma; in 1909, there were 4710 unmarried women in the field, 1948 of them from the United States. In 1861 there was one organized woman's society in our country; in 1910 there were forty-four. Then the supporters numbered a few hundreds; today there are at least two million. Then the amount contributed was $2000; last year four million dollars was raised. The development on the field has been as remarkable as that at home. Beginning with a single teacher, there are at the opening of the Jubilee year 800 teachers, 140 physicians, 380 evangelists, 79 trained nurses, 5783 Bible women and native helpers. Among the 2100 schools there are 260 boarding and high schools. There are 75 hospitals and 78 dispensaries. . . . It is an achievement of which women may well be proud, but it is only a feeble beginning of what they can do and will do when the movement is on its feet."

[Helen Barrett Montgomery, Western Women in Eastern Lands *(New York: Macmillan, 1910), pp. 243–44.]*

SUFFERING

For the Sake of Others

In China during the years before and after the Boxer Rebellion of 1900, foreigners were viewed with hostility—even those who were there in the front lines to offer sacrificial service. Indeed, many gave their lives to minister to the needy people of China. One of those was Dr. Eleanor Chestnut, a missionary serving with the American Presbyterian Board. Soon after she arrived, she built a hospital, buying the bricks with her own money. But even before the hospital was completed, she was performing surgery in her own bathroom—for want of a better place. "One such operation involved the amputation of a coolie's leg. Complications arose, and skin grafts were needed. Later the doctor was questioned about a leg problem from which she herself was suffering. 'Oh, it's nothing,' she answered, brushing off the inquiry. Later a nurse revealed that the skin graft for the 'good-for-nothing coolie' had come from Dr. Chestnut's own leg while using only a local anesthetic.

"During the Boxer Rebellion, Dr. Chestnut remained on her post longer than most missionaries, and she returned the following year. Then in 1905, while she was busy working at the hospital with four other missionaries, a mob stormed the building. Although she got away in time to alert authorities and in fact could have escaped, she instead returned to the scene to help rescue her colleagues. It was too late. Her colleagues had been slain. But there were others who needed her help. Her final act of service to the Chinese people whom she so loved was to rip a piece of material from her own dress to bandage the forehead of a child who had been wounded during the carnage."

[*Ruth A. Tucker,* From Jerusalem to Irian Jaya: A Biographical History of Christian Missions *(Grand Rapids: Zondervan, 1983), p. 421.]*

Suffering a Source of Joy

There are gains to be made through suffering. It is often difficult to see the value of suffering at the time, but such pain has the potential of building character and strengthening one's faith in God. Only through suffering can Christians truly identify with the suffering of Christ on the cross. In her book *The Spirituality of Gentleness,* Judith Lechman speaks of this kind of suffering and the spiritual benefits it can produce in a life.

"Bearing crosses can be a bitter thing indeed, if we grow afraid of letting go. Years ago I copied a striking phrase in my journal: 'and I rejoice over the falling leaves of self.' I'm not sure where I heard or read it, but it has been a reminder to me over the years that with suffering comes joy. In learning to bear our crosses in this life, we resemble trees in autumn. Layer upon layer of self is stripped away in the whirlwind and storm that is God-directed. Crying out in bitter astonishment at the unexpected pain, we are left naked and defenseless before the world. Bearing our crosses becomes a bleak and joyless journey that we wish were finished.

"Instead, we turn back to God and ask for his strength to renounce, not our suffering, not our pain, not a particular cross, but the tight hold we have on the leaves of self. As we let go of them and begin to 'live for the sake of Jesus Christ,' our suffering merges with his. In this sharing, we begin to know the terrible sacrifice that Christ made for us. Ever so slowly, our bitterness fades as we finally grasp that 'He suffered, and was a Sacrifice, to make our sufferings and sacrifice of ourselves fit to be received by God.' In a process that I can only describe as mysterious, placing our life completely in God's hands as we bear the crosses he gives us becomes an act of adoration and praise that takes us beyond suffering to joy."

[Judith C. Lechman, The Spirituality of Gentleness: Growing toward Christian Wholeness *(San Francisco: Harper & Row, 1987), p. 68.]*

SUICIDE

Asking Forgiveness for Suicide

Sharon Pierce, the daughter of Dr. Bob Pierce, who founded World Vision, struggled with depression during her teenage years that was aggravated by a broken marriage and "gnawing fears and feelings of inadequacy." After a time of serving with her father overseas, she wrote to a friend, "I feel so trapped, as if all my opportunities are quickly passing me by. I concede failure! What do you feel I should do? I'm dying. . . . Help!" She wrote how she needed "the comfort of a man, yes, a father even," but her father was too busy. "The only one who never hurt or disappointed her was the Savior she had accepted as a small child," and she expressed this feeling in her final words before she took her life. "I love you Jesus. Oh, how I beg your forgiveness for each and every time I failed you or sinned. And if you find this last act a sin, please dear God, please forgive me for my final weakness. I love you, as you know."

[Marilee Pierce Dunker, Days of Glory, Seasons of Night *(Grand Rapids: Zondervan, 1984), pp. 132–34.]*

Prevalence of Suicide among Teenagers

The incidence of teen suicide has risen dramatically in recent years and is second only to accidents as a cause of death among adolescents. It is estimated that, nationwide each year, as many as a million youngsters contemplate suicide, 400,000 make unsuccessful attempts, and some 7,000 actually take their own lives. To put it in more startling terms, "a teenager attempts suicide every ninety seconds, and another succeeds every ninety minutes." But even those figures do not tell the whole story "because many suicides are confused as accidents and others are not reported as suicides in order to save the family from embarrassment." All agree, however, that each year the numbers are rising. "California's Suicide Prevention and Crisis Center recently released statistics that reveal a tragic trend: in two short decades, the suicide rate among children ten to fourteen years of age more than doubled; among those fifteen to nineteen years of age, it tripled."

What is the profile of a high-risk adolescent? "Twice as many teenage boys commit suicide as do teenage girls." They "tend to be extremely intelligent—even gifted—young people. High achievers with drive and a high spirit of competition tend to commit suicide more often than children who are less competitive. . . . They also tend to have learning disorders, such as difficulties with reading. . . . They also tend to be advanced physically. . . . Many felt they were not liked by others or that others were unduly critical; some were described by friends and teachers as having a 'chip on the shoulder.' About the same percentage are described as quiet, uncommunicative, or difficult to get through to. An inability to express feelings and to ask for help seems to be a common personality trait among suicidal adolescents. . . . Helplessness and vulnerability always make a teenager more prone to suicide—and factors such as family violence, intense marital discord, or loss of a parent through death, divorce, or separation can significantly increase a child's sense of helplessness and vulnerability."

In these high-risk groups are children who have more specific problems that place them at even higher risk. Included here would be a child who has a distorted concept of death, who "does not believe that death is permanent but instead sees it as a reversible and temporary state of pleasantness in which to escape problems." Closely related to this problem is a more general break with reality—those youngsters who think they are failing in school or that they are overweight or being shunned by friends, when in reality they are not. An even more common problem that signifies high suicide risk is a compulsion to manipulate others. Such young people seek to control or hurt others and view suicide as the most effective way to do that.

It is a myth that says that suicides cannot be prevented. Parents and youth counselors must be aware of the high-risk groups and individuals and reach out to them by seeking to change both the mind-set and the environment that is contributing to the problem.

[Brent Q. Hafen and Kathryn J. Frandsen, Youth Suicide: Depression and Loneliness *(Evergreen, Colo.: Cordillera Press, 1986), pp. 10, 30–35, 41–42.]*

Suicide Prompted by Philosophical Confusion

Although Karl Marx sought to develop a philosophical system that would alleviate many of the social ills of society and offer a more fulfilling life to common people, he was unable to do that for his own family. He saw religion as an opiate that deadened the senses to the smells and sights of oppression, and he was convinced that only radical socialism was the answer. But the revolutionary philosophy left a void, which his daughters' distress graphically illustrates. "The story of the

Karl Marx daughters is a sad one, and points up the dilemmas faced by many revolutionary women. Eleanor committed suicide with poison provided for her by her husband, Edward Aveling. Her sister Laura committed suicide jointly with her husband, Paul Lafargue. Their mother Jenny, by being a good German *hausfrau,* had not provided an adequate role model for her revolutionary daughters. Both women had married active socialists and were deeply involved with the movement. Marriage was disastrous for both. Many revolutionary women have given poignant accounts of their desire for love and for children. Some have achieved love, some have achieved children, few have achieved both. Intellectual allegiance to the concept of love without lifetime commitment is at war inside these women with personal needs for continuing relationships. The conflict creates dark threads of tragedy in the lives of many of them."

[Elise Boulding, The Underside of History: A View of Women through Time *(Boulder, Colo.: Westview Press, 1976), p. 635.]*

TALENT

Wasted

Jane Swisshelm, a nineteenth-century newspaper editor, whose early adult life was severely restricted by a society that limited women's activities to housework, later wrote of a God-given gift she had that was wasted—painting. So consumed was she in her art that she forgot to prepare meals and do her household chores. "Again and again, the fire went out or the bread ran over in the pans, while I painted and dreamed." Finally, she realized she could not meet the demands of a housekeeper as well as be a painter.

"My conscience began to trouble me. Housekeeping was 'woman's sphere,' although I had never then heard the words, for no woman had gotten out of it to be hounded back; but I knew my place and scorned to leave it. I tried to think I could paint without neglect of duty. It did not occur to me that painting was a duty for a married woman!

Had the passion seized me before marriage, no other love could have come between me and art; but I felt that it was too late, as my life was already devoted to another object—housekeeping.

"It was a hard struggle. I tried to compromise, but experience soon deprived me of that hope, for to paint was to be oblivious of all other things. In my doubt, I met one of those newspaper paragraphs with which men are wont to pelt women into subjection: 'A man does not marry an artist, but a housekeeper.' This fitted my case, and my doom was sealed.

"I put away my brushes; resolutely crucified my divine gift, and while it hung writhing on the cross, spent my best years and powers cooking cabbage."

[Jane Swisshelm, Half a Century *(Chicago: Jansen, McClurg, 1880), pp. 47–50.]*

TEACHERS

Unappreciated

The teaching profession suffers today from lack of respectability. Teachers are not treated as real professionals in many cases, as the pay scale indicates. This is not a new trend in America, for the teaching profession has never been given the esteem it deserves. Indeed, in the nineteenth century teaching was often regarded as a women's profession, and as such the pay was very low and the benefits were few. This issue came up in the 1850s at the New York State Teachers' Association, where "more than two-thirds of the members were women, but the men ran the entire meeting, giving the speeches, voting on resolutions, and generally ignoring the women, who sat in an isolated block at the back of the room."

That meeting was noteworthy because the nationally known feminist leader Susan B. Anthony was there. During a panel discussion on the topic "Why the profession of a teacher is not as much respected as that of lawyer, doctor, or minister," she requested the floor. The men finally relented and permitted her to speak, at which time she insisted "that so long as society says woman is incompetent to be a lawyer, minister, or doctor, but has ample ability to be a teacher, every man of you who chooses this profession tacitly acknowledges that he has no more brains than a woman." She also dealt with "the disparity in the salaries of men and women teachers. It would be to the men's advantage to equalize them, she maintained, because their own incomes suffered when they had to compete with the cheap labor of women." Her persuasive arguments helped pass a resolution supporting the right of women to participate at the meetings and even hold official positions.

[*Margaret Truman,* Women of Courage: From Revolutionary Times to the Present *(New York: Morrow, 1976), pp. 148, 151.*]

TELEVISION

Its Negative Influence

A Harvard University study on the role of television in the sex education of children showed some interesting trends. Fully 70 percent of the allusions to sexual intercourse involved couples who were not married to each other. The study also revealed that much of the eroticism depicted involved violent acts against the female sex. "The television medium is also a strong promoter of alcohol. Television characters drink 3.5 times per hour on television, four times an hour during prime time. For every time coffee is consumed on TV, alcohol is consumed ten times. For every time milk is consumed, alcohol is consumed 44 times. For every time water is drunk, alcohol is drunk 48 times."

Television is also believed to affect people's aggressive behavior, a frightening thought, since studies have shown that "by age 15 the average American child witnesses between 11,000 and 13,000 acts of violence on TV." How well a student performs in school is also influenced. According to a release from the Associated Press in 1980, "A California survey indicates that the more a student watches television, the worse he does in school. California Schools Superintendent

Wilson Riles said that no matter how much homework the students did, how intelligent they were or how much money their parents made, the relationship between TV and test scores was practically identical."

[Ron Jenson, "Television: The Menacing Medium," in The Rebirth of America, *ed. Nancy Leigh DeMoss (Philadelphia: Arthur DeMoss Foundation, 1986), pp. 118–19.]*

TEMPTATION

Was Jesus Really Tempted?

The film *The Last Temptation of Christ* stirred heated controversy because of its distorted biblical portrayal of Jesus, but it also raised old questions. Was Jesus both fully human and fully divine? Many Christians are simply uneasy with the humanity of Jesus. Ours is a faith of the supernatural, the sacred, the divine, and we want a Jesus far above anything that is human. Yes, of course, we cherish the stories of his falling asleep on the boat and driving the swindlers out of the temple. But even those stories have a divine aura about them. Jesus is God, we insist. That is a doctrine we dare not diminish.

Was Jesus truly human? Did he ever throw up? Did he ever play "piggy-back" with a child? Did he ever run a race with his friends— and lose? Did he ever have sexual fantasies? Some Christians feel it is sacrilegious to even ask such questions. One Christian who does not is Marjorie Holmes, who explores the humanity of Jesus from the viewpoint of a committed Christian. In her novel *Three from Galilee,* she deals with such issues as sexual fantasies in a very sensitive way.

In one scene in her book Jesus is dreaming of finding "a woman whom he could love," a "wife who would bear him children to nurse at her breast." Then suddenly he awakes out of his restless sleep. "What was it, what was it? Jesus sat up in a cold sweat. Then to his relief it came to him: Temptation. He had been wrestling with tempta-tion. . . . He lay a few moments longer, thinking. What was temp-tation? Had he not been tempted many times? The girls at the grape treadings, young and lovely, sometimes unsteady from the very smell of the wine. The girls who came into the shop on pretext of some tool to be mended for their fathers—their flirting eyes and sometimes casually touching hands. The matrons who walked the streets of Nazareth, hips swinging seductively. . . . Was the yearning in his loins evil, or merely nature's response to the vital instinct God himself had planted in males that the race might survive?"

As a man who was fully human, Jesus can identify with the struggles and temptations that face all of mankind.

[*Marjorie Holmes,* Three from Galilee *(San Francisco: Harper & Row, 1985), pp. 155–56.*]

TIME MANAGEMENT
Awareness of Body Clock

In seeking to manage time effectively, an individual must be aware of his or her own body clock. When possible, the day should be scheduled to correspond with the body clock as closely as possible. Evelyn Christenson talks about this issue and points out that it affects not only time management but personal relationships.

"How do you start your day? Are you a 'lark' or an 'owl'? 'Larks' twitter and sing in the morning, but by the end of the day they're not doing too well; they have slowed down considerably. 'Owls' take a little long to get going in the morning. You know—'Right now I don't love anybody, but when I start loving again, you'll be first on the list.' But owls gain momentum as the night progresses. . . .

"Because our individual, inbuilt clocks function differently, I've learned that there are no spiritual 'brownie points' for being a 'lark.' Is it possible our heavenly Father created some of us to be 'larks' and some to be 'owls' so He would have somebody on the alert all 24 hours of the day?"

[*Evelyn Christenson, with Viola Blake,* What Happens When Women Pray *(Wheaton: Victor Books, 1975), pp. 90–91.*]

Problem of Procrastination

Disorganized people often seek to rationalize their lack of organization by pointing out their positive features, such as creativity, and by insisting that, if they change their routine, it will inhibit them. "They don't want to cramp their style," writes Sybil Stanton. "What they don't realize is that their style is cramping them. 'Free Spirits' fear loss of their freedom. To them, a schedule is no different than a straitjacket." She illustrates this type of person by citing the testimony of a friend, whose productivity was severely limited by her disorganization and procrastination.

"I was the least likely person for time management, because I'm the creative, spontaneous type, and creative people are usually afraid of getting organized. But I became fascinated with the idea that I could get things done.

"Procrastination was a cloud that hung over me. I was like an overeater: Left to themselves, overeaters will overeat. Procrastinators who are left to themselves will do everything but what they're supposed to do.

"I had never sat down and followed any kind of plan. I just wanted to keep moving to the next exciting thing. So I constantly put off doing the hard tasks, and then I had to face the consequences. People got mad at me because I didn't keep my word; and I couldn't sleep at night because all this stuff kept running around in my head.

"When I learned how to follow a plan, things got under control. Now I have more freedom throughout the day. And for once I can say no, which frees me to say yes later to what I really want to do. People even like me better—someone told me I am a very valuable person because I'm creative *and* organized. I was always passed by when important jobs were handed out; now I've even surprised myself by being given a responsible management position.

"In this day and age people are kidding themselves if they think they can live spontaneously. They will live with unbalanced checkbooks, unwritten letters, unanswered phone calls, broken appointments . . . and guilt."

[Sybil Stanton, The Twenty-Five-Hour Woman (Old Tappan, N.J.: Revell, 1986), 125–26.]

Stealing Snatches of Time

It is easy for a person to forfeit dreams and goals in life simply for want of time, but sometimes these dreams can be reclaimed if even a few small segments of time are snatched each day in order to reach a goal. This could involve exercising or piano practice, or it could pertain to a hobby, and the time could be snatched during a coffee break or lunch at work or during the hectic hours at home with little children. Allison Hughes's commitment to writing was not relinquished because of her busy days as a housewife. She found it difficult to fit writing into her schedule, and when she did have blocks of time, the thoughts she needed did not always come. So she snatched time from her otherwise busy days of childrearing and housework.

"Since thoughts never come to me at convenient times, I scribble them on tear sheets, which are the leftover blank pages torn from the children's scribblers at the end of the school year. These I cut in half and stack wherever I work during the day—kitchen, laundry, bedroom, living room. I even have a few blanks tucked behind the toilet paper rolls on the bathroom shelf. Thus whenever a thought hits me, I can jot it down, stuff it in my apron packet, and when I get to my desk, which isn't until after the children are in bed at night, I unload my pockets unto my typing table.

"This is the way I've collected materials for the novels I've written, stuffing files with notes for character, setting, situation, and theme. . . .

"Thoughts never come to me in any usable order either. But with loose notes, I don't have to cut, splice, or retype, I just shuffle them around, shifting the first to the last, trying them every-which-way until some shape begins to show. Then I clip the stuff that belongs together as one unit with a metal clamp. When it develops into an understandable order, I write the first draft."

[*Allison Hughes*, Love, Honor, and Frustration *(Grand Rapids: Zondervan, 1979), pp. 28–29.*]

Strict Daily Schedule

The busy schedule of a First Lady requires careful management of time. This was true in the early years of our Republic as well. Abigail Adams spoke of this while she was First Lady in Philadelphia, which was at that time the seat of government. She had learned to manage her time as the vice president's wife in the Washington administration. "I keep up my old habit of rising at an early hour. If I did not I should have little command of my time. At 5 I rise. From that time till 8 I have a few leisure hours [for writing letters]. At 8 I breakfast, after which until eleven I attend to my family arrangements. At that hour I dress for the day. From 12 until two I receive company, sometimes until 3. We dine at that hour unless on company days which is Tuesdays & Thursdays. After dinner I usually ride (drive) out until seven [for social calling]."

[Stewart Mitchell, ed., New Letters of Abigail Adams *(Boston: Houghton Mifflin, 1947), p. 91.]*

TOILET TRAINING

Influences on Later Life

Toilet training was viewed as a natural process in childrearing until modern times, when child experts began giving it much greater significance. Dr. Benjamin Spock has given considerable attention to the subject, maintaining that toilet training has a far-reaching effect on an individual's later development. According to him, proper toilet training is "actually the foundation for a lifelong preference for unsticky hands, for clean clothes, for a neat home, for an orderly way of doing business. It's from their toilet training that children get some of their feeling that one way of doing things is right and another way is not; this helps them to develop a sense of obligation, to become systematic people. So toilet training plays a part in the formation of a child's character and in building the basic trust between them and their parents."

[Benjamin Spock, Baby and Child Care *(New York: Pocket Books, 1977), p. 286.]*

TRAGEDY

Blessing in Disguise

Sometimes the worst tragedies of life turn into unexpected triumphs. Even the death of loved ones—the most bitter grief known to human-kind—can lead to blessings. This was true in 1873, when H. G. Spafford penned the lines to one of the church's most moving hymns, "It Is Well with My Soul." Spafford was a businessman who had lost much of his fortune in the Chicago fire in 1871, but that loss was not a "drop in the ocean" compared to the loss he would suffer two years later. In the fall of 1873, he bid farewell to his wife and four daughters—Maggie, Tanetta, Annie, and Bessie—and they left for Europe aboard the French passenger ship SS *Ville du Havre.* He was planning to join them later, after completing some necessary business transactions in Chicago. That reunion, however, never took place. "At two o'clock on the morning of November 22, 1873, when the luxury liner was several days out, and sailing on a quiet sea, she was rammed by the English iron sailing vessel, the 'Lochearn.' In two hours the 'Ville du Havre,' one of the largest ships afloat, settled to the bottom of the ocean, with a loss of some two hundred twenty-six lives, including the four Spafford children. Nine days later when the survivors landed at Cardiff, Wales, Mrs. Spafford cabled her husband these two words, 'Saved alone.'"

Spafford was comforted in his deep grief by his strong faith in God. That was evident as he sailed to join his wife. As the ship passed by the area where his daughters lost their lives, he once again committed his sorrow to God. "That night he found it hard to sleep. But faith soon conquered doubt, and there, in the mid-Atlantic, out of his heart-break and pain, Mr. Spafford wrote five stanzas, the first of which contained these lines:

> When peace like a river attendeth my way,
>   When sorrows like sea-billows roll,
> Whatever my lot, Thou has taught me to say,
>   'It is well, it is well with my soul!' "

Further tragedy would soon be associated with this great hymn. The well-known composer Philip P. Bliss, who put the words to music soon after Spafford wrote it, died with his wife in a train crash only three years later at the age of thirty-eight. For friends and relatives, the pain was almost too much to bear, but they, like succeeding generations of Christians, took comfort in their faith and in the words and music of "It Is Well with My Soul."

[Ernest K. Emurian, Living Stories of Famous Hymns *(Grand Rapids: Baker, 1955), pp. 66–67.]*

Enduring Tragedy with Fortitude

A prominent family that has been struck by tragedy perhaps more than any other in modern times is the Kennedys. Joe Kennedy and his wife, Rose, had nine children, and one by one, tragedy struck five of them. "The oldest child, Joseph P. Kennedy, Jr., was their pride and joy. According to most reports, Joe Jr. was a natural leader and like his father an aggressive man. The family expected great things of him, but their hopes were destroyed abruptly and painfully when Joe Jr. was killed on a dangerous bombing mission near the end of World War II." Their second child, who became President John F. Kennedy, was killed by an assassin's bullet in Dallas in 1963. Their third child, Rosemary, was born mildly retarded, a condition that greatly worsened following a surgical procedure. "The fourth child was Kathleen, a bright and vivacious girl who was always surrounded by friends and admirers." She married into English royalty and later went to England to reside—but not for long. "She was killed a few years later in the crash of a small private plane during bad weather."

The fifth child was Eunice, who is often remembered as the wife of an unsuccessful politician, Sargent Shriver, who ran on the ticket with George McGovern in 1972, and was a candidate himself in 1976. Patricia, the sixth child, had four children with her actor husband, Peter Lawford, but the marriage ended in divorce when the children were still small. The seventh child was Robert, who, as a presidential candidate, was assassinated in 1968. The eighth child was Jean, who married a successful businessman, Steve Smith. The youngest in the family was Edward M. Kennedy, nicknamed Teddy. "Beyond the deaths of all three of his brothers, Ted has coped with a long period of hospitalization after a plane crash that left doctors convinced he would never walk again; the unfortunate events at Chappaquiddick that left Mary Jo Kopechne dead and his political career shadowed; the heartbreak of discovering that his son Teddy had bone cancer, which necessitated the amputation of his leg; and his wife's alcoholism," and their subsequent divorce in 1980. There were other family tragedies as well, including a drug overdose that took the life of one of Robert's sons.

But despite all the tragedy, a spirit of optimism keeps the family going and pressing on to higher goals. In recent years the second generation of Kennedys have begun entering political service and gaining distinction in other fields.

[Barbara Gibson, with Caroline Latham, Life with Rose Kennedy *(New York: Warner Books, 1986), pp. 4–6.]*

TRANSFORMED LIVES

Religious Conversion

Women were actively involved in city mission work during the late nineteenth and early twentieth centuries, and many of their converts were wayward girls who themselves became missionaries to the inner cities. Seth Cook Rees cited many such cases in his book entitled *Miracles in the Slums.* The following are only a few of the trophies of the slum missionaries. Orpha, who "fell prey to a professional procurer . . . became a slum missionary and an ordained deaconess." Little H——, who "had been taken to men's rooms and forced to drink," was later "sanctified and went to Bible School in order to prepare to become a slum missionary." Miss M—— was put in jail for grand larceny and later "became a missionary in the New York City slums."

Lucy "was ruined by her employer who turned out to be a bartender and was put in a Negro sporting house." After she was rescued, "she began teaching a Sunday School class of nineteen scholars." Dicie, who was "a drunkard, cigarette fiend, and user of morphine, cocaine, and other drugs," later became a slum missionary. Little Ella, who was "sold as a prostitute for $5.00," later "became a Quaker and started preaching." Christine, a pregnant teenager who "was forever hopelessly ruined," was "called to be a slum missionary" and "went to Bible school for training." And Bernie, who "after trying suicide . . . decided to have a man without marriage . . . was saved, sanctified" and "became assistant matron of the Home."

[*Seth Cook Rees,* Miracles in the Slums; or, Thrilling Stories of Those Rescued from the Cesspools of Iniquity, and Touching Incidents in the Lives of the Unfortunate *(Chicago, 1905).]*

TRIUMPH

Turned to Tragedy

Winning a contest when there are 11,500 other well-qualified applicants may be the result of hard work and remarkable competence, but such remote odds turn the victory into the ultimate emotional high. So it was with a Concord, New Hampshire, high school social studies teacher, who learned in June of 1985 that she would be the civilian to be launched into space. It was a prize that Christa McAuliffe had longed for, and when her name was announced by Vice President George Bush at the White House ceremony, she could hardly contain her excitement. But in the midst of her exuberance, she could not forget those nine finalists sitting beside her, whose joy was bittersweet. They were happy for her, but they had lost the opportunity of a lifetime they had so yearned for. In accepting the honor, she acknowledged them. "I've made nine wonderful friends over the last two weeks, and when that shuttle goes, there might be one body," she said, choking back the tears, "but there's gonna be ten souls I'm takin' with me." In the months of travel and training that followed, she was too excited to be concerned about danger. When a reporter asked her if she was frightened, she answered, "Oh no, it's not like the early missions when the astronauts had no control of their destiny. Now they can make emergency landings or orbit the Earth once before landing. There's a lot less to worry about."

She did not allow worry to interfere with the excitement leading up to the launch. Indeed, it never entered her mind that the real winners at the White House ceremony were the nine finalists who were anguished over their loss. When a reporter asked her how she intended to keep her celebrity status in proper perspective, she responded, "Well, I see this as a very, very exciting time in my life, but I have thirty-six years behind me and thirty-six years more ahead of me. It's not like I'm never going to get back to earth again."

[Robert T. Hohler, "I Touch the Future": The Story of Christa McAuliffe (New York: Random House, 1986), pp. 14–18.]

UNWED MOTHERS
Bad Example

Upset by the bad example that was being displayed, a woman wrote to the Sears, Roebuck Company in 1962 objecting to the fact that "not one of the women wearing Sear's maternity lingerie is wearing a wedding ring!" The following year's catalog corrected the "error."

[Scot Morris, The Book of Strange Facts and Useless Information (Garden City, N.Y.: Doubleday, 1979), p. 78.]

VIOLENCE
Against Plantation Slave Women

The physical and sexual violence perpetrated against black female slaves by their white masters and overseers was a despicable aspect of slavery that has sometimes been overlooked by historians. Often the stories of violent abuse focus on the male slave population. But, according to historian Jacqueline Jones, "to a white man, a black woman was not only a worker who needed prodding, but also a female capable of fulfilling his sexual or aggressive desires. For this reason, a fine line existed between working related punishment and rape, and an overseer's lust might yield to sadistic rage. For example, the mother of Minnie Fulkes was suspended from a barn rafter and beaten with a horsewhip 'nekkid 'til the blood run down her back to her heels' for fending off the advances of an overseer on a Virginia plantation."

Even more shocking was the treatment accorded pregnant women, who were not spared rape and other forms of physical abuse. Not unheard of was "the whipping of pregnant and nursing mothers—'so that blood and milk flew mingled from their breasts.' " Because the offspring was considered valuable to the owner, special precautions were often taken in beating pregnant women. In some cases they were forced to lie on the ground facedown in an area where the dirt was hollowed out to protect the unborn child, and then they were whipped across the back. "Slave women's roles as workers and as childbearers came together in these trenches, these graves for the living, in southern cottonfields. The uniformity of procedure suggests that the terrorizing of pregnant women was not uncommon."

[Jacqueline Jones, Labor of Love, Labor of Sorrow: Black Women, Work, and the Family from Slavery to the Present (New York: Basic Books, 1985), p. 20.]

Justifying Violence for a Good Cause

The women who were involved in the nineteenth-century temperance crusade used a variety of means to make their position known. Many clamored for women's suffrage, convinced that it was the only way to legislate prohibition. Other women took more extreme measures—the most notorious of whom was Carry Nation. She was convinced that God had divinely called her to take violent action against the saloon keepers, and that is exactly what she set out to do. She went from town to town with her tiny band of followers and made a dramatic demonstration of force against her enemies. She described a typical incident that occurred in Kiowa, Kansas. "I threw as hard, and as fast as I could, smashing mirrors and bottles and glasses and it was astonishing how quickly this was done. These men seemed terrified, threw up their hands and backed up in the corner. My strength was that of a giant. I felt invincible. God was certainly standing by me."

[Carry A. Nation, The Use and Need of the Life of Carry A. Nation (Topeka: Stevens, 1909), pp. 130, 133–34.]

Unlikely Perpetrators of Violence

Among the least likely group of people in society to resort to violence might be expected to be nuns. In recent years nuns have been involved in protests, but none that have rivaled the violent outbreaks that sometimes occurred in medieval Europe. Many convents were located in pagan areas, and the lofty ideals and standards set by the church frequently did not correspond with reality. It was difficult for many of the women to submit to the strict rules imposed on them, and on occasion they broke out in open revolt.

Such a revolt occurred at the Frankish convent in Poitiers in the late sixth century. Gregory, Bishop of Tours, left an interesting account of how Chrodield and forty of her followers rebelled against the abbess. "The vexations sown by the devil . . . daily increased in troublesomeness. For Chrodield, having collected about her . . . a band of murderers, wrongdoers, law-breakers, and vagrants of all kinds, dwelt in open revolt and ordered her followers to break into the nunnery at night and forcibly bear off the abbess. . . . The armed bands rushed in, ran about the monastery by the light of a torch in search of the abbess, and carried off the prioress whom they mistook for the abbess in the darkness." When they realized their mistake, they returned and "secured the real abbess, dragged her away, and placed her in custody near the basilica of St. Hilary." They then returned and "plundered the monastery of all its contents." It took two years before the church was able to put down the revolt. Many of the nuns later repented, but Chroedield lived out her days a rebel of the church, under the protection of a political official.

[Lina Eckenstein, Woman under Monasticism (New York: Russell & Russell, 1896), pp. 67–68.]

VOLUNTEER WORK
Demeaning to Women

Why are most of the volunteer workers women? More and more women have been asking that question in recent years. There is concern that women are being "used" in a way that men would never allow to happen to themselves.

"Women usually say they volunteer to 'help' others, and because it is needed. Women do not necessarily analyze what doing volunteer work satisfies in *themselves*. Nor do they analyze whether their 'helping' actually helps—or not.

"The average female volunteer believes that she is not really worth taking seriously. Either her *time* is not valuable, *she* is not valuable—or she is only valuable because her time has already been paid for by her husband. She can be 'had' by society for free. More important, the average female volunteer is not, or does not feel she is, a 'professional.' And she is afraid of being judged too harshly by 'professional' standards. As a volunteer she avoids being fired, reprimanded, and competed with. She is a 'good' woman: although she is working outside her home, everyone knows that most female volunteers are *primarily* loyal to their families—and not to their unpaid volunteer work."

Volunteer work may actually have a harmful effect on women in the job market. The end result may be that opportunities for employment may become more limited.

"The volunteer does not and perhaps does not want to force private corporations or politicians into *paying* her for her work. And her unpaid presence in the job market keeps other women who are employed from earning decent wages. If volunteers can work for 'free,' then money does not have to be allocated to pay workers decent—or even low—wages for performing these tasks. Ultimately, the female willingness and *need* to volunteer make it easy for government and industry to continue assigning a low economic priority to domestic or human welfare areas."

[*Phyllis Chesley and Emily Jane Goodman,* Women, Money, and Power *(New York: Bantam Books, 1977), pp. 191–92.*]

VULNERABILITY

Prompts Deeper Trust in God

It is often only through the unpleasant feeling of being vulnerable that an individual comes to grips with the need for strength beyond human capabilities. If a person feels strong and in control of life's situations, God too easily becomes an unnecessary appendage in an otherwise fulfilling existence. Yet, it is difficult to turn that pattern around when suddenly the world caves in. This is the testimony of Judith C. Lechman.

"Several years ago, with the breakdown and collapse of my first marriage, I knew the feeling of powerlessness in almost every area of my life, and I despised it. My job, friendships, home life, financial security, and relationship with my children felt as though they were slipping beyond my control, and in anger and frustration, I not only lashed out and inflicted hurt on those around me, but I also turned my back firmly on God. . . .

"But in turning my back upon God, I had forgotten that he is omnipresent. I continued to face him, but in my pain and anguish I refused to see him. His creative power had already come into the heart of my life, but I refused to acknowledge that also. Yet, ever so slowly, the mysterious way that is the power of the Living Presence within each of us, I began . . . to hear his voice and feel his power once again, tolerant, loving, long-suffering, working quietly to strengthen me where I was weakest, to turn my anger to love and my pain into communion with and commitment to him again.

"I learned that to grow spiritually I had to embrace the powerlessness he required of me. And in becoming willingly powerless for him, I discovered that his power strengthens as no earthly power, good or evil can."

[*Judith C. Lechman,* The Spirituality of Gentleness: Growing toward Christian Wholeness *(San Francisco: Harper & Row, 1987), pp. 141–42.*]

WEALTH

Opulent Life-Style of Christian Ministers

With the news media focused for months on the opulent life-style of Jim and Tammy Bakker, many people became disillusioned about giving their hard-earned money to television ministries. Patti Roberts, the former daughter-in-law of Oral Roberts, who was very active in the ministry, writes of the image that is given to the public that is so opposite to the actual life-style behind the scenes. She writes that "in order to be accepted by those who possess wealth and influence, one has to adopt at least some of the trappings of their life style." That, at least, is the philosophy of many television evangelists—not the philosophy of Mother Teresa and others like her who are accepted by those who possess wealth and influence. Patti suggests that this life-style "inevitably creates conflicts," but such conflicts were not so disturbing as to change priorities in the Oral Roberts organization.

"Jesus said we were to be servants, but it is hard to maintain a servant's heart when you dress better than some heads of state and live better than 99 percent of the world. When you play golf with senators and vacation with heads of multimillion-dollar corporations, it is difficult to identify with the widow on Social Security who faithfully supports the ministry with her ten-dollar offering each month. The weight of success tends to remove you from the reality of the Spirit of God—from the bleeding, wounded, compassionate heart of Jesus. . . .

"We became so blinded to our own excesses that we saw nothing incongruous about singing before a Partners' meeting to raise millions of dollars for a new building, then toasting the success of our efforts with a lavish night out on the town. . . .

"None of us were evil people. We truly loved God and wanted to serve Him. We never sat down and said, 'We are going to become arrogant, calloused, and insensitive.' These maladies slip up on people. No one loved us enough to hold us accountable. No one looked beneath the glitter to see if our lives matched our performance."

[Patti Roberts, with Sherry Andrews, From Ashes to Gold *(Waco: Word Books, 1983), pp. 108–10.]*

Problems of the Rich

The rich clearly suffer many of the same problems as do the poor. They are certainly not immune to sickness and disease, and tragedies of all kinds befall the rich with the same frequency as the poor. But the problems often most associated with poverty—those associated with grimy ghetto living—are not thought to be problems of the rich. Sometimes, however, they are, and this can be seen most convincingly from a historical perspective. In his book *Rats, Lice, and History,* Hans Zinsser writers of such problems among the European aristocracy of past centuries.

"The habit of shaving the head and wearing a wig was no doubt in part due to the effort to hold down vermin. Gentlemen and ladies all over Europe resorted to this, but the wigs they wore were often full of nits. Pepys speaks of this in several places, complaining about a new wig he had bought which was full of nits. 'Thence to Westminster to my barber's; to have my Periwigg he lately made me cleansed of its nits, which vexed me cruelly that he should put such a thing into my hands.'

"Even in the highest society, the question of lice and scratching were serious problems; and the education of children, even in the highest circles, included a training of the young in relation to their vermin. Reboux, speaking of the education of a princess of France in the middle of the seventeenth century, says: 'One had carefully taught the young princess that it was bad manners to scratch when one did it by habit and not by necessity, and that it was improper to take lice or fleas or other vermin to the neck to kill them in company, except in the most intimate circles.' "

[Hans Zinsser, Rats, Lice, and History *(New York: Bantam Books, 1971), p. 138.]*

WEDDINGS

Changes in Wedding Customs

Wedding customs differ significantly from culture to culture and from century to century. Christians who look back to the Reformation as a high point in their church tradition might be shocked to discover how different morals and marriage customs really were during the time of the great Reformers. It is well known that Martin Luther married Katherine von Bora, a former nun, but the details of the wedding are less well known. Katie was forced to endure the ritual of having several of Luther's friends observe the sexual consummation of their marriage—one of the many indignities a sixteenth-century female had to cope with between infancy and death. Luther's biographer describes the ordeal. "On the evening of 13 June 1525, according to the custom of the day, he appeared with his bride before a number of his friends as witnesses. The Pomeranian [Johann] Bugenhagen blessed the couple, who consummated the marriage in front of the witnesses, as [Justus] Jonas reported the next day: 'Luther has taken Katharina von Bora to wife. I was present yesterday and saw the couple on their marriage bed. As I watched this spectacle I could not hold back my tears.' "

[Richard Friedenthal, Luther: His Life and Times, *trans. John Nowell (New York: Harcourt Brace Jovanovich, 1970), p. 438.]*

Frivolous Waste of Money

Some people view weddings as a frivolous waste of time and money. That was the position of Jim Elliot, whose single-minded devotion to missionary work among the fierce Auca Indians in Ecuador led to his death, along with four other missionaries, in 1956. Regarding weddings, he wrote, "Twentieth-century Christian weddings are the vainest, most meaningless forms. There is no vestige of reality. The witnesses dress for show. The flesh is given all the place. The songs are absurd, if one paid any attention to the words, but no one does; they simply listen to *how* it is sung, not what is means. Candles are useless but expensive trifles. Ushers help no one, but appear very officious and the ceremony itself is the most meaningless hodge-podge of obsolete grammar and phraseology. . . . And the stupid form of asking who gives this bride in marriage. Who cares? Everyone knows it is her father or uncle or some such sweating pawn standing before the altar. Talk of Romanism! We Fundamentalists are a pack of mood-loving show-offs. . . . It is no more than an expensive tedium with little remembrance. There is something in me that resists the showy part of weddings with a passion I have against few other things in life." He put his words into action when he married Elisabeth Howard in 1953 in a ten-minute civil ceremony in a "dingy, high-ceilinged room" in Quito, Ecuador. Years after his death, however, his daughter, Valerie, chose to have the very sort of traditional wedding that her father had so deplored.

[*Elisabeth Elliot,* The Shadow of the Almighty *(Grand Rapids: Zondervan, 1958), pp. 211–12.*]

WIDOWHOOD

Caring for Oneself

One reason that widowhood is so difficult to cope with is that women often fail to put enough effort into caring for themselves. They grieve without taking positive steps to heal their wounds. Jo Berry tells of her recent widowhood in light of this need. "I've been learning a lot about being good to myself since George died. George was very good to me. He spoiled and pampered me. He complimented me for little everyday things I did that often are taken for granted. . . . He also bragged to me and others about what a good writer I am. . . . Now that he's gone there's no one to do those things for me—except myself. One of the first things I learned in my widow's support group was that I have to learn how to be good to myself, because my well-being and that of those I love depends on how well I treat myself. I've also learned that being good to myself isn't being selfish or self-centered. It doesn't mean you don't reach out to others but that you respond in positive ways to yourself. . . . I've done myself a lot of little favors in these past months since George died. I get my nails manicured regularly. . . . I bought a rolltop desk for my bedroom. . . . Once a week I spend quality time with a friend I haven't seen for a while. These are all little things but they are the fiber and fabric of life. They make me feel better about myself."

[Jo Berry, Becoming God's Special Woman (Old Tappan, N.J.: Revell, 1986), pp. 69–70.]

Loss of Identity as a Widow

In her book *Widow,* Lynn Caine tells of the loss of identity she felt after her husband died—a common feeling among widows. "Our society is set up so that most women lose their identities when their husbands die. Marriage is a symbiotic relationship for most of us. We draw our identities from our husbands. We add ourselves to our men, pour ourselves into them and their lives. We exist in their reflection." She tells of a male psychiatrist who was puzzled by the "loss of self" reported by many widows. One told how she felt as though half of herself was missing, and another spoke of the "great emptiness" she experienced. He questioned why they would feel that way, unable to identify with their situations. "Only a man could ask these questions," writes Caine. In her own case, she not only felt loss of identity but also suddenly realized she "had become a second-class citizen, a member of the invisible minority of widows. And like all members of minority groups, I was deprived—sexually, emotionally, socially and financially. My very identity was shaky. At times I felt practically non-existent."

[Lynn Caine, Widow *(New York: Morrow, 1974), pp. 11, 147–48.]*

Statistics on Widowhood

"Death parts women from their lovers more often and earlier than it does men. One out of every six women in this country over the age of twenty-one is a widow. And the statistics collected by the Bureau of the Census show that women are becoming widows at younger and younger ages. The Darby-and-Joan idyll, that blissful growing-old-together, is rare, rarer, rarest. For women, that is. Men have it better. More than 70 percent of men over sixty-five are married, compared to 30 percent of the women."

[Lynn Caine, Widow *(New York: Morrow, 1974), pp. 11–12.]*

WIFE

Discontented with Role

Elizabeth Cady Stanton, the wife of a politician and lawyer and the mother of seven children, struggled with the injustices women had to endure. She wanted to move ahead with her feminist activities, but her aspirations were curtailed by household and wifely duties. In a letter to Susan B. Anthony in 1858, she expressed her discontent. "Oh how I long for a few hours of blessed leisure each day. How rebellious it makes me feel when I see Henry going about where and how he pleases. He can walk at will through the whole wide world or shut himself up alone, if he pleases, within four walls. As I contrast his freedom with my bondage, and feel that, because of the false position of women, I have been compelled to hold all my noblest aspirations in abeyance in order to be a wife, a mother, a nurse, a cook, a household drudge, I am fired anew and long to pour forth from my own experience the whole long story of women's wrongs. I have been alone today as the whole family except Hattie and myself have been out to celebrate our national birthday. What has woman to do with patriotism? Must not someone watch baby, house and garden? And who is so fitting to perform all these duties, which no one else wishes to do, as she who brought sin into the world and all our woe!"

[Elisabeth Griffith, In Her Own Right: The Life of Elizabeth Cady Stanton (New York: Oxford University Press, 1984), p. 95.]

Domineering Wife

Mark Twain enjoyed satirizing the domineering wife, and he did so with his usual humor and insight into human foibles. In his story "The McWilliamses and the Burglar Alarm," he lets Mr. McWilliams relate the frustrations of his domestic situation. "When we were finishing our house, we found we had a little cash left over, on account of the plumber not knowing it. I was for enlightening the heathen with it, for I was always unaccountably down on the heathen somehow; but Mrs. McWilliams said no, let's have a burglar alarm. I agreed to this compromise. I will explain that whenever I want a thing, and Mrs. McWilliams wants another thing, and we decide upon the thing that Mrs. McWilliams wants—as we always do—she calls that a compromise."

[Mark Twain, "The McWilliamses and the Burglar Alarm," Harper's, Christmas issue, 1882.]

Influence of Wife on Husband

Although Marabel Morgan insists that she "wouldn't dream of taking credit for the Super Bowl," she gives the following account that indicates what a powerful influence she believes a wife can have over her husband—especially if she has taken the Total Woman course. "Attending one of the first classes in Miami were wives of the Miami Dolphin football players. Mrs. Bob Griese, Mrs. Howard Twilley, Mrs. Norm Evans, Mrs. Karl Noonan, Mrs. Tim Foley, Mrs. Jesse Powell, Mrs. Mike Kolen, Mrs. Bob Heinz, Mrs. Vern Den Herder, Mrs. Jack Clancy, and Mrs. John Richardson listened well and really tackled their assignments that night. They sought to put their husbands first and bring out the very best in them." What was the result? Morgan continues: "By the way, it is interesting to note that their team won every game that next season and became the world champions! It was the first undefeated season in the history of professional football, including play-off games and the Super Bowl."

[Marabel Morgan, The Total Woman (Old Tappan, N.J.: Revell, 1973), p. 188.]

Problems of a Neglected Wife

Being married to a visionary whose dreams are as impractical as they are ingenious is frustrating for either a husband or a wife. Margaret Simpson knew this well. Her married life with A. B. Simpson, the founder of the Christian and Missionary Alliance church, was often filled with turmoil. He swam against the current and took risks, while she was left to arrange the daily affairs of life and plan realistically for the future. A. W. Tozer wrote graphically of the struggle she faced.

"The wife of a prophet has no easy road to travel. She cannot always see her husband's vision, yet as his wife she must go along with him wherever his vision takes him. She is compelled therefore to walk by faith a good deal of the time—and her husband's faith at that. Mrs. Simpson tried hard to understand, but if she sometimes lost patience with her devoted but impractical husband she is not for that cause to be too much censured. From affluence and high social position she is called suddenly to poverty and near-ostracism. She must feed her large family somehow—and not one cent coming in. The salary has stopped, and the parsonage must be vacated. . . . Mr. Simpson had heard the Voice ordering him out, and he went without fear. His wife had heard nothing, but she was compelled to go anyway. That she was a bit unsympathetic at times has been held against her by many. That she managed to keep within far sight of her absent-minded high soaring husband should be set down to her everlasting honor. It is no easy job of being wife to such a man as A. B. Simpson was."

[A. W. Tozer, Wingspread: A. B. Simpson, a Study in Spiritual Attitude (Harrisburg: Christian Publications, 1943), p. 87.]

Sacrificing for Husband's "Calling"

Many of the wives of the great nineteenth-century missionaries, though they are often lost in the shadows of their larger-than-life husbands, made more profound sacrifices for the cause of missions than did their husbands. This was particularly true of Dorothy, the wife of William Carey, the "Father of Modern Missions." She had three small children and was pregnant with her fourth when he announced to her, in 1792, that God was directing him to give his life for missionary work in India. She initially refused to go but later relented. It was an unhappy experience for her. They lived in the deadly climate of the remote interior, where one by one they were stricken by dysentery or tropical fevers, until little Peter succumbed and died. The strain was too much for Dorothy, and her mental health deteriorated rapidly until she was described by visitors as being "wholly deranged."

A similar situation occurred with Mary Morrison, the wife of Robert Morrison, the great pioneer missionary to China. She too coped with deep emotional pain. Her husband wrote of her "feeble mind" being "much harassed" and that she "walks in darkness and has no light."

Mary Livingstone, the wife of David, also made tremendous sacrifices for his highly acclaimed ministry. She was unable to endure the privations and rigors of African exploration, so she returned to England, where she was described as being homeless, penniless, and friendless. Indeed, it was rumored that she had lapsed into spiritual darkness and was drowning her misery in alcohol.

[Ruth A. Tucker, From Jerusalem to Irian Jaya: A Biographical History of Christian Missions (Grand Rapids: Zondervan, 1983), pp. 116–17, 151, 169.]

Wife Supportive of Husband

Oral Roberts, the world-famous healing evangelist, depended heavily on the emotional support of his wife. "It was Evelyn," writes his biographer, "that Oral wanted and needed by his side; she was his confidant, his 'safety valve,' his cheerleader, and his only true love. Without her he grew restless, lonely, and sometimes depressed." He found it easier to preach when she was present. "It is a thrilling thing as I preach to look out and see her shining face. She loves to hear me preach and this inspires me to preach better." She encouraged him and at times was a gentle critic, but she waited for the right time to point out his errors. "On nights when the Devil's power is strong and the sermon doesn't go over as Oral thinks it should, he goes to his room discouraged. . . . Those are times when I like to be with him and encourage him. If he had used bad English or made a mistake I do not tell him so, but try to get him to leave the results with God. Then when he feels on top of the world again I may mention a few mistakes."

[David Edwin Harrell, Jr., Oral Roberts: An American Life (Bloomington: Indiana University Press, 1985), p. 185.]

WIFE ABUSE
Not Recognized as a Crime

Although statistics indicate that one out of two wives in this country has been physically abused by her husband, the problem is often ignored or not treated seriously by legal and civil authorities, or by the church.

Indeed, the church is sometimes guilty of perpetuating wife abuse by an overemphasis on wifely submission. Esther Lee Olson writes of "a special problem that abused Christian women face: their strong doctrinal adherence to a biblical concept of marriage and submission." When this woman finally musters enough courage to take action, she finds a less-than-sympathetic legal system that "is designed to protect the batterer—the husband—not the abused wife." Many lawyers will candidly admit to the woman: "If your husband had done the same thing to a stranger, he would have been arrested and put in prison for assault and battery. But you're his wife. According to the law, you have very few rights." What is the reason for such unfairness? "First it's traditional. For centuries the legal system had extended to husbands what is called 'the right of chastisement' over their wives. Laws have changed in the last hundred or so years, sure. But attitudes haven't. Second, the law is reluctant to get involved in situations occurring inside the home. Nobody wants a government that intrudes upon the family."

Olson offers advice for battered women—especially for the countless women, many of them from strict Christian backgrounds, who are too embarrassed to admit their secret disgrace. "It is essential for a battered woman to inform other people what has been going on. Hiding the truth in an effort to protect the husband or to avoid personal embarrassment does no good. It doesn't help the batterer and it certainly doesn't help the victim. Also, it is wise for an abused wife or battered woman to seek immediate medical attention even if the injuries seem relatively mild. A doctor's examination not only can help discover more serious internal injuries that might otherwise go undetected but also can provide the written, professional verification of the nature of the abuse. This is often helpful in a legal situation, but is also proof positive to the woman herself and to her parents and friends that abuse has occurred."

[Esther Lee Olson, with Kenneth Petersen, No Place to Hide, Wife Abuse: Anatomy of a Private Crime *(Wheaton: Tyndale, 1982), pp. 9, 90, 97–98.]*

Wife-Beating and Feminism

The erroneous conclusion that wife-beating was a result of feminism was used to justify a 1977 decision in New Hampshire by the State Commission on the Status of Women not to provide shelter for battered wives. In the words of one commissioner, "Those women libbers irritate the hell out of their husbands." Are battered wives feminists? Studies indicate that they are not. According to Ann Jones, author of *Women Who Kill*, "the battered woman who kills her husband is likely to ignore feminism or oppose it. Battering may happen to any woman at any time, but many battered women marry in their teens and give up their own education or work. When marriage is not the perfect haven they've been led to expect they blame themselves; many battered women report studying Marabel Morgan's influential *The Total Woman*, the bible of self-abnegation, to learn how to please their husbands or boyfriends and stop the beatings. Then they learn that their behavior has little influence on his self-triggering violence; and in desperation they reach for the butcher knife."

[*Ann Jones,* Women Who Kill *(New York: Holt, Rinehart & Winston, 1980), p. 320.*]

WITCHCRAFT
Women Considered More Susceptible

From the Middle Ages up through the American Colonial period, women have been thought to be more susceptible to the evils of witchcraft than men. This point was made very forcefully by James I, who succeeded Queen Elizabeth I on the throne of England. Under his reign witchcraft became a "crime" punishable by hanging, and an upsurge of executions of women occurred during the early years of his rule. To justify this slaughter, he insisted that witchcraft involved a pact with the Devil, and that women were liable to fall into such snares with Satan because of Eve's deception in the Garden of Eden. He concluded that there were twenty times more female witches than male witches.

[Selma Williams, Divine Rebel: The Life of Anne Marbury Hutchinson (New York: Holt, Rinehart & Winston, 1981), p. 35.]

WOMAN'S RIGHTS
Demanded in Ancient Times

Protesting against discriminatory laws and court actions is often viewed as a modern activity for women. Indeed, it is often thought that only when they have significant rights in society do they dare protest against the rights they are denied. But long before women were perceived in any sense to be equal with men, they dared to protest—thus giving the woman's rights movement a much longer history than many people would think.

"In 215 B.C., during a critical period in the war with Hannibal, there had been enacted the Oppian law . . . which ruled that women were allowed to keep only half an ounce of gold, were forbidden to drive in carriages through the streets of Rome, and banned from wearing dyed clothes. Superficial though such a law may appear, it was the Roman world's equivalent of the clothes rationing imposed in Europe during the second world war. Gold, to a woman, meant bracelets and earrings; to the army it meant survival. Carriages cost money better spent on defense. The dyes for the blue, rose, scarlet, amethyst and violet collectively known as 'purple' had to be imported at some expense from Tyre in the eastern Mediterranean. The Oppian law, like most sumptuary laws in later history, was an attempt to limit conspicuous consumption in the only way open to legislators and was aimed at women not so much because of the perennial male belief that only women are extravagant, but because men's extravagance took different and more diverse forms. . . .

"Rome survived the crisis of 215 B.C., and 14 years later the war came to an end. But another six years passed before, in 195 B.C., there was any move to repeal the Oppian law. The die-hards were against it, and the debate raged for days. It looked as if the move were going to fail, and the women grew angrier and angrier. 'Neither influence, nor modesty, nor their husbands' commands could keep the married women indoors. They beset all the streets in Rome and all the approaches to the forum. . . . Every day the crowds of women grew, for they even came into the city from the provinces.' When they actually mobbed the offices of the two tribunes most strongly opposed to the repeal, it was too much.

" 'It made me blush,' exploded Cato in the Senate, 'to push my way through a positive regiment of women a few minutes ago in order to get here.' If a woman had something to say, she should say it in private, to her husband; and even so, she had no business even to hold an opinion about something that was a political matter. If husbands kept their wives in order, there would be no such vulgar demonstrations as he had just witnessed. 'Woman is a headstrong and uncontrolled animal, and you cannot give her the reins and expect her not to kick over the traces. . . . What [they] want is complete freedom—or, to put it bluntly, complete license.' "

[Reay Tannahill, Sex in History *(New York: Stein & Day, 1980), pp. 109–10.]*

WOMEN

Created for Men

That women were created to serve men is often thought to be a view of certain Christian theologians, but non-Christian philosophers also have maintained such positions. Jean Jacques Rousseau wrote, "The whole education of women ought to be relative to men. To please them, to be useful to them, to make themselves loved and honored by them, to educate them when young, to care for them when grown, to counsel them, to make life sweet and agreeable to them—these are the duties of women at all times, and what should be taught them from infancy."

[Quoted in Dorothy R. Pape, In Search of God's Ideal Woman (Downers Grove, Ill.: InterVarsity, 1976), p. 299.]

Cultural Hardships on Women

Ruth and Roy Shaffer began their missionary work with the Maasai tribe in Kenya during the early years of the twentieth century. One of the most disturbing aspects of what they discovered in that culture was the low estimation of womanhood. They quickly learned that "among the Maasai a woman was rated below a cow in real value to her husband. She seemed never to live in any state other than utter subjection to men, always seen but never heard." The condition of the young girls was even worse than that of the women. From the age of six to puberty, they were sent to live in a *manyatta,* "a free love kraal" set aside for the young warriors.

If life was deplorable for young girls prior to puberty, it was hardly any better during their initiation rites and following. Indeed the utter subjection of women by the Maasai tribesmen was graphically illustrated by the appalling rituals young girls were forced to endure.

"When the girl reaches puberty, she is taken back home to her parents, who arrange for her to join a group of four or more girls who are to be circumcised, in many cases against their will." Ruth vividly recalled the ceremonies she observed in the 1920s at Siyabei. Early in the morning, "the girls were led down the hill to the icy cold river, in which they sat all morning until they were numb. They were then rushed back to the hut, where screaming women carried on a frenzied ritual to build up the girls' courage, but actually it was very frightening." What followed was literally torture.

"The clinical term for female circumcision is 'clitoridectomy.' The excision of the clitoris was done by an old *Engoiboni* (female *Oloiboni*) in a dark hut. Fresh, green cow manure was used to curb bleeding. . . . Others used fat and ashes. . . . Maasai female circumcision involves not only clitoridectomy but in addition, parts of the labia minora are cut off, which has a profoundly damaging effect on fertility. It leaves a gaping vulva into which germs pass much more readily to produce inflammatory pelvic diseases. . . .

"During many days of healing, the newly circumcised girls were kept in a separate group, bedecked with beads all over their faces, necks and arms. Vivid designs were painted on their faces with white lava dirt, black soot or with red ochre which was evidence that they had completed this traditional rite. It is proof that they have been able to withstand extreme pain honorably, and have earned the status of women. They were herded like sheep, kept in motion all day long, crawling about on hands and knees. They were not allowed to sit down and they just couldn't stand up yet."

After the scarring had healed to the point where the girl could resume normal activities, she was sold in marriage to a man (often much older than she) and sent to live in his kraal. She was then expected to tend cattle and have babies—the latter being a sign of her worth, though her capability of reproducing had been severely curtailed by her circumcision, which "causes so much scar tissue that few Maasai babies can survive birth alive and mothers often die in childbirth as well."

[*Ruth T. Shaffer,* Road to Kilimanjaro: An American Family in Maasailand *(Grand Rapids: Four Corners Press, 1985), pp. 79, 97, 101–2.*]

Dignity of Women

"Since women are becoming ever more conscious of their human dignity, they will not tolerate being treated as mere material instruments, but demand rights befitting a human person both in domestic and in public life."

[*Pope John XXIII,* Pacem in Terris, *April 1963.*]

Importance of Women in Society

In the early decades of the nineteenth century, Fanny Wright was an outspoken supporter of women's education, and she was often criticized for that stand as well as her audacity in speaking to mixed groups of men and women in public. She was dogmatic in her view of the woman's role in society, which she forcefully impressed upon her hearers. "Until women assume the place in society which good sense and good feeling alike assign to them, human improvement must advance but feebly. It is in vain that we would circumscribe the power of one half of our race, and that by far the most important and influential. If they exert it not for good, they will for evil; if they advance not knowledge they will perpetuate ignorance. Let women stand where they may in the scale of improvement, their position decides that of the race. Are they cultivated?—so is society polished and enlightened. Are they ignorant?—so is it gross and insipid. Are they wise?—so is the human character elevated. Are they enslaved?—so is the whole human race degraded. Oh! that we could learn the advantage of just practice and consistent principles!"

[Emily Hahn, Once Upon a Pedestal *(New York: Crowell, 1974), p. 48.]*

Jesus' Appreciation of Women

No one can read through the Gospels without realizing what a deep appreciation Jesus had for women. They were the last at the cross and the first at the tomb, and for good reason. Dorothy Sayers, in her book *Are Women Human?* comments on Jesus' attitude and the female response.

"They had never known a man like this Man—there never has been such another. A prophet and teacher who never nagged at them, never flattered or coaxed or patronized; who never made arch jokes about them, never treated them either as 'The women, God help us!' or 'The ladies, God bless them'; who rebuked without querulousness and praised without condescension; who took their questions and arguments seriously; who never mapped out their sphere for them, never urged them to be feminine or jeered at them for being female; who had no axe to grind and no uneasy male dignity to defend; who took them as he found them and was completely unselfconscious. There is no act, no sermon, no parable in the whole Gospel that borrows its pungency from female perversity; nobody could possibly guess from the words and deeds of Jesus that there was anything 'funny' about woman's nature."

[Dorothy Sayers, Are Women Human? (Grand Rapids: Eerdmans, 1971), p. 47.]

Legal Rights of Women

Women in Colonial America had few of the legal rights that women enjoy today, and that fact was not one that could be safely ignored by the government leaders—so said Abigail Adams, the wife of the second U.S. president. She cautioned him in a frank letter that to run roughshod over the rights would spell disaster. "Remember the Ladies, and be more generous and favorable to them than your ancestors. Do not put such unlimited power into the hands of the Husbands. Remember all Men would be tyrants if they could. If particular care and attention is not paid to the Ladies we are determined to form a Rebellion, and will not hold ourselves bound by any Laws in which we have no voice, or those customs which treat us only as vassals of your Sex. Regard us then as Beings placed by providence under your protection and in imitation of the Supreme Being make use of that power only for our happiness."

[L. H. Butterfield, ed., Adams Family Correspondence (Cambridge: Harvard University Press, 1963), 1:369–70.]

Providing Opportunities for Women

A longtime supporter of women's equality, President Jimmy Carter provided greater opportunities for women than any other U.S.

president. This was evident on all levels of government. Forty-one of the forty-six female federal judges who were serving at the end of his term had been appointed by him. All his predecessors combined appointed only twenty-five women ambassadors. During his four-year term, he named sixteen women ambassadors, and of the six female cabinet secretaries in the nation's history, he appointed three of them. He likewise appointed 60 percent of the women undersecretaries and 80 percent of the women assistant secretaries ever to hold those posts in U.S. history.

[*Rosalyn Carter*, First Lady from Plains *(Boston: Houghton Mifflin, 1984), pp. 289–90.]*

Superiority of Women

> Whatever women do
> they must do
> Twice as well as men
> to be thought
> half as good.
> Luckily, this is not difficult.
> —ANONYMOUS

WOMEN IN THE BIBLE
Cultural Differences from Today

Why would the Apostle Paul, in 1 Corinthians 14:34, tell women to be silent in church and write that, if they had any questions, they should ask their husbands at home? Such admonitions almost seem out of place today. Few people (men or women) would ever think of asking a question out loud in a worship service, and a great many women know more than their husbands do about biblical issues. So, how can such a biblical injunction be explained? It is important to note that the verse in question is in the middle of a paragraph dealing with "orderly worship" (NIV). Thus, we can conclude that Paul's instructions to women relate to the overall format of the worship. In attempting to understand what sort of disorderly conduct women may have been involved in, it is helpful to look at cultures today that parallel in some respects the culture of Paul's day.

Olive Rogers, a missionary to India, in writing on "the cultural background to the Epistles," sheds light on this issue. "When in Old Delhi once, I visited the golden domed temple of the Sikhs. Being a woman, I was taken round to a back entrance and then through several rooms, till I reached the upper gallery where the ladies gathered. I sat on the richly carpeted floor and surveyed the scene. Suddenly, as so often in the East, the Scriptures became alive! We were high above the main body of the temple. The worship—intoning of the Sacred Book, and instructions for salvation—being carried on down below was pertinent only to the men, for they alone have souls to save. I tried in vain to hear what was going on, but the women were sitting around in groups gossiping, amused at the play of their children, careless of the fact that they were in a place of worship. For them a visit to the temple was merely an opportunity to escape from the monotony of an existence behind the four walls of their homes, where they reign supreme in their own quarters, but where their lives seldom encroach upon those of their men-folk, who do all the work involving contact with the outside world."

This problem, some would argue, would occur only in situations where women are not active participants in the faith. Not so, according to Rogers. Such behavior becomes part of the culture, as she illustrates through another experience she had. "Not many months later I attended one of the Christian conventions held annually in South India. Day after day thousands of men and women sat under the large leaf shelter. The men's section of the 'pandal' was quiet and orderly as they listened to the Word, taking notes with assiduous care. The women's half was another matter. All the children were there, restless, demanding and noisy, and many of the women were sitting in groups chattering." The Christian women of Corinth, whose culture did not permit them the same privileges as men, may have been guilty of the same sort of "disorderly" conduct as the Christian women of South India.

[*Olive Rogers, "The Ministry of Women in the Church," in* God's Community: Essays on the Church and Its Ministry, *ed. David J. Ellis and W. Ward Gasque (Wheaton: Shaw, 1978), p. 62.*]

The Woman at the Well

The story of the woman of Samaria is a familiar one. She talked to Jesus while she was drawing water, and then, after he had exposed her immoral past, she returned to the townspeople and said, "Come, see a man who told me everything I ever did." They came, and many believed. Many sermons have been given on her eagerness to place her faith in Jesus as Messiah, but Walter L. Liefeld, professor of New Testament at Trinity Evangelical Divinity School, has offered fresh insight on the character of her faith. "She was quite open in her attitude to her past and present and also to the perception of Jesus. But the next words convey her uncertainty: 'Could this be the Christ?' The question in the Greek . . . suggests considerable uncertainty. While one might like to celebrate this woman's bold confidence in Christ, something else is indicated that could be even more significant. Far from believing easily, or, to put it in crass terms, being gullible, as some might (wrongly) expect a woman to be, this woman was cautious about her conclusion. It is not that she was a doubter, for it is remarkable that any Samaritan would on the basis of one conversation even entertain the possibility that the speaker was the Jewish Messiah! She had ventured into the area of faith, willing to break with her own tradition but not rushing headlong and wide-eyed into something she did not understand."

[*Ruth A. Tucker and Walter L. Liefeld,* Daughters of the Church: Women and Ministry from New Testament Times to the Present *(Grand Rapids: Zondervan, 1987), pp. 31–32.*]

WORKING MOTHERS
Benefits for Family Life

It is widely acknowledged that a mother's employment outside the home can put a strain on family life, but it can also have the effect of relieving tensions. Being the sole "breadwinner" in the family can be very stressful for fathers. Their employment expectations are much greater today than they were generations ago, and this can bring pressure and conflict into the whole of family life.

"Men have been put in a terribly unfair bind since the Industrial Revolution and the end of the cottage industry. He is to be the only worker in the family. If he does well, the family does not want; if he does poorly, the family suffers. Since he 'provides' for all, he is entitled to the power that control of the purse permits. He has the last word, right or wrong; he makes all major decisions for the family; he protects them from the world. If his wife (his equal in intelligence, education, spiritual maturity, capability and wisdom) should go out to work, his ego is shattered, for his very being is measured by his financial success and how well he supports her and the children."

But if the husband is secure enough to encourage his wife's employment outside the home, he stands to be one of the greatest beneficiaries. Among other things, "the man whose wife is employed is free to explore other areas of employment, free to pursue a business of his own, or whatever. If he decides on a career switch, it does not *automatically* mean financial disaster. . . .

"Under the authoritarian system of family life, father needs to spend most of his time working. If the family lives in the suburbs, he can spend an additional two hours traveling to and from work. The family suffers. The amount of quality time a father spends with his children is minimal. In severe cases, his position deteriorates to the 'wait-till-your-father-gets-home' status of the punisher, the decision maker, the giver of orders. When he comes home, it is as though he is visiting. The house runs without him; he only pays the bills.

"When the mother too is employed, the home responsibilities have to be shared. The father as well as the mother is responsible to pick up and care for a child who gets sick at school. Both come home to face the questions from children, to share the day with them together, to clean the house and do the laundry. No longer is the head of the house shut out from the nitty-gritty of family life, nor considered merely a shadowy dispenser of funds and irrefutable decisions.

"Everybody wins."

[Millie Van Wyke, You're Hired! Insights for Christian Women Who Work Outside the Home *(Grand Rapids: Baker, 1983), pp. 16–17.]*

Guilt Associated with Working

Although many working mothers are single parents and work out of necessity, there is often a load of guilt that tortures a woman far more than it would a man in the same circumstances. This is the testimony of Mary Whelchel, who is the founder and host of "The Christian Working Woman" radio program and the author of a book by the same title. She grew up in a home where her mother modeled the traditional role of a full-time homemaker, and she learned "subconsciously that mothers should live their lives for their children . . . and anything less was second best." With that heritage she had struggles coming to grips with her own situation that forced her into the working world to support her daughter.

"I have some firsthand knowledge of what working moms go through, because I've been a career mom since my daughter, now finishing college, was eight years old. As I think back over the years, the one emotion that comes flooding back is guilt: Guilt because I was not home in the afternoon when Julie got home from school. Guilt because Julie didn't like the sitter very much, or because I could not go to her school during the day to be a grade mother, or take part in cookie sales. Guilt because the time I did have with her was occupied with housework, or work brought home from the office. Guilt when she became a latch-key kid in high school years, worrying about her feelings of loneliness. Guilt because she had to do more chores than most of her peers. The list goes on and on."

Whelchel points out, however, that much of the guilt mothers endure is false guilt. Working mothers too often blame themselves for things that are utterly beyond their control. They are prone to "assume that every problem their children have is a result of the fact that they have a working mom." Children are not altogether innocent in this regard. "All mothers have learned that kids are very good at laying on false guilt. I think children have inborn instincts for using guilt as a manipulative tool on their parents. Remember, just because your child tells you—either in words or in attitude—that you are the guilty party does not necessarily mean that they are right."

[Mary Whelchel, The Christian Working Woman *(Old Tappan, N.J.: Revell, 1986), pp. 183, 186.]*

Problems of Child Care

In her book *A Lesser Life*, Sylvia Ann Hewlett deals with the struggles mothers face in a professional world that shows no sympathy with a married woman's home responsibilities and child care, and she shares the personal difficulties she endured with childbearing while she was an assistant professor of economics at Barnard College, Columbia University. She began teaching in 1974, and three years later she gave birth to Lisa. Although her husband helped with child care, the major responsibility fell on Sylvia, who was driven by guilt and love for Lisa to be the best mother possible. She employed a part-time baby-sitter but sought to keep Lisa with her at school part of the day. That arrangement, however, was only temporary. "When Lisa was four and a half months old, I capitulated and hired a full-time baby-sitter. I did this not out of any consideration for myself or Richard (though by this stage both of us were wretchedly tired) but because I was encountering tremendous disapproval and hostility at work and knew that I could not take Lisa to my office any longer. The final straw was a note I found on my desk that spring. It was from a colleague down the hallway, and it read: 'Dear Professor Hewlett, I would like to point out that we, at Barnard, are not running a crèche but a college.' I was surprised and hurt; weren't we supposed to be providing role models for our women students? But I was also cowed. I never took Lisa to work again except for the annual Christmas party."

These problems made Sylvia realize that, despite the progress that childless career women have made in recent years, working mothers have made very few gains. And she knew well that the problems she faced as a university professor were insignificant compared to those of most working women. "I knew that I was a privileged person. Seventy percent of today's women in the labor force work out of economic necessity; they are single, widowed, divorced or are married to men who are either unemployed or earn less than $15,000 a year. I was not poor, black, or single, and I had an abundance of marketable skills. What happened to working mothers who were more vulnerable than I?"

[Sylvia Ann Hewlett, A Lesser Life: The Myth of Women's Liberation in America (New York: Morrow, 1986), pp. 22, 30.]

YOUTH

Crisis of Faith

Seeing a child grow in faith and spiritual maturity is one of the greatest joys of a Christian parent. Conversely, seeing a child doubt and question his or her faith can be a painful struggle for a parent who often feels guilty for personal failures in modeling the Christian life. And too often in their anguish, parents only make the situation worse. How should a parent respond? Marjorie Holmes addresses this issue as only she can.

"My child has lost faith in you, God, and my heart is sad.

"I hear him using all the familiar, well-worn arguments that deny your very existence. And I want to laugh and I want to scold and I want to cry.

"For I remember far too well my own young voice of arrogance and inflated learning, dismissing you. And I see my mother gazing at me with the same expression I must be wearing now.

"Only more hurt, more deeply disturbed, saying, 'I can't answer your logic. I can only say I *know.*'

"I remember all the years I kept her waiting, hurt her, rejected her, condescended to her as I stormed and stumbled along all the enticing, argument-cluttered paths to find a faith that she had never questioned.

"Waiting for a time when I would exclaim, 'Why, it's true! I know.'

"And now I see my child kicking aside the foundations, setting off on the identical stormy journey. And I can only ask you not to lose sight of him. Not to let go of him altogether. And wish him a safe return.

"Wish for the time when (I hope it won't take him so long) he too will say, with an air of discovery and relief: 'I know.' "

[*Marjorie Holmes,* Who Am I God? *(New York: Bantam Books, 1971), pp. 25–26.*]

Rejection Resulting from Cruel Joke

Youngsters are often very cruel to each other, and sometimes the damage they inflict can cause permanent scars. This is particularly true when the injury is of a psychological or emotional nature—when self-esteem is destroyed. In *Beyond Me*, Norma Kvindlog and Esther Anderson write that "even decades later the painful details can still be recalled, the hurt and humiliation still felt." They cite the story of Karen, who years later agonized over a cruel joke that had humiliated her in front of her friends.

"I was shy and quiet, one of the anonymous faces in school, and I had never had a regular date. So I was overwhelmed when one of the most popular boys in my class asked me to the prom.

"I worked extra hours for money to buy material for my dream dress, and I also made a dress for my younger sister, who had a stready boyfriend.

"By prom night I was almost sick with anticipation. And waiting. And waiting. Finally my sister's date confessed that it had all been a joke; my 'date' had never intended to escort me to the prom. He had had another date from the beginning. Going back to school the next week was one of the hardest things I have ever had to do."

[*Norma Kvindlog and Esther Lindgren Anderson,* Beyond Me *(Wheaton: Tyndale, 1987), p. 29.*]

Index